W9-BKG-908

PRESENTING

Young Adult Fantasy Fiction

Twayne's United States Authors Series
Young Adult Authors

Patricia J. Campbell, General Editor

TUSAS 699

FANTASY FANATICS AT BOULDER PUBLIC LIBRARY, COLORADO. *Back row, left to right:* Nathan Doyle, Linda Reling, Midian Crosby, Sam Walter, Mariah Iseley. *Middle, left to right:* Jonathan Singer, Eric Rice, Anne Pizzi, Galadriel Wills. *Front, left to right:* Graham Andrews, Guy Iseley, Brian Dunning.
Cathi Dunn MacRae

PRESENTING

Young Adult Fantasy Fiction

Cathi Dunn MacRae

Twayne Publishers

New York

Twayne's United States Authors Series No. 699

Presenting Young Adult Fantasy Fiction
Cathi Dunn MacRae

Copyright © 1998 by Twayne Publishers

All rights reserved. No part of this book may be reproduced or transmitted in any form or by any means, electronic or mechanical, including photocopying, recording, or by any information storage and retrieval system, without permission in writing from the Publisher.

Twayne Publishers

1633 Broadway
New York, NY 10019

Library of Congress Cataloging-in-Publication Data

MacRae, Cathi Dunn.
    Presenting young adult fantasy fiction / Cathi Dunn MacRae.
        p.   cm. — (Twayne's United States authors series ; TUSAS
    699. Young adult authors)
    Includes bibliographical references and index.
    ISBN 0-8057-8220-6 (alk. paper)
    1. Fantastic fiction, American—History and criticism. 2. Young
adult fiction, American—History and criticism. 3. Young adult
fiction, English—History and criticism. 4. Fantastic fiction,
English—History and criticism. I. Title. II. Series: Twayne's
United States authors series ; TUSAS 699. III. Series: Twayne's
United States authors series.   Young adult authors.
PS374.F27M33   1998
813'.08766099283—dc21
                                                                98-12896
                                                                CIP

This paper meets the requirements of ANSI/NISO Z3948-1992 (Permanence of Paper).

10 9 8 7 6 5 4 3 2

Printed in the United States of America

With heartfelt gratitude to the Fantasy Fanatics
who made this impossible task possible:

Graham, Allison, Ashley, Vanessa, Colyn, Dylan,
Jehnie, two Bens, Adam, Amy, Jesse, Midian,
Robin, Pixy, Jenny, Nate, Malinda, Brian, Kylin,
Nadia, Erik, Guy, Mariah, Aron, Ian, Sarah,
Jessica, Naomi, Anne, Linda, Eric, Anna,
Jonathan, Melissa, Sam, and Galadriel.

And for my father, Robert Grumbine,
whose devoted ministry to native Alaskan youth
provided the model for my own rewarding
work with teenagers.

Contents

Preface: Young Adults and Fantasy

"I enjoy the exotic presented as the everyday—fantastic characters who seem real. I also enjoy legend and fairy tale—something to do with heritage—I like links to the past."

—Rachel Scott

How Do Young Adults Respond to Fantasy?

This book could not have been written without generous support from the enthusiastic young adult readers called Fantasy Fanatics, a group of junior and senior high students who began meeting on October 25, 1991, at Boulder Public Library in Colorado. One Friday a month after school, these teenagers shared their responses to fantasy literature. Eleven attended the first meeting. At the last meeting in March 1997, two among fourteen were veterans of all five and a half years. Senior Linda Reling had rarely skipped a meeting since seventh grade. Midian Crosby sent notes during her year in Australia, returning to continue beyond high school until age 20. Fifty teenagers participated during the group's life span; a dozen turned up at each meeting.

Fantasy Fanatics endured for three reasons: they had a mission, they had a voice, and they had fun. They were thrilled to be consulted for opinions about fantasy for this book. I had been asked to choose 10 contemporary American fantasy authors enjoyed by young adults. As a young adult librarian working closely with teenagers since the late 1970s, I had never presumed to guess their reading choices. I could research authors who seemed worthy and popular, but I would never know who teenagers' own favorites were—or why—unless I asked them.

In 1990 I formulated a questionnaire to discover young adult (YA) reader preferences in fantasy. Distributing it to teen advisory boards in five libraries in Arizona, Maryland, Minnesota, Missouri, and Washington, I asked for volunteers to become Young Adult Fantasy Evaluators, or YAFEs, who would complete YAFE evaluation reports (YAFERs) on fantasy books they read. Their responses would shape this book. Twenty-three preference questionnaires came back, but only a few YAFERs about books. Soon I lost touch with these long-distance advisers, needing more local informants.

After beginning a new YA program at Boulder Public Library, I noticed a short, awkward junior high boy staggering under a teetering tower of fantasy novels, trying to escape the children's department before he was spotted by anyone he knew. He couldn't decide whether to be mortified or mystified when I asked if he would attend a new fantasy book discussion group. Sam Walter became a founding Fantasy Fanatic, remaining a member until his high school graduation in 1996, when he towered above me at well over six feet.

Fantasy Fanatics are by nature among the most voracious, curious, and imaginative young adult readers—though it's often difficult to get their attention when they read during meetings. They are undeterred by enormous tomes in endless volumes of 800 pages each. Our recruitment poster asked,

"Are you a Fantasy Fanatic? Answer these questions to find out:

— Do you sneak huge books by Terry Brooks, David Eddings, or Mercedes Lackey inside your notebook to read during math class?
— Do you get tired of waiting forever on the library's reserve list for the next book in a series, so you spend $23.95 on your own copy?
— Do you like fairy tales now just as much as when you were little?"

Fantasy Fanatics know exactly what they like to read. They are very particular about which types of books they prefer, though if someone enjoys an author, it does not necessarily follow that he or she will like another writing what appear to be similar books. Some Fanatics read in related genres of science fiction and horror. Few read realistic fiction or nonfiction. Many are writers themselves, well into their own trilogies.

As Fanatics grew older, their reading tastes changed. *Dragonlance* and other role-playing game-related series became very junior high. I had to stop senior Eric Rice, for whom Robert Jordan had become the entire universe, from discouraging an eager sixth grader from reading R. A. Salvatore. "When you were in seventh grade, you called Salvatore a god," I reminded Eric. "Could that be why you're enjoying Jordan now?" Then we dove into another heated discussion.

Still, the group could revisit childhood classics. When I praised Ursula K. Le Guin's *Wizard of Earthsea* as a classic for all ages, Dylan Burns, 16, disagreed. Required reading in sixth grade, it had left little impression on him. Spurred by my comments, Dylan picked up the book again, and by the next meeting he spilled over with reasons why *Earthsea* is the most perfect fantasy ever written.

At a YA literature conference, Diana Tixier Herald, author of *Genreflecting* (Libraries Unlimited, 1991) and *Teen Genreflecting* (Libraries Unlimited, 1997), spoke of her work on the American Library Association's young adult fantasy genre committee, which recommends fantasy titles for teens (see Lists of Recommended Fantasy Titles in Appendix A). She consulted her YA readers at Mesa County Library in Grand Junction, Colorado, while selecting titles for ALA's list; her observations of the habits of teen fantasy readers mirrored mine:

- They have specific tastes within fantasy subgenres.
- They communicate about books by word of mouth far more than other YA readers do.
- Some adore long, fat series books because they do not want the fantasy world to end.

They are acutely aware of what fantasy elements they like:

- Some see magic and wizardry as the most essential element.
- Some savor quest tales, anything with a journey or search.
- Some (mostly girls) enjoy the increasing frequency of spunky female heroines.
- Some prefer fantasy based on role-playing games.
- Some want no elements of the real world intruding, while some won't read anything without reference to our world.
- Most see no difference between juvenile, young adult, and adult books and read freely back and forth among age levels.
- Most find the element of fantasy itself more important than any subgenre.[1]

Respondents to my questionnaire, such as Rachel Scott, who supplied this preface's epigraph, identified qualities of fantasy that appear in their favorite books:

- "Talking animals and made-up creatures."
- "Creativity and originality."
- "I like the magical parts very much, and skilled warriors like elves, dwarves, and sorcerers."
- "I like anything with an element of magic, dragons, time travel, and Arthurian legend. I also enjoy all stories that deal with Robin Hood and Atlantis."

What Fantasy Types Do Young Adults Favor?

Making as many choices as they wished from a checklist of fantasy story types, 63 respondents finished the sentence "What I like about fantasy is. . . ." The top type, picked by 81 percent of the YA readers, was "alternate worlds." Humor came in second, with 67 percent; third was "magic that occurs in everyday world" with 62 percent, nearly tying with "books based on fairy tales." The fourth choice, King Arthur stories, were enjoyed by 52 percent, and 51 percent read time travel. Faerie folk and mythical creatures each attracted 48 percent; adventure or quest stories were chosen by 43 percent. Forty percent picked witches and wizards, and 33 percent selected myths and legends. In last place were "stories of normal people involved in fantasy gaming," chosen by only 11 percent. Group discussion revealed that teen fantasy fans found such stories too realistic.

Despite strong individual preferences, Fantasy Fanatics affected each other. The group had little taste for time travel, though it was popular with half the survey respondents from other sources. Our investigation of how such fantasy games as Dungeons and Dragons relate to series books inspired the creation of several gaming group offshoots. This teenaged gaming world is closed to most adults; I was privileged to observe gaming sessions, which led me to construct an additional gaming survey distributed in school classes beyond our group (see the "Fantasy Gaming" section of chapter 3).

Working with Fantasy Fanatics made me acutely aware of my own fantasy reading preferences, biases I struggled to overcome when writing this book. I was thrilled when my library hosted the touring ALA exhibit "The Many Realms of King Arthur," with related programs that tied in perfectly with the Arthurian legend—my own favorite fantasy—discussed in chapter 5. What pleasure when Fantasy Fanatics shared my enthusiasm for all things Arthurian; the group swelled to more than 20 participants during the months devoted to King Arthur. They presented their own "Many Realms" library program, an Arthur book discussion open to the public in which each Fanatic introduced his or her own favorite title. Lively discussions of Marion Zimmer Bradley's *Mists of Avalon* still resonate in my memory. It was a pivotal book for many members, heating up the ever-raging battle of the sexes among teenagers. An article by Fanatic Allison Barrett, 15, about women in Arthurian fiction, was posted on our library's Web page, sparking e-mail response from Internet cruisers, including praise from experts in Arthurian literature.

To advise me on authors to feature in this book, Fantasy Fanatics and other survey respondents from schools and YAFE groups were asked to identify authors in various ways: as those they enjoyed reading, as favorite authors, as authors deserving their own book chapter. Through an evolving outline with at least nine lives, four authors, eventually whittled down from ten, were chosen to be featured with critical biographies connecting their lives and work, one author serving as the centerpiece to each chapter about a fantasy subgenre. Though input from Fantasy Fanatics was crucial in each author choice, the final decision was mine, based on the following factors:

- Consistent literary quality in a significant body of work
- Estimable representation of a fantasy subgenre
- Lasting appeal, accessibility, and value among young adult readers
- Currently writing in America

Limitation to four featured authors was a torturous decision for Fantasy Fanatics and me. Only upon delving into this study did we discover how rich and diverse was the fantasy literature tradition. The field has exploded since Tolkien's works attracted a cult following among 1970s college students, many of whom are now fantasy authors themselves. Fantasy publishing in America has been teeming in the last two decades of this century, with no end in sight. New authors appear daily—mega-best-selling Robert Jordan had not begun publishing his blockbusters when this book was conceived in 1990. Not only is the profusion of writers dizzying, but each worthy author's works are prolific and complex, within a seemingly impenetrable rabbit's warren of fantasy subgenres. This book simply would not hold 10 authors of such depth, along with examinations of various types of fantasy. The challenging process of inclusion and elimination seemed endless.

Which Authors Made the Final Cut?

After Piers Anthony was bumped to our science fiction companion volume, the overwhelming first choice was Jane Yolen. Read by over half of my 63 respondents, Yolen was cited as favorite author by nine and was my own first choice for this book long before I distributed a single survey or met a Fantasy Fanatic. Yolen's resonant stories and essays define mythic storytelling, featured in chapter 4, "Myth: Dreams of the Soul's Adventure."

Bestselling author Terry Brooks, an unabashed disciple of fantasy master J. R. R. Tolkien, was enjoyed by over 40 percent of respondents, with four choosing him as favorite author and two mentioning *The Sword of Shannara* as best fantasy book, and one choosing *Magic Kingdom for Sale,* the initial title in his *Landover* series. Pitched for the adult fantasy market, Brooks has been adopted by teen fantasy readers and is the only male author featured here, in chapter 2, "Alternate Worlds: Beyond the Walls of the World."

The remaining featured authors are less well known. Meredith Ann Pierce's comparatively small output is exceptionally promising and original, captivating the 30 percent of respondents who discovered her two series. Three mentioned *Birth of the Firebringer,* the first volume of her unicorn coming-of-age saga, as their favorite fantasy, and two named *Darkangel,* the eerie tale of a vampire on the moon. A consummate creator of mythical creatures, Pierce graces "A Magic Bestiary," chapter 6.

When Barbara Hambly's original adult paperback *Dragonsbane* became a 1986 ALA Best Book for Young Adults, she was virtually unknown. Her utterly real human characters made their homes in richly detailed realms that just happened to be imaginary. Then Hambly transported California computer programmers to a fantasy world, opening magic realism to fresh dimensions in her *Windrose Chronicles.* The strong female protagonists of Hambly's lush adult novels appeal primarily to older adolescent girls, though boys often respond when introduced to this most underrated author, featured in chapter 3, "Magic Realism: Magic Here, There, and Everywhere."

No author stays put in only one subgenre, so works that don't fit where biographies are located appear in chapters containing appropriate subgenres. Each subgenre chapter defines the fantasy type, describes its development, and surveys noteworthy works beyond each featured author's, placing their work in context. I interviewed all four featured authors in person or by mail, focusing on life events that shaped their writing, and insights on fantasy and their young adult audience. My critical analysis of key titles cites general critical opinion while attempting my own interpretation; I also include the opinions of Fantasy Fanatics, in quotes from their YAFE book evaluations (the form they used is shown in Appendix C). Ages of the same YAFEs differ from quote to quote since evaluations were collected over a period of several years.

Two subgenres are covered in chapters without featured authors. Many authors who concentrate on other types of fantasy try their hand at Arthurian tales (chapter 5, "Legends: The Shaping of Heroes") or time travel (chapter 7, "Time Fantasy: From Now to Then").

Young adult readers' appetites for fantasy are insatiable. Fanatics list as favorites many authors who could not be ignored in this book. Modern fantasy pioneers Marion Zimmer Bradley (mostly for *Mists of Avalon*) and Ursula K. Le Guin were noted, but were not selected for biographies in this volume because they are so well known and are covered extensively elsewhere. Patricia McKillip, who trailblazed YA fantasy in the 1970s, would have been here had this book been written 10 years earlier; she writes less nowadays for the YA audience. Le Guin and McKillip are accorded their founder status among alternate worlds in chapter 2; Bradley's Arthurian expertise is acknowledged in chapter 5. Other teen favorites are more current. Margaret Weis and Tracy Hickman, the team who created the *Dragonlance* game-related paperback series, tend to be crazes with younger readers who then grow out of their work, which can be uneven, though their hardcover series *Death Gate Cycle* is in hot demand with older YA readers. Weis and Hickman are mentioned with fantasy gaming in chapter 3.

Some top young adult fantasy authors are only partially covered here, needing more detailed treatment elsewhere. Newbery award winner Robin McKinley was mentioned by just under half of the YA respondents and chosen as top favorite by seven. When readers were asked to pick the best fantasy book of all time, two chose her feminist heroic fantasy *The Blue Sword,* with its prequel *The Hero and the Crown.* This series set in the Damar otherworld is discussed in chapter 2. McKinley's unusual Robin Hood retelling,

The Outlaws of Sherwood, appears with legends in chapter 5. Two survey participants chose as best all-time fantasy McKinley's *Beauty,* a groundbreaking retelling of the "Beauty and the Beast" fairy tale that opened the way for other novel-length retellings. The fairy tales that McKinley so vividly reimagines are such a vast topic that a future volume is proposed to study them in depth, within a history of fairy tale and a critique of other modern retellers, along with related novels about inhabitants of faerie realms. Also belonging in such a study are teens' beloved *ElfQuest* comics by Wendy and Richard Pini, and urban fantasy. The popularity of urban fantasy about faerie creatures coexisting with us parallel to and sometimes in our cities is a recent phenomenon, and its Canadian proponent Charles de Lint emerged as a top favorite Fanatic author too late for inclusion here.

Mercedes Lackey is a recent and incredibly prolific phenomenon whose first original paperback, *Arrows of the Queen,* was a 1987 ALA Best Book for Young Adults. Since then she has become an adult hardcover bestselling author with nearly 50 titles published in just one decade. She has coauthored books with everyone from her husband, Larry Dixon, to the shining stars of fantasy, including Piers Anthony and Andre Norton. Many Fantasy Fanatics are committed Lackey fans who have read most of her books, three citing *Arrows* as the very best fantasy. She writes in most fantasy subgenres as well as horror, science fiction, and even song lyrics; her works are mentioned here with heroic fantasy and magic realism. Although inconsistent in quality, Lackey writes her best novels with intense compassion for her teenaged protagonists. Lackey's YA characters, some of whom are abused or gay and many of whom are misunderstood, are authentic. Due to her immense output and appeal to young adults, Mercedes Lackey deserves a whole biography of her own.

Two '90s newcomers with strong YA followings also did not make the cut. Fanatics were so disappointed that David Eddings and Robert Jordan were not included, that they wrote justifications why they should have been, which appear in chapter 2, "Alternate Worlds." Piers Anthony also earned two essays, and Tad Williams almost did. Other authors beloved by Fanatics include Orson Scott Card, Parke Godwin, Robert Holdstock, and Brian Jacques; all appear somewhere in this book. Giants Andre Norton and Anne McCaffrey fall beyond our scope; Norton writes science fantasy, and McCaffrey, who detests being labeled a fantasy author, considers her writing science fiction. Still, both are mentioned.

Limited to contemporary American authors, this book could not focus on British writers, preeminent among them being Tolkien, who created the modern fantasy novel now embraced by so many Americans and who does appear in a section of chapter 2. British roots are traced in discussions of each subgenre, and some authors from other countries coexist with American counterparts in subgenre overviews. Teen survey respondents stated that they had little recognition of author nationalities; they simply read what they like. Such is not the case in realistic fiction, where YA readers may complain of difficulty in understanding foreign teen culture and slang. Glaringly absent here are the humorous British fantasies of Terry Pratchett and Neil Gaiman, who use that madcap Monty Pythonesque tone American teens so appreciate. Humorous fantasy receives short shrift, since a "light fantasy" chapter bit the dust when this book grew overlong.

Because it was impossible to discuss every worthy title, each chapter contains its own recommended reading list, suggesting related books in addition to those discussed in the chapter, and a selected bibliography containing primary and reference sources relating to the featured author or subgenre discussed in the chapter. Additional selected references appear in the back. Chapters with a featured author contain a chronology of that author's life and works. Appendices include "Literary Awards and Fantasy Fiction," "Best Fantasy Books for Young Adults," and "Surveys and Questionnaires Used in This Study."

Whose Book Is This?

The purpose of this book is to portray fantasy as a complex genre in great demand by many of the most motivated teenaged readers and to describe its subgenres clearly so that YA readers—and those who connect them to books—may map the journey to another good book. To be effective advisors who can steer YA readers to the exact type of fantasy they want, librarians must know the right questions to ask. Yet librarians are often unfamiliar with fantasy literature; many assume they dislike fantasy when perhaps they have simply not discovered the kind they could enjoy. Like librarians, teachers also recommend reading to teenagers and may find in these subgenre studies the background needed to teach a literature with ancient roots, certain to provoke appreciative responses from students. In college or graduate adolescent literature classes, the fantasy genre often foxes instructors who are not its personal fans. This book makes a bid for fantasy to earn more coverage in classes that teach professionals to use literature with teenagers; not only is fantasy so often their literature of choice, but it also has profound messages especially for youth.

For young adult readers, this book is intended to provide compelling information about some of your favorite authors and to introduce you to new ones. Comments from your peers, my Fantasy Fanatic consultants, will spark your interest. You will see how writers use their own imaginations to stimulate yours; perhaps you will be inspired to try writing yourself. You will see how the fantasy you have loved since childhood fits into the ancient world of myth and legend, how it is a hero's journey like the life you are now embarking upon. As a young adult reader, you appreciate fantasy because you see yourself in it, facing the risks of the world out there—another world, and our world, too.

Acknowledgments

The most rewarding aspect of writing this book was the opportunity to interview writers previously met only through their work. Much of the flavor of this study is due to their time and care, for which I thank them. My impression of Terry Brooks during our interview at the historic Boulderado Hotel was reinforced by his warm reception of his fans at a bookstore signing in Boulder, Colorado. After Barbara Hambly sent her interview by mail, we discovered our paths would cross in New Orleans and shared an atmospheric meal in a steamy courtyard restaurant while she researched her historical mystery set in that city. One interview was done entirely by mail, in flowing words from a writer who loves the language; someday I hope to meet in person fellow librarian Meredith Ann Pierce in Florida. I met Jane Yolen during an American Library Association conference in Chicago for a breakfast interview—a time of day when I am not at my best. Not until afterward did I realize I had made the classic blunder of novice interviewers, failing to check that my tape recorder was recording properly. Jane Yolen graciously refilled me in by mail during her extended stay in Scotland. Our orbits continued to cross at ALA, where I was pleased to meet her characterful sons, Adam and Jason. These critiques of their work are the best way of thanking "my" authors—even if they disagree with my conclusions!

Many publishers gave me practical assistance. Ann Flowers from *Horn Book Guide* sent me her syllabus from the fantasy literature course she teaches. Many publicists arranged interviews or sent press kits, author photographs, catalogs, review books, and precious information on forthcoming—or not so forthcoming—publications. The folks at TSR were especially accommodating as I puzzled out how their books relate to their fantasy games. Tom McMahon at Gale Research, editor of the reference work *Authors and Artists for Young Adults*, sent me prepublication biographical sketches and other background information on authors. I am grateful to everyone who made sure I kept up with their authors.

Many librarians volunteered expert service. Fellow members of ALA's Young Adult Library Services Association (YALSA) shared their knowledge of fantasy. Di Herald, Dolores Maminski, and Merilyn Grosshans sent early notice and insight into their booklist selections. Bonnie Kunzel prepared a fantastic set of fantasy handouts for a genre preconference that reduced my own research.

I cannot imagine how anyone could accomplish this sort of project without insider contacts in libraries. Old colleagues at Pratt Library in Baltimore, one of the finest public libraries in the country, located resources impossible to find elsewhere. When I worked at Boulder Public Library in Colorado, it became my research lab. I especially thank Judy Volc for unrestricted access to her superb children's literature reference collection, and Marcelee Gralapp and Randy Smith for time off to write. Fellow staff Carol Heepke, Chuck Lomis, Colleen Miller, Mary Jane Holland, Margaret Furumo, Patty Kessler, Jennifer Fakolt, Sherri Ostergren, Diana Siemer, and Mary McCarthy supported me as I led the double life of a librarian/writer.

The last two also served as my research assistants. I have a vivid image of determined Diana, after she threw out her back, lying on the library floor searching indexes for book reviews. Mary worked miracles during the hectic countdown toward deadline. She meticulously transcribed my Terry Brooks interview tape, sprinkled with her own sharp comments. She organized a mountain of Mercedes Lackey material before we realized there was too much to fit. After I moved to Maryland, she sent overnight mail references from the CU library. I miss indispensable Mary more than I can say.

There is nothing like research to reveal libraries' strengths and weaknesses. Norlin Library at the University of Colorado seems to have every periodical on earth, and was so well organized for self-service that I never met any librarians. In my new Maryland home, just before deadline, I had to become acquainted with smaller, unfamiliar public libraries in a hurry, encountering exemplary service at Anne Arundel County and Prince George's County libraries. I commend the first for unmatched patron computer access and the second for hanging onto rare "hard copy" references. I needed both libraries to complete this job and regret that public libraries make choices favoring either new technology or old research methods when *both* go hand in hand.

In the final year of this endeavor, I began editing the young adult library journal *Voice of Youth Advocates* (*VOYA*), where access to reviews and annual "Best Science Fiction, Fantasy, and Horror" booklists (begun by visionary founders Dorothy Broderick and Mary K. Chelton) became crucial. I thank my stalwart staff, Avis Matthews and Linda Benson, for keeping *VOYA* afloat during my mad rush before deadline.

This long and challenging project was made bearable by the enormous support I received from friends and family. Richard Strompf encouraged me to make the initial leap. Old friends Linda Myers Vitello, Eileen Zeller, and Joy Savage patiently listened to me rant by long-distance telephone. These friends shared both empathy and professional expertise: publisher/librarians Martha Franklin and Shirley Lambert, writers Frank and Lavinia Reno, school librarian/fantasy aficionado Nancy Moore, YA librarian/writers Joni Bodart, Pam Spencer, and Mary K. Chelton—who in synchronicity finished her dissertation the moment I finished this book. Each one lent willing ears and unerring advice, and I owe them all, big time. Patty Campbell walked the treacherous tightrope between being my editor and friend, managing never to be intrusive, and I deeply appreciate her efforts.

Too long separated by thousands of miles, my family was nevertheless always there for me. Brother Ed, who beat me in publishing his own books, was another source of writing wisdom. Vermont siblings Carol and Richard put up with my ventilating by phone and e-mail; professional therapist Carol earned her place as first in the family to hear the book was finished. My mother,

Fern, was unfailingly loyal and encouraging, and stepped in heroically to lend her cataloging expertise to the creation of my index. My father, Robert, and my stepmother, Edna, forgave me for having so little time to spend with them. I thank all other Grumbines and extended family for continuing to care and never passing judgment during the years when the book ruled my life.

My computer expert brother-in-law, John Dunn, saved this book's life four days before deadline when my computer crashed due to an insidious "stealth" virus. John's hours talking my husband through computer "brain surgery" by overseas phone from London, while holding my hysteria down with his calm assurances, can never be adequately repaid. Another "computerhead" pal, Dick Geldof, chipped in good counsel and a new computer. Lyn Hurst and John Peacock also gave antivirus assistance. Every unwary home computer owner needs such an expert team.

Beyond computer surgery, my husband, Robin Dunn's, contribution was inestimable. As a publisher, bookseller, and fellow writer, he understood my process, giving immeasurably valuable counsel. He kept his head during every crisis, forsaking his own work to become my editor, bibliographic expert, library researcher, and right hand. There are no words to thank him enough for being there. Rhubarb, our only "child" cat, was also an anchor and is probably my only assistant who got back as good as she gave, in long hours luxuriating on my lap as I read more books than ever in our life together.

Beyond all these gifts is the vital involvement of this book's official consultants, 85 young adult fantasy evaluators (YAFEs), especially the Fantasy Fanatics at Boulder Public Library. The contribution of these talented teenage fantasy readers is detailed in the preface, and this book is dedicated to those who were most deeply involved. The book itself, with all their names in print beside their many quoted comments, is my heartfelt thanks to them. I am especially grateful to Fanatic artist, Galadriel Wills, for producing the marvelous cover illustration on a very tight deadline, knowing she is as happy as I am to see her art in print.

Young Adult Fantasy Evaluators (YAFEs)

Fantasy Fanatics, Boulder, Colorado

Graham Andrews
Allison Barrett
Ashley Besel-Gregg
Silas Bowler
Vanessa Bowler
Colyn Bulthaup
Ashley Burns
Dylan Burns
Jehnie Burns
Ben Cameron
Ben Cantrick
Adam Chapin
Amy Coffelt
Jesse Coffelt
Noah Cohen
Midian Crosby
Robin Deeter
Alison (Pixy) Dougherty
Jenny Dowe
Nathan Doyle
Tiernan Doyle
Malinda Dunckley
Brian Dunning
Nicole Fardi
Kylin Follenweider
Nadia Haddad
Erik Hansen

Alysia Hayas
Guy Iseley
Mariah Iseley
Justin Kantor
Aron Kelly
Ian Kelly
Marc Langford
Genevieve Lawrence
Sarah Luna
Jessica Lundie
Alex Pelton
Naomi Perera
Natalie Marie Petrarca
Annie Pettigrew
Anne Pizzi
James Potts
Masharey Preston
Linda Reling
Eric Rice
Anna Salim
Jonathan Singer
Maria Taylor
Melissa Tolve
Sam Walter
Nicholas Williams
Galadriel Wills

Ken Caryl Middle School YAFEs, Littleton, Colorado

Alysia Ahlin

John Beachem

Michelle Boudreau

Zack Brackney

Sara Hibschweiler

Becca Kreidler

Sarah "Otto" Marxhausen

Kate McCrimmon

David Proctor

Mesa Public Library YAFEs, Mesa, Arizona

Christy Boyd

P. J. King

Katie Maher

Arvind Sundar

Enoch Pratt Free Library YAFEs, Baltimore, Maryland

Ron Araujo

Tricia Brissett

Megan Corrigan

Raymond Drummond

Bill Henry

Deirdre Kambic

Alisa Kotmair

Amanda Krotki

Rachel Libonati

Domenica Mirarchi

Ann Rodavitch

Matthew Wernsdorfer

Duluth Public Library YAFEs, Duluth, Minnesota

Crickett Lancaster

Gary Virta

Ray Privett III

Springfield-Greene County Library YAFE, Springfield, Missouri

Sara McCorkendale

Spokane Public Library YAFEs, Spokane, Washington

Nicki Crocker

Joel Singer

Rachel Scott

1. Defining Fantasy:
The Impossible Made Real

Fantasy literature is so diverse and so entangled with other imaginative fiction that defining it seems as impossible as its own stories. In her essay on the history of fantasy literature that introduces *The Faces of Fantasy*, editor Terri Windling avoids a definition, since "it is the nature of faery ... to be elusive and mutable. Those readers well versed in fantasy know the feel, the look, the distinctive smell of a fantasy story when they come upon it."[1] Fantasy author Orson Scott Card describes the allure of fantasy for adolescent readers as a survival instinct. Beloved fantasy books, says Card, satisfy teens' "deepest personal hungers; kids know what they're hungry for."[2]

What are young adults hungry for in what Card calls "the literature of the strange"? Highly regarded for both his science fiction and his fantasy writing, Card explains that something in these two related "strange" types of stories "must violate reality as we know it." Adult readers who crave such stories have intuitive temperaments, Card asserts, and are always searching for new identities and possibilities. There is also a "huge audience among adolescents who grow out of it," he says. Adolescence is "a natural time for science fiction and fantasy to be the literature of choice, especially for the best and brightest" (Card).

The reason is simple, Card continues, for most SF and fantasy is about the search for identity by a "romantic hero ... going through the adolescent phase of human life." This hero "is unconnected. He belongs to no community; he is wandering from place to place, doing good (as he sees it), but then moving on. This is the life of the adolescent, full of passion, intensity, magic, and infinite possibility, but lacking responsibility. . . . Who but the adolescent is free to have the adventures that most of us are looking for when we turn to storytellers to satisfy our hunger?"[3]

In her article "Fantasy: Why Kids Read It, Why Kids Need It," Tamora Pierce, another fantasy author, declares that young adults "respond to the idealism and imagination they find in everything they read. . . . They take up causes, . . . are also dreamers. . . . Their minds are flexible, recognizing few limits. Here the seeds are sown for the great visions, those that will change the future for us all. . . . [The] fuel that fires idealism . . . [is] in the mighty symbols of myth, fairy tales, dreams, legends—and fantasy." Pierce identifies elements of fantasy that attract teenagers:

- The impetus to challenge the way things are.
- The creation of a unique place in the world [to belong].
- Empowerment. . . . however short, fat, unbeautiful, weak, dreamy, or unlearned individuals may be, they find a realm in which those things are negated by strength.
- [Ordinary or] very junior people become heroes.
- [Magic is] that great equalizer between the powerful and the powerless.
- Hope and optimism.[4]

These elements are not limited to fantasy novels that target teenagers; they also appear in much adult fantasy. Critics Marshall B. Tymn, Kenneth J. Zahorski, and Robert H. Boyer make a case for "all-ages fantasy" without age restrictions (see chapter 2), which Pierce echoes in her observation that fantasy has "a large crossover audience, with YAs reading the adult shelves once they deplete their part of the store or library, and adults slipping into the youth section" (50). Ruth Nadelman Lynn, whose annotated fantasy bibliography was a major aid to this study, notes that in the 1960s, YA fantasy literature began developing alongside new YA realistic fiction; adolescent protagonists coped with coming-of-age issues in both.[5]

Some try to define fantasy by differentiating it from its sister science fiction. "Fantasy, along with science fiction, is a literature of *possibilities*," proclaims Pierce (50). "Science fiction is the literature of the thinkers, and fantasy is the literature of the feelers," says Card, noting jokingly that one can tell the difference simply from book jacket illustrations: "Science fiction has a lot of rivets and fantasy has a lot of trees" (Card). Rosenberg and Herald, authors of the *Genreflecting* guide, see their fantasy and science fiction sections as "symbiotic," since they share a preoccupation with "other" worlds.[6]

Straddling both genres in her writing, Emma Bull regards science fiction and fantasy as a single genre of fantastic literature. "I'm one of the heretics who think science fiction is a subset of fantasy," she says. "It can be tremendously subversive. For the few hours it takes to read a book, you get somebody else's idea of what's important, of the moral stance to take, of how one treats other people. When you've spent several hours immersed in someone else's value system and culture, you'll come out looking at yours differently. . . . all literature should do it, but science fiction and fantasy are able to deliver it to you in a way that gets around the barriers you set up against receiving information you don't agree with."[7]

Three YAFEs expressed differences between fantasy and science fiction:

Fantasy is an exploration into what our minds wish might be, whereas science fiction searches for what our minds know might be.
                                        —Sarah "Otto" Marxhausen, 14

Fantasy is things that can't happen. Science fiction is stuff that can happen but isn't happening right now.
                                        —Galadriel Wills, 14

Fantasy: a story that uses magical rather than mechanical means to make miracles.
                                        —Anne Pizzi, 14

A Menu of Fantasy

Taste this intriguing menu from many chefs, describing the "feast" of fantasy that Orson Scott Card recommends librarians and teachers prepare for the "hungry" young adult.

Critics on Fantasy

[Fantasy is] a body of stories that deals in the marvelous, the magical, and the otherworldly. . . . The "truest" fantasies present us with an inner landscape, one might almost say a spiritual landscape, which may well have psychological and mythological depths.

—David Pringle[8]

"Fantasy literature" is a broad term used to describe books in which magic causes impossible, and often wondrous, events to occur. . . . Such themes as the conflict between good and evil, the struggle to preserve joy and hope in a cruel and frightening world, and the acceptance of the inevitability of death have led some critics to suggest that fantasies may portray a truer version of reality than . . . realistic novels. . . . The two elements . . . given the greatest weight by critics and fantasists alike are the presence of magic and of the impossible or inexplicable.

—Ruth Nadelman Lynn (xxiii–iv)

[The fantasy genre] is composed of works in which nonrational phenomena play a significant part—without scientific explanation.

—Marshall B. Tymn, Kenneth J. Zahorski, and Robert H. Boyer[9]

The essential ingredient of all fantasy is "the marvelous," . . . anything outside the normal space-time continuum of the everyday world.

—Ann Swinfen[10]

The writer of fantasy goes beyond realism to disclose that we do not live entirely in a world of the perceived senses, that we also inhabit an inner world of the mind and spirit where the creative imagination is permanently struggling to expand vision and perception.

—Sheila Egoff[11]

[Fantasy] attempts to convince the reader that the unlikely or improbable or impossible matters being narrated are true—at least for the duration of the reading of the story. . . . When the fantasy elements are given a scientific or pseudoscientific rationale, you've got science fiction. When they're evoked to terrify or horrify you, you have the classic ghost story or tale of the supernatural. And when it's neither, you have the rarest of the subgenres, that which could be called pure fantasy.

—Baird Searles, Beth Meacham, and Michael Franklin[12]

Writers on Fantasy

Those epic tales and fairy tales that speak to us from centuries long past have often taken the form of a quest: The hero is torn from hearth and home and set on a strange unpredictable road, where a trial must be endured, a riddle solved, a monster overcome, a future claimed. By the time of the quest's completion, something or someone has been transformed . . . most often the heroes themselves. Modern fantasy fiction also often takes the form of a quest: [heroes] undergo rites of initiation . . . and, in the process, effect the transformation of the world in which they live.

—Terri Windling (25)

[Fantasy] is a different approach to reality, an alternative technique for apprehending and coping with existence. It is not anti-rational, but pararational; not realistic, but surrealistic, a heightening of reality. . . . It employs archetypes, which, as Jung warned us, are dangerous things. . . . Fantasy is nearer to poetry, to mysticism, and to insanity than naturalistic fiction is. . . . It is a journey into the subconscious mind. . . . Like psychoanalysis, it can be dangerous, and *it will change you.*

—Ursula K. Le Guin[13]

Fantasy . . . comes from and appeals to the unconscious. . . . [T]he fantasist . . . deals with the substance of myth: the deep archetypal patterns of emotion and behavior which haunt us all whether we know it or not. . . . Fantasy, unlike real life, offers amazing adventures with no price tag; all you have to do is open a book. And afterwards, if one of its adventures does ever happen to overtake you, somewhere in your unconscious mind you will be equipped to endure or enjoy it.

—Susan Cooper[14]

The fantasy book, like the fairy tale, may not be Life Actual, but it *is* Life in Truth. . . . It tells us of the world *as it should be*. . . . [T]he fantasy tale . . . becomes a rehearsal for the reader of life as it *should* be lived. . . . The reader, caught in the tale, . . . is unable to get free of the spell. . . . Yet in the end, . . . this acting out in fantasy frees the reader from the fear of failing, the fear of powerlessness, the fear of fearfulness and shame. . . . The fantasy book pushes the reader on to a confrontation with life's greatest mysteries, the great unknowns that frighten us all.

—Jane Yolen[15]

While real life may not call upon us to battle darkangels or wyvern queens, the lessons of perseverance and self-confidence learned in a myth or a fantasy story may help us survive other sorts of conflict. My stories contain a lot of mythological monsters because I'm well aware that not everyone one meets in the real world is a nice, compassionate, ethical person. Life is full of ravenous beasts eager to gobble up the unwary. *En garde!*

—Meredith Ann Pierce[16]

One of the paradoxes lying within the nature of fantasy is this: Though it contains assumptions no sane person would be willing to admit, and though it assaults and breaks the scientific laws of our world, all fantasy that lives and continues to live possesses a strange, private, yet powerful and convincing, reality of its own.

—Eleanor Cameron[17]

True fantasy . . . aims to define the universe. . . . If science has been unable to explain our beginnings to everyone's satisfaction, and if the world's religions disagree . . . about our ends, we can turn to fantasy, just as we have always done. Fantasy doesn't exactly explain these things, but it does give us a variety of systems by which we can at least catch hold of them and examine them for possibilities.

—Natalie Babbitt[18]

If science fiction proclaims itself "the literature of ideas," then fantasy might be called "the literature of ethics." These days we have gotten away from the dualistic insistence that characters be all-bad or all-good, but the foundation of a good fantasy is the conflict between good and evil *forces*. In fantasy, you can not only tell the difference between them, but it makes a difference which you choose.

—Diana Paxson[19]

Most fiction is like a pane of glass, a window that we look through to see another view of the world outside ourselves. It is not a tale of real events, but it *looks* real. . . . The events in a fantasy novel are not simply things that *have* not happened; they are things that *cannot* happen. . . . Fantasy takes the window and coats the outside with the silver of wondrous impossibilities—elves, dragons, wizards, magic. And that window becomes a mirror that reflects both ourselves and all the things in the shadows behind us, the things we have tried to turn our backs on. More: In the best tradition of magic mirrors, fantasy reflects not only ourselves and our shadows, but the truth of our hearts. I think this is one of the reasons some people fear fantasy.

—Patricia C. Wrede (*Faces,* 190)

The job of a storyteller is to speak the truth. But what we feel most deeply can't be spoken in words alone. At this level, only images connect. And here, story becomes symbol; symbol is myth. And myth is truth.

—Alan Garner (*Faces,* 38)

YAFEs on Fantasy

Fantasy is reaching beyond the societal standards of normality and finding an adventure which has the capacity to elevate you toward understanding yourself.

—Linda Reling, 18

Fantasy is overflow of the imagination. It transports us from the flat sameness of mundane reality into the dark corners of the author's mind.

—Nathan Doyle, 18

A good fantasy book is a journey to a place you know you could never reach simply by heading down the interstate. It involves magic, and often analyzes good versus evil, and has creatures your parents told you could never exist. But I don't think those three items define it.

—Rachel Scott, 20

Fantasy takes place anywhere, Past or Present, Near or Far, in a world where anything is possible, and everything that is possible usually happens.

—John Beacham, 14

Fantasy stories take place in worlds which could be if history had been different.

—Noah Cohen, 12

Fantasy is politics, science fiction, fiction, romance, adventure, mystery, poetry, mythology, humor, all together.

—Becca Kreidler, 14

Fantasy is where magic and normal life combine. Mix in a little comedy and you have the ultimate book.

—Kate McCrimmon, 13

Fantasy is a walk on a beach. . . . [T]he strangest, most inane objects wash up . . . and every so often it feels really good.

—Jonathan Singer, 17

A fantasy world is one in which the outrageous is commonplace, a world where you can eat bratwurst for dinner and your dreams that night make sense.

—Eric Rice, 17

Fantasy is an expansion of our reality, the things that we don't expect to happen in our everyday routine. Fantasy is turning on the TV and finding out a dragon ate the Mets.

—Dylan Burns, 16

Before one word of this book was written, a working definition was devised: "fantasy literature takes place in the realm of magic, where happenings defy rational explanation. Beyond mere escape from the real world, the finest visionary fantasy gives wings to its readers' imaginations. The universal archetypes or symbols employed to describe the classic conflict between good and evil expand our awareness of reality. While exploring fantasy's other-worlds, we probe our own inner landscapes." As work progressed, the definition faded, becoming ever more elusive. At the end of this project, Le Guin's dangerousness, Wrede's magic mirror,

YAFE Dylan Burns's dragon eating the Mets, seemed far more apt descriptions of fantasy. Its meaning shapechanges with every chapter of this book.

How Do You Organize a Magic Mirror?

To render fantasy's vast landscapes more navigable, many critics have drawn maps proposing categories of fantasy. Tymn, Zahorski, and Boyer, authors of *Fantasy Literature: A Core Collection and Reference Guide,* note enormous confusion among critics and writers, who disagree when defining terms such as "heroic fantasy" or "sword and sorcery." After careful analysis of others' fantasy classifications, they use their own three broad categories based on high fantasy, which occurs entirely in a secondary or alternate world, and low fantasy, where magical happenings intrude in everyday life. Ruth Nadelman Lynn acknowledges their system in her exhaustive annotated bibliography *Fantasy Literature for Children and Young Adults,* but she chooses to divide her 4,800 titles into 11 narrow categories, some relating only to children's stories or to the dark fantasy left out of this book. In *Genreflecting,* Rosenberg and Herald also use 11 categories, different than Lynn's. Searles, Meacham, and Franklin use 6 types in *A Reader's Guide to Fantasy.* Gale's *What Do I Read Next?* treads a more narrow path with 17 fantasy categories.

Other critics found fantasy such an amorphous stew that they threw every type of tale in the pot together. While picking *The Hundred Best Novels* of modern fantasy, David Pringle concluded that fantasy is a "formless" genre "wholly without good manners and literary decorum." This "swamp" is "the breeding ground for all other popular fictional genres" (Pringle, 14).

Since no one has declared unbreakable rules of fantasy classification, this study merges existing systems to make yet another to fit our requirements. Its primary aim is to offer useful categories for young adult readers, educators, and librarians searching for the type of fantasy story they want, illuminating fantasy's elusive meaning through careful description of its varieties. Critical biographies of the four featured authors are placed within subgenres they represent: Terry Brooks in alternate worlds, Barbara Hambly in magic realism, Jane Yolen in mythic fantasy, and Meredith Ann Pierce in "A Magic Bestiary." Each subgenre is further defined and refined within each chapter. As previously noted, the subgenres of legend and time travel are in chapters without featured authors. Of course, many books classify in more than one category; a mythic fantasy could be set in an alternate world, thereby fitting in both chapters 2 and 4. For clarity, each book is assigned to one category.

Though arranging fantasy by subgenre facilitates the reader's location of the type of book desired in a critique such as this, library and bookstore displays still present problems. Publishers argue over the increasing tendency to market fantasy in subcategories, identified by cover designs and tag lines that lump together titles not similar in content, perhaps excluding some potential readers or disappointing others. Terri Windling observes that "serious literary endeavors and light adventure novels for teenage boys ... sit side by side upon the fantasy shelves, often with identical dragons and swordsmen leering from the covers. ... [O]ne must come equipped with reviews and recommendations in order to wade through the deluge of titles published every year" (Windling, 23–24).

A 1993 *Publishers Weekly* article examines "packaging cues" and issues in science fiction's and fantasy's proliferating subcategories. Some booksellers believe they limit sales if they separate fantasy and science fiction at all, while others feel they help customers with display breakdowns of fantasy game tie-in books, epic fantasy, dark fantasy, even "elfpunk." Librarians also struggle with these issues and would likely agree with Tor editor Neilson Hayden's observations that "An enormous part of the field falls between the various subgenres," that "Subcategories are only useful to the extent that they actually hook up with a definable clump of readers with similar reading tastes," and that "Ultimately, the history of literature is the history of authors, not subgenres."[20]

Is there a last word on the subject? There is merely the most recent. As the final chapter of this manuscript was being written, a brand-new 1,000-page *Encyclopedia of Fantasy* appeared. Would it have made this task any easier? Its introduction revealed that editors John Clute and John Grant struggled with the same impossible definition to limit their far fatter work. Capitalizing each word or phrase used in their subject headings, they declare, "Tales involving DREAMS and VISIONS, ALLEGORY and ROMANCE, SUR-REALISM and MAGIC REALISM, SATIRE and WONDERLAND, SUPERNAT-URAL FICTION, DARK FANTASY, WEIRD FICTION and HORROR—all of these and more besides, sometimes expressing conflicting under-standings of the nature of fantasy, were theoretically within our remit." They settled on this "rough" definition: "a fantasy text is a . . . narrative which, when set in our REALITY, tells a story which is impossible in the world as we perceive it; when set in an OTHER-WORLD or SECONDARY WORLD, that otherworld will be impossible, but stories set there will be possible *in the otherworld's terms.*"[21]

When encyclopedia editors can find a definition so rational for the irrational, we must pause yet again to consult an artist. Famous for his marvelously real illustrations of literary aliens in the 1980 ALA Best Book for Young Adults, *Barlowe's Guide to Extraterrestrials* (Workman, 1980), Wayne Douglas Barlowe introduces his fabulous new *Barlowe's Guide to Fantasy* with these words: "What is it about fantasy that has so captivated the minds of people since time began? . . . I think that through fan-tasy, people—both primitive and civilized—have the sudden abil-ity to ask for and be granted all things. The realm of fantasy is one in which absolutely anything can and does happen. And as such, it is as fulfilling as anything can be."[22]

2. Alternate Worlds: Beyond the Walls of the World

> It is by such statements as, "Once upon a time there was a dragon," or "In a hole in the ground there lived a hobbit"—it is by such beautiful non-facts that we fantastic human beings may arrive, in our peculiar fashion, at the truth.
>
> —Ursula K. Le Guin, "Why Are Americans Afraid of Dragons," in *The Language of the Night*

High fantasy, heroic fantasy, epic fantasy, alternate or secondary world fantasy, adventure fantasy, fantastic romance, sword-and-sorcery: all are the same, most popular type of fantasy, set entirely within an author's invented otherworld. Though otherworlds have many landscapes, one usually detects a striking resemblance to home.

Visit any library or bookstore to be amazed at the abundance of otherworlds proliferating in countless writers' imaginations. Be further amazed that just over 30 years ago, these teeming choices in otherworld travel were not available. The fantasy travel agency of multidestinations did not open in America until the landmark publication of J. R. R. Tolkien's trilogy, *The Lord of the Rings*. Tolkien still inspires new creations long after his death. As he began his trilogy in 1938, Tolkien delivered a university lecture, "On Fairy-stories," which called fantasy writing a "sub-creative art";[1] writers' world building mirrors God's creation of our world. The successful sub-creator "makes a Secondary World which your mind can enter. Inside it, what he relates is 'true': it accords with the laws of that world. You therefore believe it, while you are, as it were, inside. The moment disbelief arises, the spell is broken; the magic, or rather art, has failed. You are then out in the Primary World again" (*Tree,* 36).

So it is the reader's belief in the writer's Secondary World that makes it real. When we put down the book to return to the everyday Primary World, our life here is enriched, Tolkien believed, by perceptions of magic from the Secondary World. The reading experience brings us awareness of the mystical that colors our reality, "giving a fleeting glimpse of Joy, Joy beyond the walls of the world" (*Tree,* 60).

To invest the construction of a world within a book with such momentous inspiration has been Tolkien's legacy to fantasy writers (see "Writers on Fantasy" in chapter 1). In a doubting modern world, otherworld creators labor to "induce 'Secondary belief' " in readers, declares critic Ann Swinfen.[2] A secondary world must have its own "essential inner consistency," and readers must recognize its basics in their own world in order to sympathize with otherworld characters and understand the ways of that world (Swinfen, 75–76). These elements of world building make it "acceptable to readers":

- Its physical laws of nature should seem comprehensible and logical (77).
- Its history must relate to its geography (often with actual maps) through facts or fables (80).
- It must take place in a defined cultural period, often related to earth (82).
- Language and literature must be specified and detailed (85).
- A belief system must contain religion, philosophy, and values (88).

Young adult literature experts Kenneth L. Donelson and Alleen Pace Nilsen list similar qualities of good fantasy, including real-world relationships, "internally consistent" physical laws, and these additional elements:

- A smooth, unhackneyed way of establishing the imaginative world
- An originality of concept
- Something that stimulates readers to participate in the author's creative thinking and to carry the story further in their own minds.[3]

Incorporating all these elements into a brisk and involving plot with sympathetic characters is not the only daunting task facing otherworld creators. If they succeed that far, authors have "complete artistic freedom" to explore their own philosophies of life without our reality's restrictions (Swinfen, 76, 92). The best alternate world fantasies, beyond mere escapism or battles between good guys and bad, have "profound moral purpose" that critiques our own society and makes readers think (2). Otherworld inhabitants face spiritual or moral dilemmas that parallel ours, sometimes posed more clearly as good versus evil (91). Swinfen sees the challenge for fantasy writers as convincing readers of their created reality and its relevance to them (99). The finest works offer readers provocative ways to see their own world from an alternate viewpoint.

Each author's unique otherworld somehow converts science to magic. Many writer-creators explore, almost scientifically, exactly how magic works, what forces control it through its witch or wizard masters. Humorists parody classic fantasy elements, their playful irreverence making a point. No matter how magical or madcap, alternate world fantasy is always about us.

Otherworld Foundations: Before We Heard of Tolkien

For most of human history, all stories have been more or less fantastic. When tales were told instead of written, myths, legends, fables, and fairy tales featured gods, creatures, and superheroes beyond reality. When stories became literature, supernatural characters persisted; Shakespeare brims with ghosts, witches, and fairies. When the novel debuted in the 1700s, realism appeared for the first time, but the most popular novels were gothic tales of terror, in which horrors lurked in scary old mansions. Gothics formed the root of one of fantasy literature's cousins, horror or dark fantasy.

By the nineteenth century, however, realism reigned supreme, flourishing in the works of the great English novelists Thackeray, the Brontës, Dickens, and Eliot and in novels by Americans Mark Twain and Henry James. Fine literature was supposed to tell the truth about human nature, which society believed could be done only through realism. Fantastic tales were banished to children's nurseries or trashy dime novels.

Yet some visionary 1800s writers bucked the trend. Edgar Allan Poe wrote macabre stories, Robert Louis Stevenson wrote about Dr. Jekyll and Mr. Hyde, Bram Stoker wrote *Dracula,* and Mary Shelley wrote *Frankenstein;* Cosette Kies explores their modern descendants in this volume's companion *Presenting Young Adult Horror Fiction* (Twayne, 1992). Jules Verne and H. G. Wells pioneered another cousin of fantasy, covered in a different companion volume, *Presenting Young Adult Science Fiction* by Suzanne Elizabeth Reid (forthcoming, 1998). Fantasy itself was born again when its fathers blazed trails to different subgenres. Lewis Carroll's Alice escaped our real world down a rabbit hole in an early exercise in magic realism (see chapter 3). The American Bulfinch and the Scotsman Frazer collected ancient myths in best-selling anthologies (see chapter 4). Tales of legendary King Arthur and Robin Hood were retold for young readers early in this century (see chapter 5). Rudyard Kipling and Kenneth Grahame portrayed sentient or talking animals (see chapter 6), and E. Nesbit sent her child characters through time in time fantasy (see chapter 7).

The best-selling heroic or alternate world fantasy at the heart of fantasy literature today was one of the last types of fantasy to develop. It began casually, a small part of the voluminous artistic output of William Morris. To counteract the materialistic Industrial Revolution, this English utopian socialist became a "one-man Renaissance," designing architecture, furniture, fabrics, wallpaper, costumes, and hand-printed books while fathering the Pre-Raphaelite art movement.[4] We still use the Morris chair, and his repeating design patterns appear on modern gift wrap.

Adding scribbling to his pastimes, Morris foreshadowed Tolkien's interest in Norse sagas, translating them into English. After composing new romances in the old medieval style, he decided to invent his own type of medieval world; in so doing, William Morris invented heroic fantasy. In 1895 he published *The Wood Beyond the World*, "the first great fantasy novel ever written" (Carter, ix).

Because hero Walter sails from his earthly city, Langton, to the otherworld, this study would categorize Morris's novel as magic realism, echoing *Gulliver's Travels*. Yet once Walter arrives on otherworld shores, there is no returning home. Several sightings in his own city of a curious trio of "alien wayfarers," a Maid, a Mistress, and a Dwarf, propel Walter to search for them; his ship seems fated to land in their country, where a solo quest across rugged mountains leads to a glorious pastoral forest. When Walter finds the Maid sighing beside a pool, it is love at first sight. He must help her escape from her cruel Mistress, whose evil Dwarf tortures her and whose bored lover pursues her.

Instead of acting as dashing knight in shining armor, Walter must wait agonizingly for the Maid's instructions as she spins a web—secret even from Walter—to trap the powerful Mistress, since her wizardry endangers them both. As the Maid employs wisdom to trick the Mistress, the Mistress treacherously woos Walter. Nothing is as it seems in this wood, where Walter must keep his wits about him to win a future for his Maid and himself.

Morris never explains the Mistress's powers, though she and her hideous Dwarf are the epitome of evil. The Maid, though pure and good, is tormented by her need to employ guile and betrayal to become free and must confess these sins to Walter before they can be together. Every decision Morris's hero and heroine make involves an ethical choice. When Walter and the Maid finally achieve their destiny, they realize they have escaped "the razor-edge betwixt guile and misery and death" on their truly fraught hero's journey (Morris, 233).

Morris keeps readers on that edge of suspense, while his archaic, quaint language (antique even in his time, so stylized it was never realistic) propels us into his isolated otherworld. One cannot read endless *forsooths, meseemeths,* and *bedights* without feeling foreignness. The hidden magic of the wood and its residents is never revealed, so Morris's enchantment never lifts. Readers who enjoy being ensnared in such spells will persist in Morris's mysterious otherworld. He also wrote a coming-of-age quest, *The Well at the World's End,* and *The Water of the Wondrous Isles.*

Morris's work inspired Lord Dunsany, who was 18 when Morris died in 1896, to write his later spellbinding tales of faerie. E. R. Eddison also followed Morris's example; claims author Lin Carter, "[F]rom these three master storytellers derive almost every important writer of adventurous fantasy" (Carter, xiv). Considered "one of the true originals of fantasy,"[5] Eddison published *The Worm Ouroboros: A Romance* in 1922. From his bedroom, Englishman Lessingham is whisked away by a winged horse and chariot to Mercury, not a planet but a true otherworld where epic battle rages between a sorcerer king and demon lords. Loosely connected to Eddison's first novel is the *Zimiamvian* trilogy, written from the 1930s to the 1950s.

Eclipsed in America by his contemporary Tolkien but also popular among British students was Mervyn Peake, Tolkien's worthy rival in otherworld creation. *Titus Groan,* the first volume of Peake's monumental *Gormenghast* trilogy, is "one of the greatest fantasy novels in the language."[6] Published in 1946 between Tolkien's *Hobbit* and *The Fellowship of the Ring, Titus Groan* was followed by *Gormenghast* in 1950 and by the final volume, *Titus Alone,* in 1959 (delayed in America until 1967). The trilogy is well worth rediscovery by readers today. Peake's vivid but magicless parallel world, over which looms crumbling Gormenghast Castle, is unforgettable. His characters, whose eccentricities include such Dickensian names as Rottcodd, Flay, and Dr. Prunesquallor, hover near the edge of caricature. Yet they are individual and brilliantly drawn, representing infinite varieties of human nature enmeshed in the tragicomic human condition. The trilogy opens with the birth of Titus Groan, the 77th Earl of Groan, who must make his mark through the crushing weight of inherited meaningless ritual and handle the revolt of the sly kitchen boy Steerpike.

Peake's background as a printer and illustrator informs his lush descriptions, every detail visualized. He began writing *Titus Groan* as a World War II gunner and bomb-disposal expert (Pringle, 28); a dread suspense tingles through the labyrinthine plot like the unbearable moment before a bomb is defused. By the time he wrote the last volume, Peake was suffering from a degenerative illness that also defused the power of his writing. And Tolkien had arrived.

YAFEs on Foundations

Peake—*Titus Groan*

Each character portrays human weaknesses, and no one is entirely good or evil. Almost all the seven "cardinal" sins are represented in Gormenghast: envy, vanity, greed, lust, ignorance, revenge. I liked the author's rich wording. The story itself is very intense, lightened only where he stopped to describe a sunset or something else, as if painting a picture. This is not the usual light fairy tale romance fantasy with big men wielding swords and killing dragons. I would recommend it to anyone dedicated and broad-minded enough to read it.

—Tiernan Doyle, 13

English Inklings and Weird American Barbarians

In "the poverty-stricken 1930s and the war-torn 1940s . . . when fantasy was at its lowest ebb," a "wonderfully symmetrical" pattern appeared with the emergence of six writers divided equally into two sets, one British, one American. These two groups of fellow writers enormously influenced the development of two divergent strands of fantasy, separated by an ocean (Searles et al., 172).

The Inklings were a group of students and professors who gathered at England's Oxford University to discuss writing, literature, and philosophy, often over beer at the pub. In 1937, one Inkling published *The Hobbit,* based on stories he had spun for his children. Only after his books about Middle-earth achieved cult status in the late 1960s was J. R. R. Tolkien recognized as the founder of modern heroic fantasy. Two fellow Inklings, C. S. Lewis and Charles Williams, explored Christian themes in their fantasy writings. *War in Heaven,* published by Williams in 1930, blends murder mystery in a contemporary church setting with a search for the Arthurian Holy Grail. Lewis achieved more lasting fame with his *Chronicles of Narnia* (see chapter 3).

The American trio of writers who began their own fantasy strand had less scholarly origins. Robert E. Howard, H. P. Lovecraft, and Clark Ashton Smith lived in locations spread across the continent. They became pen pals but never actually met. All published short stories in the pulp magazine *Weird Tales,* launched in 1923. Within its lurid covers was a wild mix of supernatural, science fiction, and fantasy stories of varied quality, some shoddy, some now classic. None of the three writers became famous in his lifetime; all were flawed. New Englander Lovecraft's often purple prose gloried in the occult, his creepy pseudoscientific creatures bent on taking over the world; his writing veered into dark fantasy and horror. Smith, a Californian, remains the least known but most polished and poetic of the three.

Texan bodybuilder Robert E. Howard, whose "major contribution to fantasy was the barbarian hero" (Searles et al., 174), has achieved cult status since his tragic 1936 death by suicide at age 30, portrayed in the 1996 film *The Whole Wide World,* which stars Renée Zellweger and Vincent D'Onofrio. Inspired by the adventure stories of Jack London and Edgar Rice Burroughs's *Tarzan,* Howard started a series of stories in 1926 about Kull of Atlantis, a Stone Age savage who becomes a king. In 1932, Howard created his most enduring character, Conan the Cimmerian, a "gigantic barbarian adventurer" who becomes a king, like Kull, "after a lifetime of wading through rivers of gore and overcoming foes both natural and supernatural,"[7] according to L. Sprague de

Camp, a fantasy author who helped revive Conan almost 30 years after Howard's death. During his lifetime, about 160 of his stories were published in various magazines. Only 17 stories and one serialized novel, *The Hour of the Dragon,* were about Conan, who lived in the Hyborian Age, conceived by Howard as an amalgam of primitive societies before the Ice Age. The Hyborian Age, which expanded in his vigorous imagination to include demons, sorcerers, and damsels in distress, became, in all its gory glory, a true otherworld.

Howard also wrote about other heroes: Puritan Solomon Kane and Irish foe of the Vikings Cormac Mac Art. Nonfantasy writings included sea stories, boxing stories, Westerns, and poetry. Many of his 250 stories were published only posthumously. Other writers including de Camp have edited or rewritten Conan stories or created their own. Paperback reissues finally made Howard a bestselling author long after his death. In 1950, serial installments of his only novel were gathered in one volume under a new title, *Conan the Conqueror.* Among heroic fantasists in the 1970s, he was "surpassed in sales only by Tolkien—who once told me," says de Camp, "that he rather liked the Conan stories" ("Barbarian," 176). Everyone knows Conan now, from Marvel Comics and Frank Frazetta art and Arnold Schwarzeneggar movies. But Howard's stories are still difficult to find. A 1994 paperback of the one novel, reprinted under its original title, *The Hour of the Dragon,* is already unavailable. Some new Conan tales by Robert Jordan and Sean Moore are listed in this chapter's Recommended Reading.

De Camp's essay "The Miscast Barbarian" reveals much about the shadowy, tragic young writer. Howard's hero was a barbarian because Howard believed that primitivism was humanity's natural state; civilization was decadent. Howard's writing could be excessively violent, derivative, repetitive, racist, and careless. Yet it continues to attract readers to Howard's "distinctive intensity—a curious sense of total emotional commitment, which hypnotically drags the reader along" (141). Tortured, unstable Howard saw Conan as his idealized self.

Not until the late 1960s did Fritz Leiber, a writer following the form that Howard invented, coin its label, "sword-and-sorcery."

Leiber began writing the humorous, earthy adventures of his own rogue barbarian hero, Fafhrd, and the thief Gray Mouser soon after Howard's death. The only novel about them, *The Swords of Lankhmar,* wasn't published until 1968. Leiber was one in a trio of second-generation writers following in the footsteps of Howard and his *Weird Tales* originators, in the fantasy magazine *Unknown,* published from 1939 to 1943.

Leiber's cohorts were L. Sprague de Camp and Fletcher Pratt, who coauthored the Harold Shea stories. Harold Shea is a psychologist who studies paraphysics, which postulates that infinite otherworlds coexist with ours. If we could only fill our minds with the assumptions of another world's natural laws, we could visit there. Bored with his life, Harold does just that. Aiming for mythic Ireland, he lands instead among the Norse gods in "The Roaring Trumpet." Harold, astonished that his matches, flashlight, and gun won't work, instead has the magical skills of a warlock, handy when confronting trolls and giants. Quick wits are Harold's survival tool, and the thrill of adventure has improved his temperament by the time he lands back home due to a fluke. Now his boss wants to join him in proving the existence of otherworlds, so together they hit the England of Spenser's *Faerie Queene* in "The Mathematics of Magic." Both lengthy stories were first published in *Unknown* in 1940, were revised to appear together in a 1941 book, *The Incompleat Enchanter,* and became "compleat" in various editions with three other Shea tales, "The Castle of Iron," "The Wall of Serpents," and "The Green Magician," most recently in a 1989 paperback entitled *The Complete Compleat Enchanter.* These humorous adventures reveal human foibles while poking fun—the stinky Norse giants pick their noses, spit, and speak like Chicago gangsters. Yet de Camp and Pratt meticulously describe the settings and mythic characters they parody quite entertainingly, inspiring the later "light fantasy" of Gordon R. Dickson (see chapter 6), Robert Asprin, Terry Pratchett, and others.

Pratt and de Camp also collaborated on a 1942 novel, *Land of Unreason,* reprinted from *Unknown,* in which a wounded American in World War II England slips into *A Midsummer Night's*

Dream. On his own, historian Pratt published a complex medieval fantasy in 1948, *The Well of the Unicorn,* influenced by British fantasists Eddison and Dunsany but also a subtle political commentary that preceded other fantasy writers' similar attempts. In 1953 de Camp, an engineer and patent law expert, published his own epic sword-and-sorcery novel, *The Tritonian Ring,* set in a Bronze Age alternate Earth, with his trademark humor and Howard's influence.

How do these British and American strands of fantasy, launched 60 years ago by Tolkien and Howard, fare near our century's close? Both have come to be regarded as heroic fantasy. Searles et al. helpfully differentiate: "Where the English trio made heavy use of traditional myth and religion and folklore, the Americans were making up their own; it was obvious that the Americans felt the weight of their past much less" (174). The sword-and-sorcery label for "Conanesque thud-and-blunder" got mixed up with the Tolkienesque; eventually sword-and-sorcery was regarded as a "pejorative epithet," whereas heroic fantasy was acceptable (178). Attempting to clarify these indefinite terms, critics Tymn, Zahorski, and Boyer suggest that "high fantasy" be used to describe most heroic fantasy, while "sword-and-sinew" could replace "sword-and-sorcery" to cover escape literature with little redeeming value that features barbarian superheroes, flat characters, all action, little theme, colloquial style, and gratuitous violence.[8]

Sword-and-sorcery is now a label for imitative fantasy, often connected with role-playing, computer, and video games. Eminent editor David G. Hartwell explains the genesis of current derivative fantasy by tracing fantasy publishing since the 1970s, when Ballantine editor Lester del Rey set up an adult fantasy novel formula for what had previously been confined to children's books: "In invented worlds in which magic works, . . . a male central character . . . triumphed over the forces of evil . . . by innate virtue. . . . It was nostalgic, conservative, pastoral, and optimistic." This formula was so successful that other publishers insisted that their authors convert every fantasy into a trilogy. "Trash writing . . . mediocrity . . . and repetition" resulted.[9] Over the next 20 years, the quality of fantasy writing steadily improved as the field widened. Hartwell applauds the many fine and original fantasy authors now writing, and Searles et al. celebrate "the incredibly rich mosaic" of our current "Golden Age of fantasy" (178).

How do readers sort the original from the derivative, the rich themes from mere blood-and-guts action? Young adult readers, rarely allergic to formula, often find predictable, ongoing series comforting and familiar. Yet they also recognize good story. Resonant themes speak to them as deeply as they do to more experienced readers. The critics who suggest "sword-and-sinew" propose another category, "all-ages fantasy," explaining how fine fantasy appeals to readers of different ages at different levels. Unlike mainstream literature, fantasy can have either child or adult protagonists without limiting readers' identification to characters their own age. Sophisticated issues, elaborate settings, archetypal characters who grow, many layers of meaning, an elevated writing style—"poor style is the surest giveaway of a second-rate fantasy"—all are found in all-ages fantasy. It is defined as "works that can be read with equal (though different) appreciation by the child, the adolescent, and the adult" (Tymn et al., 25–28). A perfect example is C. S. Lewis's *Chronicles of Narnia,* YAFEs' most-read fantasy series, first encountered as young as age nine, when it is beloved as a great adventure story. When the series is reread in adolescence or adulthood, Christian symbolism and other deep themes emerge. The heady variety of fantasy books from which young adults choose today are flowers of every hue, a harvest gathered from seeds sown by Tolkien and his contemporaries on both shores of the Atlantic.

J. R. R. Tolkien:
Founder of Modern Heroic Fantasy

I am in fact a hobbit in all but size. I like gardens, trees; . . . I smoke a pipe, and like good plain food, . . . and even dare to wear . . . ornamental waistcoats. I am fond of mushrooms; . . . have a very simple sense of humor, . . . I go to bed late and get up late. . . . I do not travel much.
—J. R. R. Tolkien, in Carpenter, *Tolkien: A Biography*

When rotund, furry-footed hobbit Bilbo Baggins emerged from his round doorway to embark on a perilous adventure, the face of fantasy literature forever changed. J. R. R. Tolkien's children's story *The Hobbit* drew conventional peace-loving Bilbo into a harrowing mission to recover the dwarves' treasure stolen by Smaug the dragon. Tossed headlong by Gandalf the wizard into treacherous forces he hardly comprehended, Bilbo survives through his untested courage and instinct for good, arriving safely home again.

Bilbo's story was published almost accidentally, when a London editor heard that a distinguished Oxford professor was entertaining colleagues with his own amusing "fairy tale." Publisher Sir Stanley Unwin put the manuscript to the supreme test: he asked his 10-year-old son Rayner's opinion. The boy dubbed *The Hobbit* very exciting and appealing to young readers, so his father published it, in 1937. (Young Rayner earned a shilling for his written report.) The next year it reached America. On both shores, it became so popular that readers clamored for a sequel. Burdened with obligations of lecturing, research, and grading papers, Tolkien was more interested in working out his own mythology than in writing children's stories. His own children had grown too old to practice on. What more could be said about hobbits?

Yet Middle-earth, the Secondary World of Bilbo's Shire, was part of this mythology, holding irresistible allure for Tolkien. Since adolescence, he had been inventing languages sparked by ancient northern European tongues, and he had become a professor of philology, the study of linguistics and the history of language, which connected with mythology. Tolkien wished his native England had its own myths to match the robust Icelandic *Eddas*. In his mid-20s, during a long hospital recovery from trench fever caught as a World War I soldier, Tolkien began to construct his imaginary English mythology by writing stories peopled by immortal elves and other magical creatures for *The Book of Lost Tales*. Tolkien added to those tales and associated maps, languages, alphabets, chronologies, and lineages for over 50 years. Only after his death would his son Christopher gather and edit this sprawling mythology into a book, *The Silmarillion,* published at last in 1977.

The Hobbit revealed but a tiny portion of Tolkien's mythic world, already under construction for 20 years when the book was first published. Struggling to produce the requested sequel, Tolkien realized that the magic ring Bilbo had found in slimy Gollum's cave could be the focus of a quest. Sauron the Dark Lord could be searching for his lost ring, which he needed to rule the world. Ignorant that the treacherous ring not only makes its wearer invisible but exerts control over its owner, Bilbo's young nephew Frodo inherits it.

As Tolkien delved deeper into *The Lord of the Rings,* Frodo's adventures turned darker. The wizard Gandalf tells Frodo he must journey to the Crack of Doom to fling the ring into it, the only way to destroy its evil power. Pursued by the Black Riders, Sauron's terrifying faceless servants, and by Gollum, who also wants the ring, Frodo and his band carry danger with them as the ring starts to possess Frodo's soul.

Tolkien labored on *The Lord of the Rings* for over 12 years. It grew in length, seriousness, and style far beyond a children's story. Its publisher, Unwin, had no idea who would read it. Would adults be interested in such an adventure quest? Never intended as a trilogy, it was so long that Unwin could not afford to print it as a single volume. The story had been structured as six "books" in one; Tolkien reluctantly broke it into three parts of two books each. In 1954, four years after he finished writing it, the first volume was published in Britain as *The Fellowship of the Ring.* A few months later, *The Two Towers* appeared, then *The Return of the King* the following year. The three volumes were published separately in America in 1955. Having waited 17 years since asking Tolkien for a *Hobbit* sequel, the publishers expected to lose money on the trilogy. Hadn't public interest in hobbits died down? Yet a trilogy—and with such cliff-hangers at the end of each part—was very unusual. Fans panted for each new installment. It gained momentum until the 1965 publication of all three volumes in one. By the late 1960s, it had become a U.S. campus cult classic; its epic struggle of good against evil, of the ordinary against the powerful, struck a chord with youth rebelling against conservative authority. Students wore buttons proclaiming "Frodo Lives!" or "Gandalf for President."

What was it about *The Lord of the Rings* that captured the imaginations of a generation of youth and many more since? Is it true that critics either loved it or hated it? How did an otherworld creation by a scholarly, stodgy language professor become "the norm according to which all other fantasy works must now be judged" (Tymn et al., 163)? Some answers might be found in Tolkien's Secondary World of Middle-earth. Tolkien proved to be a genius at the "sub-creative art" defined in his famous essay "On Fairy-stories" (found in both *Tree and Leaf* and *The Tolkien Reader*). Readers who enter Middle-earth believe in it while they are there, partly because Middle-earth is our earth's ancestor. One critic calls Tolkien's world "the backward extension of the one we know from romance, legend, folklore, and fairy tale."[10]

"Middle-earth is *our* world," Tolkien admitted, but "in a purely imaginary . . . period of antiquity, in which the shape of the continental masses was different."[11] He based the Shire landscape on his family's home county of Worcestershire, in England's West Midlands—his Aunt Jane's farm was called Bag End, borrowed for his hobbit's house. Hobbiton village is actually Sarehole, in the neighboring county Warwickshire, where Tolkien lived happily as a child for four years near the turn of the century, savoring trees, plants, and contours of the English countryside before being uprooted to attend school in the sooty city of Birmingham.[12]

Many who observed or wrote about Tolkien noted his curious attitude toward Middle-earth. His biographer Humphrey Carpenter visited Tolkien at home in an Oxford suburb in 1967. As they discussed revisions for *The Lord of the Rings,* Carpenter realized that Tolkien saw "his book not as a work of fiction but as a chronicle of actual events," with himself as "a historian who must cast light on an obscurity in a historical document" (Carpenter, 4). Often a vision of an episode, character, or place would come to Tolkien unbidden, and he searched for explanations as if "Middle-earth was a world discovered rather than dreamed up" (Lawler, 800). He felt, corroborates Robin McKinley, a fantasy author who also wrote a penetrating critique of Tolkien, that "he was only recording a story, a history, that existed somewhere, perhaps not in our world as we know it, but somewhere" (McKinley, 562). Tolkien convinces readers of Middle-earth's reality because he is himself convinced of it.

Tolkien was, of course, utterly familiar with Middle-earth because he had been visiting there for so long, building the mythology that became *The Silmarillion,* which he called the prequel to *The Lord of the Rings.* Critics have called *The Silmarillion* "elvish scripture, ... the foundation of ... Middle-earth and everything in it" (Lawler, 800), or Middle-earth's "Bible—the mythopoeic account of the creation of Tolkien's land and the compendium of its cosmology and history" (Tymn et al., 167). Carpenter suggests that Tolkien could not finish *The Silmarillion* because his endless revisions and digressions were satisfying; "sub-creation had become a sufficiently rewarding pastime in itself" (285). What other fantasy author has devoted as much time, concentration, and expertise as Tolkien did to creating an otherworld? He sits alone atop heroic fantasy's pinnacle, inspiring other writers to attempt his achievements though he may be an impossible act to follow.

Many critics have tried to express why Tolkien was such a fantasy master, while acknowledging that his work of genius is flawed. There is little undiluted praise of Tolkien's work by anyone other than devoted fans. Even C. S. Lewis, Tolkien's friend and Inkling colleague, who claimed in a sincerely laudatory review of *The Fellowship of the Ring* that it was a revolutionary "book like lightning from a clear sky" (Carpenter, 248), had reservations—especially about Tolkien's poetry. (Tolkien and Lewis had a complicated relationship, as they were intolerant of each other's criticism; Tolkien did not disguise his contempt for Lewis's *Narnia* series.) Poet W. H. Auden reviewed the first two volumes of *Lord of the Rings* in the *New York Times,* claiming, "No fiction I have read in the last five years has given me more joy" (Carpenter, 250). But Auden also observed that opinions about Tolkien were polarized: "[E]ither, like myself, people find it a masterpiece of its genre, or they cannot abide it" (253). American critic Edmund Wilson soundly slammed *The Lord of the Rings:*

> The wars are never dynamic; the ordeals give no sense of strain; the fair ladies would not stir a heartbeat; the horrors would not hurt a fly. . . . These characters who are no characters are involved in interminable adventures, the poverty of invention displayed in which is, it seems to me, almost pathetic. . . . Now, how is it that these long-winded volumes of what looks to this reviewer like balderdash have elicited such tributes . . . ? The answer is, I believe, that certain people . . . have a lifelong appetite for juvenile trash.[13]

After quoting Wilson, fantasy author L. Sprague de Camp offers his own more measured analysis of Tolkien, whom he finds "occasionally awkward, occasionally eloquent" ("Merlin," 219). He sees Tolkien as very successful when interpreting traditional mythology, less so with original concepts. Despite inconsistencies, de Camp concludes that "in this genre, few have equaled and none has surpassed *Lord of the Rings* in vividness, grandeur, and sheer readability" (251).

Robin McKinley meticulously and often hilariously lists Tolkien's flaws:

- "Samwise Gangee, . . . a maudlin recreation of a phony element of a way of life that never existed"
- "That embarrassing creation Tom Bombadil, [who] capers [and] refers to himself in the third person"
- Poetry that is "little more than doggerel"
- Stolid, stilted, cliché-ridden prose
- "Characters . . . too heroic . . . to be human or interesting"
- Unsuccessful "anxious attempts at humor" (McKinley, 565)
- "Virtually no women of any species," none "ever enough of a character even to be called cardboard" (566)
- "The relentless quaintness of the hobbits"

- "The blunt confrontation between Black and White with no patience or subtlety for the presence of shades of gray" (570)

McKinley finds it much easier to point out flaws than to explain why Tolkien's work "rises above its failures, . . . why it is, finally, grand." Her reasons:

- Tolkien translates his scholarly knowledge of myth and language "into utterly convincing place-names and proper names and geographies and cultures."
- His strong feeling for landscape "as three-dimensional as his own back garden" is paralleled by belief "in his God . . . the struggle between Good and Evil [as] a real question fought daily in the hearts and lives of real people" (566).
- "It is Tolkien's genius that the singular fire of myth burns in his own work, that the liveliness of Story entered what he had made" (568).

These are reasons people continue to read *The Lord of the Rings,* why it caused "a revolution in both popular fiction and serious literature." McKinley concludes:

> *The Lord of the Rings* is one of the finest books . . . to put in the hands of any eager, wistful junior high school student who has begun to suspect there's something more to life than Steven Spielberg; and it will lift the heart and touch the soul of anyone of any age who can suspend disbelief long enough to step through Tolkien's enchanted portal and welcome what will be found on the other side (570).

A more mundane key to his fans' fanatical devotion evidenced in over 50 Tolkien societies around the world and countless Internet Web pages is his story's accessibility, its familiarity. Hobbits are us. Frodo's cozy Shire is our own home, safe and snug, secure from the ravages of the crazy world "out there." We know, however, as Frodo learns, that we aren't really safe, that evil and chaos threaten our cherished way of life. Tolkien insisted that he was not writing an allegory about the two world wars he personally endured. Yet his childhood as an orphan and his experience of those wars did affect his sense of safety, his conviction that we must protect ourselves. In the epigraph to this section, he admits to identifying with his own hobbits.

Tolkien had a deep, wistful attachment to English country life because it was snatched from him by poverty in childhood and because the pastoral England fought for in the wars was disappearing in front of his eyes as industry and population encroached. In the midst of dire danger, Frodo longs for his unreachable Shire. Readers recognize that they, too, must find courage to fight the powers that shatter their peaceful homes, their natural landscape. Like ordinary Frodo, we are the only ones who can save our world. "Such is oft the course of deeds that move the wheels of the world," wrote Tolkien; "small hands do them because they must, while the eyes of the great are elsewhere."[14]

According to 1990 statistics, *The Hobbit* and *The Lord of the Rings* are among the 20 best-selling paperbacks of all time. Tolkien's books are available in 40 countries, and over 40 million copies of his works are in print.[15] They endure, shining a beacon for imaginative readers everywhere.

YAFEs ON TOLKIEN

The Hobbit

The Hobbit is the prototype upon which the majority of fantasy books are based. It is one of the first fantasy books I ever read, at age nine (C. S. Lewis was first). *The Hobbit* gives a great start to a young person's journey into fantasy reading.
—Jonathan Singer, 16

It was very black and white—though Gollum and Smaug as bad guys were very interesting. It showed me, at 12 or 13, that getting pressured into something you don't want to do can turn out to be really cool. It read very smoothly, a fabulous book that can't be judged in relation to other fantasy—it's high on its own pillar.
—Midian Crosby, 19

The Lord of the Rings

My name came from this book [Galadriel was the tall, golden-haired princess of Noldor, staunch foe of the Dark Lord Sauron], written by the father of modern fantasy. His made-up languages and maps are really well thought out. Everyone now takes ideas from him—his races are sort of "generic fantasy races." The only thing I didn't like was certain races were set permanently on good and others on evil—so annoying! But you can't say anything bad about Tolkien without feeling guilty.

—Galadriel Wills, 15

Incredibly imaginative and original, it was very engrossing, though you need patience to get through the long parts.

—Eric Rice, 16

Tolkien started the fantasy genre; this excellent book became the basic standard for all current fantasies. The pace never left you feeling impatient to get on with it. He used his style at a level few have reached.

—Erik Hansen, 16

Lord of the Rings was the first fantasy book, basically. This classic will be around long after its imitators are gone.

—Brian Dunning, 15

Superbly written, this is a standard "David vs. Goliath" type book, good always being a small party against incredible odds. Tolkien added more to it, making both sides fallible, though the seeming invincibility of some characters was predictable. I enjoyed the great descriptions and the poems immensely.

—Gary Virta, 12

This is the book that hooked me on fantasy—I have not met any equal. One becomes intoxicated with it—it is enthralling, full of intrigue, the procession of events is timed well. More than anything else, I liked the language—the runes, the diagraphs—and the poetry was also magnificent. Tolkien's Middle-earth has been commended as one of the best-developed fantasy worlds; Fonstad's indispensable guide *Atlas of Middle-earth* (Houghton Mifflin, 1981) is based on it and is a tremendous help as I am writing a dream into a story taking place in Middle-earth.

—Ray Privett III, 12

Tolkien was beautiful. He created the Fantasy Epic, he created the Elf and the Dwarf and the Goblin that were not child's toys but PEOPLE—good, bad, and ugly. The books flowed together, as did the chapters, which ended with masterful hooks to keep you reading. Yet each new chapter started off fulfilling the hunger that you had, two pages back, beckoning you forth. In *The Two Towers,* the characters split up into three groups, all hundreds of miles away from each other, yet you kept track of everyone with minimal confusion. The characters all had their parts: they changed, they loved, they hated and sometimes lost. They were just plain beautiful, and I am still in love with them. Out of all great books I have read, these were the greatest, the very best. It takes a masterpiece to create a genre. This is worth two.

—Dylan Burns, 16

The Tolkien Legacy in America

The Tolkien craze that swept American college campuses after the 1965 paperback reissue of *The Lord of the Rings* coincided with the appearance of the first realistic young adult "problem novels": S. E. Hinton's *The Outsiders* (Viking, 1967), Paul Zindel's *The Pigman* (Harper, 1968), and Robert Cormier's *The Chocolate War* (Pantheon, 1974). As youth of the '60s rebelled, so did their literature. Tolkien's fantasy seeds fell on fertile American soil, where for the first time since the pulp magazines of the '30s and '40s writers were creating fantasy worlds with unique American flavor. Today, teenaged fantasy readers are unfamiliar with writers from Tolkien's period, such as Eddison, Peake, Howard, and de Camp. Yet American writers following Tolkien from the late '60s onward are avidly read. What has changed?

Tolkien started two major practices in fantasy literature that have not only become requirements for other writers but have continued to develop beyond his vision: (1) Secondary world building must be based on a rigorous mythology, with nothing left to the capriciousness of fate or a writer's whim. Little can be left unexplained, as it was in William Morris's ethereal Wood. In a logical otherworld, magic works as meticulously as science. (2) Tolkien's conviction that we ordinary folks (or hobbits) are the only ones who can save our world has become an axiom. Against evil forces, reluctant human heroes have a moral obligation to use their power within for the good of society.

In this post-Tolkien age of psychology, writers carry his instincts further, so that a hero achieves growth as a whole and integrated self. A hero's journey is archetypal, part of the mythic cycle since Story began (see chapter 4), but today young readers expect to find a model of their own reaching toward maturity in every fantasy saga. Youthful idealism is also nurtured in fantasy. An integrated heroic leader uses ethics as a force for overpowering evil—the corruption, violence, and pollution that plague us in reality.

Contemporary morality since Tolkien is based on the self that modern fantasy reflects. In her 1981 essay "The New Fantasy," children's literature critic Sheila Egoff identifies "new rules for an old game" among modern fantasists:

> there can be felt a powerful, even an awesome, seriousness together with an uncompromising perception of reality, a command of mythology, an emphasis upon the individual, a complex concept of time, an elliptical style, and a cinematic vision that separate them from the fantasists of an earlier period. There is also a sense in which most writers of modern fantasy are the moral arbiters of our time.[16]

It is not chance that Tolkien, so affected by two world wars, led the way to a revised view of the nature of good and evil. In earlier ages, one believed in a natural instinct to fight for good, but Egoff points out that "modern fantasists see evil in a metaphysical way; it must be battled with, but it will always abide." Until we "experienced two world wars and Nazism ... it had probably never been seen so clearly that ordinary people could become agents of malevolence ... that seemed beyond the power of the individual to combat." The battlefield settings of fantasy novels are no accident (Egoff, 91). Just as ordinary people can be swept into evil, "everyday . . . kids next door can uphold the good. . . . Modern fantasists seem to be saying, 'The good is what we have, so hold fast'[;] . . . however, both sides are balanced. There can be no Light without Darkness, no Darkness without Light" (92).

Nearly 25 years after the publication of *The Lord of the Rings,* fantasy author Diana Paxson dissected Tolkien story elements later writers utilized in her 1979 lecture "The Tolkien Tradition." Paxson built a clear case for Tolkien's work as "not only the foundation of a new tradition but the culmination of several older ones," making many elements "accessible to the contemporary reader" for the first time.[17] These elements include extended length in trilogies, the epic sweep of large casts in a broad field of action, complete mythologies, archetypal motifs and figures representing standard roles, sentient species such as elves or talking animals interacting with humans, symbolic talismans, recurring plot motifs such as the Quest, and "moral struggle . . . on a global scale" (Paxson 1984, 23–25). Paxson constructed a chart with these elements along the top and titles of post-Tolkien fantasies through 1979 along the side, checking items appearing in each work. Her conclusions concerning worthy inheritors of Tolkien's mantle will be noted here where those authors are discussed. Readers may find Paxson's published lecture worth perusing for details.

A striking development since Paxson's study is the proliferation of both female writers and female characters in fantasy. One of Tolkien's weaknesses was his scarcity of female characters; still, young writer Robin McKinley took inspiration from one fleeting glimpse of a Tolkien warrior woman to create revolutionary female protagonists in fantasy, with a fresh feminist twist to the concept of heroism (see the section on feminism later in this chapter). Three of the four featured authors in this book are female.

A 1993 study analyzed 15 critically acclaimed young adult science fiction and fantasy novels for images of women during three time periods, 1970, 1980, and 1990. Though male characters outnumbered females in all three periods (66 percent of all characters were male in the 1970 sample and 56 percent in 1990),

female characters increased significantly, and female protagonists became more frequent. "Only three out of fifteen books analyzed had female protagonists in 1970, while in 1980 and 1990,
the number . . . jumped to seven and nine out of fifteen, respec-
tively." Women characters also grew less passive: "[T]he number
of active female characters increased from 45 percent of the total
number in 1970 to 78 percent in 1990." Finally, intelligence in
women began to rate higher than beauty.[18]

Though there are no statistics yet to prove it, we suspect that
these figures have increased in favor of females throughout the
'90s and that female fantasy *readers,* as well as writers, have also
flourished. Not only are female YAFEs willing to read about male
escapades, but contrary to teen readers of realistic fiction, male
YAFEs do not shun female adventurers in recent fantasies by
Robin McKinley, Mercedes Lackey, or Tamora Pierce—or even
the raging feminism in Marion Zimmer Bradley's *Mists of Avalon*
(see chapter 5). Girls both glory in increasing evidence of female
strength in stories and express discomfort with older titles dis-
playing sexism. Girls always notice when writers stint female
characters, and writers seem to be responding to this more
numerous and vocal female force among their readers. Like the
metaphysical balance of good and evil, the balance of male and
female in recent fantasy more accurately reflects the state of our
world. Male authors are also becoming egalitarian; Terry Brooks,
the sole male author featured in this book, portrays strong female
characters Brin and Wren Ohmsford, among others, who have no
trouble keeping up with the guys in magical powers, intelligence,
warrior skills, or sheer guts and determination (see the section on
Brooks later in this chapter).

Ursula K. Le Guin's
Men and Women of Earthsea

The first significant American fantasist to follow Tolkien embodies both these emerging concerns, the quest for self and the inclusion of the female. Ursula K. Le Guin's watery otherworld of

Earthsea shimmers with its creator's carefully fashioned words and philosophies in a dimension all its own. Paxson's chart of Tolkien elements shows that Le Guin has incorporated all but "epic scope," for her work is not sprawling but "highly focused, confined in scale, and her style has a classical economy that is very different from that of Tolkien. Yet. . . . certainly she is just as concerned with the relationship between language and culture as he is, and perhaps even more concerned with the link between words and one's perceptions of reality" (Paxson 1984, 25).

Le Guin's first volume, *A Wizard of Earthsea,* was published in 1968 during the Tolkien craze. Having published adult science fiction, Le Guin was asked by an eminent editor to write for young adults. She had written a 1964 short story, "The Word of Unbinding," about a wizard on an island, and "The Rule of Names," defining magic more clearly on another island near the one introduced in the first story. (Both stories are anthologized in *The Wind's Twelve Quarters.*) She had never considered writing for teens so began wondering about what wizards were like before they reached the ancient age of Gandalf or Merlin. They must have been young once; did they attend wizard school? The faint map of an archipelago of hundreds of islands in a world where magic was natural law began to emerge more clearly in her mind, and the goatherd boy Duny was born on the island of Gont, show-ing early aptitude for magic. Le Guin tells the story of Earthsea's genesis in her essay "Dreams Must Explain Themselves," insist-ing that "I did not deliberately invent Earthsea. . . . I am not an engineer, but an explorer. I discovered Earthsea."[19]

The island's mage, Ogion, instructs Duny in wizardry, telling him his true and secret name, Ged. Others call him by his "use-name," Sparrowhawk, since he calls wild hawks to his hand. Finding Ged impatient with his quiet ways, Ogion sends the boy to the famous wizard school on the island of Roke, where Ged soon distinguishes himself as a gifted student. The complex sys-tem of magic that keeps Earthsea in Equilibrium is based on the Taoism Le Guin admires, on its concepts of yin and yang, light and dark, making and unmaking. Earthsea's existence relates to the Power of Names; a convention of magic is that one's name embodies one's essence and so can be used to ensorcel someone. By learning the true names of things and people, Earthsea mages make or unmake them, careful to keep the Equilibrium.

As a young wizard learns to control weather, healing, and other ways of keeping the world in balance, youthful passion can interfere. Ged cannot resist a dare from student Jasper to perform the forbidden rite of calling a spirit from the dead. The dark, taloned Shadow thus unleashed attacks Ged and would kill him but for the intervention of the Archmage, who closes the door between living and dead and so sacrifices his own life.

With grave injuries of body and soul, Ged suffers crippling guilt for his careless pride. He knows the terrible Shadow is loose, lurking unseen until his chance to claim Ged. Embarking on official wizard duties, Ged wins a dragon's true name to become a dragon lord, but he cannot erase his fear of the pursuing Shadow. Deciding to chase rather than be chased, Ged searches for the Shadow in his enchanted boat, *Lookfar,* beyond all known islands. At last Ged faces his nightmare, to call the Shadow by his own true name. Instead of being consumed, he consumes the Shadow, which merges into him as the dark part of himself, making Ged whole.

In this perfect all-ages fantasy, the literature grew up; Le Guin presents ultimate horror and ultimate truth to young readers, that such a monster is part of us all, our shadow self. Every reader will picture—or resist picturing—this Shadow, but artist Wayne Douglas Barlowe's black, clawed watercolor shape in *Barlowe's Guide to Fantasy* (HarperPrism, 1996) brings shudders to any *Earthsea* reader.

A Wizard of Earthsea is also a classic coming-of-age tale. Ged achieves adulthood by accepting the metaphysical truths of his universe and incorporating them into his being. Le Guin's characterization of Ged wins readers' understanding of his isolation and intensity, his pride and ambition, his struggle for self-mastery and skill. Recognizing his weaknesses, readers experience why it is essential to cultivate courage, determination, and the pursuit of truth. Yet never does Le Guin preach. Instead, she carries readers along as witnesses to these insights, on waves of sparkling words.

A Wizard of Earthsea won the 1968 *Boston Globe-Horn Book* Award and became an ALA Notable Children's Book. It also won Le Guin her first high critical acclaim. In the *Times Literary Supplement,* John Clute called *Wizard* "as polished and word-perfect a tale for older children as could be imagined."[20] In his recent definitive *Encyclopedia of Fantasy* covering thousands of authors, Clute still finds *Earthsea* "central to Le Guin's reputation" as "one of the two or three most important U.S. [science fiction] authors of the second half of the 20th century."[21]

The Tombs of Atuan: The Second Book of Earthsea, published three years later, is a brilliant, tightly structured novel seen through the eyes of a solitary character. At age five, Tenar is removed from her family to become the One Priestess of the Tombs of Atuan on a desert island of holy women, the Place. The tiny girl goes through a ritual "beheading," giving up her name to become the Eaten One, Arha, dedicated to the Nameless Ones, rulers of the world before men. Their tombs are nine standing stones above a labyrinth of underground caverns, where no light is allowed. These caverns contain Treasure, open only to Arha and a few of her highest priestesses and eunuchs. They become Arha's haven; the young girl learns to navigate their twisted passages in the dark. Keeping the rituals that serve the silent forces—including burying alive prisoners sent by the Kargish godking—Arha withdraws from her few companions into isolation.

One day a glow appears in a cavern, and Arha spies a man searching for treasure to steal. This violation of her sacred Place by a forbidden male is so repugnant to Arha that she cannot face him. Closing the door to the only way out, she watches him from various spy holes above. He seems to work some sort of magic, lighting his staff without fire and saying futile charms at the blocked doorway. Fascinated by the first man she has seen, Arha finally bribes him with water to spill his secrets.

It is Ged, of course, and Arha cannot comprehend his mission or respectful attitude. Just as she is tempted to kill him, Ged calls her by her forgotten childhood name, Tenar. Reawakened, her true self realizes that the Nameless Ones have done nothing to stop him. Here is the truth about the spirits to which she has dedicated her life: Ged explains that the Nameless Ones are immortal earth spirits of the dark, but they are not gods. "They have no power of making. All their power is to darken and destroy."[22]

With nothing left in which to believe, Tenar has only one way to go, out of the caverns with Ged. He has found the treasure he sought there, the other half of the amulet he wears around his neck. Now the Ring of Erreth-Akbe, Earthsea's ancient hero-king, is whole. When they emerge from the caverns into the light, the earth spirits are so enraged that the Tombs implode in an earthquake, and they flee in Ged's boat to a world Tenar has never seen. They deliver the ring to the empty throne in the city of Havnor to await a new king to restore peace to the kingless kingdom. Stripped of the only life she knows, Tenar is sent by Ged to his first master, Ogion, on Gont, for he sees enormous power in the confused young woman.

Through almost half of this taut tale, Arha's warped perceptions are the only realities. In her isolation, Arha's spirit struggles for release, but only Ged's light pierces her darkness. She has endured two deaths, once as a child "eaten" by the gods and now, after Ged has shattered her false gods. How will she be reborn? For this tortuous coming of age, Le Guin places the reader inside Arha's perceptions; we realize the truth as she does.

Twenty years after his feats in *Wizard,* Ged has matured. Though his life hangs in the balance, he never imposes his will on Arha but guides her with tact, patience, and kindness to her own realization. It is Tenar who takes charge, leading Ged out of the underground trap of her whole misguided life. At the end, hope mixes with grief as Tenar contemplates her false self and the evil she has done, facing the new undefined person she is free to become. Though Tenar's situation was imposed upon her without her will, she must summon the will to change. As always, Le Guin shows the double face of light and dark.

Seeking her lost self in unrelieved sexually charged tension, Arha coils back and forth through her dark tunnels. "The subject of *The Tombs of Atuan* is, if I had to put it in one word, sex. . . . [T]he symbols can all be read as sexual," Le Guin declares. "More exactly, you could call it a feminine coming of age" ("Dreams," 55). This daring depiction won the 1972 National Book Award and became both a Newbery Honor Book and an ALA Notable Children's Book.

Though *Tombs* won acclaim when it was published, with critics applauding its mythic "universal patterns"[23] or recognizing its significant treatment of the theme of change,[24] some later analysts faulted the work for portraying the feminine as passive. In an essay marking its 1991 choice as a Phoenix Award Honor Book for standing the test of time 20 years after its original publication, Millicent Lenz relates her initial disappointment with the story's ending, in which Tenar holds Ged's hand in childlike dependency.[25] Lenz cites another critic, who found the contrast between Ged's active male heroism and Tenar's twisted community of women suspect (Lenz, 94). Now Lenz lists Tenar's worthy nonpassive qualities: endurance, resistance of temptation to kill Ged, acceptance of responsibility, and courage to go forward into unknown change (95). Realizing that Tenar's deprived upbringing could only have left her unformed, Lenz makes a case for Le Guin's vision of the wholeness of Earthsea's entire story cycle (96), which continues in what was once the ending, *The Farthest Shore*.

Le Guin calls *The Farthest Shore* "the most imperfect of the three, but . . . the one I like best" ("Dreams," 56). She claims that "strong-minded" Ged "took over completely in this book. He was determined to show me how his life must end." While author and protagonist wrestled for control, the book endured many rewrites (55–56). Death was necessary to discuss, for Le Guin believes that "the hour when a child realizes . . . that he/she, personally, is mortal, will die, is the hour when childhood ends, and the new life begins. Coming of age again, but in a larger context" (55).

Having known about death since his own coming of age, Ged must impart that awareness to someone younger, to carry forward a new generation. This young man is Prince Arren of Enlad, sent to Roke to inform aging Ged the Archmage that magic is disappearing. Ged and his Council of Mages have received such reports from many islands. People have lost their will to work and create, and mages are forgetting the words of their spells. On a voyage mirroring his youthful search for the Shadow, the Archmage himself searches for the hole in the world where magic is leaking out, taking Arren because it is clear that the boy has some great purpose.

As they sail in *Lookfar* from island to island to find evidence of magic's weakening, the islanders go from unfriendly to hostile. A madman, Sopli, comes along to show them the source of the evil, which promises immortality. When they are attacked while trying to land, Sopli drowns himself, Ged is badly wounded, and Arren becomes crippled with despair as they drift beyond shore. Just as they are nearly dead of thirst, Ged and Arren are rescued by a huge tribe of primitive people who live year round on rafts. So begins a time of restoration, as Arren swims with the carefree young people and Ged slowly heals. To Arren, it feels like an afterlife, sharing simple joys with those living freely on a sea both bountiful and unforgiving, without the safe haven of land. (Le Guin's raft people appeared years earlier in a short story that got scrapped except for this "lulu" of a colony ["Dreams," 51].)

Part of their healing is Arren's confession that fear of death, and some unreachable dream of living forever, immobilized him in the boat. Arren had succumbed to the magic stealer's lure, but immortality is a lie, Ged explains. Longing for it while fearing death made Arren incapable of living. Only to humans, says Ged, "is it given to know that we must die. And that is a great gift: the gift of selfhood."[26] Now they can face death itself.

Ged's dragon friends come to their aid; enormous Orm Embar carries them from the rafts to the farthest shore, where they confront the stealer of magic, the long-dead wizard Cob. By leaving the door open between the worlds of the living and the dead, Cob has found eternal life. Following him into the "Dry Land," Ged closes "the door through death" with every morsel of his power (*Shore*, 135). So life that is no real life ends for the dead, including Cob, and the living are freed to live fully with magic—and the promise of eventual death restored. The oldest dragon, Kalessin, carries Ged and Arren, thoroughly spent, back to Roke. Arren will be crowned the new King Lebannen of Earthsea with the ring restored by Ged and Tenar in *The Tombs of Atuan*. But just as Arren comes into true selfhood by accepting death, Ged loses his.

The encounter with the dead drained Ged's mage power. He is merely a man again, exhausted, and the book ends with Kalessin carrying him home to Gont.

In her thoughtful essay, critic Ann Welton celebrates the trilogy's wholeness:

> Taken as a whole, the books sing . . . [with] the deeper poetry of the truth being spoken with beauty, clarity, and economy. The ending of *The Farthest Shore* reconciles a loss. Ged's power is gone, he has returned to the state of a common man, but with an incomparable gain: his full, worthy, and sufficient sacrifice in the interests of wholeness has restored balance to his world. . . . The dragons wheeling in the light, the young king's wisdom, born in pain and loss, provide symbols of hope and assurance of the validity of the sacrifice.[27]

This "final and most powerful and substantive book" of the trilogy won the 1973 National Book Award (Tymn et al., 111). Yet for Le Guin, Earthsea was still "the dream I have not stopped dreaming" ("Dreams," 56). Eventually she reexamined Earthsea, publishing its 1990 conclusion, *Tehanu: The Last Book of Earthsea.*

"The first books are written totally within the classic western tradition . . . a vaguely medieval, vaguely European context of an unquestioned patriarchal system where only men are wizards, only men have power," Le Guin explains. "They keep saying, 'weak as women's magic, wicked as women's magic.' " As feminism progressed in our world after her trilogy ended in the early '70s, Le Guin wondered, "What's going on in Earthsea? How is it that not only men do all the big magic, but they have to be celibate to do it?" Even Arha's community of women in *The Tombs of Atuan* is under the male godking's control, and when *The Farthest Shore* ends, it "looks as if in some way the wizards are going to be replaced by the king. The secular, earthly power is going to replace the more magical or spiritual power." Subconsciously pondering these questions for years while "a great shift in fantasy" occurred, Le Guin realized "I had to learn to see Earthsea through these other eyes."[28]

When *Tehanu* opens, no time has passed in Earthsea. At last we learn how Tenar has fared on Gont, where Ged sent her at the end of *Tombs*. Instead of Ogion's lessons, Tenar chose a traditional woman's role. She became the wife of a successful farmer, Flint, and the mother of two children, enjoying the "power that a woman was born to, the authority allotted to her by the arrangements of mankind."[29] Now she is widowed, her children are grown, and Tenar has adopted Therru, a tragically abused little girl left to burn in a bonfire by her father and another man after they raped her. Horribly disfigured, Therru has only half a face and one good hand, and her soul is wounded even more deeply. Tenar tries to heal her with love, but Therru's progress is slow, and everyone is afraid of her. On his deathbed, Ogion tells Tenar to teach Therru everything.

When Ged arrives from Roke on the dragon Kalessin's back after facing Cob, Tenar tries to heal him too, for his strength is gone in both body and spirit. Few realize that this faded Hawk is the Archmage Ged, for he has no power and is unable to stop grieving its loss. When the new King Lebannen, once the boy Arren, sails to seek him, Ged flees into the mountains to become a goatherd once again. Tenar must explain Ged's absence to Lebannen, who is searching for a new Archmage, led by only one clue: "a woman in Gont." Though she is famed for her role in recovering the ring years ago, Tenar has no magic, so she cannot be that woman.

Missing Ged, Tenar raises Therru on her husband's farm. In a scene of sudden horror, the men who abused Therru break into Tenar's farmhouse one winter night. Long-absent Ged materializes with a pitchfork, pinning Therru's father, Hake, to the ground. The villagers catch the rest of his gang, who have just murdered Therru's mother. After this dreadful shock, normality returns, for Ged has accepted his loss and can finally share Tenar's life as her lover and Therru's new father, teaching her the philosophy behind Earthsea's magic, for which she obviously has aptitude.

This fulfillment late in life for Tenar and Ged is sweet and satisfying, but Tenar still questions why mages must be male, why men's and women's powers are different, why men can be so afraid of women that they seize power over them through abuse. Unencumbered by magic, Ged ponders these issues with Tenar until both face the worst evil yet. Unknown to them, the wizard Aspen has been practicing Cob's dark arts of immortality right there on Gont. To destroy his greatest threats, Aspen binds Ged and Tenar in a deadly spell.

But like everyone else, Aspen is ignorant of the only true power on Gont. To save her parents, Therru calls the dragon Kalessin in the Language of the Making, her native tongue, which no one realized she knew. Soaring through the air to crush Aspen just before he pushes Ged and Tenar off a cliff, Kalessin recognizes Therru as one of his own ancient race. Calling her by her true name, Tehanu, Kalessin promises to return to take her to the dragons "on the other wind" when her work is done in Earthsea (*Tehanu*, 249). Now we know Tehanu is "the woman of Gont" who will become the first female Archmage, and that magic will work a bit differently in Earthsea forevermore.

Le Guin took a risk reenvisioning her otherworld, so beloved by readers of several generations. Tampering with such an exalted work as *The Earthsea Trilogy* seemed sacrilegious to some, who wondered how a fourth book could "complete something already whole in itself" (Welton, 15). How could Le Guin describe the trilogy as "a four-legged chair missing a leg"? (*Tehanu*, 255). Would young readers respond to a fantasy that places a middle-aged woman and a burned-out wizard at its core? Is it fair to say that *Tehanu* is a "more different book" than its predecessors, one that "pleases feminists and students of Le Guin's maturation as a thinker more than those who are looking for more of the same in Earthsea" (R. Herbert, 477)?

Welton articulately details why she sees *Tehanu* as "basically unsuccessful." For her, it jars with the atmosphere, philosophy of magic, and harmony of the trilogy. Though *Tehanu* has powerful insight on the roles of men and women, they are imposed upon Earthsea; "the message comes from someplace else, and the effect is deleterious to both *The Earthsea Trilogy* and to *Tehanu*. It dilutes the strength and force of the former, while reducing the message of the latter to a form of axe-grinding" (Welton, 16).

There is merit in Welton's deeply felt criticisms. Many feminists believe that the pendulum must swing in the opposite direction to redress inequalities between men and women, and Welton finds such swinging inappropriate for Earthsea. But Earthsea *is* a male-dominated society in which women such as Tenar are ignored, overlooked, denied the full exercise of their own power. Even in the domestic arena, where Tenar has chosen to excel and which Le Guin shows is admirable, she has no rights. Her husband's farm reverts to her insensitive seafaring son Spark, who merely tolerates his mother's presence, taking for granted her upkeep of the property he ignored for years while at sea.

What Le Guin calls a "shift" in fantasy over the last 20 years has mirrored the shift in society; otherworlds like Earthsea aren't so other anymore. Earthsea was always remarkably real; in 1971 critic Eleanor Cameron declared, "[I]t is as if Ursula Le Guin herself has lived on the Archipelago, minutely observing and noting down the habits and idiosyncrasies of the culture from island to island."[30] As in many patriarchal cultures, Earthsea's tensions between male and female are unacknowledged. What is new in *Tehanu*'s Earthsea is that through the character of Tenar, these concerns are voiced, just as they are in our world. In the original trilogy, Tenar was young, abused, and undeveloped in the only book in which she appeared, *The Tombs of Atuan*. She had no chance to consider her feminine power. While Ged's development progressed through each book of the trilogy, Tenar's growth was unknown, unwatched. Her fate is the fourth leg of Earthsea's chair.

Only in caring for the deeply wounded Therru, cruelly used by men to assert their own power, does Tenar come to see that in her own youth, she too was wronged, not wrong in her forced exile as priestess. Welton is not immune to Therru's immense power: "The burned, abused child represents Everyone in the state in which she has been held by men. She has been made to be afraid . . . because of men's fear of her. . . . She has been told that she is powerless. The entire thrust of the book indicates that the author believes that it is past time for both the oppression and the suppression to end" (Welton, 16).

Earthsea is an otherworld, not the ideal world Welton hopes for, where differing strengths of men and women are merged into a human whole. Yet Welton misses how Le Guin begins to bring male and female into harmony through the thoroughly human, unmagical union of Tenar and Ged. Once they become lovers, they share the parenting of Therru with their separate gifts, Tenar's nurturing and Ged's teaching. They openly discuss how to meld their different perceptions of power. They protect each other from danger in the world around them, they heal each other's hurts. Their attuned relationship is one of the most uplifting in all of literature, not just in fantasy alone.

Because it is fantasy and because they are only human, they still need Tehanu's magic to save them. The magic that offers ultimate deliverance *is* different than the magic Ged practiced in the earlier books, but it is still native to Earthsea. It is older than Ged's magic, for Tehanu comes from the dragon race that preceded humans, described in the first book. Tehanu embodies the natural, unschooled power that Tenar has sensed all along, an "emptiness" or "potentiality" present in anyone with the gift to develop it, "what true doing rises from, and the freedom to be one's true self" (*Tehanu,* 216). It is time for a female Archmage, but that means that anyone, male or female, can hold power, even the most damaged. When Therru becomes Archmage Tehanu, everyone will face the worst in themselves whenever they see her ravaged face, half destroyed, half perfect. Overcoming the evil we do to each other, beyond gender, is what *Tehanu* is all about. It is cause for celebration in a world like ours and Earthsea's, for devastating evil can appear anywhere—in the form of sexual abusers, terrorists, political dictators, or those who seek "immortality" in notoriety, fearfully reacting to their own lack of power by stealing it from others. *Earthsea*'s last leg, *Tehanu* stands firmly as one of Le Guin's most distinguished accomplishments.

In Tenar's youth in *The Tombs of Atuan,* Lenz points out, a "psychologically whole woman mentor" is missing, which "Tenar herself becomes" in the last book of Earthsea. "*Tehanu* supplies the missing link, helping young readers see the young Tenar of *Tombs* in the perspective of a woman's entire life story" (Lenz, 96). Le Guin's enduring theme of change, of becoming, is enhanced by Tenar's "full embracing of the human condition of . . . always undergoing transitions. . . . Whereas the Tenar of the earlier book holds potentiality and promise, the Tenar of the last book is the completed human being. Young readers are richer than those of twenty years ago, for they can avail themselves of both the promise and the fulfillment" (97–98).

Famous for her own feminist fantasy (see the later section in this chapter), Robin McKinley reviewed *Tehanu* as "a novel rich in the ways of humanity . . . not . . . the grand world-threatening passions . . . in much traditional fantasy. . . . It requires a certain quietness of mind . . . to recognize and appreciate the subtler world-threatening passion here. . . . The astonishing clear-sightedness of *Tehanu* is in its recognition of the necessary and life-giving contributions of female magic—sometimes disguised as domesticity. This book would be admirable and evocative by itself, but it has the advantage of the resonance it gains from the three that went before, and our memories of them. Young readers of the *Earthsea Trilogy* should be obliged to wait a decade or two before they read it. Adults may read the quartet as a finished work."[31]

Including *Tehanu*, Clute and Grant call the *Earthsea Cycle* "one of the most deeply influential of all 20th century fantasy texts" (Clute and Grant, 573). To all of *Earthsea*'s awards was added the 1978 Gandalf Award for lifetime fantasy achievement. At the time of *Tehanu*'s publication, in an imaginary interview by her 15-year-old self with her self at 60, Ursula Le Guin tells an unpublished teenaged writer about her later success doing work she was "born to do." The woman tells the girl, "I wish you could read the Earthsea books and tell me what you think of them. But then, you haven't even read Tolkien." Young Ursula asks, "Who's he? Hey, do you still like Frankie Sinatra?" Young adult readers respond to this most integrated of writers, well aware of her own young self within: "You are the only person that ever interviewed me that didn't ask where I got my ideas from."[32]

YAFEs on *Earthsea*

A Wizard of Earthsea

A teacher forced it on me in seventh grade, so I didn't get much out of it.

—Erik Hansen, 16

I read it three months ago and found it more sophisticated than hack-and-slash fantasy. I liked the archipelago where magic took energy.

—Nathan Doyle, 18

My best friend considered it one of the most influential books in her life, but it didn't grab me.

—Allison Barrett, 17

After reading Tolkien, I read *Wizard* in sixth grade, and it didn't compare with his greatness. But I just reread *Wizard* and loved everything about it: the writing style, the descriptive sailing scenes, the concept of magic, how Le Guin captured Ged's despair, and how his last voyage seemed to go on forever, the great climax. It's a really dark book in which Ged seems doomed for his whole meaningless existence, but it has an uplifting ending. It turned me on to the idea of rereading books I read when I was a kid.

—Dylan Burns, 15

It stood out from all the other books I read for last summer's reading game. Its simple language conveyed profound ideas and images, beyond authors with vast vocabularies who don't say much.

—Jonathan Singer, 17

When I read it in seventh grade, I got scared by the supernatural stuff—too scared to put it down.

—Galadriel Wills, 15

The Tombs of Atuan

Le Guin shut out the rest of Earthsea to focus in on one desolate area so well, I almost felt as if I was there in the undertomb. My sympathy for Tenar derived from my own view of the world as a place to explore and experience, not from any longing of hers to get out. The theme was that forces of decay, death, and destruction exist and always will, but it is not man's task to serve them. Man ought always to live. But while the simplicity of the writing style added to the ambience, it also felt very shallow. Ideas were not explored in full, characters were left superficial. Le Guin hints of a theme in *1984:* that you cannot comprehend something if you cannot speak of it, and you cannot speak of it without a name. This book frustrated me because it seemed to toy with a deeper idea and then pull away. It had a grim and barren aspect. I enjoyed the rest of the series more.

—Rachel Scott, 20

The *Earthsea Trilogy*

I read this trilogy right after Tolkien, in middle school when I was miserable. They really impacted me; I enjoy dark books. Her powerful writing gripped me.

—Brian Dunning, 15

I just read the trilogy and found that each individual book lacked closure, but taken as chapters of one book, they were about life itself.

—Colyn Bulthaup, 19

I loved everything about them. In eighth grade I presented a booktalk on *The Tombs of Atuan* for English class. I'm currently inhaling *The Wind's Twelve Quarters*.

—Ashley Burns, 17

Tehanu

While it was very different from the other three books, I thought that *Tehanu* finished things off very well. I love the book by itself, as a wonderful story with character development and mystery. I wish she had written another book about Tehanu herself, but I've always wanted to know more about Le Guin's dragons. As the fourth book in the series, I also thought it was good, if not what I expected. Portrayals of Ged and Tenar were lovely: Tenar's acknowledgment of her love for Ged, and her contentment as an ordinary woman instead of a high priestess, Ged's dealings with what it means to be a wizard no longer and what it means to become a man, Therru's past and present and how she interacts with their lives. I especially like the fact that the ending seemed not an ending but another beginning. They're all alive and well, safely hidden in the mountains of Gont, where Ged himself began the first book.

—Ashley Burns, 17

The Magic Kingdoms of Terry Brooks:
Responsibility and Choice

Chronology: Terry Brooks's Life and Works

1944   Terence Dean Brooks born January 8 in Sterling, Illinois, son of Marjorie Gleason Brooks, a housewife, and Dean O. Brooks, a printer.

1958   Publishes first piece, "Lincoln's Final Hours," in eighth grade for Illinois State Historical Society competition on Abraham Lincoln.

1961   Member of Illinois State Champion Debate Team at Sterling High School.

1962   Graduates from Sterling High School.

1965   Interns for the summer with Congressman John Anderson in Washington, D.C.

1966   Earns bachelor's degree in English literature from Hamilton College in Clinton, New York.

1969   Receives LL.B. degree from School of Law at Washington and Lee University in Lexington, Virginia. Begins practicing law in Sterling.

1972   Marries Barbara Ann O'Banion, an office manager.

1973   Becomes partner in firm Besse, Frye, Arnold, and Brooks, Attorneys at Law.

1974   First manuscript, *The Sword of Shannara,* accepted in November by Lester del Rey at Ballantine Books.

1975   Daughter Amanda Leigh is born.

1977   Publishes first novel, *The Sword of Shannara,* which becomes first fiction work to hit the *New York Times* trade paperback best-seller list and is an American Library Association Best Book for Young Adults.

Terry Brooks
Harvey Wang

1982   *The Elfstones of Shannara* (*Shannara* 2) is published and selected by *School Library Journal* as a Best Book for Young Adults.

1983   Son Alexander Stephen is born.

1985   *The Wishsong of Shannara* (*Shannara* 3) is published.

1986   *Magic Kingdom for Sale—Sold!* begins new *Landover* series and is chosen as both American Library Association and *School Library Journal* Best Book for Young Adults. Brooks leaves law practice to write full-time and moves to Seattle.

1987   Marries bookseller Judine Elaine Alba on December 11; *The Black Unicorn* (*Landover* 2) is published.

1988   *Wizard at Large* (*Landover* 3) is published.

1990   *The Scions of Shannara* is first installment of the *Heritage of Shannara* quartet.

1991   *The Druid of Shannara* (*Heritage* 2) and movie novelization of *Hook* are published; short story "Imaginary Friends" appears in anthology *Once Upon a Time*.

1992   *The Elf Queen of Shannara* (*Heritage* 3) is published.

1993   *The Talismans of Shannara* (*Heritage* 4) concludes the quartet.

1994   *The Tangle Box* (*Landover* 4) is published.

1995   *Witches' Brew* (*Landover* 5) is published; computer game Shannara is issued.

1996   *The First King of Shannara*, prequel to *Sword*, is published.

1997   *Running with the Demon* is first contemporary fantasy.

One of the good things about writing fantasy is that you are able to suggest certain things without having to spell it all out. You

can suggest the way things are and the way things are maybe
going to end up. You can leave a lot of loose ends hanging about
the way people's lives go on after your story is completed. How
bad are these monsters? Well, they're just as awful as every
reader imagines in his mind. So I never explain.
                        —Terry Brooks, from personal interview

Since the publication of his first fantasy novel, *The Sword of
Shannara,* in 1977, Terry Brooks has never been off the best-
seller list. He was the first post-Tolkien American fantasist to
become a best-selling author, and his success opened the fantasy
publishing market to countless new writers. Fifteen books later,
his name is one of the few recognized even by nonfantasy readers.
Though his books are published for adults, Brooks has legions of
loyal young adult fans, whom he values far more than adult readers. He admits he owes a great debt to Tolkien, and he never apologizes for obvious Tolkien influences in his writing.

Brooks writes very differently from Tolkien, with his own motivations and themes. Like Ursula K. Le Guin, Brooks follows the
revised American version of the Tolkien legacy rather than
Tolkien himself. Also like Le Guin, Brooks takes young readers
on a hero's journey with his characters. Through that mirror they
face the bewildering array of choices in their own world, tangle
with ethical and social issues, and ponder questions of our responsibility to those with whom we live. Not as literary or philosophi-
cal as Le Guin, Brooks writes rip-roaring adventure yarns, their
message never intruding upon entertainment value. As his characters consider different alternatives, often on a razor's edge of
suspense between a monstrous creature on one side and a
precipice on the other, readers identify with their fully human
motivations. The post-Tolkien earmarks are here, for it is only
Everyman—or Everywoman—who can save the world.

Terry Brooks believes he was born a writer, but it took a while
to discover the right form in which to communicate with readers.
In the small southern Illinois steel-making town of Sterling, Terence Dean Brooks was born on January 8, 1944. Since his father
owned a small printing business, Terry felt comfortable around
books and words and cannot recall a time when he was not writing

and reading. In small towns, a child creates his own entertainment, and Terry Brooks played happily in his imaginary worlds. As soon as he learned to read, he devoured *The Hardy Boys, The Black Stallion,* and *Boys' Life* magazine. By eighth grade he had progressed through *Tarzan* to the science fiction of Heinlein and Bradbury.[33] In high school, Terry discovered the classic European adventure novels of the last century, reading everything by Sir Walter Scott, Robert Louis Stevenson, and Alexandre Dumas, with the Sherlock Holmes mysteries of Sir Arthur Conan Doyle mixed in. These adventure stories were "huge influences when I was floundering about trying to find something that I could write."[34]

For almost as long as he has been reading, Terry has also been writing. "I can't remember when I started," he says. "I still have the first story I can remember from fourth grade, about aliens in a haunted house, and I can remember the teacher's response to it." In eighth grade, he won the Illinois State Historical Society competition on Abraham Lincoln, a native son of Terry's state. His winning submission, "Lincoln's Final Hours," was also Terry Brooks's first publication. In high school, Terry began experimenting with novel writing. "I finished a science fiction novel, now too awful to contemplate, but it was the first piece of long work that I had completed, and I managed to wrangle a review out of a children's book editor who was a friend of a friend. That encouraged me to continue writing" (*SATA,* 15).

Teenaged Terry attempted to write every kind of novel. "I tried the great white whale story, the great moors of England love story, the last showdown western. I'd get several chapters into it and I'd toss it aside and say, 'Ah, this isn't going anywhere.' When I read those European adventure stories, I knew *this* was the way to go. But how could I do it? I didn't want to write historical fiction. There's nothing like *The Three Musketeers* happening right now, so how could I make this topical and in what form?"

While Terry was struggling to find the right fictional form, his high school experience was providing him with ample material for what would become an enduring theme in his writing: being an outsider. "As a kid growing up, I never really fit in," he recalls. All that writing and reading was "weird stuff that other kids didn't necessarily do. I was a little short dorky guy with glasses and I never had any luck with girls. I was never part of the [culture] that was commonplace in those days, growing up in the '50s and early '60s. I was real good at schoolwork." Terry was one of four members of the Illinois State Champion Debate Team from Sterling High School, from which he graduated in 1962.

Terry left the Midwest to go to Hamilton College in Clinton, New York, where he majored in English; it was during this period that he encountered the works of Thomas Hardy, Herman Melville, and Joseph Conrad and absorbed the pivotal influence of William Faulkner's writing. In his junior year, a fateful event occurred: a friend gave him a copy of *The Lord of the Rings* by J. R. R. Tolkien. The Tolkien campus cult was in full swing that year, 1965, when the trilogy was first published in one volume. It changed Terry Brooks's life.

"This is *it!*" said the young writer searching for a form for his stories. "This is what I will do. I will cut out all of Tolkien's appendices, all his language and historical concerns, and just go for the heart of the story. I want my book to read like *Dune*. I want it to be a story that you get into and *cannot* put down. You have *got* to find out what happens from one page to the next, one chapter to the next. It will be the kind of adventure story I admired so much, only it will be in a fantasy setting. We won't know where it is, that Tolkienesque world. Magic will be the driving force in place of science. I'll discuss all of these topical issues. Everything that is happening right outside my door, I'm going to put into this world and explore."

The year Terry discovered Tolkien, he also did a summer internship in Washington, D.C., with Congressman John Anderson. Despite his dreams of becoming a writer, the practical student knew that he would have to earn a living in a more conventional career. After earning his bachelor's degree in 1966, Terry went into law school at Washington and Lee University in Lexington, Virginia. That did not mean he was giving up writing. When law school began, so did Terry's novel, the one modeled after Tolkien that would become *The Sword of Shannara*. He was to work on it for seven years.

After receiving his law degree in 1969, Terry Brooks returned home to Sterling to practice law. Three years later, he married office manager Barbara O'Banion. The next year, 1973, he got his name on the door by becoming a partner in the law firm Besse, Frye, Arnold, and Brooks, practicing mostly family law. All this time, while being a lawyer by day, he was creating his own world of Shannara by night.

At last, in 1974, the labor of creation was complete. Terry Brooks sent his manuscript of *The Sword of Shannara* to a paperback publisher who enjoyed the book but felt that publishing it would be too risky. He suggested that Brooks send it to Tolkien's publisher, Ballantine, where new editor Lester del Rey, a respected fantasy writer and critic, just happened to be looking for an epic novel to launch his new fantasy imprint.

The maverick del Rey was unlike other publishers at that time "when Tolkien was *extremely* revered and *nobody* would publish fantasy that was anywhere near Tolkienesque because they were afraid of the comparison," explains Brooks. "Though there was a hidebound belief within the industry that fantasy wouldn't sell, Lester was convinced it would sell as well as any category of fiction out there if it was marketed and distributed right." Though naive Brooks knew nothing of this situation at the time, del Rey spied two cartons stuffed with an 850-page manuscript on the unsolicited "slush pile" and performed a fateful rescue mission. He decided it was the best fantasy since Tolkien, just the ticket to prove his point about selling fantasy.

In an interview with *Publishers Weekly* drawing attention to this new fantasy phenomenon three months before it appeared, Lester del Rey characterized the audience for *Sword* as fantasy fans who had already fallen for Tolkien. "There's nothing else out there for them to read," he declared. "They just have to reread their Tolkien." He described the *Sword* manuscript's two-year trip from acceptance to publication. Written 10 years before when Brooks had just finished reading Tolkien, "the older half, the first box, was much too close to Tolkien in part. . . . [A]nd it sprawled, but through the editing Terry always managed to take my ideas and shape them into his own."[35] The second half had been written more recently.

At the time, Ballantine published only paperbacks. It attempted to find a hardcover publisher for *Sword,* and though some liked it, no one seemed willing, in del Rey's opinion, to put the necessary muscle behind the book. So del Rey and Ballantine's science fiction editor, Judy-Lynn del Rey, decided to publish it larger than pocket size, as a trade paperback with illustrations. Their choice of the Brothers Hildebrandt as artists was deliberate; everyone would recognize their work from Tolkien's book and calendar. Along with the cover, they produced a color foldout centerfold and eight black-and-white paintings.

The del Reys also convinced the Literary Guild book club to feature *Sword* as an alternate selection, "which meant we had to have a hardcover," said Judy-Lynn del Rey. "We went to Random House, and now we'll both be publishing it simultaneously," with a larger run of copies in paperback (Dahlin, 39). At the time, such a joint venture between a paperback and hardcover house was rare. Also rare was the effort del Rey put into publicity, marketing, and hand-selling the book with Ballantine's sales representatives, who convinced booksellers to stock it. They even printed posters and preview booklets. While he waited to see his first novel in print, Terry Brooks became a father; his daughter, Amanda, was born in 1975.

When *The Sword of Shannara* hit the market in April 1977, it proved del Rey's point explosively by staying on the best-seller list for 26 weeks, selling hundreds of thousands of copies. *The Sword of Shannara* made publishing history as the first work of fiction ever on the *New York Times* trade paperback best-seller list. It was also named as a Best Book for Young Adults by the American Library Association, which listed few fantasies at that time.

What captivated so many readers? Just as Brooks hoped, *Sword* was an epic adventure story set in a world based on ours but altered. It is a world rebuilt after nuclear holocaust, where magical races of Trolls, Dwarves, Gnomes, and Elves are reborn from legend to dwell among humans. In the Four Lands, magic has replaced science, but it has been misused by power-hungry Brona, once a wise Druid, now corrupted by magic's power to become the Warlock Lord. The only other Druid left, the mysterious Allanon, knows that just one magic is strong enough to stop the Warlock Lord from controlling the world. That magic resides in the long-forgotten Sword of Shannara, which can be wielded only by someone with ancient royal Elven blood of the Shannara line. Its single descendant is ordinary part-human, part-Elf young man Shea Ohmsford. Shea's story is enough like Tolkien's hobbit Frodo's but sufficiently different to capture all the readers who had so little to choose after Tolkien.

The Sword of Shannara is now widely known as the title that "brought fantasy novels into the mainstream. Until *Shannara,* no fantasy writer except J. R. R. Tolkien had made such an impression on the general public," says critic Louise J. Winters.[36] Brooks himself credits Lester del Rey as "the Svengali of this whole thing," knowing he was merely lucky to be in the right place at the right time. His own accomplishment has been "to keep the stories consistently good over the years," and he is pleased that *Sword* "opened the doors to everything that has followed in the field of modern fantasy, to the success that every writer has enjoyed since then. Now nobody questions whether or not a fantasy writer can sell as well as a horror writer, or a mystery writer, or anything else. It's an accepted fact, so we're not fighting these battles anymore. And that's a big plus for every writer."

Brooks was such a novice that he did not realize what a fluke it was to hit the best-seller list with a first novel. Looking back, he is glad he was so naive, because he did not kick back and relax, which would have been a mistake, but "really got up my head of steam and started up the next two" in the *Shannara* series.[37] Terry Brooks still had much to learn about writing. He began working on *The Elfstones of Shannara* as soon as *Sword* was accepted for publication. After practicing law in the mornings, Brooks wrote in the afternoons. Ignoring his editor Lester del Rey's requests to see the manuscript along the way, Brooks zoomed through 450 pages until he reached a dead stop. "Suddenly I thought, 'I don't know how to end this and I don't know where this is going.' "[38] It was time to ask Lester for advice.

"He sent back the manuscript with pieces of legal size yellow paper stuck in about every third page analyzing the book all the way through. After I got done getting steamed and I really took the time to study it and see what he was doing, it turned out he was right" (Narvaes). The result was that Terry Brooks learned the fundamentals of storytelling, which became his guiding principle and the secret of his success. "I believe that telling a good story is a fantasy writer's first obligation to his readers," he declares. "I was first told that by my editor, and it's the best piece of advice I ever received about writing. I also believe in writing for myself; that is, if I write something that I would enjoy reading, it will find an audience" (*SATA*, 15).

Brooks recalls how difficult it was to incorporate del Rey's advice. "He beat the living bejesus out of me, verbally and critically, . . . had me do extensive rewrites and taught me hard lessons, but boy, were they worth it! Every writer should have that kind of editor early on in their career to help them understand what it is that drives a story and makes it strong, how to pace and how perspective works and all those things I didn't learn in writing classes, which were a waste of time for me."

While Brooks was learning how to make all the suspenseful elements of classic adventure work in his own writing, he was also finding out how to convert such adventure from realism to fantasy. His editor's philosophy guided him. "Lester del Rey used to argue that fantasy was the most difficult form of literature to write because it had to be the most realistic," says Brooks. "What he meant was that if the reader couldn't suspend disbelief long enough to accept the possibility of the story, then the writer had failed. . . . Most of what I write is, metaphorically, about our own world. The plots . . . are almost always inspired by what I read in the newspapers. By putting the story in a different world, I can take a fresh look at the particulars and perhaps bring to the reader a different perspective. My first goal is to tell a good story, but my second is to make readers think about their own lives."[39]

In his much-rewritten second novel, *The Elfstones of Shannara,* his concern for the environment emerges; it pervades the rest of his writing. The central character is Wil Ohmsford, the grandson of Shea from *Sword,* who is also pressed into service by the Druid Allanon. The Ellcrys, a magical tree that guards the land from ancient evil demons, is dying, and Wil must help the Elf girl Amberle to preserve it and their beloved land from decay. Entwined with this issue is how men should use magic, its power a metaphor for science, which Brooks continually explores. In *Elfstones,* Brooks breaks away from the constraints of following Tolkien conventions and so comes into his own voice. He admits that *Elfstones* is "probably my favorite book because it was the hardest book to write" while del Rey raked him "over the coals. . . . [M]ost of the readers I speak with to this day say it was the book that made the biggest impact on them. . . . I like what I did with *The Elfstones* very much. I don't think I would change anything" (Francisco, 175–76). *School Library Journal* recognized *The Elfstones of Shannara* as a Best Book for Young Adults.

Appearing throughout his writing, "environmental issues are a major part of my life," Brooks explains. "I live in the Pacific Northwest, where we are dealing with all kinds of problems, from the spotted owl and the loggers to the extinction of the salmon runs, to the pollution of the earth through nuclear waste and our own toxic fumes. . . . I pick up the paper and I read about [the environment] almost every day. And I live here too, so I don't particularly like what I see happening." His writing has become a way for Brooks to place such issues into his readers' consciousness.

Brooks's second novel also marked the beginning of another constant concern: the reactions of his readers. He takes his fan mail very seriously. After *Sword* made such a fanfare, he received many letters noting the absence of leading female characters—perhaps another Tolkien influence. In response, Brooks developed female characters more fully. In *Elfstones,* Amberle and Eretria both love Wil. Brooks did not want "the standard love story, so I decided to do a triangle. I decided to have two women, strong characters each but in different ways, involved with one of the Ohmsfords. . . . You're always looking for different types of characters to develop and explore because that's what you do when you're a writer. Then you open that up to the readers" (Francisco, 177).

His third book, *The Wishsong of Shannara,* was his first to feature a teenaged female protagonist, Brin Ohmsford, the daughter of Wil from *Elfstones.* Like the rest of her clan, Brin cannot resist the summons of Allanon to awaken her magic within. Only her wishsong can destroy the source of dark magic that has corrupted the Mord Wraiths, the once-human monsters who pollute the land and seek control over other races. Brin easily takes her place beside Robin McKinley's strong heroines (see her section later in this chapter) and is the equal of any male Brooks hero; all question their enforced quests and grow stronger as a result.

While he was writing *Wishsong,* in 1983, Brooks's son, Alex, was born. By 1985, when *Wishsong* was published, Brooks was taking a break from the Ohmsford saga to explore a new type of fantasy that mirrored his own life and paved the way for major changes to come. Knowing that he wanted to write something shorter and lighter unconnected with Shannara, with "somebody from this world as a protagonist, . . . a *John Carter of Mars* kind of story where he leaves this world," Brooks consulted his editor, del Rey. Years later, Brooks loves to tell the famous story of "how Lester del Rey *enticed* me into writing *Magic Kingdom for Sale— Sold!*" According to Brooks, del Rey refused to tell him his idea for a book because "he didn't think I was the right writer for it. And then he led me on and on, and I was saying *just tell me* what the idea is." Finally, del Rey revealed

> this whole scenario about this guy who gets one of these Christmas wish books from a major department store. It's got the goldfish in the clear bathtubs. It's got the voyages to Bermuda fully crewed. And in there is this ad for this magic kingdom which he thinks can't possibly be, but he decides to go ahead and buy it. Then it doesn't turn out to be what he thought. Lester envisioned it as a Xanth kind of story. He says, "You can have this idea for a year, and if you write the story, it's yours, but if you don't, you have to give the idea back." So I took it home and I mulled it over. I knew where Lester was going with it and thought, I don't want to do that. I have to have much darker things working there. So I thought, who is this guy? Well, he's a lawyer, that's who he is, and he hates practicing law. I said, "I know who this guy is! I know what this story is about!"
>
> I started to develop it metaphorically from the point of view of a lawyer who wanted out because he was burned out. Which was where I was at the time. It progressed from there and all the other things started to fit into place.

In *Magic Kingdom for Sale—Sold!* Ben Holiday is a Chicago lawyer grieving for his wife, Annie, who died two years earlier. He sees an irresistible ad in a posh catalog and, for a million dollars, he buys the Kingdom of Landover and its kingship. When he disappears through its gateway in the Virginia mountains, leaving his old life behind, Ben has no idea what he will find. His subjects include Abernathy, the court scribe, a man turned into a talking Wheaten terrier with human hands and feet—based on Brooks's own dog—and inventive new breeds of magical and faerie creatures who give Ben enormous challenges in ruling. With a fresh twist and doses of humor, Brooks explores his favorite themes of the use and misuse of power and the care of the environment while working out his own personal issues through writing.

Magic Kingdom was published as the first volume in the *Magic Kingdom of Landover* series in 1986 and named a Best Book for Young Adults by both the American Library Association and *School Library Journal*. On an author tour promoting the book in Seattle, Brooks met Waldenbooks district manager Judine Alba. He recognized his true partner immediately. At the same time, he was finally able to give up law for writing.

> I wrote *Magic Kingdom* . . . specifically on a metaphorical level to talk about my transition from being a practicing attorney to being a full-time writer. What happens to Ben Holiday is sort of a mirror of what that meant to me, and it allowed me to work through some issues while writing it. Interestingly enough, I didn't (retire from practicing law) until after I wrote the book, but after I'd written the book and worked through the transition, I decided I was ready to do it. I still like that book for what it revealed to me, what the possibilities were. (Francisco, 178)

Ben Holiday, openly the alter ego of Terry Brooks, sees himself as the outsider, as Brooks always has. No longer the nerdy bookish kid, Brooks has "metamorphosed over the years into a different kind of personality, but I never lost that sense of what it was to feel like you just didn't fit in anywhere. I'm *sure* that readers of science fiction/fantasy fit right in with that. . . . [W]e all are just looking to stretch the imagination and find a way to belong to something. In that sense, Ben is certainly part of who I am."

As the result of writing a story about a man changing his life, Brooks changed his own life dramatically. Not only did he leave his law career but he also left his whole life in Illinois behind, moving to Seattle in 1986. He confessed that "[t]he toughest thing I've ever done was to leave my kids," who moved to Pittsburgh with their mother but flew to Seattle regularly to visit him.[40] In December 1987, Terry Brooks married Judine. It was the same year that his second *Landover* novel, *Black Unicorn,* was published. Ben Holiday's Landover rule continued in the third volume, *Wizard at Large,* in 1988, though the series was not to stop at a trilogy.

After 17 years of law practice, Brooks missed the courtroom not at all. Since childhood he had identified himself as a writer, while law was merely a way to make a living. When economics became less important, he was reluctant to let go of his practice mostly due to fears that "maybe if I had all this free time, I wouldn't be able to write. If you're not grounded in something, what keeps you from just falling apart? I waited and had four books before I said, 'OK, you're a writer now, you can quit practicing (law) and just write' " (Francisco, 178).

His daily schedule as a writer is "fairly straightforward," Brooks says. "Judine works three days a week in a bookstore, from 8 to 4:30. When she works, I work. It's a logical thing to do. I drive her to work, go home at 8:05. I'm at the computer until two or three in the afternoon. I usually put in six or seven hours of concentrated effort, but I do a lot in that time period. I'm a very quick writer; I do my editing as I go. I didn't always write that way, but I've learned to be that kind of writer. I usually work those three days and then I throw in a fourth day, sometimes a fifth day or part of a day, when I'm working hard at a book. I do a book a year. That's the pattern that is comfortable to me now."

In 1990, Terry Brooks returned to his *Shannara* world with the publication of *The Scions of Shannara*. Three hundred years after *Wishsong* ends, this first installment of a new series, *The Heritage of Shannara,* introduces descendants of previous characters who will become the scions to restore magic to the Four Lands. The military Federation now ruling has abolished the old kings and outlawed magic. The last Druid, Allanon, is dead, the Elves have completely disappeared, and people hardly remember the sword. The Shadowen are the new enemy, dreadful creatures made of magic's residue gone awry, who can possess others from inside and destroy their souls. Three Ohmsfords are given a new charge by Allanon's shade: Par must find the sword once again to discover the secret of the Shadowen, his cousin Wren must find the missing Elves, and their uncle Walker Boh must restore the Druids. It will take four books for these various quests to be accomplished and for the scions to come together to restore magic. In successive years, each *Heritage* title appeared: *The Druid of Shannara* in 1991, *The Elf Queen of Shannara* in 1992, and the conclusion *The Talismans of Shannara* in 1993. Unlike the first *Shannara* series, which featured separate characters in each volume, momentum builds in *Heritage* as the story continues from book to book.

Just after he began the *Heritage* series, Brooks took a break for two writing projects unrelated to either *Shannara* or *Landover.* For *Once Upon a Time,* a modern fairy tale treasury edited by Lester del Rey, Brooks wrote an uncustomary short story, "Imaginary Friends." After seventh grader Jack is diagnosed with leukemia, he meets a real elf named Pick, who takes him flying on the back of Daniel the barn owl for a unique view of the world that others cannot see. The story collection was published in 1991, the same year as Brooks's other project, the novelization of the feature movie *Hook,* which starred Robin Williams as an aging Peter Pan who has forgotten his once-eternal youth. How could Terry Brooks, originator of two otherworlds, write a book based on someone else's screenplay sequel to a fantasy classic? Brooks answers:

> I liked the concept of doing a sequel to *Peter Pan* and I thought I was the writer to do it, in my arrogance. So I asked for permission when my publisher bought the rights. My editor said, "You'll be sorry. I'm telling you right now, don't do it." But I insisted. I gave him all my reasons that I thought it was a good idea, and he said, "Your reasons are sound but the experience will be different."

And it was extremely different. It was *hard* working with people who do movies, because they don't know books. It was very difficult to get them to agree to do *anything* that deviated from the script, or even to flesh out what was there. Or even to let them understand the differences between writing words on paper and showing images on screen. They don't get it. So it was a pain to do it, and it took an inordinate amount of time. I wrote the whole thing in 45 days. They were still filming and changing, so I rewrote. Then they filmed and rechanged some more—they can't make up their minds and they make all these silly mistakes. Fortunately, my editor fought very hard to keep my story intact. I was very happy with the way it worked out, but it wasn't worth it.

Fans often wonder why no Terry Brooks novel has been made into a movie. Though Hollywood often approaches him, Brooks is not eager to see his work translated to the screen, because "the movie industry doesn't really understand fantasy, and doesn't know how to do it." He has heard many horror stories from authors who have sold their rights and hated the resulting movies, but only "maybe two that have turned out well, Kinsella's *Field of Dreams* being one. I sold the rights to *The Sword of Shannara* early on, and that was also destroyed, but I got it back before they could do anything. If I sell rights, I have to be prepared to give up *all* control and any chance that anything will happen other than a movie will drive up sales of the books—which is a big commercial consideration. So the question is: how much is it worth? I've decided it's worth a whole bunch of money, and if they're not going to pay that, or give me control over the way in which the storyline is developed, then I *don't* need the money, and I *don't* need the movie, and I *don't* need it in my life."

The year *Hook* was published, only about three years after Terry Brooks married Judine, they faced a severe setback to their newfound happiness, when Judine was diagnosed with breast cancer. "It seemed unfair. We had known each other for such a short time," says Judine. "But Terry and I are forward-looking people and we refused to dwell on it" (Achiron and Gallo, 54). Fortunately, Judine responded well to treatment, beating the disease.

In 1994, readers could return to Landover after a six-year absence, with the fourth title in the series, *The Tangle Box*. Ben's beloved sylph has conceived a child; Willow is a green-skinned "once-fairy" whose mother is a wood nymph and father the River Master. While Willow must go alone to a fairy ritual for the child's birth, Ben is trapped in the limbo of the Tangle Box. Brooks devoted this book to "the relationship of Ben and Willow" and "the pregnancy, because this is obviously not going to be your average birth, dealing with a sylph and a human. Will the baby be Twig or human?"

The following year, *Witches' Brew* appeared, exploring the growth of Ben and Willow's remarkable daughter, Mistaya. "I've got all kinds of things to say about kids," says Brooks, "about the way kids affect the lives of their parents and vice versa. Everybody can immediately relate to that in some fashion. But this child's formative years aren't the same as they are here." When asked in 1994 if another *Landover* book might cover Mistaya as an adult inheriting Landover's throne, Brooks replied, "There are no more *Landover* books this decade."

In 1995, the year of the last *Landover* novel, Brooks ventured into a new format with the computer game Shannara. At first, self-described "control nut" Brooks was reluctant to sell rights to a game developer, for the same reasons he has declined movie offers. But he was impressed with the approach of Legend Entertainment Company: "[A]ll the people involved were readers of the books who knew and appreciated . . . the story, and we were all on the same wavelength. . . . They basically presented me with a script, a synopsis of the story line, and a workup of the characters. They said, 'If you want to make any changes, we'd like you to say so now.' I did, and they made some changes. Then I said, 'That's it, I'm out of it. . . . I'm not the expert on putting this together, I put my faith in you, and go ahead and do it' " (Francisco, 171).

He agreed to do three Shannara series games, as long as players responded well. Brooks was pleased that the games used not actual stories from his books but ones based upon his world. The new stories "created the whole generation of Ohmsfords between

The Sword and *The Elfstones of Shannara*," taking advantage of the gaps Brooks likes to provide so that the history of the Four Lands will have authentic flavor, and avoiding other complications arising from licensing Brooks's own work (Francisco, 171–72).

Brooks also feels that fantasy adventure fits naturally into the medium of computer games. "It lends itself very well because you're operating in an imaginary world, so you can create all of the visual effects around the world without being tied in any way." Though Brooks himself has played computer games, he stopped when he found "it eats up too much time." He isn't a computer expert, though he writes using computer word processing. It is his teenaged son, Alex, who "eats, sleeps, and breathes computers, and most of what I know about computers I've learned from him" (Francisco, 170).

A review of the Shannara game reads, "You're Jak Ohmsford, called upon to take up the Sword of Shannara against the War-lock Lord. Players are challenged by puzzles and tested in combat. Controls are intuitive; you assemble a subject-verb-object command with a few mouse clicks. Puzzles are easy enough not to interrupt the story's flow; that, plus engaging characters and plot, make it a good kids' choice."[41]

The computer age also offers a fitting way for fans to partici-pate in Brooks's otherworlds through their own expressions on personal Internet home pages. In 1997 there were at least 15 fan-produced home pages, most about *Shannara*. Some featured their own creative writing with new characters in *Shannara*'s world or produced enhanced maps of the Four Lands or original art. One site concentrated on the computer game; one was in Swedish, another in Italian. Only one focused on Landover.

Terry Brooks openly encourages his fans' feedback and involve-ment in his stories. He won't even dictate to readers how to pro-nounce *Shannara*. (He himself accents the first syllable.) He answers all fan mail except inquiries about how much money he makes. One of his most engaging traits is his commitment to his young readers and his respect for their opinions. At a busy book-store signing in Colorado that drew over 100 readers, mostly teenagers, Brooks personally inscribed every copy of each young fan's towering Brooks collection, often amounting to over 10 tattered paperbacks per person. Sitting at a table with Judine, Brooks gave undivided attention to each reader. Able to overcome shyness with such warm reception, many teens asked questions. Despite the length of the line of fans awaiting autographs and the fact that he had heard each question countless times before, Brooks patiently answered them all.

Not surprisingly, many asked for advice on becoming writers. Brooks obviously relishes sharing secrets of his craft and enjoys the mentor's role. He dispenses strong encouragement:

> If you're going to be a writer, then keep writing. You have to want to write. If you're a writer, you will write even though everybody is telling you that you should be a ditch digger. That's what's going to happen. People will look at your work and say, "Is there anything else you think you might do with your life?" You're going to get rejected over and over. That's my whole history. With the exception of one slim eighth-grade article, I was rejected for every single thing I ever did as far as I can remember. But it doesn't matter. You just figure, "They don't know. I'm going to show them and I'm going to find a way to get published."

Brooks knows such words will inspire the true writers to keep at it, and he sees hope in the current fantasy market. "Publishers do support young, beginning writers. There's a commitment, at least on the part of some, del Rey fortunately being one, to find new writers and publish them each year, on the theory that some of those will strike a common chord. You can't become too moribund with the group of writers that you have. This is an area where there is a lot of change and opportunities because the readership is growing, and is strong, and reads quickly. Kids go through one of my books in a week."

Brooks understands his young fans, who are so often versions of his writer self:

> I've been writing stories forever, all through high school, all my life, and I can't imagine doing anything else. If I didn't write, I'd probably just die. It's just as simple as that, and I think that's the way writers are. My wife says that writers are born. You're

either a writer, or you're not. You have to discover whether this
is true about you or not. You have a special kind of drive for
what you do, and you just never back away from it.

Even now that he commands seven-figure advances for his
guaranteed best-sellers, Brooks sees himself as "a work-obsessed,
compulsive Midwestern moralist" (Achiron and Gallo, 54). Three
of his books have hit the number-two slot on the *New York Times*
best-seller list, but he has never attained slot number one. "If I
could get the kind of coverage that John Grisham gets, I could
double my readership tomorrow," Brooks declares. But that top
slot is elusive unless "I . . . show people that I'm not just writing
about elves and dwarves. I'm touching themes that affect our
lives" (53).

Brooks sees fantasy pigeonholing as limiting his readership. "I
don't talk about my work as fantasy," Brooks asserts. "That's the
category that it's shelved in and marketed as, but really, I write
adventure stories. Yes, they have fantasy trappings, but there's
not a whole lot of difference between my stories and Tom
Clancy's. There are dozens and dozens of different kinds of fantasy writers. You can't dismiss the whole category as one thing."

Brooks often borrows from other genres. "I can reach over into
that horror genre and pull out a little bit of Stephen King or John
Saul. . . . I can reach over into the romance field and I can develop
a story that involves great love between two of the characters. Or
I can do something contemporary. I can take issues like the environmental issue . . . in a metaphorical fashion and people will recognize them without being beaten over the head with what's
going on" (Narvaes).

As a "commercial animal," Brooks hopes to extend his readership, already young and older readers of both sexes. "I can't
expand with these series," he admits. Figuring out how to draw in
audiences who enjoy Anne Rice, John Grisham, or Stephen King
is "a challenge, and that's also what writing is about. If you're
any kind of writer, you want everybody, every man, woman, and
child to pick up these books and read them. I don't write for any
other reason except to be read. I'm not writing for the ages. I

don't want to be discovered when I'm dead. I want to be read right here and now. I want to be here to enjoy it."

When people ask that irritating "where do you get your ideas?" question always posed to writers, Brooks tells a secret. "There are no new ideas. There are no more original ideas out there, they've all been discovered a long time ago. There are new approaches to old ideas, new ways to look at things, and that's what makes a writer successful in my field particularly. It's good storytelling with a different slant."

Surprisingly, Brooks reads very little fantasy, though he did write a sincerely admiring introduction for one of the hottest new fantasies in recent years, *The Golden Compass* by Philip Pullman, which is "chock-full of the most innovative concepts in fantasy storytelling that I have come across in years."[42] Brooks confesses that only Tolkien "has been a major influence on my life. I take my inspiration as a writer, and my impetus to do better, from writers outside the fantasy field."

Nurtured on adventure classics in his youth, as an adult Brooks finds

> the best adventure stories in history, and also contemporary fiction. . . . I read a lot of different stuff, a smorgasbord. In mysteries and detective stories, I admire Ed McBain as a stylist and James Lee Burke very much. Paul Watkins, an English writer of adventure stories, has done really interesting things about historical England and Europe. I like Alice Hoffman. *The Birthday Boys* by Beryl Bainbridge is wonderful because it explains, from the five different voices and views of the members of the Scott expedition who perished on their way back from the South Pole, exactly how this debacle took place, and why they all died. You can see it from the composite, she's done such a good job. *That's* the kind of thing that I would like to do as a writer.
>
> I also read everything about the French Foreign Legion, everything about the exploration of Africa, everything about Alexander the Great and the Greeks and the Romans. A lot of military history stuff, too.
>
> Then my wife brings home a whole 'nother perspective because she reads southern fiction, short stories, black women's fiction, stories about people's lives and the way they rub up against each other. She'll say, "You have to read this." And I'll

read it, and it will be wonderful. It will be the kind of thing that
will open your eyes, that I wouldn't have picked up on my own.
I like to read things that inspire me to do a better job.

First King of Shannara, a prequel to the whole series that tells
how the Druid Bremen forged the Sword first used by Elf King
Jerle Shannara, with tantalizing tidbits about the boyhood of
Allanon, was published in 1996. After working on the two series
of *Shannara* and *Landover* for 20 years, Terry Brooks was ready
to try "something different." To open a new series set in our own
world, he published *Running with the Demon* in 1997. It features
Nest, a feisty 14-year-old orphaned heroine drawn into a cosmic
battle between good and evil when a demon takes over her small
town of Hopewell, Illinois, based on Brooks's own hometown,
Sterling. Reusing the huge park, the crusty six-inch elf, Pick, and
the barn owl, Daniel, from his 1991 short story "Imaginary
Friends," Brooks is likely to snag that new audience he is looking
for in this riveting tale of evil infesting our secure everyday world,
which reads more like the horror of Dean Koontz than fantasy.
He plans two more volumes of this "big series of issues and characterization." The new series will carry him through the nineties.
After that, there will be another two-book *Shannara* series.
Brooks has not decided yet when or if *Landover* will continue.

Meanwhile, Terry Brooks enjoys life with Judine and their cat,
Phoebe, in their "incredible" lavender cliffside house overlooking
Puget Sound in Seattle, complete with sweeping views and a tele-
scope. He loves meandering through Pike Place Market to buy
fresh fruit, eating in great restaurants, and attending the sym-
phony and ballet. He also owns three forested acres of Oregon
coast where he and Judine savor the outdoors. For a change of
pace from the Northwest, they stay in their luxury second home,
in Hawaii, or just travel, a pleasure that has recently hooked
Brooks (Achiron and Gallo, 53–54). Readers will appreciate the
rare photos of Brooks and his wife accompanying the 1993 *People*
interview, especially the one in which his grinning form is
dwarfed by an enormous troll sculpture under Fremont Bridge in
Seattle. Yet would Terry Brooks, a man of slight stature with sil-

ver hair, who dresses in neat conservative slacks and shirts, appreciate the interviewer calling him "elfin"?

Brooks dislikes impersonal questionnaires sent by reference biography publishers, preferring face-to-face interviews in which he can discuss his work. Possibly because critics have not always been kind to him, treating his writing as merely "popular," he may not see any point in appearing in reference works in which scholars may study him. He was receptive to this interviewer because he believes there is merit in addressing a young adult audience about writing, since they "take a lot more inspiration away from that kind of thing than adults do." This critique was stymied in small, annoying ways by a perception that Brooks's work may not be worth serious study. Few references exist (perhaps with Brooks's collusion), and one standard index seemed to have made a policy decision not to list his reviews after 1985. Yet following the development of his writer's consciousness and skill can be satisfying, as readers will see in the following section. His exciting adventures offer fine entertainment that grows ever more meaty but never less accessible to devoted YA readers. Some might outgrow Brooks, but they would understand his statement: "I'm very proud of my work. I'm prepared to defend it. I think I write good stuff. It's not meant to be certain things, but for what it's meant to be, I think it pretty much succeeds."

The Sword of Shannara Trilogy

The Sword of Shannara, the sprawling epic fantasy of over 700 pages that launched both the career of Terry Brooks and the popularity of modern heroic fantasy, is difficult to digest or summarize quickly. Its pivot is the enigmatic Allanon, the only surviving Druid in the Four Lands, who holds all history and knowledge, forgotten by the world's inhabitants. Only Allanon knows that the evil Warlock Lord, once the Druid Brona, actually survives 500 years after everyone presumed him dead, threatening again to control the world. Only Allanon knows that hope lies in the fabled Sword of Shannara, now lost. Only Allanon knows the true heritage and destiny of young half Elf/half human Shea Ohmsford, adopted son of an innkeeper in the peaceful Southland town of Shady Vale. Only Allanon knows all is in jeopardy in the Four Lands, where races do not mingle as they should. The people have come to believe that most of their history is mere legend or fairy tale.

When the Druid suddenly appears, Shea Ohmsford sees Allanon as a myth come alive. Few have ever seen "the mysterious wanderer of the four lands, historian of the races, philosopher and teacher, and some said, practitioner of the mystic arts." Allanon is seven feet tall, hooded and cloaked in dark robes, ageless.[43] Before he can tell Shea the purpose of his visit, Allanon must correct Shea's false impressions of the past. Among humans living isolated from other races in the Southland, Shea knows little about the Trolls and Gnomes and soulless creatures of the Northland, or the Dwarves in the Eastland. He is even unacquainted with his own race, the Westland Elves, whose pointed ears and slanted eyebrows Shea inherited from his Elf father, who died when Shea was very young. Shea knows only that when his human mother died, he was adopted by distant cousins, the Ohmsfords.

For both Shea and readers entering this fantasy realm, Allanon encapsulates 1,000 years of history in 20 pages. During the long history lesson, identifying with Shea is all that stops this violation of the storytelling rule "show, don't tell" from losing us. We soon discover, with Shea, that Allanon never tells the whole truth. His mission is to make others enact his vision, so he constantly judges how much is safe to reveal. The questioning this policy evokes in Shea and others who must jump to Allanon's tune can become tiresome to both characters and readers but also breeds the suspense that keeps pages turning. Brooks walks a narrative tightrope with Allanon, and his novice skills in this first novel do not always allow him to hold the rope taut.

Yet the world Brooks constructs is fascinating, even if we must navigate it through Allanon's long-winded sermons. Over 100 pages after his introduction to Shea, Allanon revises his initial explanation. He describes a vanished world 2,000 years before populated only by Man, a "fabulous, exciting time to live" in which Man "was on the verge of mastering the secrets of life itself" through the "science of machines and power, one that divided itself into infinite fields of exploration, all of which worked toward the same two ends—discovering better ways to live or quicker ways to kill" (*Sword*, 154).

Readers recognize our familiar world, precursor to the Four Lands, and are hardly surprised when Allanon recounts that "the same elements of power that made life free from sickness and infirmity nearly destroyed it altogether" (155). The Great Wars of our future began with small disputes among human races, until immense power was unleashed that destroyed human life and altered the land's surface. The few survivors of the holocaust were flung back into primitive existence, shared with new races of Dwarves, Gnomes, Trolls, and Elves.

Those who recalled science's secrets were few, retaining small bits of vast knowledge that eroded as rare books decayed and memories faltered. To save knowledge, the first Druid Council called all learned men to "reconstruct the old means of harnessing power" (158). But some sought easier answers in the study of a more ancient power, the mystic arts. The Druid Brona uncovered secrets of sorcery so alluring that he sacrificed his goal of understanding science, his ideals of making a better world, his identity, his soul. Corrupted by mystic power, he became the Warlock Lord, starting the First War of the Races to dominate all others. When he was defeated, the world split into the Four Lands. Still Brona secretly fed his spirit on mystic powers, becoming immortal and enslaving mindless followers who sacrificed their humanity to become winged black destroyers, the Skull Bearers.

Relaying this history to Shea, Allanon states Brooks's thesis for the entire *Shannara* series: "The fact that these unfortunate Druids stumbled onto the very opposite of what they were seeking is in itself a lesson to Man. Perhaps with patience, they might have pieced together the missing link to the old sciences rather than uncovering the terrible power of the spirit world that fed eagerly on their unprotected minds until they were devoured. Human minds are not equipped to face the realities of nonmaterial existence on this sphere" (160). Like science, the mystic arts are dangerous when taken to excess, and humanity is unable to control its own use of either power. A strong related message is that we are doomed to repeat the errors of history if we forget it or dismiss hidden truths in our stories and legends.

Suspecting that the Warlock Lord would return, another Druid Bremen began studying the forbidden mystic arts in order to defeat him. Disapproving fellow Druids banished Bremen from their Paranor stronghold, so he did not perish with them when the 500-year-old Warlock Lord destroyed Paranor in the Second War of the Races. To protect the other races, Bremen forged the Sword of Shannara as a great talisman with mystic power. "The Sword was to draw its strength from the minds of the mortals for whom it acted as a shield—the power of the Sword was their own desire to remain free," Allanon explains (163). In the hands of Elven King Jerle Shannara, the Sword did defeat the Warlock Lord. Then it was preserved in a vault in the Druid's Keep, set in a block of Tre-Stone with an inscription indicating that when the Warlock Lord appeared again, a son of the House of Shannara would take up the Sword against him.

After Allanon relates this forgotten history—none of which Brooks presents in story form until his eighth and most recent *Shannara* volume, the prequel *The First King of Shannara*— Shea is flabbergasted to learn that he is the last descendant of Jerle Shannara. He must retrieve the Sword from the vault in Paranor and use it against the Warlock Lord. If Shea refuses, the Warlock Lord is sure to win the greatest war yet. Legend decrees that only Shea can wield the Sword, which works only if he believes he can use it. Brooks thereby launches another ongoing theme; part of Shea's quest will be for belief in himself, a search that every Brooks hero undergoes.

Allanon's history is essential for understanding the *Shannara* books, but Shea's adventure has hardly begun. Brooks slowly assembles a huge cast of characters to accompany reluctant hero Shea. First, Shea's sturdy adopted brother Flick stays bound to Shea through fierce loyalty, a trait of other Ohmsford siblings to come. Then Shea's old friend Menion Leah, prince of the Highland Kingdom of Leah, joins him—as future Leahs will always bond with Ohmsfords in friendship. As the three head for the

Dwarf city of Culhaven to meet Allanon, menacing Skull Bearers stalk the skies. Another of Brooks's horde of horrific monsters, a "huge, unspeakable bulk" of the Mist Wraith rises from slimy marsh waters to grab them with its green tentacles. So Shea learns why Allanon gave him three blue Elfstones, whose "dazzling blue light" cuts into the monster with knife-edged flames (*Sword,* 106). The Elfstones will accompany Ohmsfords throughout the *Shannara* series.

Brooks conducts all journeys as ballets, their dancers coming together and moving apart in rhythms that pace the plot. The first separation occurs when Menion Leah is lost in thick mists, lured by a Siren, that mythic temptress who possesses men's souls— quite a treacherous first female to appear after over 100 pages of story! The only other woman in the book, Shirl Ravenlock, remains a minor player as the love interest of two of the men.

Rescued from the Siren by taciturn Dwarf Hendel, prince and Dwarf find the Ohmsford brothers in Culhaven, where all join Balinor Buckhannah, charismatic commander of a Border Legion that protects the Southland from the Warlock Lord's Northland invaders. Allanon brings two Elf brothers, Durin and Dayel Elessidil, cousins of the Elf King Eventine, to swell their ranks; Elessidil descendants will remain allies of the Ohmsford clan. This Band of Eight, which includes members of three races who have not fought together for hundreds of years, must rescue the Sword from the Gnomes, who have just seized it in Paranor, before it reaches the Warlock Lord. This effort occupies them through the rest of the book, the Eight operating more apart than together. Less than halfway through, Shea is on his own, a ploy Brooks repeats in most *Shannara* volumes to force his hero to rely on inner resources. Unlikely new allies rescue Shea from the Gnomes: con man and thief Panamon Creel, one of whose hands has been replaced by an iron pike, and his odd companion, huge mute Rock Troll Keltset, representing the final race in the coalition. Even Flick goes solo, helping King Eventine escape from the Northland army.

The breathtaking climax of this massive novel is played out on three simultaneous fronts: the Warlock Lord's immense army attacks Balinor's walled city of Tyrsis while Flick and Eventine await Elf reinforcements, and Shea confronts the Warlock Lord. Whenever such separations occur, each character's longing to reunite with the others proves a major force; the bonds of loyalty and common cause are strong. When the Band disperses at the story's end, readers knows the cause will rise again in future volumes.

Shea's crowning discovery is the Sword's power to reveal truth, which, for Brooks, signals what the epic struggle is all about. This talisman's protective power was forged through belief in freedom. These twin forces for truth and freedom are our only resources against our own weaknesses. In his postholocaust world of our future, Brooks parallels the mystic arts—never called magic until later volumes—with science, two powers that are not good or evil in themselves but become either by the way we use them. Evil is a corruption of truth, erupting from the selfish use of power for one's own ends. Good arises from insistence on truth, allowing us to realize our indelible bonds with others of all races, and our connection with nature and the earth. Anything unnatural is evil, such as the Warlock Lord's immortality, which recalls similar abuse of nature by Le Guin's Cob and by Barbara Hambly's wizard Suraklin (see chapter 3).

One of Brooks's strengths is his plot's momentum, maintained through cliffhangers, unexpected twists of fortune, and the dance of many characters' constant movements. This brisk pace alters when characters pause to ruminate, which draws out suspense and reveals motivation. However, first novelist Brooks as puppet master is not always in control of the strings. With no single point of view centered in one character, his focus is diffused, and the anxieties and realizations of each character begin to sound the same, blurring their identities with repetition. This effect occurs to some extent in the *Shannara* series as a whole, as characters continually reveal similar motivations in each quest toward wholeness.

In later volumes, Brooks develops better control of novelistic elements. As his "everyman" and "everywoman" characters engage readers through feelings we readily share, Brooks becomes more skillful in differentiating personalities, showing how people with various natures explore themselves. The Ohmsfords, Leahs, and Elessedils of Brooks's stories do confront their inner weaknesses, but readers are always sure they will eventually make the right choices, no matter how rough the path. Seeking his readers' identification with characters, Brooks never ventures into the viewpoints of any of his evil creatures, so they remain one-dimensional, lacking the true horror of villains in other fantasies whose depth depends on self-recognition of dark characters as well. (It should be mentioned that since his villains are subverted humans based on illusion, they are not human enough to identify with.) For Brooks, magic is corrupting and addictive; we must develop the ability to control it before it controls us. There is little forging of dark with light, as with Le Guin's multifaceted Ged and Tenar. It is this rather surface treatment of the riddles of existence that separates Brooks's rousing yarns from literary fantasies.

Still, Brooks urges readers to make their own connections between his fantasy world and reality. We wonder if we are certain to destroy ourselves through abuse of science. If we do, how will the world rebuild? Will old patterns repeat? Does human nature shape its greatness while simultaneously seeding its own destruction? Can we cooperate with other races?

Every so often, Brooks inserts an enigmatic symbol or two to keep us wondering. Breathless after barely eluding a Skull Bearer, Shea and Flick rest beside a river where a light suddenly moves to their side from the opposite bank. An ancient man with silver hair and beard appears, carrying a strange flameless light that goes out to reveal "a cylindrical object gripped in the old man's gnarled hand." The old man tells his amazed witnesses that he holds "a toy of people long since dead and gone" (*Sword,* 117). This is the first appearance of one of Brooks's most elusive and mystical characters, who returns for brief moments throughout the series. Unnamed at this point, he is the King of the Silver River; readers later learn that he guards the spirits of the earth that keep it bountiful; he is a benevolent sort of faerie king. Here he soothes Shea and Flick to sleep, sending them dreams in which they float over the earth, touching each creature and plant, understanding for the first time the interconnectedness of all nature. While reassuring and enlightening the brothers at a time of doubt, this spirit being carries an artifact of long-dead technology that readers guess is a flashlight, with symbolic overtones of lightbringer. Here Brooks allows readers to make their own connection between the scientific and the mystical in an inspired touch well left unexplained.

Of course the wise immortal sending visions of the secrets of nature to young heroes recalls T. H. White's Merlin instructing young Wart, who will grow up to be King Arthur (see chapter 5). Brooks borrows Arthurian motifs to underline his points. The King of the Silver River is a suitably subtle Merlin meshed with faerie, whereas Allanon is a more open relative, as is any man of wisdom since the Merlin legend. Writers continually mine this most powerful myth of Western culture, partly because Arthur is so familiar. At first one groans at the obviousness of the Sword of Shannara stuck in a stone awaiting the destined leader's discovery. Has Brooks descended to the level of animated Disney? On reflection, Brooks is not so crass; his Sword of Shannara in the stone shows history repeating itself in our future world.

Brooks is less measured in his liberal borrowings from Tolkien. He began writing *The Sword of Shannara* in response to Tolkien, just after reading *The Lord of the Rings* as a college student. The riddle of his own direction in writing was answered by what Tolkien did, and *Sword* is openly and admittedly his homage. Readers spot dozens of Tolkien references large and small. Allanon, for instance, is Gandalf with his message to "everyhobbit" hero Frodo (Shea). Still, Brooks converts Tolkien's ideas to his own uses:

> Tolkien's books were founded on his interest in a history and a language. The appendices, for him, were as important as the story. He was a classicist; his scholarly background was altogether different than mine. I've never been much of a scholar. I'm a straightforward, go-for-the-throat kind of person with storytelling, and that's the one thing we have in common. I thought his creation was wonderful, and that's what I needed to do, but with no little furry-footed hobbits, even though sometimes my work gets billed that way.

In his Landover book *The Tangle Box,* published 17 years after *Sword* and never compared to Tolkien, Brooks cannot resist a fond

comic reference. Landing in Landover by mistake, myna bird Big-
gar suggests to his hapless conjurer crony, Horris Kew, "How about
going to the place with the little people with the furry feet?"[44]

Brooks hears many young readers declare he is better than
Tolkien. "In that age group, I probably am," he says. "Tolkien
didn't write *The Lord of the Rings* for kids, let's face it. To be
ready for his complexities, I think you need to be in college, at
least. I'm a lot more accessible as a writer than Tolkien is." On
another occasion he referred to the *Shannara* novels as a "primer"
for those who go on to read Tolkien (Narvaes). In response to critics who say *Sword* is too derivative, Brooks concedes that they are
"partially right. The first half of this book is too Tolkienesque,
much so. The second half is much stronger. It was my first book,
and it wasn't perfect. It was a real sound story, and the second half
was all my own creation and owed nothing to Tolkien." Few have
picked up Brooks's equal indebtedness to classic adventure tales;
he confides, "Panamon Creel was drawn directly from Rupert of
Hentzau in *The Prisoner of Zenda*" by Anthony Hope.

Dune science fiction author Frank Herbert wrote what Brooks
considers "the seminal review" of *The Sword of Shannara* in the
New York Times Book Review. Herbert picked up what Brooks
admits:

> the first half runs a poor second when compared with the last
> half. . . . The debt to Tolkien is so obvious that you can antici-
> pate many of the developments. In spite of that, you're held by
> the numerous hints at what will happen if and when Brooks
> reverts to his own style. This he does somewhere around Chap-
> ter 20.
>
> Don't fault Brooks for entering the world of letters through
> the Tolkien door. Every writer owes a similar debt to those who
> have come before. . . . Tolkien's debt [to Norse myth] was
> equally obvious. . . .
>
> Brooks demonstrates that it doesn't matter where you get
> the idea; what matters is that you tell a rousing story. . . .
>
> [To] a strong mixture of allegory. . . . Brooks adds his own
> leavening. It's as though he were unwilling to leave out any ele-
> ment of our long mythic history, not even . . . movies and sci-
> ence fiction. This goes far beyond the usual fantasy, and the
> marvel is that he makes these elements essential to his story.[45]

Other reviewers were less perceptive or forgiving. *Choice* found *The Sword of Shannara* an "exceptionally well-written, very readable, totally derivative entrance into the genre . . . [that] will be most accepted by bright teenagers."[46] *Saturday Review* charged Brooks with crowding "his ponderous tome with all manner of bloody adventure and derring-do . . . never . . . [using] one word where he can use two. Thus . . . silence becomes 'mute silence,' a person doesn't think, but 'thinks inwardly.' "[47]

Fantasy author Diana Paxson was so scathing in her criticism that she would not allow Brooks a place on her chart of authors following the Tolkien tradition. "It is pointless to indicate the aspects of the book that show Tolkien's influence—setting, characters, plot etc. are as closely modeled on *Lord of the Rings* as could be managed without actually committing plagiarism. Where imitation is impossible, . . . some equally well-worn archetype is employed. . . . [B]latant derivation is not the same thing as developing a tradition" (Paxson 1984, 26).

In their fantasy reference guide, Tymn, Zahorski, and Boyer found *Sword* a "problem book" but one worth considering. Despite its "close imitation of Tolkien" noted by "most . . . critics" in "strongly negative reviews, ... the book is basically well-written. . . . Does Brooks offer any worthwhile additions to Tolkien's construct? He does, but whether these additions justify the work as a whole is hard to determine." The guide cites the postholocaust setting and its resulting races, the "entertaining con artist, Panamon Creel, . . . and . . . an unexpected ending springing from the nature of the sword" (Tymn, 55).

This same ending was "a distinct letdown" to *Choice* (678), but in her thoughtful essay, Christine Watson finds that "it is in the nature of the Sword itself that Brooks makes one of his most interesting statements"—that its power works only when it is believed. So believing, Shea destroys the unconquerable Warlock Lord with the truth-revealing Sword; "by forcing [him] to see himself as he actually is—long ago dead—[so] Shea makes it impossible for the illusion to be continued."[48]

Watson lists reminders of the Tolkien model: the Skull Bearers, reminiscent of the Black Riders; Allanon, who is like Gandalf; and

"Gollum-like gnome" Orl Fane, who covets the Sword as Gollum does the ring (Watson, 1866). His snatching of some exact names "is sometimes quite jarring. These small annoyances are troublesome chiefly because they loosen the hold of Brooks's engrossing story. *The Sword of Shannara* does not recapitulate a tale already told; instead, it uses the ideas of the artifact-centered quest and the final confrontation between good and evil in ways which make them very much the author's own" (1867). So Watson echoes Herbert, and much seems to ride on a sequel that might make or break Brooks's promise.

The Elfstones of Shannara, the second volume of the *Sword* trilogy, opens 50 years after *Sword* ends. The Elven blood in Shea's grandson, Wil Ohmsford, is more diluted, but young Wil has inherited the power of the Elfstones. An orphan like Shea, Wil is similarly accosted by Allanon when the Elfstones are needed to aid the Elves, whose true origins Allanon reveals at last. They did not first appear with the other races after the Great Wars nearly destroyed humanity but always lived parallel to humans. Descendants of old-world faerie, the Westland Elves have lost their magic. In the world before the Great Wars, an earlier war determined which power of magic would hold sway: the good, to preserve, or the evil, to destroy. When the forces for good won, they imprisoned their foes in a black hole called the Forbidding, sealing evil away forever. To keep the evil locked in the Forbidding and preserve the land's health, the Elves' ancestors created a sentient tree called the Ellcrys from the earth's life source, the Bloodfire. Still standing in the Elven city of Arborlon is the Ellcrys, now dying. As its protection weakens, demons have begun to escape the Forbidding. A complex ritual will restore the Ellcrys, but only the Elven princess Amberle Elessidil, once a Chosen maiden who attended the tree in the Garden of Life, can perform it. For some reason Amberle has fled Arborlon and must be persuaded to find the Bloodfire, which can restore the Ellcrys; Wil must protect her during her quest.

Though Amberle consents to search for the Bloodfire, she will not confide to Wil why she left the Chosen. The journey of two reluctant heroes through a decaying landscape that reflects evil's encroachment alternates with another scene of action as demons assault Arborlon. Joining the Elves in their city's defense are Trolls, Dwarves, and the Legion Free Corps, led by human borderman Stee Jans in shades of the Foreign Legion. Endless battle scenes underscore the limitless flow of faceless demons who rush unconcerned to destruction as Elf King Eventine Elessedil sickens, leaving command to his sons, Arion and Ander. Brooks skillfully handles the conflict between the different natures of this second set of Elf brothers since *Sword*. Wil's and Amberle's progress across the Wasteland, where they find feuding witch sisters Mallenroh and Morag and their stickmen slaves, offers welcome relief from repetitive battle. Voluptuous gypsylike Rover girl Eretria also creates tension between Wil and Amberle. Brooks portrays this love triangle with aplomb and without graphic details.

Before their quest can be successful, Wil and Amberle must face their fear of magic by helping each other cultivate belief in themselves. Wil is able to use the Elfstones, one for heart, one for mind, one for body, only when he can integrate himself. Confessing that she left her service to the Ellcrys because she feared the tree's absorption of herself, Amberle finally chooses to sacrifice that self in another surprising Brooks ending. One force absent in the Shannara world is religion, so it is striking that Amberle's gift of herself to preserve the forces of good has such Christian overtones, recalling the crucifixion of Jesus.

The publication of *Elfstones* prompted critics' judgments on how it stood up to or surpassed its *Sword* predecessor. Louise J. Winters found that *Elfstones* "breaks new ground," since it is a "very environmental novel" and "Brooks's writing is strongest when dealing with problems that relate to present concerns." Winters applauds Brooks's characters as "extremely well done, giving the reader friends to agonize over and cry for. The women are generally portrayed more sympathetically; the witches in *Elfstones* are both menacing and pathetic, and Amberle is an exceptionally endearing character" (Winters, 80–81).

Library Journal predicted that *Elfstones* would likely repeat *Sword*'s "moderate success" without being so reminiscent of Tolkien. Instead, "*Elfstones* has a tinge of Stephen Donaldson's grim ambiance, although the squeaky-clean romance keeps it at the YA level."[49] *Booklist* still found "an overpoweringly strong influence of Tolkien," though "his world building is improving, likewise his characterization. Brooks would still have to be classified as a 'promising' fantasy writer, but his new book is sure to be popular with those who loved his first."[50]

The last volume of the trilogy, *The Wishsong of Shannara*, introduces Brooks's first female protagonist. Brin Ohmsford is the daughter of Wil and Eretria. Her father, Wil, has hidden the Elfstones, swearing never again to use them. But he cannot control his legacy to his children. Within Brin is a magical power discovered in childhood, which she named the wishsong: "Wish for it, sing for it, and it was yours."[51] Whenever she wanted something, an unrehearsed melody and words flowed out of her, affecting the behavior of living things. She could call wild beasts, or change a tree's spring green leaves to autumn colors. Knowing that magic always exacts a price, Wil forbids Brin and her impulsive younger brother, Jair, to use it, letting them believe it is only a toy.

Twenty years after Wil helped save the Ellcrys, Brin and Jair are grown, and their parents are away. Allanon appears yet again to drag an Ohmsford into a world-saving quest. Though Brin's great-grandfather Shea indeed destroyed the Warlock Lord, the power he misused still exists within a book of dark magic, the Ildatch. The Warlock Lord's remaining followers used it to become Mord Wraiths, who drain others' minds and souls. They have poisoned the Silver River, which pollutes the land as it flows. Allanon cannot reach the Ildatch, the source of this plague, because he cannot cross the Maelmord, a living swamp created by the Mord Wraiths to protect the book. Only Brin's wishsong can alter the Ildatch's dark magic. Jair cannot accompany Brin because his wishsong has a different nature, creating illusion but not actual change. Leaving disappointed Jair at home, Brin consents to Allanon's mission, as all Ohmsfords must, taking along her childhood friend Rone Leah, descendant of *Sword*'s Menion Leah, whose sword Allanon invests with protective magic.

Disgruntled Jair grabs the Elfstones his father thought were hidden, following after Brin and acquiring the touchy tracker

Gnome Slanter and almost superhuman Weapons Master Garet Jax as his cohorts. As he once came to Shea and Flick, the King of the Silver River intercedes with Jair, trading the Elfstones for silver dust to cleanse the polluted river. The dust might also help Brin, if Jair ever catches up to her. On his way to purify the water, Jair gathers other helpers, a Dwarf, a borderman, and Elf King Ander's son Edain Elessidil. Action flits between the two groups led by Brin and Jair.

Readers are as shocked as Brin when the seemingly immortal Allanon actually dies, drawn into a lake by the specter of his Druid father, Bremen, in an echo of King Arthur's death. Brin and Rone find new allies in old Cogline, his adopted granddaughter, Kimber Boh, and a 10-foot-long moor cat, Whisper, who can become invisible. Old man, girl, and cat live isolated in a cozy cabin in a lovely glen, an oasis of calm where Brin and Rone find new direction. Kimber urges Brin to consult the oracle the Grimpond, and although it tells her of a safe way past the Wraiths, it also forecasts Brin's death through her use of the wishsong, which makes her both "savior and destroyer, mirror of life and death. The magic uses all" (*Wishsong,* 346).

Despite this disturbing prophecy, Brin persists to a confrontation with the Ildatch, which nearly subverts her to its dark purposes. It is only Jair's loving intervention that saves her from the corrupted wishsong. The trilogy satisfyingly closes as Allanon's shade goes to rest, leaving Brin to pass old-world magic on to future Ohmsfords.

Through profound personal testing in the dark and light of magic, Brin is more fully developed and sympathetic than any previous Brooks character. Winters calls Brin "the focus of the story in a way that no female character has been in fantasy literature before" (81). Critics concede Brooks's improvement: *Wishsong* is "less obviously derivative of Tolkien than the earlier books and shows improvement both in plotting and characterization," says *School Library Journal*.[52] "While this is a vast improvement over the first book, especially in making a teenage girl the heroine," agrees *Voice of Youth Advocates (VOYA),* "there are still some cardboard characters and cartoony dialogue. The world of Shannara is a mish-mash of Celtic, Norse, and Germanic legend. Still, followers of these tales—and they are legion—will sic their trolls on you if you don't buy this."[53]

YAFEs on the *Sword* Trilogy

The Sword of Shannara

With lots of surprises, a fast pace, and a climactic battle between good and evil, this is a really great book.
—Dylan Burns, 12

This book is a good example of good vs. evil on many planes. The story fills you with emotion: love, devotion, determination, sorrow, and triumph. It is easy to identify with Shea because he is so well developed, if a little stereotypical. It's a bit slow starting out, and Brooks does stretch the story out, but the plot is good and it's easy to read once you get into it. The idea of the Skull Bearers is one of my favorites, as is the Sword that reveals truth, defeating a creature of evil whose power is based on illusion.
—Jenny Dowe, 16

Though I like the concept connecting this world to the environment of modern earth, this is classic good vs. evil at its hokiest. The characters are beautifully realistic, but the fantasy realm is stereotypical. The style is superb enough to prevent one from realizing that there is virtually no plot.
—Ben Cameron, 16

The Elfstones of Shannara

One of the best in the series, since the relationships between males and females were interesting.
—Nathan Doyle, 18

The Sword Trilogy

The idea that the use of magical items can be hereditary is imaginative. The Prince of Leah, if you can forget that he is a prince, seems to be the only average joe, just trying to make his way in the world and burbling along. Good and evil are very well defined; I cannot think of any case where I was

unsure about the polarity of any character. This is one of the
most blatant rip-offs of Tolkien I have ever seen, almost pla-
giaristic. After a while, the repetitive books become boring.

—Nathan Doyle, 18

The Heritage of Shannara Quartet

The fourth *Shannara* book, *The Scions of Shannara,* which opens
the new series *The Heritage of Shannara* 300 years after
Allanon's death in *Wishsong,* introduces the scions, who must
return magic to the Four Lands. Under the harsh rule of the Federation, the land is decaying, magic is outlawed, the Dwarves are
enslaved, the Elves have disappeared, and Par Ohmsford is the
only descendant of Jair to carry the wishsong. With his skeptical
brother Coll, Par is a traveling storyteller keeping alive the magical past as his wishsong creates images in his audience's minds.
When they are nearly arrested, a leader of the rebel free-born
movement warns the brothers that First Seeker Rimmer Dall
from the Federation is after them. They must hide their use of
the only real magic left. Par has no intention of stopping the
storytelling, perhaps the only antidote to attacks of the Shadowen, rumored to inhabit people's bodies and turn them into
mindless monsters. Dreaming often of the destruction of their
land, Par is unsettled when old Cogline, who should have been
dead 300 years ago, arrives with a message that Allanon's shade
has been sending the same dreams to their cousin Wren Ohmsford and their uncle Walker Boh. All must meet this ghost at the
Hadeshorn to learn the dreams' meaning.

When the entire reluctant crew is assembled, Allanon's shade
rises from Hadeshorn waters to decree impossible missions: Par is
to recover the Sword of Shannara so it can reveal the truth about
the Shadowen, Wren must find the Elves and return them to
their old Westland home, and Walker Boh must overcome his lack
of belief to restore Paranor and the Druids. Even after death,
Allanon is still summoning Ohmsfords, still speaking in riddles. It
will take four volumes for this crew to enact their roles as Shannara's scions. With them will be descendants of old allies, Morgan
Leah, whose family has been ousted by the Federation from their

Highland rule, and outlaw Padishar Creel, many-greats grandson of thief Panamon Creel, who aided Shea. In Padishar's band of free-born is lovely redheaded Damson Rhee, another strong Brooks female who will fall in love with Par, and Steff, leader of the Dwarf underground.

By the end of *Scions,* Par has obtained the Sword from a treacherous pit full of Shadowen, where it has lain forgotten. Like all Brooks heroes, Par must accept that he is in control of neither his destiny nor his magic until he understands it and himself. The Ohmsford magic changes with subsequent users, and in Par the Elfstone power to find the hidden and defend against danger has evolved in the wishsong. It is available only if Par can overcome his doubt to believe in it. When he locates the Sword in its block of red marble, Par must face the Satan-like temptation of Rimmer Dall, who reveals himself as a Shadowen, claiming he is not evil but simply carrying the magic the Druids left behind. He says Allanon has been lying just to get the magic back for himself. The truth, he insists, is that anyone with power, including Par, is Shadowen. If Par joins him, Rimmer Dall will teach him all magic's secrets.

While Par pursued the Sword, Coll has been possessed by the Shadowen, and now Par is forced to kill his brother before the Shadowen absorb him as well. Shattered Par realizes both Allanon and Rimmer Dall tell mixtures of lies and truth. As the volume ends, readers learn that Coll is not dead but imprisoned in the Shadowen stronghold of Southwatch.

This first book of the new series "magnificently follows the earlier *Shannara* trilogy . . . by totally captivating the reader in its magic," declares Gene LaFaille of *Wilson Library Bulletin.* It "mixes danger, treachery, bravery, horror, fidelity, and love in large quantities, along with a strong plot, great character development, and an outstanding cliffhanging conclusion. *The Scions of Shannara* is a reading experience that is not soon forgotten."[54]

School Library Journal's Barbara Lynn agrees: "Brooks weaves an action-packed tale set against a richly detailed fantasy world and readers will be quickly drawn into this survival adventure. The main characters are all well-developed and the tale is sprinkled with many interest-generating elements: romance, suspense, magic, and evil vs. good. . . . The book ends with a cliffhanger; teens will be clamoring for the sequel."[55] *VOYA*'s Nancy Choice echoes these votes of confidence: "It's packed with plenty of adventure, intrigue, magic, hellish creatures, and unexpected twists. It's a riveting tale."[56]

The King of the Silver River makes one of his brief appearances to create, literally, the pivotal character of *The Druid of Shannara,* volume 2 of *Heritage.* As faerie guardian of the Eden-like garden that nourishes the earth in the Four Lands, the King forms his own daughter from elements of plants and creatures and faerie magic. Naming this elemental being Quickening, he sends her to heal the Shadowen blight beyond his garden. Her mere touch transforms ruins into blossoms, and the lovely, serene miracle worker soon attracts a following of worshipers desperate for something in which to believe. She also attracts Pe Ell, an assassin who works for Rimmer Dall. He agrees to help her find some talisman but dreams of the ecstasy of killing her at just the right moment. When Quickening asks Morgan Leah to join their search, he is captivated by her stunning perfection, by her "long, silver hair that shimmered like captured light, and a softness to her that invited protection."[57] Morgan and Pe Ell, protector and traitor, become instant rivals for Quickening. She adds another to their party, Walker Boh, who by resisting Allanon's charge to restore the Druids lost one arm to a poison serpent, the Asphinx, and witnessed the Shadowen's fiery destruction of his old mentor, Cogline, and his devoted Moorcat, Rumor. Healing his arm stump, which has turned to stone, Quickening tells Walker he cannot confront himself or the Shadowen without her.

When she explains to her three companions that she needs their help to recover the Black Elfstone, readers learn more about her father, the King of the Silver River. Thinking himself the only faerie creature to have survived from the old world, he recycled his strength derived from the earth's waters back into the land. Now he has discovered that his brother Uhl Belk, the Stone King, still exists. "Where my father found strength in fluidity and change, his brother found strength in constancy and immutability," explains Quickening (*Druid*, 103–4). Obsessed with permanency, Uhl Belk hid from the earth's cataclysms, forgetting his purpose to protect the land. Having stolen the Black Elfstone, the Druid talisman that Walker Boh must recover, the Stone King commands Eldwist, an abandoned old-world city, turning it and the surrounding land to stone. Uhl Belk is invincible unless Quickening and her company take the Elfstone from him.

Adding stout tracker Horner Dees and sentimental bard Carisman, Brooks constructs an unusually tight group for this quest to Eldwist. At their core is imperturbable faerie creature Quickening, "incandescent, a creature of overpowering brilliance. . . . [S]he spun them in the vortex of her being" (*Druid*, 139). Each of the three main players has a unique bond with her; each believes his relationship with Quickening is the most special to her. Addicted to the thrill of killing with his cherished blade, Pe Ell tries to control his craving to possess her through murder, putting it off until later. Brooks's compelling psychological portrait of Pe Ell contributes enormous tension to the band's already precipitous situation. Morgan Leah falls in love with Quickening. Her awakening love for him steadily turns her more human, enhancing her mystique as we sense her secret, tragic purpose. With Walker Boh, Quickening shares pure fellow feeling, for both cope with the vagaries of using magic and a mission imposed upon them. Brooks's characterizations, and his ability to interweave them with plot and pacing, have never been stronger.

Strong too is his setting of Eldwist, a haunting landscape with an "endless procession of obelisks and gleaming black ribbons . . . a stone forest filled with shadows and secrets . . . empty and lifeless" (*Druid*, 211–12), which we recognize as a dead city of our own skyscrapers, frozen in the future. Uhl Belk hides, leaving on patrol his offspring, the Maw Grint, an enormous blind worm whose shiny trail turns everything to stone. His lair is the underground subway tunnels where ancient train cars, unrecognizable to Quickening's band, rust. The streets above are swept clean of intruders by the Rake, a machinelike beast with metal legs. Subverting technology to nightmare, these monsters are among the most original and relentlessly terrifying in Brooks's catalog of horrors, which has consistently developed in the eight novels since Frank Herbert remarked in his *Sword* review, "Ah, the monsters. . . . Brooks creates distillations of horror that hark back to childhood's shadows, when the most important thing about a fearful creature was that you didn't know its exact shape and intent. You only knew that it wanted *you*" (Herbert, 25).

The search for the Stone King stretches interminably in this stone purgatory, where Brooks's clear images resonate with his theme of changelessness vs. change, the lifelessness of stone contrasting with the energy of living, in opposing magics. Quickening, whose name means "to come alive," is a potent force here. Her healing of Walker's stone arm awakens his first acceptance of the magic within him, combating his fear of Brin Ohmsford's legacy, which he has so strenuously resisted. By the end of the book, Quickening's ultimate sacrifice—recalling Amberle's in *Elf-stones*— makes it possible for Walker to choose his fate to become the Druid of the title.

In "the rousing second book in the *Heritage* . . . series . . . is plenty of excitement and horror for any fantasy fan," said Choice in *VOYA*. "The metal and flesh machine . . . with its vicious tentacles, uncanny tracking abilities, and amazing speed is one of my favorite fantasy monsters."[58]

Brief genre reviews have little room to explore relative merits of various series titles. In each volume of *Heritage,* Brooks displays steadily growing expertise and confidence with his material, until the third volume, *The Elf Queen of Shannara,* which rises head and shoulders above the rest. It stands apart from all his writing to achieve truly tragic proportions.

With Amberle Elessedil, Brin Ohmsford, Damson Rhee, and Quickening, Brooks honed his considerable skills in creating credible, independent, and engaging female characters, each a unique individual. In *Elf Queen*'s Wren Ohmsford, Brooks reaches his pinnacle. Wren lives and breathes, carrying readers with her in unquestioning empathy. Beyond the struggle for identity and destiny that every fantasy hero undergoes, beyond dauntless grappling with the most inhuman and implacable monsters Brooks can create, Wren faces the ultimate trial of every human life: the loss of those nearest and dearest, together with the realization that each of us is utterly alone. Wren's roots are in her cool-headed ancestor Brin, but she is far more emotional and approachable.

To fill Allanon's charge to find the missing Elves and return them to the Westland, Wren traces them to remote Morrowindl island, where they emigrated secretly 100 years earlier to avoid the Federation threat to their magic. Wren is yet another Ohmsford orphan, knowing little of her parents except that they gave her into the care of Garth, the massive muscled Rover who has assiduously taught her the wilderness survival, tracking, and hunting skills of his wandering people. Garth is solid, utterly loyal, and mute; they communicate with signing and intuition born of lifelong closeness. Garth is Wren's only companion on the journey to Morrowindl, where they fly with Wing Rider Tiger Ty, an Elf from a small separate colony, on the back of his Roc, named Spirit. On the island where he sets them down, the volcano Killeshan threatens imminent eruption, and the two must trek through miles of wasteland full of deadly creatures that besiege the Elves' walled city of Arborlon. This island where the Elves escaped is in worse ruin than the Four Lands, and the culprits seem to be beings similar to the Shadowen.

Wren marshals every resource to reach the city. "She could not remember a time when she had been afraid of much of anything. It simply wasn't her nature. . . . No matter the danger, whatever the uncertainty, she remained confident that somehow she would find a way to protect herself. This confidence was innate, a mix of iron-willed determination and self-assurance that had given her a special kind of inner strength all her life."[59] Wren carries the Elf-stones, reluctant to use their unpredictable power. Beset by unspeakable creatures who spin webbed traps or shoot poison, Wren and Garth find two odd allies created by Elven magic. Stresa the Splinterscat speaks, has humanoid eyes, a cat face, porcupine quills, and superb tracking skills through the booby-trapped landscape. Faun the Tree Squeak is a tiny furry creature who falls for Wren through her kindness, riding along inside Wren's clothes; they become inseparable. Despite their assistance, Wren is forced to use the Elfstones against the monsters, experiencing a frightening exhilaration when using their power.

When they reach Arborlon, Wren needs a new kind of strength. The secret of her heritage is revealed but comes with conditions she never expected. Wren learns she is Queen Ellenroh's granddaughter, of pure Elven blood. When her mother, Alleyne, was pregnant with Wren, a prophecy that they would die if they stayed in Arborlon sent Alleyne back to the Four Lands. The rest of the prophecy was that Wren would grow up to return and save the Elves. Ellenroh has been waiting for her, since the danger is dire. The demons are assaulting their walls, which will be breached at any moment—if the volcano doesn't erupt first. Ellenroh won't explain how the demons invaded their once-paradise island, where the Elves did not simply migrate but were carried with their entire city inside the Loden stone on the Elf ruler's magical Ruhk staff. That is now the only method by which they can escape back home, and Ellenroh is determined to carry the staff.

Within days of their hair-raising trek across the island, Wren and Garth must escort Ellenroh, her few chosen companions, and the staff containing the entire Elf civilization back to the shore, where Tiger Ty will pick them up on his Roc. Though it would seem impossible to crank up the island's horrors to new heights, Brooks does so. One at a time, members of their party perish. First Owl, the seasoned Elf tracker who was Wren's first Arborlon friend, is shot full of poison by a plant. Then her grandmother Ellenroh, the first family member Wren has ever known, succumbs to a fever, naming Wren Queen and giving her the staff. Devastated and overwhelmed by this new role, Wren finally hears the rest of the truth of her heritage. Ellenroh's friend and seer, Eowen, explains that when the Elves arrived on Morrowindl, they experimented to regain their understanding of the old magic of faerie. To make new and stronger beings, they combined animal and human life forms to produce oddities such as Stresa. They progressed to making human replicants for border guards, not realizing the guards would become demons because wild magic is beyond control unless it regenerates from the earth.

Brooks's warnings about cloning and overuse of natural resources are not lost on Wren. Learning the worst, that the Elves
who stayed behind in the Four Lands subverted magic to become
Shadowen, Wren confronts the horror that her own people created. Can she in good conscience carry Arborlon back into the
Four Lands and risk setting free Elves who still insist on experimenting with magic, perhaps worsening the horror they have
already unleashed?

As Wren agonizes, Brooks switches the scene to Walker Boh,
who has used the Black Elfstone to find the Druid's keep, Paranor, in limbo between "being and nonbeing" (192). Walker is
trapped there with Cogline and the Moorcat Rumor, who entered
this half-life instead of dying, as Walker assumed in *Druid*. To figure out how to return Paranor to the world, Walker must not only
study Druid lore but search within himself. Instead of the merely
convenient scene switch Brooks often employs to spin out plot
and heighten suspense, his occasions of focus on Walker parallel
and comment upon Wren's situation. Like Paranor, Morrowindl
operates as a limbo, and Walker's unwanted Druid role shadows
the Queenship thrust upon Wren. Both are inexperienced initiates wrestling with a destiny they did not choose.

Wren's testing is far from over. She loses Eowen to the Drakul
vampires. Then her charming cousin Gavilan, with whom she is
falling in love, steals her staff in a bid for rule and control of the
magic—a heartbreaking betrayal. Even that is not enough. The
few survivors find Gavilan's body ravaged by the Wisteron, a
clawed, spiky-haired monster whose "hideous insectlike face" has
"an odd sucking maw" (*Elf Queen,* 358). While retrieving the
staff—and Arborlon contained within it—beneath Gavilan's body,
Garth is infected by the Wisteron's poison. Facing the irretriev-
able loss of Garth, her adopted father and protector, Wren must
do the unthinkable when Garth asks her to help him die, for the
poison is turning him into a Shadowen. Looking into his eyes, she
sees the evil red gleam dawning.

When Wren plunges Garth's own knife into his heart as his
hands cradle hers, Terry Brooks's writing moves us to tears. No
longer is this only a fantasy adventure. Wren is truly and terribly

alone in facing a challenge she never bargained for, to save and rule and change her Elven people into more responsible healers of the land than they can be without her, to teach them to use well the treacherous magic she herself does not yet understand. She must wrest life from the death surrounding her.

When a writer produces superior work that so carefully scrutinizes our ultimate fear of aloneness and death, one speculates that his own life gave occasion for soul searching. Could Brooks's experience of his wife Judine's cancer the year before *Elf Queen*'s publication have led to this overwhelming depth of feeling, this confrontation of the precipice? The poison seeping into Garth's soul is a cancer. Like Wren, Brooks contemplated the possibility of being alone. Perhaps Judine's healing allowed Brooks to turn Wren's story into one of affirmation. She goes on doggedly, despite nearly debilitating grief, carrying her staff home to the Westland, where she plants it firmly in the ground to restore Arborlon. Shouldering her responsibility, Wren embraces her destiny of guiding her people to renewed life. Walker Boh also takes on new life as he mystically subsumes Allanon's identity and knowledge into himself, releasing his resistance at last to become the only Druid, accepting "the weight of responsibility that came with power" (*Elf Queen*, 351). As Arborlon appears back in the world, so does Paranor.

When asked why religion is absent in his fantasy realm, Brooks replied, "What I'm concerned about is the way we behave towards one another. That's my religion. The things I have to say where any kind of religion is concerned have to do with how we react to the conditions into which we're put. Do we *assume* responsibility for the lives of others and their problems? How far do we go with that? Will we be honorable in the way we approach things? Is it right to lie in certain situations? Is the truth always the best thing? These issues are perhaps as political as they are religious, but those are the things that to me are crucial."

In another interview, Brooks disputes the notion that his books are merely escapist. "They're supposed to give you a break from your world, but they're not supposed to relieve you of your obligations and responsibilities to this world. . . . [T]hey . . . make you aware of what [responsibilities] are by showing them to you in a slightly different light" (Narvaes).

The Elf Queen of Shannara is far too wrenching to be escapist, clearly demonstrating the obligation of responsibility through the trials of Wren and Walker. Some readers resist this use of fantasy, especially from authors such as Brooks, often assumed to be lightweight. Says critic Louise J. Winters: "Wren Ohmsford is a highly intriguing character. . . . [Her story] has the potential to be one of the best in the series. Unfortunately it fails. Wren's journey is riddled with gloom [and] doom. She is . . . forced to face unpleasant truths about everything she believes. This does not make her a better person, only more resigned to the will of fate" (Winters, 81).

Yet other reviewers agree that *Elf Queen* is Brooks at his best. "Wren is Brooks's most successful character to date—tough and self-sufficient without being abrasive, trusting, and caring. Part coming-of-age story, part journey toward the self," observed *Library Journal*.[60] It is "among the best of Brooks's growing list of excellent novels. Characterization, plot, setting, and story flow are all superb," said *VOYA*.[61] *Publishers Weekly* recognized that Brooks turned a corner: "Finely tuned and occasionally elegiac, ... Brooks's prose becomes more fluid and his world becomes more complex, ambiguous, and credible with each volume."[62]

As final volumes do, *The Talismans of Shannara* ties up loose ends and brings all the players of the *Heritage* series together to complete their missions. When it opens, all the scions have fulfilled Allanon's charges, but they have not shared their experiences to work out how they connect and how to destroy the Shadowen. As the only living Druid, Walker Boh is in Paranor with Cogline and Rumor. Wren has no sooner set Arborlon on its old foundations than she spies an enormous Federation army marching to besiege them. Par has the Sword, but his brother Coll, whom he thinks he killed, has been allowed by Rimmer Dall to go free to lure Par to the Shadowen stronghold Southwatch.

Action swings from one front to another. Coll wears a stolen magic cloak, the Mirrorshroud, which Rimmer Dall has fooled him into thinking will protect him. Instead, it turns him into a

Shadowen. When Par sees what his brother has become, he shows him the truth through the grasp of the Sword. Just as Coll comes back to himself, Rimmer Dall and his Shadowen appear, and Par loses control of his voracious wishsong. As he did when their journey began in *Scions*, the King of the Silver River returns to the brothers, but he can only rescue Coll, for Par's wishsong blocks him. Rimmer Dall carries Par away, and his attempts to make Par believe he is Shadowen punctuate the rest of the volume.

Rescue follows rescue, until Damson Rhee, her nearly executed father, Padishar Creel, with his army of free-born and Dwarves, Morgan Leah, and Wren and her Elves are brought together for a final Shadowen showdown. Cogline's sacrifice helps Walker escape the fearsome Four Horsemen of the Apocalypse, which Rimmer Dall sent to trap him inside Paranor, and join the others.

The scions still don't understand the Shadowen power caged deep below Southwatch, where Par battles insanity under Rimmer Dall's incessant assault on his wishsong and his will. At the climax, when his compatriots reach Southwatch to set him free, Par lets his wishsong loose, wreaking destruction in "a dangerous mix of casual disregard and pleasure born of the magic's use. . . . He was shedding his humanity."[63] Once again, only the touch of the Sword can restore Par's true self, reveal Rimmer Dall's lies, and destroy Shadowen magic leached from the core of the earth. With the Four Lands free of subverted magic, the Elves will flourish as healers and the Druid Walker will be "the land's conscience" (*Talismans*, 435). All seems settled until our own millennium, when Brooks plans to produce another *Shannara* duet.

In this "resounding, action-filled conclusion" to the tetralogy, says *Publishers Weekly*, "the three searchers must be tempered by disaster, conquer their self-doubts and discover within themselves the true nature of their quest and the means of salvation for their people. Cutting from one group to another, Brooks builds tension and suspense, weaving a rich and complex tale."[64] *Library Journal* reports, "Brooks orchestrates an exciting, though predictable, conclusion to his second *Shannara* series. Brooks's appeal lies in his fidelity to tried-and-true quest fantasy and his ability to create engaging protagonists."[65] *Booklist* is not quite convinced: "[T]his volume, like so much of Brooks's work, drags in spots and reaches compelling power in others. Overall, the tetralogy may well have been loading more on the Shannara universe than it can bear, particularly in the face of competition from such better-wrought worlds as those of David Eddings and Robert Jordan's multivolume sagas."[66]

Shannara Prequel: *The First King of Shannara*

Having completed two *Shannara* series, Brooks produced a stand-alone prequel to expand *Shannara*'s history and the origins of the Sword so condensed by Allanon in his recaps for Ohmsford recruits. Taking place back during the Second War of the Races when man was isolated from other races, it centers around how the Druid Bremen forged the Sword for Elf King Jerle Shannara. The Warlock Lord emerges from hundreds of years of the Druid Sleep to attack the Druids, Dwarves, and Elves with his North-land army of Trolls, Gnomes, and netherworld creatures. Bremen tries to warn his old Druid comrades at Paranor, but they will not heed the Druid they banished for studying magic. Having heard of Paranor's destruction repeatedly throughout the saga, readers will be gripped by the actual horror of the Druids' massacre and dismayed at the arrogance that caused it. Bremen's doomed efforts to stop it and his stoic acceptance despite his grief at the loss of his roots generate our sympathy for this solitary old man, from whose commitment and vision the entire saga will unfold. The Paranor scenes, early in this novel, are the most intense and moving, reaching tragic dimensions. The two Druids who escape with Bremen, the Elf Tay Trefenwyd and the Dwarf Risca, are the only ones who also know magic. Tay is one of Brooks's most likable Elves, made vulnerable by his lifelong friendship with Jerle Shannara and his hopeless love for Preia Starle, a fearless warrior Elf woman promised instead to Jerle.

The small band of three Druids, with Bremen's longtime scout, Kinson Ravenlock, and a tormented young female Druid apprentice, Mareth, who seeks control of her overwhelming inborn magic, must unite the races against the Warlock Lord. With this new set of appealing characters, Brooks explores more fully how

Shannara's magic works. Before Brona stole the Ildatch book (later sought by Brin) to learn magic's secrets, the Druids warned him, "[T]here had never been a form of power that did not evoke multiple consequences. There had never been a sword that did not cut more than one way."[67] Even though Bremen uses magic for good, it damages him when he uses his own dark side as a cloak in order to spy inside the Warlock Lord's Skull Mountain or consults ancient Druid spirits of the dead for counsel at the Hadeshorn. Brooks also describes other types of magic: the boundless empathic magic of Mareth, which can overpower her, and Tay's elementalist skills, which balance magic and science with the basic elements of earth, air, fire, and water. When Tay retrieves the Black Elfstone from its ancient plant guardians, Brooks shows its treacherous negation of other magics with tragic consequences.

Readers who have stuck with *Shannara* will be interested in *First King*'s firsthand depictions of what has become legend in other volumes: the Druid massacre and Jerle Shannara's first use of the Sword against the Warlock Lord. Yet smaller revelations are also savored. Smith Urprox Screl's forging of the Sword using Cogline's scientific formula in the nightmarish Industrial Revolution–like factory town of Dechtera is a memorable scene with an unexpected tidbit at the end: Screl changes his name to Creel, becoming an ancestor of all rebel Creels to come.

And what of Allanon's origins? Disappointingly, he does not appear until page 375, when at age 12 he is discovered by Bremen as the only survivor of the Warlock Lord's sacking of the town of Varfleet. The traumatized boy mutely follows Bremen and will not be parted from him. Their affinity soon becomes apparent, as does Allanon's enormous talent and hunger for magic. Declaring that he wants to be like Bremen, he learns so quickly that he becomes a strong force in Jerle Shannara's battle, allaying Bremen's anxiety about who will be his successor. But the scenes with Allanon are so brief and lightly sketched, always from a distance, that readers longing to know more about him will be more teased than satisfied. Brooks is not about to make his most enigmatic character any less mysterious.

This "very satisfying beginning to his fascinating series," says *VOYA*, "is an exciting page-turner ... [with] many vividly detailed battles and skirmishes before the final confrontation between good and evil."[68] Yet *Publishers Weekly* finds Tolkien's influence too strong once again. "Brooks's prose generates a breakneck pace, but it lacks depth of characterization and also the wealth of linguistic invention that the most satisfying high fantasy offers. ... Brooks's mythical universe also suffers from a crucial dearth of those magical moments of heart-stopping revelation when, against all hope, against all reason, against all the forces of evil, salvation comes at last."[69]

First King is definitely not Brooks's strongest *Shannara* book; it seems somewhat of an afterthought to quell fan demands. Few critics have paid enough attention to Brooks's work to mark the nuances and variations of individual books. Critical judgment that penalized *The Sword of Shannara* for Tolkien imitation is slow to fade, prejudicing opinions of later books. Some critics who failed to note Brooks's early promise did notice improvements during the eight-book *Shannara* cycle, especially the strengths that come to such culmination in his finest work, *The Elf Queen of Shannara*. In hindsight, many credited Brooks with opening the fantasy market into the mainstream. Brooks chuckles when observing that his editor Lester del Rey's determined press finally worked years later as "revisionist history." His reviewers often go to one extreme or another. "Either I have been the salvation of fantasy, or the biggest rip-off that anybody ever saw in their lives. Early on, there were only a couple of really good balanced reviews. It's changing a little bit now. I'm doing much better. People are starting just to say, 'This is good storytelling and it does this and it does that,' and I can live with that; that's reasonable."

Clute and Grant's definitive new *Encyclopedia of Fantasy* takes rare note that Brooks's other "main influences are writers like Alexandre Dumas, which may account for the ease with which he translated the complex Christian fantasy of *Lord of the Rings* ... into a series of morally transparent genre fantasy adventures.... The initial tale is simple, but told with happy clarity ... [in a] post-Apocalypse Earth, a venue whose potential for change substantially undercuts the fantasyland surface of the tales. . . . [A]t points, the dependence upon a familiar cast and standardized motifs becomes mechanical" (Clute, 142–43). These distinguished critics do not note any variations in quality among *Shannara* titles.

When asked what he found satisfying about such detailed exploration of one world, Brooks responded:

> The *Shannara* books are multigenerational sagas. What's interesting to me is that they involve members of certain families who have been a) blessed or b) cursed with an inheritance of magic that affects their lives and keeps evolving, taking different members of different generations in different ways. While there is similarity of story lines and plots, still, what they have to deal with from one book to another does undergo some changes. That intrigues me enough that I don't feel as if I'm getting flat on the story line. . . .
>
> Each member of this family inherits something from the history of the past like we all do. We carry around the baggage of our ancestors, and we are responsible for the baggage of our descendants.

How do young adult readers rate the *Shannara* books? As they progressed from junior through senior high school, Fantasy Fanatics' opinions on Brooks evolved. During our last Brooks discussion, senior Nathan Doyle, currently reading more sophisticated fantasy, looked back on the seven *Shannara* books and jokingly pointed out plot patterns:

Book 1—Little dork gets hugely magical item and saves the world.

Book 2—Little dork is given hugely magical item from hugely magical being and saves the world.

Book 3—Two little dorks, sister and brother, are born with immensely powerful magical ability and go out and save the world.

Books 4 to 7—Previous books recapped and strung out with several little dorks.

Sophomore Dylan Burns agreed that when one reads too much Brooks, the books all start to look the same. But Dylan felt that

Brooks "made a huge impact on fantasy, and is great reading for middle schoolers, since he's easy to read and very enjoyable. In your progression as a fantasy reader, as you get more experienced, you get more critical."

Another senior, Sam Walter, did not burn out on Brooks but appreciated his "extraordinarily well-developed setting for his deep characters to live in. The characters have so many sides to them, and in many cases the real struggle is within the character and not with the external enemy. That speaks well to young adults who are going through internal changes and have to know themselves before they can even hope to know the world."

YAFEs on *The Heritage of Shannara* and the Prequel

The Scions of Shannara

People either love this book or they hate it with a passion—I loved it. Par's moral ideals were similar to mine, and I liked the way the characters were portrayed as having many faults. All fantasy readers should read the whole series.

—Sam Walter, 15

This is my favorite fantasy at the moment. It has a nice fast pace, great detail, and the Shadowen give a creepy feeling to the book. It's easy to tell which characters are good or evil.

—Dylan Burns, 12

The Druid of Shannara

The best thing about this book is the idea that genetic heredity rules the forces of magic. It's great that direct descendants of the Shannara family are the only ones who can use the magic.

—Nathan Doyle, 16

The main character, Walker Boh, really kicked butt!

—Dylan Burns, 12

The Elf Queen of Shannara

More exciting than *Scions,* this is a truly superior, awesome book. The half cat/half porcupine Splinterscat was really weird. Queen Ellenroh had to abandon the greatest magic of the Elves to save her race. I would have done that.

—Dylan Burns, 12

The Talismans of Shannara

Not much was new here. The best scene was the Four Horsemen of the Apocalypse, a major plus, though Walker Boh defeated them in a really cheesy way. Walker Boh is a rusty antihero with a very nice life, living in the wilderness in solitude, when some ancient Druid comes to send him on a very dangerous quest. Boh did exactly what I would have done: "Are you kidding? What's in it for *me*?"

After six books, Terry Brooks's style got very tiring. He stretched out too many plot lines too long. The concept wasn't bad though, and Brooks is a very good writer. The much-acclaimed ending of the *Heritage* series was incredibly disappointing. I predicted it by the third book. Still, a few of the characters were a lot of fun to read about.

—Dylan Burns, 15

The Heritage of Shannara Quartet

At first glance this was a solidly written fantasy series about the problems in the Four Lands after the last war. Then I looked again and . . . ack! It's a takeoff of a takeoff. No, no, it can't be! Sob! It's so sad. These four books are basically a retelling of any one of the first three stories. The only differences are the time and the characters' names. Most of the personalities are just recycled from the first series. Pe Ell was the only person in the series who I thought was cool. There was no incident in the *Heritage* series that I couldn't reference back to the *Sword* series and make an analogy for. The more I think about it, the more amazed I become that this series is hailed as great fantasy fiction when it is so vapid and free of original ideas.

—Nathan Doyle, 18

Prequel: *The First King of Shannara*

Predictable and boring, this book had none of the power of Brooks's other work. Even though the section dealing with the fall of the Druids is interesting, the book on the whole is a disappointment.

—Ashley Burns, 17

The Magic Kingdom of Landover Series

Because the fantasy realm of Landover is entered through a gateway in Virginia's Blue Ridge Mountains, this series rightly belongs with "Gateway Magic" in chapter 3. Yet *Landover* has so many concepts in common with *Shannara* that it is more naturally discussed here. In the opening volume, *Magic Kingdom for Sale—Sold!*, Ben Holiday is grief stricken over his wife, Annie's, death and burned out in his lawyer career. So he buys a magic kingdom from a Christmas catalog for a million dollars and changes his life at age 39. He can hardly believe Landover actually exists, but through the fairy mists shielding it from our world is the perfect escape, complete with a castle, a wizard, and loads of mythical creatures.

One would hope a lawyer would read the small print, but the reality of Landover is not as advertised. Its sale was a scam by the ex-king who abdicated 20 years before and continues to sell and resell it to would-be kings from Ben's world, who just can't hack it. Left rulerless for so long, Landover has no government, no laws, no money in the treasury, no taxes, and no army, and its magic is failing, blighting the land. As new king, Ben must not only restore law and order but heal the land, figuring out how the king's role relates to its health and the restoration of the magic, which makes it live. But first he must win the loyalty of subjects tired of a succession of "play-kings," cope with power-hungry magical beings, and accomplish all with a small oddball staff. Even his wizard, Questor Thews, is inept; his scribe, Abernathy, is a man turned into a dog, and his servants are two sharp-toothed monkeylike kobolds and two filthy cannibalistic gnomes. Brooks treats this motley crew with a light, humorous touch, but Ben's situation is serious.

What Ben really wants is a meaningful life, so the challenge of governing and healing this ailing magical kingdom becomes his mission, his route to his own fulfillment and healing. Terry Brooks unabashedly admits that Ben's story is "all about my life," closely paralleling his own experiences. *Magic Kingdom* was "wish fulfillment in the truest sense," for Brooks, like Ben, left his law practice, moved to a new home, and found a new life partner after writing about it here.

While Brooks became a full-time writer who investigated magic worlds in his books, Ben becomes a successful king by investigating how magic works. In Landover is Brooks's perfect opportunity to explore a system of magic he first created in the *Shannara* series, one that relates closely to the environment. Images resound between the two series, showing our abuse of the land. As Ben flies in a jet over New York, he watches the city's bones and skin "materialize beneath him as if by magic." Yet "the city had the feel of a corpse."[70] One cannot help but flash back to *Shannara*'s Skull Mountain, commanded by the Warlock Lord, or Morrowindl, decimated by demons and a volcano, or Eldwist, a lifeless city of skyscrapers turned to stone. This "deadness" of our modern urban world, where not even a blade of grass shows, connects to the land's decay in both the Four Lands and Landover. Brooks works through the metaphor of "magic substituting for science. In our world," he says, "we do not have a magic that heals and nurtures, or destroys. We do have science, which does both. It can work either way." In his books,

> magic is that two-edged sword that in some instances can be destructive and in some instances can be healing. It works in mysterious ways; nobody can be sure how it's going to turn out. It's very powerful, like electricity, or nuclear power. It's just out there. The problems that exist are very clear in my stories, but writers should not propose solutions. Writers should explore their nature; then it becomes the reader's job to decide which way things ought to go, whether it is good or bad, make the judgment calls.

In *Magic Kingdom,* Ben must figure out how to harness magic's healing power. His Sterling Silver Castle, a living building that provides for all of its residents' needs, is under a Tarnish, and Ben learns that it is the absence of a king that threatens the nurturing magic—a ruler quite literally maintains the vigor and health of the land. In Landover, magic is the natural law, sustained by the king. Ben's seeking of his own purpose and self-knowledge is inextricably tied to his ability to keep the healing magic flowing. Brooks's concept of Ben's warrior alter ego, the Paladin, is an effective way for Ben to achieve the inner unity needed for such a goal.

Combining a more engaging premise than *Shannara's* with similar heartfelt exploration of moral truths by a believable and accessible hero, *Magic Kingdom for Sale—Sold!* was a 1986 Best Book for Young Adults for both ALA and *School Library Journal.* Reviewers may limit the book by classifying it as "humorous" fantasy. Says *Booklist,* "Brooks does not possess the wide range of gifts required for this sort of fantasy tale—his ear for dialogue is not wholly true, and he is still a creator of scenes rather than of coherent stories. Nonetheless, the book remains enjoyably imaginative, marking Brooks's first move beyond the rather derivative limits of the *Shannara* saga and into the creation of original visions."[71] *Library Journal* observes, "Despite a slow, pretentious beginning, Brooks displays an unexpected flair for light comedy in this not-so-standard fantasy quest."[72]

Landover's second volume, *The Black Unicorn,* continues to explore how magic connects with Ben Holiday's identity as king. Ben's identity is stolen by Meeks, the broker who sold him the kingdom, who turns out to be a wizard with his own dark intentions. Meeks disguises Ben from his subjects, impersonating the king while Ben wanders as a peasant, confused and lost. Meeks has sent cryptic dreams to Ben and his closest colleagues, Questor the court wizard and Willow, the lovely part-human, part-tree sylph, which propel them on separate quests and isolate them from Ben. Questor must find lost books of magic, and Willow seeks an evil black unicorn and its fairy-spun gold bridle. But the puzzles can't be solved until illusion is separated from reality. Willow's fairy instincts lead her to the black unicorn, from which she senses compelling goodness, not evil.

Ben's only companion in his wanderings is Edgewood Dirk, a prism cat sent by the fairies to help Ben see beneath his own mask, for Meeks's magic disguises Ben even from himself. The cat tells Ben that his purpose is "to arouse your consciousness—to make you think! I was not sent to provide salvation! If you want salvation, you will have to find it within yourself!"[73]—a neat précis of Brooks's thesis.

Once again, responsible use of the land is essential; the Earth Mother rises up from her swamp to tell Ben that humans must stop dominating the land, for it "is a trust to be shared by all of finite lives and never to be taken for private use." To preserve the bond between Ben and Willow, she must make him understand Willow's earth connections and how not all healing is advisable, since "a recycling of life is a part of being" (*Unicorn*, 141).

Eventually all come together to discover why Meeks wanted the unicorn, the books, and Ben's identity. Brooks uses the traditional fantastical unicorn in a fresh way. In Landover's history, wizards imprisoned a herd of white unicorns in two books, separating their bodies from their spirits to draw on the unicorns' magic power. The spirit alone broke free, embodied in the black unicorn, a mere shadow, as is Meeks's wizardry, based on deception—like the Warlock Lord's in *Shannara*. When Meeks disappears as the illusion he is, Ben regains his kingship and himself. In an epilogue, a white unicorn flies over Chicago; the few witnesses are not sure they saw it yet are left with the sense of being "part of something magical" (*Unicorn*, 307). So Brooks sends magic to our world, for Landover is "where the dreams of fairy world and mortal world come together and are channeled one to the other. Reality in one is fantasy in the other" (*Unicorn*, 13).

Asked to discuss how magic fits into the real world, Brooks replied,

> Magic serves two purposes for me. It's a metaphor for science. But also there's the kind of magic that happens when you meet somebody, like I met my wife, and the first time you meet you *know* that after 42 years you've found the right person. Everything clicks into place and you can't believe it. And there's magic that happens in the way we relate to each other and the way people respond to challenges, such as the kid who pulls the woman out of the river. There's magic in the fact that people can rise above themselves, like Schindler. There are all kinds of examples that to me represent forms of magic. They're not the traditional fairy tale magic where we stir up a kettle or cast a spell—even if those are the ways in which we talk about it.
>
> Religion is magic—what else is religion but our answer to things we don't understand? Magic is just the way in which things happen that are so wondrous and incredible that we can't put words to the reasons behind them. We can't fully comprehend why it happens.

The Black Unicorn's reviews were nearly identical to those of the first volume. Brooks "is attempting a multivolume work in the difficult category of humorous fantasy," says *Booklist*, "and he has achieved a respectable degree of success."[74] Agrees *Library Journal*, "This sequel has the same welcome touches of humor as its predecessor, and confirms Brooks's talent for light fantasy."[75] Says *Publishers Weekly*, "Like Brooks's other novels, this is smoothly spun but highly derivative (Dirk, for example is closely patterned on the Cheshire Cat), and, even in this genre, unusually escapist."[76]

In *Wizard at Large*, the third *Landover* book, Ben takes Willow back to our world, a trip made necessary by the title wizard's incompetence. Questor Thews is sure he can reverse the spell that long ago turned scribe Abernathy into a dog, but his sneeze at just the wrong moment spins Abernathy off to captivity on Earth. Ben follows to rescue Abernathy, taking Willow, who suffers from our toxic environment, fading without the nourishment her tree self needs from Landover's soil. That his true love cannot survive in the poisoned world Ben left behind underlines how he no longer belongs there.

Unlike early, lighter volumes, *Wizard at Large* has a tense aura of anxiety as both Ben and Questor face unpleasant truths about themselves. Ben broods about how little he feels like a king as he tries to come to terms with his dark side in the Paladin, and Questor tries to prove himself a decent wizard while carrying a burden of guilt. *Booklist* does not note the darkness but concedes that "Brooks may go on amusing both himself and his committed audience for quite a few more volumes before we see the last of Landover."[77] Ann Welton in *VOYA* is more specific: "From the attention-grabbing opening sentence, the pacing is implacable, the narrative gripping. . . . [T]he snappy dialogue, making the most of the contrast between everyday English and the fairy tale setting of Landover, has considerable charm and carries the story over the rough patches caused by the occasionally wooden characterization. Brooks is not a particularly inspired writer, but he is a breathtakingly competent storyteller."[78]

Landover's fourth volume, *The Tangle Box*, is its most well constructed, sophisticated, and stylish. Finally Ben has worked out how to run his benevolent dictatorship of Landover's feudal system, introducing new democratic ideas. His resource management includes land, water, air, and magic—no need for science. Ben utilizes his law background to govern, and his success feels "like being able to start over before so much was poisoned" in our world (*Tangle*, 69). He and Willow have committed to each other, and Willow tells him she is expecting their baby. Though Ben is overjoyed, it is difficult for him to understand why Willow must go alone to see her nymph mother dance their unborn baby's future. What she does not tell him is that she must also collect the "soils of the three worlds to which her child's blood could be traced," earth, human, and fairy, to nourish her roots when she reverts to tree form to birth the baby (*Tangle*, 236). Ben still does not grasp how his Landover child's birth must connect with the land her mother's people tend and heal.

It is in Willow's absence that Ben once again encounters trouble. As in *The Black Unicorn*, he loses his identity, this time through allowing exiled sorcerer con artist Horris Kew back into Landover from Earth. Horris unwittingly frees a vengeful spirit, the Gorse, from the Tangle Box, where fairies imprisoned it. Intent on taking over Landover, the Gorse traps Ben, his witch enemy, Nightshade, and the dragon Strabo in the box, where they lose their memories to become merely the Knight, the Lady, and the Gargoyle. The box is an endless labyrinth where the three wander as who "we most fear we might really be," with no idea where they are (*Tangle*, 241). Meanwhile, the Gorse sends the kingdom into pandemonium.

Brooks employs decidedly Christian imagery here: his medieval symbols of the mythic Knight, Lady, and Gargoyle confront their worst fears while lost in the labyrinth, as Christ was lost in the wilderness. A Haze appears as "divine retribution for their sins," a sort of Purgatory. There is also a prophecy regarding Ben and Willow's special unborn child, and though we know Ben was involved, the baby's birth in his absence through a sacred earth ritual has parallels with the virgin birth of Christ. And there is final redemption for all, even the most undeserving, selfish character, Horris Kew.

However, *Publishers Weekly* found *The Tangle Box* "slower and less charming than its predecessors. . . . This rather haphazard tale" is "for hardcore readers who like their fantasy lite."[79] Ruth Dishnow Cox of *VOYA* perceives more depth: "Battles rage in Landover, in the Tangle Box, and in the fairy mists. Some are battles of sword, some of mind, and some of heart. Good triumphs over evil, but not before the reader is entranced by the fantasy world of Landover, involved in the innermost turmoils of the fantastical yet believable characters, and delighted by Brooks's three-tiered adventure."[80]

Witches' Brew, the last *Landover* volume to date, features the intriguing new character Mistaya, Ben and Willow's unusual daughter, who two years after her birth has matured to the age of 10. Beyond precocious, Mistaya, who senses her difference from others and her untapped magic within, longs to be free of her overprotective parents, to get on with growing up. Mistaya receives her wish, which is also a grueling trial. The cruel witch Nightshade, who harbors bitter resentment toward Ben for the time she spent with him as Lady in the Tangle Box, kidnaps Mistaya to train her as an apprentice. She teaches Mistaya to create monsters, which the child unwittingly sends to destroy her father. But knowing Mistaya's magical destiny, her benefactor, the Earth Mother, has already given her a protector, the mud puppy Haltwhistle, and the warning that she must be careful with her special mix of several heritages: "There is no one like you in all of Landover."[81] Nightshade holds Mistaya hostage for Ben's kingdom, and he must once again become his dreaded alter ego, the Paladin, to save her.

With this fifth volume, *Booklist* continues to find *Magic Kingdom* books "ingenious, witty, and generally fun to read,"[82] while *Publishers Weekly* complains of an "increasingly convoluted narrative. . . . Despite entertaining passages (Mistaya's training in witchcraft) and moments of depth (Holiday's struggles with his inner demons), the novel still feels cobbled together, a kind of prelude for . . . later installments. Fortunately, the familiar characters remain as appealing as when they first appeared, despite their involvement in these transparent and hackneyed situations."[83]

Will there be later installments of the *Magic Kingdom of Landover?* Not this century, according to Brooks's publication schedule. Even the *Encyclopedia of Fantasy* cannot help speculating: "[T]he *Kingdom of Landover* series . . . has been less popular than the bestselling *Shannara* books, but although Terry Brooks is clearly an uneasy humorist, the underlying premise of the sequence has some interest. . . . [T]here is ongoing rumination on the costs of wish fulfillment. The series . . . may darken" (Clute, 143).

When asked which series he prefers, Brooks responded, "I like things about both of them, or I wouldn't be writing them. I suppose that my preference deep down inside is for the longer, darker, more complex issues in the *Shannara* books. But *Magic Kingdom* is intriguing because it's so personal. I think the one balances the other. I can't do what David Eddings does, which is 12 books linked. I need to back away and go somewhere else for awhile. And I don't want to see any more *Magic Kingdom* books after *Witches' Brew.* I've got other things to talk about that I can't fit comfortably into either of these worlds, so it's time to take it another way."

Teenaged readers have not embraced the *Landover* books as they have the *Shannara* series. Perhaps the midlife crisis aspect does not speak to those still coming of age. Still, diehard Brooks fans may find rewarding his humorous forays into another version of magic in Landover.

YAFEs on *The Magic Kingdom of Landover* Series

Magic Kingdom for Sale—Sold!

It's exciting and funny and dramatic, all rolled into one non-boring book. It also shows that the author is flexible and able to keep from stereotyping his stories.

—Ron Araujo, 18

It's a gripping, adventurous, intelligent, funny mystery story. It's solid, probably due to the fact that it comes across as a setup for future books.

—Bill Henry, 18

The simplistic style allows a person to enter the world of
Landover. I had to remind myself that I was not Ben.
                                        —Matthew Wernsdorfer, 16

It is very humorous, with much adventure and mystery. Most
kids would love it because of the wizardry.
                                        —Domenica Mirarchi, 13

Odd Brooks Books Out

In 1991 Terry Brooks took some writing detours. His novelization
of the movie screenplay for *Hook* was an update of the classic
Peter Pan story from an early 1900s play by Scotsman J. M. Barrie (see chapter 3). Like the *Landover* stories, *Hook*'s characters
move from our world to an otherworld, in this case Neverland.
The boy who refused to grow up has done so; Peter Pan has
become Peter Banning, a driven American business executive,
played in the movie by Robin Williams. He married Wendy's
granddaughter Moira, and Wendy has become Granny Wendy to
Peter's children, Jack and Maggie. Not only has Peter forgotten
all about his long Neverland childhood, but he is so obsessed with
work that he is missing his children's childhood. His son, Jack,
resents his father's absence from his baseball games, and Peter is
late to his daughter's school play, *Peter Pan,* in which Maggie
stars but which fails to trigger Peter's memories.

A family trip to visit Granny Wendy in London sparks a crisis
when Jack and Maggie are stolen from their beds and whisked to
Neverland. To rescue them, Peter is yanked protesting back to
Neverland by tiny fairy Tinkerbell and still has trouble recalling
his enchanted past. Saucy Tinkerbell, played by Julia Roberts,
has been in love with the oblivious Peter since before he left
Neverland. She must help him recall how he fearlessly led the
Lost Boys so he can challenge his old nemesis, pirate Captain
Hook, played with suitable villainy by Dustin Hoffman. It was
Hook, of course, who stole the children.

Brooks reports difficulty with his assignment to stick to the
screenplay, and its novelization reveals movie director Steven
Spielberg's influence. Spielberg's favorite movie theme has al-

ways been the magic of children's imagination, and a pure Spielberg moment is revealed in the passage in which overweight, out-of-shape Peter is relearning how to fly. To do so, he must grasp one happy thought, all too rare for adult Peter until he recalls a moment of joy as a new young father: "He was transformed, become the essence of the spirit that lives within us, that wondrous spark of childhood we all too frequently manage to leave behind in growing."[84] Brooks barely manages to resist turning such sentimentality into schmaltz. Yet with the authority of a writer whose milieu is abstract magic, so difficult to put into words, he beautifully describes Peter's returning memory: "There was a shifting within him of time and place, of memories and dreams, and the boy and the man readjusted their positions, the boy giving back some of what he had taken, the man accepting what was offered without feeling the need to ask for more" (*Hook,* 179).

Brooks's descriptive powers suit the Neverland setting and the action-packed battles between Hook and Peter. He is less comfortable with silly Lost Boy tricks and warm, fuzzy family feelings, though he does convey the desperate tension of Peter's tenuous hold on his child self while he saves his children. Unhappy writing to formula, Brooks copes well with its limitations. The book was not widely reviewed, but *VOYA* observed that "Brooks was well-chosen as the author. . . . He uses descriptive language that allows the reader to enjoy the book without having seen the movie. It is a better-than-average retelling of a movie plot."[85]

Around the same time, Terry Brooks contributed a rare short story to *Once Upon a Time: A Treasury of Modern Fairy Tales,* commissioned by his longtime editor, Lester del Rey. "Imaginary Friends" is his first writing specifically addressed to young readers; its protagonist, Jack McCall, is in seventh grade. It is also his first work taking place entirely in our own world, with Jack experiencing hidden magic, as in earthbound tales in chapter 3. It has strong Peter Pan echoes about retaining childhood wonder.

When Jack is diagnosed with leukemia, he recalls a forgotten encounter, seven years earlier, with an elf named Pick, who took him flying high above the huge park near his house on the back of a barn owl named Daniel. The delighted child saw a wondrous landscape of nature tinged with magic, including a troll hiding under a bridge and the lair where the dragon Desperado is imprisoned. Pick explained he was not a fairy tale elf, for which he had great disdain, but a real Elf, whose job is to keep magic balanced in the world. Jack has never seen Pick or Daniel since; his mother patiently explained that they were just "imaginary friends."

Now 13, Jack confides his fears about dying to his best friend, Waddy. Supportive Waddy seems to think that Jack will survive, believing in "some kind of magic out there that saves people from dying."[86] Waddy's faith opens Jack to a return visit from Pick, who sends him alone to drive the escaped dragon back into his prison.

The timing of this story's publication makes it probable that Brooks used Jack's cancer to grapple with his wife's. Magic in this everyday world reflects his own declaration that "magic" is our name for what we cannot understand. The story is charming but for one fatal flaw. Instead of allowing the reader to conclude that Jack's confrontation with Desperado is his way of facing his fear, Brooks tells us directly: "That was what the fight to lock away the Dragon had been all about. It had been to lock away Jack's sickness" ("Friends," 46). We're glad that Jack's illness is cured, but young readers may feel patronized. It is surprising that Brooks, who encourages his young fans to interpret his stories for themselves, has violated his own rule. But we might forgive him, since vulnerable Jack could be young Brooks himself, "only a little taller than most fire hydrants and a lot shorter than most girls" ("Friends," 26).

The new path Brooks proclaimed he was ready to take in his 1994 interview has come to fruition at this 1997 writing, in *Running with the Demon,* the first volume of an unnamed new series of contemporary fantasy, set in our "earthbound" reality. Its heroine is 14-year-old Nest Freemark, who lives in the fading steel factory town of Hopewell, Illinois, the setting from "Imaginary Friends." Nest has always known she is different from others. Her grandmother has told her since early childhood that she has the inborn magic of all the women in her family, the only ones who can see the malevolent faceless feeders hovering at the edge of vision in the huge park nearby. Nest has become a keeper of the balance of magic with grouchy twiglike Pick, resurrected from Brooks's short story and now called a sylvan. In adolescence, however, it is hard for Nest to control the magic within that she must not let others see, especially when the balance is tipping dangerously. Multiplying wherever there is dark emotion, the Furies-like feeders have become more daring, and Nest has rescued several children from their devouring clutches. Now a boy's unwanted attentions have forced Nest to zap him in public, turning him into a gibbering idiot in front of all her friends. She knows her grandparents have not told her the truth about her missing father or her mother's death, but she doesn't know that a demon has arrived in town, hell-bent on its destruction, or that another newcomer, John Ross, is a Knight of the Word, and she will be fighting on his side with everything she has to preserve what she loves.

Brooks introduces a fascinating new cosmology of light and dark, which rules the magic unseen all around us, defining his "religion" of magic in a fresh, compelling way. This normal, idyllic small town unknowingly poised on disaster's edge is charged with a menacing aura of tension reminiscent of Dean Koontz or Stephen King, making us wonder what lurks in our own parks and streets, our own family squabbles or factory strikes. Young adult readers will effortlessly identify with Nest, as dauntless as Wren Ohmsford but as tormented by inner turmoil as any teenager. Brooks's masterful control of pacing and suspense has never been better.

Reviewers' reactions range from halfhearted to excited about Brooks's venture into magic realism. "Brooks forsakes the medieval settings, but not the cosmic plot implications of his very popular *Shannara* and *Landover* sagas in a romance that may launch a contemporary fantasy series, or, considering that it is rather bland and predictable, may not," pronounces *Booklist*.[87] *Kirkus Reviews* finds "an intriguing and well-balanced scenario with believable characters, but undermined by uninspiring story developments and therefore little or no narrative tension."[88] But

Publishers Weekly is pleased: "The genius of Brooks lies in his inspired joining of different worlds in one intricate tale. Here, for instance, are teen romance, satanic horror, elfin fantasy, and Native American mythology, among other plot elements. . . . Brooks's pacing is fabulous, and he manages to surprise and yet to maintain a feeling of inevitability. . . . As his first novel to be set in the modern world, this volume represents a significant development for Brooks; but his fans should embrace it . . . eagerly."[89]

Terry Brooks will certainly continue to please his readers, who are far more important to him than critics, and seems destined to expand his own boundaries, always striving for further challenges in his superb storytelling. Brooks hopes that his stories "suggest different things to different people. If it generates discussion, I think that's when the writer is really doing his job."

Ordinary Heroes:
American Fantasy until the Millennium

The groundswell that began with Terry Brooks has continued to sweep American fantasy publishing for 20 years, as more and more writers create otherworlds, seemingly without end. Some authors achieve monumental status, though literary and popular acclaim do not always go hand in hand. Some authors write in related subgenres for years until they achieve a special niche.

Feminist Fantasists
Marion Zimmer Bradley

Long before she became known as a feminist fantasist, Marion Zimmer Bradley began writing science fiction in the 1950s. Her *Darkover* sequence of over 20 related novels about human colonists on the planet Darkover, which opened in 1962 with *The Planet Savers,* is still going strong. One *Darkover* title, *Hawk-mistress!,* was a 1982 ALA Best Book for Young Adults. Later volumes, which stress psychic powers rather than technology, are often labeled science fantasy. In the 1970s, Bradley borrowed

Tolkien's Middle-earth for settings of *The Jewel of Arwen, The Parting of Arwen,* and related *Atlantis Chronicles,* which celebrate warrior women. In 1982 she broke new ground with *The Mists of Avalon,* a breathtaking reimagining of the Arthurian myth in terms of the clash of matriarchal pagan Celtic religion with the new patriarchal Christianity (see chapter 5). It established Bradley as the preeminent force in feminist fantasy, a movement Ursula K. Le Guin, Robin McKinley, and others have joined since the 1980s.

Patricia A. McKillip

Contemporary with Terry Brooks in the 1970s, Patricia A. McKillip made a quiet but more critically appreciated debut with *The Forgotten Beasts of Eld,* in which sorceress Sybel lives isolated with her legendary talking beasts, whom she controls telepathically. The intrusion of a royal baby heir and two men who wrestle for Sybel's love and power force her to learn about herself in relation to others (see chapter 6). This young adult fantasy won the 1975 World Fantasy Award for Best Novel. Her masterful *Riddle of Stars* trilogy, which expanded the same themes in 1976 through 1979, was recommended to teenagers as a seminal work on ALA's YA fantasy genre list nearly 20 years after its publication. Also called the *Star-Bearer* trilogy, it is set in a world where solving riddles is the ultimate intellectual pursuit. Unraveling the work's many intertwined strands requires its readers to be agile riddle solvers themselves. In its opener, *The Riddle-Master of Hed,* young Morgon plans a peaceful life leading his simple farming people until he wins the hand of Raederle, daughter of the King of An, in a riddle match. Shipwrecked while sailing to claim his bride, Morgon's course is altered; he must seek the answer to the riddle of himself and the destiny encoded in his birthmark: three stars upon his forehead. Morgon is just as reluctant a hero as Tolkien's hobbits and Brooks's Ohmsfords; he simply wants to go home to be a farmer. Instead, he is pursued by shapechangers and a mysterious harpist until he disappears altogether.

Heir of Sea and Fire, the second volume of the trilogy, follows Raederle's search for Morgon as well as for her own identity as magical mistress of the two elemental powers in the title. In the conclusion, *Harpist in the Wind,* Morgon and Raederle are united to learn how Morgon's mastery of earth and air complements Raederle's use of sea and fire; together they integrate creation's four basic elements as well as male and female.

In this multilayered trilogy, embroidered with rich symbolism and language, McKillip's magic is knowledge of the true nature of things, with the balance of love and power. Her deliberate pace gathers every nuance, too slowly for some. Critics Tymn, Zahorski, and Boyer note that *"Riddle-Master* moves rather slowly at first while McKillip develops her characters and creates a detailed and believable secondary world, but the pace quickens in the second half" for Morgon's "perilous journey" (Tymn et al., 137). They find *Heir of Sea and Fire* carrying "too much dialogue and not enough action," its pace "rather sluggish until the very last episode." Yet they praise McKillip as "a rare talent: she knows how to create believable secondary worlds; she understands the nature of magic; she presents us with richly delineated and memorable characters; she invests her novels with substantive thematic import; and she has a smooth and polished writing style" (Tymn et al., 138).

In a long essay that exhaustively analyzes McKillip's trilogy, feminist critic Charlotte Spivack describes McKillip's pace as part of her prose style, which has "a unique, painterly quality. Not a dramatic, fast-paced writer, she has a flare [sic] for the sharp unexpected simile . . . but tends to visualize a scene detail by detail."[90] *The Encyclopedia of Fantasy* declares that *Riddle* is a "well-wrought" trilogy: "The intellectual and emotional maturation of its mild-mannered hero and independent-minded heroine are handled with scrupulous delicacy" (Clute, 607). Critic Donna R. White sees McKillip as "one of the best contemporary fantasy writers for young adults. . . . Her distinctive writing voice sets her books apart from more traditional fantasies. A mood of dreamy mysticism pervades most of her works, and her heroes and heroines are loners isolated from others by their own immense supernatural powers and/or by their search for some ultimate truth. . . . No one is better at exploring the imperative of truth and its high personal cost."[91]

McKillip herself recalls, "When I was a teenager writing, I remember thinking this was the one place—where I had that pen in my hand and that paper in front of me—where I could tell the truth."[92] She follows the modern fantasy preference for the ordinary hero: "I like taking ordinary people with simple problems and sticking them in a situation in which extraordinary things happen" ("Moving," 5). She was one of the first to examine women as heroes in the '70s, with headstrong Sybel in *The Forgotten Beasts of Eld* and a trio of lively women around Raederle in *Heir of Sea and Fire,* "a work to delight feminists," says Spivack, "with its range of resourceful, independent, capable, and appealing female characters" (Spivack, 118–19). Spivack pinpoints major feminist themes that McKillip incorporates: renouncing traditional routes to power, integrating the masculine and the feminine, and connecting humans with nature in harmony (125).

After her early success, McKillip sampled other formats, from fairy tale parody to young adult realistic fiction, science fiction, science fantasy, and adult contemporary fiction, before settling back into fantasy. An accomplished creator of mythical creatures, she featured memorable sea people in the YA fantasy *The Changeling Sea* and the adult *Something Rich and Strange,* and a wolf shapechanger in *The Book of Atrix Wolfe* (see chapter 6). Her recent atmospheric faerie romance is *Winter Rose.* Now over age 40, McKillip has lost interest in writing for teenagers but remains concerned with women. *The Sorceress and the Cygnet* and its sequel *The Cygnet and the Firebird* feature two different viewpoints of two women. *The Encyclopedia of Fantasy* proclaims, "Patricia McKillip is one of the most accomplished prose stylists working in the fantasy genre; she always brings a keen and refreshingly idiosyncratic intelligence to her employment of its motifs" (Clute, 607). Teenagers who discover her early YA books may persist with McKillip's measured pace and intellectual focus for rare rewards.

Robin McKinley

Throughout her body of work in retold and composed fairy tales and heroic fantasy, Robin McKinley has never strayed from her feminist ideal of "Girls Who Do Things" which she claimed in her acceptance speech for the Newbery Medal was "the only thing I . . . talk about."[93] As she avidly reread Tolkien's *The Lord of the Rings* in junior high, its lack of women characters did not escape her. She latched onto a rare female image in *The Return of the King:* a warrior, Éowyn, masquerading as a man but finally revealing herself as a golden-haired woman on horseback with hard gray eyes, holding a sword. "I will always be grateful," declares McKinley, "for the hard pure light this one scene shed on my own girls-saving-the-universe fantasies (Newbery, 402–3)." She carried this image around subconsciously for years as it seeded creation of her otherworld of Damar and its revolutionary female heroes, Harry in *The Blue Sword* and Aerin in *The Hero and the Crown*. In her published critique of Tolkien, McKinley notes how his characters were "too heroic to be human or interesting" (McKinley, 565; see the section on Tolkien earlier in this chapter). Her own heroic fantasy novels seem designed to put right those failings of her beloved Tolkien, to portray in depth the woman with the sword as a hero both ordinary and utterly human.

From Robin McKinley's earliest writings, the land of Damar sprawled and grew in her imagination, demanding expression in what would become "a series of indefinite length."[94] Everything McKinley writes is set in Damar, even her fairy tales. Its landscape was heavily influenced by McKinley's almost obsessively repetitive viewings of John Huston's *The Man Who Would Be King,* a very male film whose portrayal of heroism based on "idealism and loyalty" McKinley applied to her women, Harry and Aerin (Newbery, 401). Says McKinley:

> *Sword* as *Sword* was a late addition—even the name Damar was—to a cacophony of stories rattling around in my brain. . . . But the first disentangled thread of story was Aerin's—or rather the thread of story that led me to the tangle was Aerin's. . . . I recognized that there were specific connections between Harry and Aerin, and I deliberately wrote their stories in reverse chronological order, because one of the things I'm fooling around with is the idea of heroes: real heroes as opposed to the legends that are told of them afterwards. Aerin is one of her country's greatest heroes, and by the time Harry comes

along, Harry is expected—or Harry thinks she is—to live up to her. When you go back and find out about Aerin in *Hero,* you discover that she wasn't this mighty invincible figure with a cult of acolytes; she had a very hard and solitary time of her early fate. (*AAYA,* 197–98)

So McKinley's first heroic fantasy of Damar was Angharad Crewe's story—Harry's—in *The Blue Sword,* which takes place two generations after Aerin's story in the prequel, *The Hero and the Crown. Sword* is set in Damar's land of Daria, reminiscent of a British colony, whose white Homelanders have conquered the Arabian-like Hillfolk. Harry is an orphaned Homelander staying with diplomats near her soldier brother's outpost. Soon after her arrival in this barren country so unlike her lush green home, Harry is kidnapped by the Hillfolk leader Corlath, who follows a vision informing him that this pale-skinned foreign girl will be instrumental in the Hillfolk's coming battle against invading Northerners.

Corlath has the visionary power of kelar, common to his people but unknown among Harry's. Yet on the first night after her capture, when drinking the Water of Sight, Harry surprisingly demonstrates kelar herself. Speaking "the Old Tongue, . . . the Language of the Gods,"[95] which few understand anymore, she describes a detailed vision of a past battle in which the Hillfolk's ancestor Aerin fought the Northerners who plague them now. Later Corlath's whole camp sees Harry's second kelar vision, when Lady Aerin emerges from the fire to greet Harry with a wry and intimate smile, holding her legendary blue sword, Gonturan, which won their people's crown back from its wizard thief. These visions confirm that Corlath must convince this reluctant and ignorant young girl to take up Aerin's blue sword for his people.

Though at first she is afraid even to touch the sword, Harry cannot resist the call of her destiny on the first day of grueling warrior training, when "her heart rose up, despite her fears, to greet the adventure she rode into" (*Blue Sword,* 97). This line could be an epigraph for all of McKinley's heroic fantasies. Both Harry and Aerin instinctively recognize their natural calling to unassuming heroism, no matter how unexpected or outlandish it seems at first.

Both persist in overcoming lack of aptitude or experience to train doggedly for the warrior skills they need, for heroism is the only role that makes sense in lives that heretofore have been lived as misfits. Here McKinley reveals her own background of feeling different; both Harry and Aerin feel alien among their people and surroundings, even in their ungraceful, unfeminine bodies. Though she borrowed her sword-wielding heroine image from a glimpse in Tolkien, McKinley admits that "the large clumsiness of Harry and Aerin is certainly an addition by this author" (Newbery, 403), one that reflects her own youthful awkwardness.

The Blue Sword, which became a 1982 ALA Best Book for Young Adults and a 1983 Newbery Honor Book, was a warm-up exercise for her remarkable next novel, *The Hero and the Crown,* which won the coveted Newbery Medal in 1985 and became another ALA Best Book. Revealing the background of Damar's legendary hero Aerin, *Hero* predates Harry's story. Aerin is the daughter of the dead second wife of King Arlbeth, who lives in his fortress in an unnamed city in the Damarian hills. Since her mother was regarded as a witch from the enemy lands of the North, her father's subjects are suspicious of the gangly red-haired girl so unlike them. Aerin is Giftless, lacking the psychic power other members of the royal family share, a power that mends broken dishes, opens locks, and provides visions when the surka plant is chewed. Internalizing her people's doubts about her, Aerin defiantly eats a whole mouthful of surka, which makes her desperately ill for months.

Her only friends and comforters are her older cousin Tor, heir to the throne (since women cannot rule), and her father's retired war horse, Talat, whom Aerin nurses and revives from lameness, teaching him to accept her riding with a technique she invents. Without fondness for feminine clothes or graces, Aerin enjoys the swordplay Tor teaches her, but she has no real purpose or place. She secretly experiments with an old formula for kenet, an ointment that protects from dragonfire, though dragons have not been seen for years.

Arlbeth supports her but cannot let her publicly flout restrictions on females. Furious that he will not allow her to accompany his warriors to quell a rebellion in the North, Aerin takes Talat dragon hunting instead. With the kenet's help, her success in slaying two small dragons finally gives her a position in court and in the hearts of the people, who fondly name her Aerin Fire-hair, Dragon-killer. When the great dragon Maur decimates the countryside, Aerin faces him with no idea of how much more enormous and deadly he is than the small dragons she quickly dispatched. Her kenet offers little protection. In a heart-stopping battle, Aerin persists even after realizing she cannot win. She somehow slays the vicious beast. Mortally wounded, she crawls away with Talat.

McKinley's account of Maur's slaying is extraordinarily vivid. Having always asserted that Damar stories came from somewhere outside her, set down beyond her control through "virtually automatic writing," McKinley cites this scene as proof:

> I've certainly never killed a dragon. When I wrote the first dragon scene in *Hero* I was shocked by how graphic it was. I didn't know . . . that there was going to be the second dragon, any more than Aerin did. My hand kept moving across the page. . . . I was just following along, with my mouth a little open, wishing I could write faster, because I wanted to know how it was going to end. . . . I don't know where it all came from, but they sure know about dragons there. I went around the house for weeks after Aerin kills Maur with my left arm cradled next to my body, and dragging my right foot a little—yes, I do tend to identify with the heroes. (*AAYA*, 200–201)

Killing Maur is the turning point of Aerin's story. Though she has asserted herself to the utmost and earned respect, Aerin cannot heal. In a feverish deathbed dream, a red-clad man seems to threaten, while a blond man calls her to come to him. Leaving a note for Tor—who has declared his love for her—Aerin leaves to follow the call. Talat unerringly leads her to the isolated mountain hall of the blond man, the mage Luthe (who appears in many Damar stories, including fairy tales). Luthe heals Aerin and teaches her that the family Gift she thought she lacked is stronger than ever in her; it has merely bloomed late. Luthe instructs her in how to use what will be called kelar in Harry's time. After a plunge in the Lake of Dreams, where Aerin sees images of her future, she is "no longer quite mortal," explains immortal Luthe.[96] Giving her Gonturan, the blue sword, he explains that she has a mission to restore her father's crown, stolen long ago by her mother's brother, the wizard Agsded, who destroyed her mage mother but whom no one even remembers. Agsded is behind every threat to Damar, even Maur's attack; only one of his blood can defeat him. Aerin does not hesitate, for now her history makes sense. She is her mage mother's daughter, and Luthe has taught her the skills she needs.

The most surrealistic passage in *Hero* comes as Aerin climbs endless steps up Agsded's tower to confront the red-robed mage wearing the crown, her only weapons the sword, the bloodstone from Maur's body, and a wreath of surka. In the swirling battle between uncle and niece who look so much alike, Aerin realizes she fights her own dark side and her deepest fear. It seems to be a draw until Aerin impulsively flings at him her hard-won talisman, the wreath containing the bloodstone. All disappears in blinding fire as the tower walls tumble down. Only later does Aerin learn she was flung forward in time. But Luthe brings her back to reveal the rest of her destiny and allay her remaining fear. When Luthe becomes her lover, Aerin gives up her fear of loving Tor. She must take the crown back to Damar now, marry Tor, and rule, knowing she will share a future part of her not-quite-mortal life with Luthe. With a magical army of wild cats and dogs, Aerin returns to her city to turn the tide of a raging battle the Northerners have been winning. She also rids the castle of the trophy of Maur's head, which has infected everyone, unknowingly, with despair.

McKinley thought *Hero* would end with the battle, but

> then there was all this business with . . . Maur's head. I went on writing, thinking . . . what next? And I went on, and on, and then it occurred to me that I'd passed up the end of the book I was writing, and was into another book. Whereupon I stopped and went back and tidied off, and that's the first time I knew that there would be another book about Aerin. (*AAYA,* 200)

Since *Hero* appeared in 1984, that other book has not been published. Its working title is *Kirith,* and it has mushroomed in nearly

15 years to at least three more unpublished Damar books as McKinley has been sidetracked by shorter, more attainable writing projects. *The Hero and the Crown* stands as one of the first and finest YA novels featuring a consummate female hero. Its characters are entirely real. Readers ache with Aerin as she parts from her beloved Luthe, as she faces battles with all the fears and doubts anyone would have. One of McKinley's huge strengths is her instinct about which details to delineate and which merely to suggest. She does not give the content of Luthe's teachings in magery, keeping the magic mysterious and showing the powerful mage with human faults. His teaching talents are imperfect; he is careless and forgetful and worries that he may skip some essential lesson that could endanger Aerin. McKinley's description of the inhuman creatures who fight on the Northern side does not go beyond a shivery suggestion of crawling, so our imaginations supply the details. Like Aerin, we take magic on faith when it comes through such a human context. Aerin's story has a classic mythic structure stretched into fresh fields envisioned through feminine eyes.

School Library Journal starred *Hero* as a "splendid high fantasy . . . with perhaps the most vivid and realistically described fire-breathers in all fantasy . . . filled with tender moments, vivid characters, satisfying action and sparkling dialogue."[97]

In a lucid essay, literature professor Anna E. Altmann outlines exactly how *The Hero and the Crown* challenges readers' assumptions about whether a woman can be a hero. Altmann traces how *Hero* follows the classic form of the mythic hero's journey to selfhood (see chapter 4). Her careful analysis of this book that spoke so deeply to her about women's roles was spurred by a student's negative reaction to McKinley's story. The student complained that *Hero* was "just another case of welding brass tits on the armor. . . . A book that really has a woman as hero would validate women's lives as we live them, would recognize that what women actually do and are is worthwhile and central. I don't ride warhorses and fight dragons and wear armor. I'm sick of books that make women heroes by turning them into men."[98] Responding to this charge, Altmann constructs a clear case for how McKinley is not "welding brass tits on the armor but reclaiming the metaphor of the heroic quest for women as Aerin reclaimed the lost traditions of Damar" (Altmann, 154)—much as Marion Zimmer Bradley reclaims the matriarchal Celtic code behind the male Arthur myth in *Mists of Avalon*. How much of women's strength and versatility has our male-oriented society forgotten? Altmann's essay is worth pondering, and it also reveals how astute was McKinley's awareness when she wrote her Newbery winner *The Hero and the Crown*. Says McKinley, "I wished desperately for books like *Hero* when I was young: books that didn't require me to be untrue to my gender if I wished to fantasize about having my sort of adventures" (Newbery, 403–4).

YAFEs on the *Damar* Series

The Blue Sword

One of the most engrossing classics of the fantasy world, which I liked better than its fellow, *The Hero and the Crown;* somehow the plot was too clichéd for my tastes, though headstrong, determined, inventive Aerin was a thoroughly enjoyable character to follow.

—Ashley Burns, 17

The Hero and the Crown

Aerin is a heroine who actually takes part in the action. Full of unique and original ideas, the book also uses elements I recognize from old myths and tales, such as special gifts, the healing lake of immortality, and the bane for dragon fire. Some parts were fast paced and others were slow and boring.

—Domenica Mirarchi, 16

McKinley creates very vivid images that linger still, such as Aerin climbing the tower stairs for a very long time and Maur's head driving her from the banquet hall with mockery. A woman who once believed herself insignificant saves her nation; her perspective widens as she grows older. It reminds me of Pierce's *The Woman Who Loved Reindeer* for its mythic quality and McKillip's *The Forgotten Beasts of Eld* for its strong female characters.

—Rachel Scott, 20

Barbara Hambly

Though Barbara Hambly, the author featured in chapter 3, usually sets her fantasies in otherworlds reached through our own world, her paperback *Sun Wolf* trilogy takes place entirely in her otherworld of the Middle Kingdoms; some regions bear resemblance to McKinley's Arabian-inspired desert lands of Damar. Sun Wolf leads a mercenary band of soldiers who winter in the isolated town of Wrynde, where he runs a training camp for warriors. A barbarian by birth, 40-year-old Sun Wolf makes no apologies for his ruthless code of loyalty to whoever is paying him, for his endless concubines, and for his savagery in battle. Brawny and tawny haired, Sun Wolf is golden eyed, lionlike, crude—and nobody's fool. As the trilogy progresses, Sun Wolf learns wisdom, magic, and love, becoming a far more refined barbarian than Conan could ever be. His second-in-command is a woman, Starhawk, who is colder, fiercer, and more pragmatic than Sun Wolf and, despite her seeming detachment, a superb judge of human character possessed of a wicked wit. With cropped platinum hair and pewter eyes, Starhawk is "steely and enigmatic, . . . a tall cheetah of a woman."[99] The unfolding characters of this unusual pair, who have fought together for eight years before the story starts, do much to drive the tension of the trilogy from one breathless and brutal escapade to another.

Sun Wolf's credo is "never fall in love and never mess with magic" (*Ladies,* 133); he violates both rules in the opening volume, *The Ladies of Mandrigyn*. Kidnapped by a band of women from Mandrigyn, a city conquered by the Wizard King Altiokis, Sun Wolf must train them as warriors to free their men, who are imprisoned in the mines as forced laborers. He learns much in the process about women and also about magic. Altiokis systematically destroys other mages to hoard all power for himself. Sun Wolf must understand his odd, corrupt power in order to confront it. How has Altiokis, so "trivial, . . . spiteful and vicious" (*Ladies,* 228), gained so much power, and why is "his soul literally rotting" (274)? How is he using the Hole between worlds as his power source, a "gap of nothingness that led into a universe beyond the

ken of humankind" (277), a concept explored by Hambly throughout her many fantasy series? And what is Sun Wolf to do when his
own unsuspected magic talent suddenly rages inside him?

In *The Witches of Wenshar,* Sun Wolf and Starhawk, now committed lovers, have forsaken their mercenary band to search for
someone to teach Sun Wolf to control the unschooled magic
within him. Mages are scarce in kingdoms scoured by Altiokis,
now dead, but they track one to the Fortress of Tandieras, near
the abandoned city of Wenshar, which is haunted by the ghosts of
evil witches destroyed generations ago. Coldly beautiful Kaletha
has recently emerged as a teacher of magic, but her first meeting
with Sun Wolf is not cordial. When Kaletha claims to be able to
awaken magic even in those who are not mageborn, Sun Wolf
calls her a fool. They are instant enemies; she insists that magic
comes from the mind and cannot flourish without bodily purity,
whereas Sun Wolf believes "magic is born in us. . . . Its presence
doesn't make us better or holier people." According to how mages
choose to use it, magic can be pure or foul.[100]

Staying in King Osgard's fortress to mend his fences with the
teacher he so desperately needs, Sun Wolf agrees to instruct
Osgard's "cowardly" nine-year-old son, Jeryn, in the arts of war,
and Starhawk, without a trace of magic in her, joins the king's
guards. Soon after they arrive, a series of gruesome murders
starts; bodies are hacked to pieces with unearthly force in the
ruined old quarter of the fortress. In a community seething with
political intrigue around the betrothal of Princess Taswind to the
foreigner Incarsyn, desert Lord of the Dunes, Sun Wolf and
Starhawk discreetly investigate these murders, which seem
fraught with magic. Could they have anything to do with Kaletha,
the first admitted witch since the evil Wenshar coven was massa-
cred, despite her claims of purity?

Amid a cast of many colorful and deftly drawn characters,
including the scarf-swathed, braid-bedecked, Arabian-like shirdar
people, a tense supernatural murder mystery winds to a shocking
and unpredictable conclusion. Readers drawn by Hambly's controlled, nail-biting pace, which combines cerebral and physical
action, must be able to stomach some exceedingly gory scenes.

Hambly displays immense capability for drawing intense detail that gives definition to a haunted atmosphere often merely suggested by lesser writers; one believes in Hambly's otherworldly horrors. Beyond suspense, rewards include tender moments for Sun Wolf and Starhawk, whose relationship grows with Hambly's careful rendering until Sun Wolf becomes a barbarian with a heart and Starhawk reveals her compassion. Sun Wolf even acknowledges fatherly feelings for the young prince and princess he has mentored so well that they can get along without him.

Booklist found that *The Witches of Wenshar* "is not up to the standards of its predecessor, but still shows Hambly to be a superior fantasist" due to her "characterization and world building."[101]

The final *Sun Wolf* volume, *The Dark Hand of Magic,* begins as soon as Sun Wolf and Starhawk leave Wenshar. Ambushed by the still-angry shirdar, they are unexpectedly rescued by a party from Sun Wolf's old war band. Though no longer their commander, Sun Wolf is urgently needed to help the mercenaries out of their latest fix. Their assault on the city of Vorsal is being hampered by a hex bringing unrelenting ill luck to their camp. If there is a hex, reasons Sun Wolf, there must be a wizard—and perhaps a teacher at last.

Yet unearthing the source of the sorcery proves as frustrating as finding it in Wenshar. As he searches for traces of magic, Sun Wolf is drawn once more into the life of the camp he gave up to learn wizardry. It's a rough, unsavory crew of thugs named Pinky, Cat-Dirt, Dogbreath, and Battlesow, and camp whores such as Opium, who tempts him to betray Starhawk. When his men sack Vorsal, the cruelty of their treatment of innocent citizens repels him, and he can hardly believe he once participated. Mistaking a gentle philosopher, Moggin, for the mage he seeks, Sun Wolf unwittingly brings on the brutal rape and murder of Moggin's wife and daughters before Moggin's eyes. Then the real wizard, still unknown, enslaves Sun Wolf's will with his spells, turning him against his own band. As usual with Hambly, her mystery's solution is impossible to forecast. Sun Wolf must confront his own nature to save Starhawk, his new friend Moggin, and his warriors. Yet there is no happy ever after even then, for

Sun Wolf has lost his home, his old pals, his heart for war, and even his magic. What can replace them?

As Sun Wolf's new principles evolve, he swears off war against the innocent but still keeps his fighting skills in shape. "The arts of combat were one thing to him, a meditation, an art, a need which could not be explained to a non-warrior. War was another matter."[102] Even Moggin learns swordplay, though it is too late to prevent his family's deaths. As Starhawk explains, "He's decided that his philosophic principles against taking life don't extend to letting his life be taken because he's too helpless to prevent it" (*Dark Hand,* 290). These philosophies reveal Barbara Hambly's own as a devoted student of karate; she dedicates the first *Sun Wolf* volume "To my fellow members of the West Coast Karate Association BROAD SQUAD: Anne, Gayle, Helen, Sherrie, Janet, Georgia, With Love." Her depiction of the taming of a barbarian is informed by her own self-defense skills, so her portrait of Sun Wolf and Starhawk is not only compelling but authentic. Readers who think they abhor barbarian sagas will be converted by this one.

YAFEs on the *Sun Wolf* Trilogy

The Ladies of Mandrigyn

Sun Wolf was just a mercenary, who became more than he ever dreamed he would. Hambly did a good job of portraying how the characters felt, in an interesting plot that kept my attention—a great story about wizards.
—Vanessa Bowler, 16

I enjoyed the solid writing in this very addictive page turner. Once you started, you knew something was going to happen—and it did. The characters seemed real. I didn't like the ending, though—it seemed to be thrown together.
—Melissa Tolve, 16

The Witches of Wenshar

I enjoyed the mystery, but there was no action accompanying it. It was too much like an Agatha Christie novel with magic. The characters were just walking around wondering "Whodunnit?" When Sun Wolf was arrested, it was the only action part where you wondered what the outcome would be.

—Melissa Tolve, 16

Tamora Pierce

Sparked perhaps by McKinley's Damar in the early '80s, fantasies by female authors about spirited heroines began to proliferate. A favorite writer with junior high girls is Tamora Pierce, whose quartet *Song of the Lioness* opened with *Alanna: The First Adventure* in 1983. The work plunges immediately into a lively plot with classic switching of identities between 10-year-old twins Thom and Alanna of Trebond, in the Kingdom of Tortall. Since Alanna has always wanted to be a knight and Thom longs to be a sorcerer, they secretly masquerade as each other to get the schooling they desire. In the second volume, *In the Hand of the Goddess,* Alanna becomes squire to Prince Jonathan, who knows she is a girl. By the third book, *The Woman Who Rides Like a Man,* Alanna has come of age and sets out to become a knight errant. In a duel of magic she earns acceptance by a desert tribe, which she revolutionizes by training two women to be their shamans instead of men. Her love life complicates when Prince Jonathan assumes they will marry and she turns instead to George, King of Thieves. In the last volume, *Lioness Rampant,* Alanna undergoes a quest to save her land by finding the powerful Dominion Jewel.

About Pierce's adventurous romps without the symbolic overtones of McKinley, *Horn Book* says: "Although the reader must feel that the odds run very heavily in favor of Alanna—not only is she hard-working, sensible, and modest, but she is blessed with beauty, intelligence, apparently invincible martial skills, and possesses supernatural abilities—the stories are lively and enjoyable, a happy blend of fantasy and adventure with a strong, vigorous heroine."[103]

Once Alanna grew up, Pierce began another quartet, *The Immortals,* with a new heroine, Daine, who communicates with animals. *Wild Magic* opens when Daine is 13 and homeless. Taken in by a horsemistress who needs her to drive a pony herd to Tortall, Daine discovers a deeper talent, the ability to sense dangerous immortal creatures invading the land. Eventually she meets King Jonathan, Queen Thayet, and his champion, Alanna, but most importantly she meets the mage Numair, who teaches her to use her magic. In *Wolf-Speaker* and the third volume, *The Emperor Mage,* the only Pierce title to be named a Best Book for Young Adults by ALA, Daine's mind-speaking skills grow so she can heal animals and shapeshift into their forms. In a starred *Booklist* review, Sally Estes comments that "as Daine grows in her powers, so does the power of the narrative. . . . The climactic scenes in which Daine brings to life the bones of the long-dead dinosaurs . . . in the great natural history hall and leads them in the destruction of the castle and downfall of the emperor are truly riveting. This impressive entry in Pierce's saga will leave fans clamoring for more."[104]

The quartet ends when Daine is 16, in *The Realms of the Gods,* in which Daine and her mage teacher, Numair, flee for safety from attacking creatures. It is a classic journey to the underworld to discover her origins, for Daine meets her dead mother, Sarra, and learns that she was illegitimate because her father was the god Weiryn, who is a bit unsettling to meet with his crown of antlers. But Daine and Numair, now aware of their love for each other, cannot stay and must find their hazardous way home. Says *VOYA,* "It is the detailed descriptions of the characters that etch the tale in memory. . . . Daine is a feisty, liberated lady. Her human problems provide special spice not found in conventional teen fantasy."[105] Pierce leaves Tortall for a new universe, the Namorn Empire, in her new series, *Circle of Magic.* Its first two volumes, *Sandry's Book* and *Tris's Book,* follow the fates of four young misfits as they learn to use their magical powers in a strict temple community.

YAFEs on Tamora Pierce

Song of the Lioness Quartet

Pierce's writing style is nearly perfect. With all their twists and turns, plots are innovative, and the story moves fast enough to keep the reader spellbound but slow enough so that you feel as if you are living the story, down to the finest detail, and you come away feeling fulfilled. I have been reading this quartet for nearly 10 years, and I still enjoy it immensely.

—Jenny Dowe, 15

The Immortals: Wild Magic

The way Pierce describes wild magic, and its differences from what she calls "the Gift," makes one think she actually possesses this power. This charming story makes you laugh out loud, while it's straightforward and easy to understand, with enough unexpected twists to make it thoroughly enjoyable.

—Jenny Dowe, 15

Wolf-Speaker

This touching story is like none other; not even Pierce's other books have similar plots. It teaches some environmental and humanitarian lessons.

—Jenny Dowe, 15

It moved along at a pretty good pace, but it did get over a little too fast, leaving lots of questions unanswered. I don't think the *Immortals* series is as interesting as the *Lioness* series; the characters aren't as well developed, and it was just a bit disappointing.

—Mariah Isely, 13

The Emperor Mage

Even after reading seven of her books, Pierce's writing style continues to impress me. You are always meeting new characters and having new adventures. The descriptions in this book were wonderful but not tedious—a lot said in a few words. It makes you cry and laugh, fume about the foolishness, and jump up and down for joy.

—Jenny Dowe, 15

The Realms of the Gods

Pierce is very consistent with her clear and simple style. She brings the series to a good end, but I find the plot getting stale and stereotypical.

—Jenny Dowe, 16

Mercedes Lackey

Since her first novel, *Arrows of the Queen,* was one of the few original paperbacks to make ALA's Best Books for Young Adults list in 1987, Mercedes Lackey has enjoyed a meteoric rise in the world of fantasy. In only 10 years, she has published nearly 50 books, many as collaborations, which include horror and science fiction. Like Barbara Hambly, she has graduated from paperback to hardcover editions. Her character-driven tales usually focus on teen protagonists who quest for identity and a place to belong, often under difficult circumstances of abuse or hardship. Her independent heroines are in the new feminist fantasy tradition, but Lackey does not limit herself to that mode. Her male heroes too must fight the odds. In her *Last Herald Mage* trilogy, often considered her finest work, Vanyel must confront his gay identity in addition to overcoming all the trials of a throne's heir. Vanyel's story, which joins realistic YA literature that insightfully and sympathetically depicts coming to terms with homosexuality, also earns credibility with devoted Lackey readers through its place among her 20 heroic fantasies set in Valdemar.

Because she is so popular with teenaged readers, Mercedes Lackey was a strong contender for a featured-author biography in this volume, but her prolific output makes her worthy of an individual volume. Little is published about "Misty" herself, an ex-computer programmer who lives in Tulsa, Oklahoma, where she rehabilitates injured hawks, owls, and falcons with her husband, fantasy illustrator and writing partner Larry Dixon. In this volume, Lackey's books are integrated wherever they fit. Her magic realism and computer game–based books are introduced in chapter 3 and her mythical *Firebird* is listed in chapter 6's Recommended Reading. Here we cannot manage full exposition of her extensive Valdemar books, but we can briefly outline them with some of her other works and support those outlines with YAFE evaluations, which poured in for years. Perhaps what is most remarkable about Mercedes Lackey is the response she generates from her teen readers, who argue passionately about her books; Fantasy Fanatics Ashley Burns and Allison Barrett became so embroiled in a disagreement that they left a meeting to continue their wrangle by e-mail, some of which appears at the end of this section.

Readers who want to know more are referred to Lackey's 1992 interview in *Voice of Youth Advocates,* in which Larry Dixon reveals how deeply he is involved in creating Lackey's books, from his first coplotting and editing effort for *Magic's Price* in 1990 to "heavier co-writing on *Winds of Fate* and *Jinx High* [Tor, 1991; in her *Diana Tregarde Investigations* horror series]. . . . *Born to Run* is about my fourth or fifth co-written book (silently, with Misty), but is the first with a cover credit."[106]

Lackey is also a very active presence on the Internet, and her long-standing fan club Queen's Own has an online version. One can send snail mail to the official club by writing to Judith Louvis, Queen's Own, P.O. Box 132, Shiloh, NJ 08353, or send e-mail to annes3832@aol.com, using the subject header "***FOR JUDITH***." Its informative newsletter contains special messages from Lackey, forecasts upcoming publications, lists convention appearances, allows fans to communicate, and suggests writing opportunities in such venues as zines, in which Lackey got her start.

Lackey also produces "filk," folk music set in science fiction or fantasy worlds. The appendix of her third Valdemar book, *Arrow's Fall,* contains her song lyrics relating to the *Heralds of Valdemar* trilogy. In one *Queen's Own* newsletter, Lackey explains how songs relate to her writing:

> One of the reasons I write song lyrics is because I see songs as a kind of "story pill"—they reduce a story to the barest essentials or encapsulate a particular moment in time. I frequently will write a lyric when I am attempting to get to the heart of a crucial scene; I find that when I have done so, the scene has become absolutely clear in my mind, and I can write *exactly* what I wanted to say. Another reason is because of the kind of novels I am writing: that is, fantasy set in an otherworld semi-medieval atmosphere. Music is very important to medieval peoples; Bards are the chief news bringers. When I write the "folk music" of these peoples, I am enriching my whole world, whether I actually use the song in my text or not.[107]

Recordings of Lackey's songs relating to her various novels, often performed by other artists but which include a live performance of Lackey herself, may be ordered through Firebird Music Catalog at P.O. Box 30268, Portland, OR 97294-3268. The catalog includes other items related to her writings, such as prints of her Jody Lee book jackets, jewelry, stationery, and T-shirts. Lackey has also inspired other musicians. New Age composer and performer David Arkenstone created a concept album trilogy about heroic quests, winning a Grammy nomination for its opener, *In the Wake of the Wind* (Narada). The trilogy continues with *Quest of the Dream Warrior: Kyla's Journey* and *Return of the Guardians*. Each compact disk includes full text of the Mercedes Lackey stories on which his compositions are based.

Lackey's affinity with bards led to her only heroic fantasy series not set in Valdemar, *Bardic Voices,* which takes place in a medieval world where magic works. Its first volume, *The Lark and the Wren,* focuses on teenaged Rune, who refuses to follow her unmarried servant mother's model but persists with her fiddling until she wins a competition to enter the Bardic Guild, disguised as a male for safety. When her secret is discovered by the judges, Rune is beaten and disqualified from the contest but finds a place for herself, and a new love, in the anti-Guild group the Free Bards.

While criticizing its awkward construction, *VOYA*'s Mary K. Chelton praised Rune's tale: "All the usual engaging Lackey trademarks are here—an abused, alienated teenager with latent magical powers, music and medieval faires, a wonderfully realistic medieval fantasy setting, elves, evil mages, and mature (though not explicit) sexuality, with the addition of the Church as an institutional, omnipresent menace."[108] *The Lark and the Wren* became Lackey's only title besides her first novel, *Arrows of the Queen,* to be listed as a Best Book for Young Adults by ALA, in 1993. The series continues to follow the affairs of the Free Bards in *The Robin and the Kestrel, The Eagle and the Nightingale,* and *Four and Twenty Blackbirds,* with a related title, *A Cast of Corbies: Bardic Choices,* coauthored by Josepha Sherman.

Lackey's writer mentor C. J. Cherryh taught her the extended outline system of writing, which allows her to convert one page of detailed story outline to 10 pages of written text (Taylor et al., 214)—and to meet a grueling publication schedule of one finished novel every three months, with Dixon's help. With Cherryh, Lackey did her first book collaboration, in 1989, *Reap the Whirlwind,* an addition to Cherryh's *Sword of Knowledge* series.

In 1991, Lackey began one of her most successful collaborations, with Andre Norton, in *The Halfblood Chronicles.* In the unnamed otherworld of the best-selling first volume, *The Elvenbane,* cruel Elvenlords and greedy humans are repulsive to Alara, the spirited shaman dragon who shapechanges into elf or human form to spy on these other species who share her world, unaware she exists. When the Elvenbane prophecy comes true with the birth of Shana, the halfblood elven human who will be more powerful than either, it changes all three cultures. In the 1995 sequel *Elvenblood,* Elvenbane Shana struggles to find a weapon impervious to the magic of ruthless elven oppressors.

Known for meshing well with coauthors, Lackey describes her partnership with the venerable Andre Norton. "We worked on the outline, then I passed her three-chapter chunks and she added what she wanted to see. . . . I did most of the physical pounding on the keyboard because I'm half Andre's age and I don't have her vision and health problems. The way I see it, she did her share and more of the real work, which is outlining" (Taylor et al., 214). The result, according to *VOYA,* is a smooth blend: "In style, in characters, in mood and tone, it is so precisely halfway between the worlds of Norton and Lackey that it would be no surprise to find this place fixed on a map exactly as far from Valdemar, say, as it was from the Witch World." Both writers "have attracted well-deserved accolades for skillful handling of young protagonists"; available here for YA readers are "a wealth of adolescent central characters" of all species.[109]

In 1993, three collaborations with other giants in the field were published: the science fiction *The Ship Who Searched* (Baen) with Anne McCaffrey, the science fantasy *Darkover: Rediscovery* with Marion Zimmer Bradley, and a fantasy set in a world where women lord over men, *If I Pay Thee Not in Gold,* with Piers Anthony. Working with both Bradley and Norton again in *Tiger*

Burning Bright, Lackey created a triumvirate of female fantasy characters who protect their city-state from an emperor's invasion.

The Valdemar books at the core of Lackey's work do not occur in that otherworld's time line in the order in which they were published. Lackey's first novel, *Arrows of the Queen,* falls halfway through Valdemar's history. Its series *The Heralds of Valdemar* covers 13-year-old Talia's escape from a dull patriarchal community to become one of the Queen's Own, her chosen adviser, and a Herald ambassador to other realms on her psychic Companion horse, Rolan. By the end, Talia learns to control her Gift of empathy and use it ethically to help the queen's difficult daughter, Princess Elspeth. In the second "page-turner" volume, *Arrow's Flight, Booklist* noted, characters "spend a good deal of time discussing their emotions, but in the context of a world where empathy is a recognized gift, this makes a good deal of sense."[110] Lackey wrote two other Valdemar series before *Mage Winds,* which follows *Arrow's Flight* chronologically with Elspeth as central character.

Lackey's second series, *Vows and Honor,* published in the late '80s, features swordswoman Tarma and sorceress Kethry, who swear to battle evil together in *The Oathbound* and *Oathbreakers.* The series seemed to have no connection to other Valdemar stories until 1991, when the single volume *By the Sword* became what *VOYA* rejoiced in as "this great huge chunk of story" bridging the *Oath* books with the original *Herald* series through Kethry's granddaughter Kerowyn, who becomes Elspeth's arms instructor in *Mage Winds.* Yet *VOYA* notes that not only is *By the Sword* unintelligible to anyone unfamiliar with other books in the series, but "Kerowyn never comes as alive as Talia, or Vanyel, or even Tarma and Kethry have in their own books."[111]

Vanyel appears in *The Last Herald Mage,* the third Valdemar series published, a prequel set 600 years before *By the Sword.* One critic considers this series to be "among the strongest of [Lackey's] work. . . . The author's crowning triumph in characterization is the protagonist . . . Vanyel Ashkevron."[112] Of its last volume, *Magic's Price, VOYA* declared, "Lackey has written another intensely wrought, finely detailed story of heroic victims struggling to do the best with their fate."[113]

The most recent series, *Mage Wars,* coauthored by Lackey and Dixon and published between 1994 and 1996, is earlier prehistory, 1,000 years before Valdemar's founding, when the gryphon race evolves and interacts with humans. *Publishers Weekly* criticizes its first volume, *The Black Gryphon:* "[T]he tale soon bogs down in fantasy clichés. . . . [T]he plot is predictable and the overwritten battle scenes are difficult to follow."[114] Reviews improve through the series until *VOYA* says of the final, "more introspective" volume, *The Silver Gryphon,* "[T]he writing is solid and thought-provoking, exploring the themes of parent-child relationships and coming of age within the context of the survival story."[115]

The *Mage Storms* series, which follows *Mage Winds* chronologically and in publication through the early to mid-'90s, was issued simultaneously with the *Mage Wars* prehistory. The latest stand-alone Valdemar title is *Owlflight,* which follows *Mage Storms* in time but with all new characters, including a rebellious misfit orphan boy, Darian. Another 1997 title, *Swords of Ice and Other Tales of Valdemar,* a "Friends of Valdemar" shared-world anthology edited by Lackey, contains three stories she cowrote with newcomer writers and other stories by such familiar contributors to Lackey's worlds as Josepha Sherman, Mark Shepherd, and Larry Dixon, among others. For readers' convenience, all Valdemar series appear in time line order, rather than by publication date, in this chapter's Recommended Reading. A fan's Internet home page, *Firesong's Guide to Mercedes Lackey's Work* (http://www.firesong.demon.co.uk/misty.htm), was a help in deciphering the order of the books.

YAFEs on Mercedes Lackey

Lackey has strong female lead characters. She really puts women in higher places but doesn't make a big deal about doing it. I like the way this speaks toward gender equality. Her views on homosexuality are also very liberal, and she incorporates that too.

—Sam Walter, 17

If *Forgotten Realms* are the dime novels of fantasy, then Lackey's are the quarter novels. She writes the same story over and over. All her books have stock characters dancing around in different patterns. It's hard to feel sympathy for perfect people like heralds. Being shy or pompous is the only flaw they're allowed to have.

—Allison Barrett, 17

No, Lackey's books are not dime novel fantasy where the plot is always, "Oh, no, we've got to save the world!" Instead they focus on character development, which is probably why I read them, because I *only* read for characters, how they change, and the ideas they come up with in the process. Often people pay so much attention to plot that they miss all the subtle, wonderful details characters come up with. I don't think Lackey goes on and on . . . or if she does, I find it interesting. We're actually *seeing* the characters think. Her action tends to be quick and to the point, which is also true of real life. We spend more time thinking than doing.

—Ashley Burns, 17

The Last Herald Mage Trilogy: *Magic's Pawn*

Vanyel's feelings were more than real—so lifelike I felt that I know him inside and out. This exciting true fantasy had so much feeling in it, but I think it brooded too much on the affair between the two boys and didn't explain why. People who are unfamiliar with it or think it's bad may not want to read it. But others are still looking for understanding about why someone would do it.

—Melissa Tolve, 16

Vanyel felt that nobody cared about him. He didn't know what love was. Lackey's development of Vanyel was magnificent. It is one of my favorite books.

—Vanessa Bowler, 16

Vanyel just kept getting hurt and then getting healed. His internal conflict got old—at one point I wanted to say to him, "Get over it already." He was pathetic, just feeling sorry for himself. I have trouble reading books when I can't connect with the main character.

—Midian Crosby, 18

I could not connect with pathetic little dweeb Vanyel.
—Allison Barrett, 17

Magic's Promise

I love tearjerkers—when Vanyel saved everyone at the end and was willing to give up his own life, it broke my heart. I felt for him and wished I could possibly be like that someday.
—Melissa Tolve, 16

Magic's Price

The evil characters are dark, dripping with witchcraft; the evil is unrelenting. You can feel in the descriptions that evil masked in beauty is sinister. The story is dramatic, like a legend, and would even interest teen romantics—the love between Vanyel and Stefan would keep them in suspense. But the emotionalism went on far too long; their fight takes up some 50 pages. The end was the best, when Vanyel realizes he is destined to die for Valdemar. Then, unleashing all his power, he kills the Dark One. The climax left me yelling out loud!
—Christy Boyd, 15

I liked the loving connection between Vanyel and Stefan. Sometimes the sections didn't fall into place very well, though. It was very jumpy. The ending was kind of dumb. What?—they turn into ghosts and haunt the forest?—NOT!
—Melissa Tolve, 16

After Vanyel's poor start in the first volume, this book saved the series. Now *Last Herald Mage* is my runner-up to the best Lackey series, the *Arrows* books. The scene where Vanyel finds his soul mate is the best in any Lackey book!
—Allison Barrett, 17

Vows and Honor Series: *Oathbound*

Tarma and Kethry are two of Lackey's most famous and loved characters. The first book is mostly stories we've seen in the *Sword and Sorceress* books, which is annoying. The tales themselves are good, but the reading is a bit disjointed. Nevertheless, it's lovely to watch Tarma and Kethry interact, though the plot consists mostly of running around saving

helpless women and killing a demon or two on the side. *Oath-breakers* has a more interesting plot and is less stereotypical.
—Ashley Burns, 17

It's great, finally, to have a book about two female mercenaries. I really got a feeling of the friendship between Tarma and Kethry with every passing adventure. But the beginning was repetitive: meet the characters, read the adventures, and in the next chapter, meet the characters again and have another adventure. From the middle to the end it finally got exciting.
—Melissa Tolve, 16

By the Sword

The story started with Kero's training. Then there was a giant leap to her joining the mercenary company. I hate skips. The story was a bit too tactical, and some would find it hard to follow. The battle at the end was resolved too quickly—a whole other book could be written about the ending.
—Melissa Tolve, 17

I like the way Lackey writes with just enough detail, but not overly descriptive. She has a very interesting mind, as I can see in her writing style. This is a fun book with a catchy plot which moves very well.
—Sam Walter, 14

This book is a bit different from most of Lackey's other work because Kero is so different, a creature of unbelievable determination, ambition, and spunk. As a result, there's a bit more adventure and a lot more humor than in Lackey's other tales.
—Ashley Burns, 17

Heralds of Valdemar Trilogy: *Arrows of the Queen*

It's one of the best stories I've read. Everything that happens is depicted down to the last detail. This wasn't any old fantasy story but contains major elements of love, joy, sadness, and adventure, which all come together to form the story.
—Raymond Drummond, 15

This story reminded me a lot of Pierce's *Alanna* series, which I also liked very much. I especially like the scene when Talia finds out she has to straighten out the queen's snotty daughter Elspeth.

—Domenica Mirarchi, 14

It moved kind of slowly, without much adventure, since Talia was learning more about how to express herself and make friends than how to conquer the world with magic. *The Last Herald Mage* trilogy had more magic and is for more advanced readers. Talia's story is for young adults.

—Melissa Tolve, 16

Arrow's Flight

Lackey creates her own legends and world, and general life is well defined. I like her humor and her way with words; it comes very close to the poetic phrases in McKinley's *Beauty*. It's a little slow to climax, with a big letdown afterward. It really relates to teenagers, creatively dealing with our problems in different worlds.

—Christy Boyd, 15

I enjoyed Talia's and Kris's intimacy but disliked the story's formation—the beginning did not relate to the end. There wasn't much adventure and too much conflict in Talia's mind. You get used to what the people are feeling and start to feel with them, therefore making it very un-fantasy.

—Melissa Tolve, 16

Entire Series

Talia was my gender and age, and her character was so well developed that I could be her. It's a warm, loving story that will make you laugh, cry, smile, blush, anything you would do in life because her life is so real.

—Jenny Dowe, 15

What I enjoyed most about Lackey's style was the building up of *Arrows of the Queen* into the next two books, making it seem like one book split into three. It's a total fantasy where Lackey gets into Valdemar realistically. Nothing was boring or slow. Lackey gets across to young readers the value of integrity and honor. It's an unusual idea to tell a fantasy story about a people's duty to their king, and the songs on a companion tape were original too. The only other book it reminds me of is McCaffrey's *Dragons of Pern* series; the Dragon/Rider bond and the Companion/Chosen bond is very similar.

—P. J. King, 17

Lackey presented Heralds as imperfect, so they were believable. But the books don't sparkle. I don't feel she loved it with all her heart.

—Sarah Luna, 17

Lackey's most acclaimed series is a perennial favorite among fantasy readers. Talia is altogether lovable. It's impossible not to feel for her as she struggles to master her magical Gift, not to mention her insecurities, to become a Herald. I have memories of reading it underneath my blanket with a flashlight, very late on a school night, too engrossed in the book to care about sleep and half afraid my dad would figure out that I was reading when I should be sleeping and force me to stop, in which case I still wouldn't sleep, as I'd be too busy wondering what happened next!

—Ashley Burns, 17

Mage Winds

This series has gotten a lot of criticism, even from diehard Lackey fans who feel that Lackey's style had become predictable, boring, and clichéd. Still, Falconsbane made a cool villain, and I liked the development of characters such as Nyara, An'desha, and the sword Need. Unfortunately, it is true that the main characters, Elspeth and Darkwind, were much too stereotypical. Much of the story was lost as a result.

—Ashley Burns, 17

Mage Storms: Storm Warning

This series restored my faith in Lackey (whew!). The plot is incredible, the characters are intriguing, and the action comes quick and hard and unpredictably. The main character is a Karsite secretary who has trouble believing that Heralds aren't demonspawn and Companions aren't going to drag him down into hell. Comparisons between different races and countries are unbelievably interesting: the Shin'a'in and the Native Americans, the Karsites and the Egyptians, the Empire and China, the Tayledras and Elves, the Heralds and medieval chivalry. I honestly have not been able to put this incredible book down. I'm buying the next two tomorrow.

—Ashley Burns, 17

The Epic Proportions of Heroic Fantasy
Piers Anthony

Outside the borders of feminist fantasy for the past 20 years, a huge array of solid epic fantasy has claimed loyal YA readers. In 1977, the year Terry Brooks paved the epic highway with *The Sword of Shannara,* another writer modestly known for science fiction wrote the first volume in a still-running fantasy series that would propel him to astounding popularity. *A Spell for Chameleon* by Piers Anthony won the British Fantasy Award for best fantasy novel of 1977, introducing the magical land of Xanth, which cannot tolerate any nonmagical resident older than 25. When his magical talent won't reveal itself, hero Bink is exiled to unmagical Mundania, where he finally learns that his talent is that he cannot be harmed by magic. In their reference guide, critics Tymn, Zahorski, and Boyer found this first *Xanth* novel "highly entertaining," showing "that it is possible to inject humor into a fantasy novel without necessarily destroying the seriousness or credibility of its magic. . . . One of the strong points of the novel is its exploration of the nature and uses of magic, although the reader should be warned that Anthony has a tendency to overuse magical paraphernalia" (Tymn et al., 46–47).

Developing in the tradition of de Camp's and Pratt's irreverent Harold Shea stories, Anthony found a formula that worked phenomenally well, with puns, madcap humor, and wild leaps of imagination, which proved addictive to many readers, especially teenagers. *Xanth* novels, however, are an acquired taste; some never acquire it at all. Girls who enjoy feminist fantasy may find some of his attitudes or jokes at the expense of women offensive. Some find *Xanth* books just plain silly. Beginning with the stronger, early books in the series, fans put up with inconsistent quality for that familiar wacky dose of *Xanth.* It is amazing that 20 years and 21 volumes into this endless saga, Anthony has not gone more than a little stale. Reviewers point out what fans don't mind anyway. Reviewing *Demons Don't Dream,* a 1993 novel about teens playing a fantasy role-playing game in which they actually enter Xanth through their computer, *VOYA* notes that "subtlety is not a Xanthian concept and the audience seems com-

fortable with his approach." The puns "come at you in a somewhat relentless and overcute fashion, but it's the kind of humor
the average fourteen-year-old appreciates, there is a logic at work
beneath the silliness, and the narrative style echoes a role-playing
game master's patter."[116] *Booklist* characterizes *Xanth*'s 1995
entry, *Geis of the Gargoyle,* as unlikely to "change anybody's
mind from loving or loathing Anthony's creation, . . . zany, light-
hearted, occasionally flat-out silly," and "absolutely unignor-
able."[117]

Anthony also produces prolifically in more serious subgenres.
Both critics and teens appreciate his *Apprentice Adept* series featuring two interlocking worlds. Since magic reigns in one and science in the other, it qualifies as science fantasy. "*Split Infinity*
and its original two sequels, *Blue Adept* and *Juxtaposition,*
remain among Anthony's most successful works," says critic Don
D'Ammassa, though later additions "lack the impact of the first
trilogy."[118]

The only Piers Anthony book to win a place on ALA's Best
Books for Young Adults list was *On a Pale Horse,* the 1983 introduction to his *Incarnations of Immortality* series, mentioned with
myth in chapter 4, in which Death and other mythic forces are
personified. The series remains a teen favorite. Anthony's magic
realism *Mode* series, mentioned in chapter 3, utilizes the favored
Anthony strategy of entering one universe from another. Also
mentioned in chapter 3 is *Through the Ice,* which Anthony completed from a manuscript sent by a teenaged fan, Robert Kornwise, who later died. It is Anthony's openness and empathy with
his teen readers, revealed in lengthy author's notes in his books,
that endear him to so many. When Anthony was not chosen as a
featured author in this book, some YAFEs were disappointed
enough to write justifications of why he should have been
included, which appear at this end of this section. *The Encyclopedia of Fantasy* puts the problematic nature of Anthony's writing
in a nutshell: "The fantasy work of Piers Anthony constantly
enthralls with its scope and frustrates through the pun-ridden,
excessive facility of its telling. It sometimes seems difficult for . . .
Anthony to find worlds of the imagination that are sufficiently

gritty to engage his full attention. When his imagination is properly involved, however, his work is explosive" (Clute, 47).

YAFEs on Piers Anthony

Xanth was a horrible reason to get famous. It is chock full of bad writing, stereotypical characters, and an even more stereotypical setting.

Incarnations of Immortality was also a stereotypical setting, a future Earth of magic and science. However, Anthony's writing about the godlike incarnations is beautiful, fascinating, and imaginative. A fabulous use of hooks, intrigue, and foreshadowing keeps you with a carefully woven plot that ties up perfectly (to use the title of the third book) *With a Tangled Skein,* from book 1's introduction of Zane, soon to become Death, to God's last words in book 7.

Use of mythology from every source imaginable, with Anthony's own twist, makes for an exotic series. Some of the finest points are jumps between scenes; for example, seeing Satan corrupt a friend of Gaea's and watching Gaea's angry reaction to this treachery, with Satan laughing in book 5, then seeing it through Satan's view in book 6 as an act of necessity, not of malice, his laughter a facade to keep an evil, imposing image. Anthony uses this technique extensively throughout the series, letting us see the characters perfectly and helping the complex plot stay within the mind frame of the average human being. One cannot express how beautiful this series is; it is a masterwork in modern writing and gave me faith that there really are good writers after Tolkien.

—Dylan Burns, 15

Piers Anthony is a most prolific writer with a varying style. He is most renowned for the *Xanth* series, which is a fun and easy read as long as you can stand all the puns. *Incarnations of Immortality* is also a fairly easy read but is much more serious and appealing to those who like philosophy, with numerous arguments about the nature of God, Satan, time, and nearly everything else under the sun. Music lovers will adore the fifth book in the series, *Being a Green Mother.*

More controversial than either of these series are the *Mode* books, my personal favorites, which deal with interdimensional travel and in which the heroine is a depressive, suicidal 14-year-old girl who has fallen in love.

Anthony also has several solitary books that do not belong to any series, such as *The Caterpillar's Question,* the story of a man and a young crippled girl who are drawn into another world, and *Through the Ice,* cowritten with Robert Kornwise, a story about four people from four different Earth planes who go on an adventure and increase their understanding of each other and the different dimensions they come from.

Piers Anthony has an easy writing style that goes along at a fast pace, and he writes very well about difficult subjects, such as suicide, abuse, Creationism vs. Evolution, and strange magicians asking enigmatic riddles.

—Ashley Burns, 17

Terry Pratchett

Another humorous fantasy series of similar size and longevity is Terry Pratchett's *Discworld,* which could be considered *Xanth*'s British counterpart. Discworld is held up by four elephants atop an enormous turtle who swims through space, but its bizarre structure matters little. What is fuel for endless hilarious gags and parodies is that Discworld is a distorted mirror of our world. Through the inept wizard, Rincewind, the canny witch, Granny Weatherwax, and the straight man, Death, Pratchett comments farcically on every human foible and social issue imaginable, from war to feminism. His delightful romps attract teen readers who like their humor British, the same ones who appreciate Monty Python and Douglas Adams. Like Anthony, Pratchett seems inexhaustible; *Discworld* opened with *The Colour of Magic* in 1983, and its 19th and latest work, *Maskerade,* appeared in 1997. The full set is listed in this chapter's Recommended Reading, as are Anthony's *Xanth* books. Pratchett's books are an astonishing one percent of all books sold in the U.K., reports *The Encyclopedia of Fantasy,* which devotes pages of serious attention to him, concluding: "The *Discworld* books are a remarkably fine set of fantasy comedies whose popular success derives not only from inventiveness with words and ideas but from understanding of how darker issues can, by contrast, intensify the comic highlights" (Clute, 785).

Young Adult Fantasists

Another British fantasist known for imaginative humor is Diana Wynne Jones. Specifically targeting young adult readers, she is mistress of the deliciously intricate plot that still manages to be down to earth, in which magic infects our everyday world, producing matter-of-fact witches, or sends characters spinning into faerie or time travel. Her noted otherworld fantasy is the *Dalemark Quartet,* which opened with *Cart and Cwidder* in 1977 and concluded with *The Crown of Dalemark* in 1995. Five of her YA fantasies have been honored as ALA Best Books for Young Adults: *Homeward Bounders* (1981), *Archer's Goon* (1984), *Howl's Moving Castle* (1986), *Castle in the Air* (1992), and *Sudden Wild Magic* (1993). Humor infuses even Jones's serious books; some are laugh-out-loud funny. *Howl's Moving Castle* is especially riotous, as teenaged Sophie tries to get rid of the curse that has turned her into an old woman while coping with the wizard Howl and his alarming castle, whose doors keep opening onto new landscapes.

Several other noteworthy YA fantasists have commanded attention on the Best Books list. Lloyd Alexander, whose *Chronicles of Prydain* are covered as Celtic roots of Arthur in chapter 5, also wrote several classic adventure fantasies, appealing to readers as young as middle grade. All three volumes of his *Westmark Trilogy,* a political adventure thriller in the alternative Kingdom of Westmark, were named Best Books in their publication years: *Westmark* in 1981, *The Kestrel* in 1982, and *The Beggar Queen* in 1984.

Calling her otherworld simply the Kingdom, realistic YA author Cynthia Voigt, acclaimed for her Tillerman family saga, imports realism into an otherworld without magic, where three loosely related dramas occur. *Jackaroo* echoes the Robin Hood legend in chapter 5, featuring innkeeper's daughter Gwyn, who masquerades as the fabled deliverer Jackaroo. Gwyn's granddaughter Birle makes her own bid for freedom by stowing away on a fishing boat stolen by a handsome young lord in *On Fortune's Wheel,* a 1991 Best Book. Tied to the first two titles only by the Kingdom, *The Wings of a Falcon* is a dark and tragic tale that explores "how people survive in the face of overwhelming cruelty and yet maintain integrity"[119] through the story of Oriel, who inherits a dictator's role but makes his own choices.

Much more lighthearted is Mary Frances Zambreno's 1993 Best Book, *A Plague of Sorcerers,* featuring apprentice wizard Jermyn and his skunk familiar, Delia. Their adventures continue in *Journeyman Wizard.* New Zealand author Sherryl Jordan creates a memorable, viscerally icy otherworld in the 1994 Best Book *Winter of Fire,* in which a young girl rises from slavery to improve her people's fate.

Two newcomers in YA fantasy reassure us that inventive new worlds continue to be created by rising new authors. In *Sabriel,* a 1996 Best Book, Garth Nix presents a resourceful heroine who must journey from her unmagical border town to the magic Old Kingdom on the other side of the Wall to rescue her necromancer father, who refuses to bring the Dead back to life. In a world recalling ancient Greece in *The Thief,* lowly Gen, removed from prison by a king who needs him to steal a fabled stone, reveals his surprising true identity in a clever twist in this 1997 Best Book by Megan Whalen Turner.

David Eddings

Two authors of adult fantasy have recently emerged to capture the hearts of teen fantasy readers, who made strong bids for their inclusion here long after this book was planned (see their arguments later in this section). Like Terry Brooks, David Eddings was inspired by Tolkien to create his own otherworld through a rereading when he was over 40 of the trilogy he loved in high school. Also like Brooks, Eddings was nurtured through his first fantasy series, *The Belgariad,* by Lester del Rey. Its five volumes contain one continuous story, from 1982's *Pawn of Prophecy* through 1984's *Enchanter's End Game,* selling easily in original paperback editions. Just as *Shannara*'s ordinary Ohmsfords are thrust into magical quests not of their choosing by the Druid Allanon in Brooks's series, so is Eddings's young farm boy, Garion, propelled by Belgarath the Sorcerer and his daughter Polgara to search for the Orb of Aldur, the magic jewel that is the only salvation from Torak, the evil god about to awaken. Appreciating the leisurely unfolding of Garion's world through his naive eyes, critic Michael Cule notes, "Gradually we see his sensible, workaday, limited world expand to include stranger and stranger things. Particularly entertaining is his slow discovery of his own sorcerous powers." In a "standard-issue" otherworld where "analogues" of various human cultures and time periods interact in unlikely proximity, Cule asserts that world building and cultural conflict are not the point of Eddings's work; instead, he focuses on "the comedy of character." Eddings contrasts personalities among his band of heroes, paying special attention to the blossoming love between Garion and Princess Ce'Nedra "and the growth of a sense of responsibility in the two adolescents."[120]

Published in 1987, *The Guardians of the West,* the opening volume of the second continuous quintet, *The Mallorean,* was both the first hardcover and the first best-seller for Eddings. Garion is now the Rivan King who must learn new roles as ruler, husband, and father, protecting his kingdom and heir from new threats of sorcery. Reviews continued to be enthusiastic. Reviewing the series's first volume, *Booklist*'s Roland Green proclaimed Eddings "a natural and extremely gifted storyteller, with a keen eye for interesting characters and sound world-building."[121] In its concluding volume, *The Seeress of Kell,* Green found "no shortage of action, suspense, or reader satisfaction at the resolution of the struggle."[122] However, having noted that Eddings's "chief flaws come when the artifice fails and one becomes aware of the lack of depth in the illusion"—as when characters revert to modern American speech and values—Cule found that *The Mallorean* "unhappily has the faults of the first sequence in exaggerated form and lacks fresh invention" (Cule, 234).

Fans seemed not to notice, for between *The Mallorean*'s third book, *Demon Lord of Karanda,* and its fourth, *Sorceress of Darshiva,* Eddings made an unprecedented nervy move: he launched a new series before the old one was completed. *The Elenium* trilogy opened with *The Diamond Throne* in 1989, and *The Ruby Knight* followed in 1990 before *The Seeress of Kell* ended *The Mallorean* in 1991. All became best-sellers, but the result was fan frenzy, described in a publicity packet from Del Rey. Some readers thought Eddings was holding back, some demanded a whole story in one hefty volume, and countless callers begged for forthcoming dates of new volumes, even offering bribes for pre-publication copies. Teenagers are among this swarm, offering their testimonies in the comments at the end of this section.

The Elenium introduced a new protagonist, the Pandion (church knight) Sparhawk, in search of yet another magical jewel. The jewel is the only cure for the poisoned Queen Ehlana of Ele-nia. Sparhawk is on a quest beset by "diversions and endless problems," including "treachery, ambushes, and church politics," notes Gene LaFaille in his review of *The Ruby Knight*. "Eddings continues to present his stylish prose, gentle humor, and frequent action scenes, but the characters and their detailed development are this work's main strength."[123] Of the last *Elenium* volume, *The Sapphire Rose*, *VOYA* declares, "This is fun fantasy."[124]

A second trilogy, *The Tamuli*, follows the characters from *The Elenium* after Sparhawk marries Queen Ehlana. In a land of many gods vying for their followers' worship to empower them, the rulers become pawns of one supernatural entity, and their daughter Danae is really the child-goddess Aphrael. *Publishers Weekly* describes the series's second volume, *The Shining Ones*: "Neatly blending simplicity and complexity, this tale of comrade-ship, dastardly doings, multiple gods, strange races, and noble and ignoble humans is vintage Eddings."[125]

Eddings's most recent series is a prequel to *The Belgariad*. Its 1995 opener, *Belgarath the Sorcerer*, contains an author's note recognizing his wife, Leigh, as "hitherto unacknowledged co-author" all along, ever since their first book in 1982.[126] At last she receives credit on this series: the jacket reads "by David and Leigh Eddings," as does the cover of its 1997 sequel, *Polgara the Sorceress*.

YAFEs on David Eddings

David Eddings left out of this study? This is an outrage! A horror! A travesty! Eddings has written 17 fantasy novels, a long series divided into two sets of five books apiece (*The Belgariad* and *The Mallorean*), a prequel to these (*Belgarath the Sorcerer*), and another series divided into two sets of three books apiece (*The Elenium* and *The Tamuli*) that deal with a different universe.

Many people claim that David Eddings is not worth reading because his plots are mundane and clichéd. Not so! Take *The Belgariad:* true, the idea of a band of adventurers setting out to save the world, complete with warriors, thieves, magicians who have lived for thousands of years, and a missing princely warrior, is clichéd—yet somehow the characters avoid being clichéd themselves. Each is given detailed backgrounds and subplots, and their lives are as complicated as real people's. In addition, the interaction between them makes one swear they are alive. It is beautiful to read, and Eddings has a descriptive writing style that allows you to see the entire scene set before you in vivid detail. David Eddings is a phenomenal writer.

—Ashley Burns, 17

As I was growing up reading fantasy novels, there was one author with whom I could identify the most. His writing gripped my attention and stimulated my imagination in ways that not many other fantasy writers could. His characters were individual and alive. The plots were solid and not overly complicated. This author was David Eddings.

When I first read *The Belgariad,* I was struck with how long it stayed with me. Weeks after I had finished it, I found myself thinking of the characters and what they might be doing after the last book ended. I was sad when *The Mallorean* was over that I could not follow these characters further. Eddings's strength lies in his characters; I knew them personally. I could relate and emote with every single one. I cared about what happened to them.

His writing style is very engaging. The plot is there to supplement the characters. It could be considered a little simple, but there are subplots and twists. Things follow logically without jumping around, and there aren't a lot of surprises.

I thoroughly enjoyed everything that Eddings wrote, though I liked the first two series better than the last two. His writing still continues to entertain and stimulate me four or five years after I first read David Eddings.

—Sam Walter, 17

The Belgariad

All five books build toward a final confrontation of good vs. evil, but the journey toward that point is far more interesting. One already knows that good will triumph. In everyday, amusing conversations, detailed characters are shown through actions and words, not told. Fantasy books often seem too grim. Although the plot is clichéd, this funny series is memorable. I don't recommend *The Mallorean,* which continues with these characters, because Eddings only repeats the earlier books.

—Rachel Scott, 18

The Mallorean

A giant game is played in which the end result is the joining of good and evil parts into one, which is what is supposed to be. All the characters are pawns but still very good characters. I identify with them very well, especially Belgarath the Sorcerer, because he has almost the exact same personality that I do. I could picture myself in many of his situations. This excellent series is my favorite, and David Eddings is the best author.

—Erik Hansen, 17

The Elenium

I enjoyed the subtle way Eddings put magic into the story. It's there, but it's casual. The land he creates is very real—he even found a wonderful way of telling its history through a lesson to a pupil. Centering on the corruption with the hierarchy of the land, and how hard but rewarding it is to fight against it, the conflict was very political. Brawls were frequent, but they got old fast. In *The Diamond Throne,* Eddings seemed to be keeping the bad guys from getting killed to save them for the other two books. It was frustrating; I didn't think it was necessary to make this story into a trilogy.

—Midian Crosby, 16

The writing is similar to Terry Brooks. The books are humorous, move at a fast pace, and are hard to put down. The descriptions and action keep you involved.

—Jehnie Burns, 17

Robert Jordan

The most recent epic fantasist to create a full-blown new other-world as a best-selling phenomenon is Robert Jordan. After a distinguished military career, Jordan was forced to leave his nuclear engineering job with the navy due to injury. According to his publishers, Jordan spent his time reading and began writing only when he became frustrated with the quality of what was available. Since *The Eye of the World,* the first volume of his massive chronicle *The Wheel of Time,* debuted in 1990, Jordan has proved to many readers that he can indeed do it better. Among his devoted fans are older teenagers who savor the rich complexities and teeming characters in his universe. A YAFE essay in tribute to Jordan appears at the end of this section. Many *Wheel* fans are unaware that Jordan wrote many previous works, including Conan stories (see this chapter's Recommended Reading).

Like Brooks and Eddings, Jordan targets an ordinary and innocent young man from a farming village, shepherd Rand al'Thor, to battle powerful forces of Darkness when myth suddenly becomes all too real in his world. Everyone believes that the Dark One was imprisoned by male witches called saidin, in a long-ago time known as the Breaking of the World. Ever since, men have been unable to use the magic poisoned by the Dark One's revenge without going insane. A sudden attack by the Dark One's troll-like beast-men on Rand and his friends Matrim and Perrin marks them as instrumental, and their long journey to confront the Dark One begins. By the second volume, *The Great Hunt,* Rand has been identified as the messianic figure the Dragon Reborn. By the third volume, *The Dragon Reborn,* he is adjusting to his perilous role as a saidin with his friends, who are joined by three female friends with new roles as Wise Women. Entangled in the Wheel of Time, the six young reluctant heroes must follow their fates set up in the mandala-based philosophy: "The Wheel weaves as the Wheel will."

Without knowing the fate of the *Wheel* series in her review of its first volume for *VOYA,* Laura Staley correctly forecast to librarians that "the size of the book may put some off, but if you can get one good reader to try it, word-of-mouth will sell it to the

rest." Her description is apt: "With well-drawn, believable characters; an intelligent plot; and something significant to say about
the range of good and evil and the effects of fear and obsession on
the human character, 670 pages is hardly long enough. While certain aspects of his world aren't outstandingly original (names,
characters, and scenes reminiscent of Tolkien, the Arthurian
mythos, Troy, the Spanish Inquisition, and *Return of the Jedi* all
appear), the author weaves his many strands into a memorable,
highly enjoyable tale."[127]

The fourth volume, *Shadow Rising*, "is a huge sweeping novel
full of maidens in distress, heroic battles, great loves, and tragic
deaths. Jordan has completely envisaged the world of *The Wheel
of Time*[;] its geography, races of people, and history are laid out
in magnificent detail," says *VOYA*. Yet "sections of the novel are
almost incomprehensible if one has not read the earlier volumes.
The glossary in the back is a tremendous help but it is incom-
plete."[128] The fifth volume is *The Fires of Heaven*. Reviewing
book 6, *Lords of Chaos, Publishers Weekly* observed that "while
Jordan's prose is sometimes bloated, he rises above his Tolkien-
influenced contemporaries, (Brooks, Eddings, et al.) with his skill
at narrative pacing and his ability to create fully realized characters (though his treatment of sexuality will appeal primarily to
adolescents)."[129] With the 1996 publication of book 7, *A Crown of
Swords,* there is still no end in sight on the long and winding road
of Rand and his followers.

What tangled webs are woven by Tolkien-inspired writers who
surpass each other in ambitious world building as our century
draws to a close! Each new generation of YA fantasy readers has
more to choose from; youth of the '90s cannot imagine our world
without Bradley or Brooks, McKinley or Eddings, just as they
cannot visualize the "olden days" without computers—which now
assist them in making sense of their favorite fantasies and com-
municating with other readers. With more fuel for boundless
appetites, additional otherworld fantasies are listed in this chapter's Recommended Reading, all familiar in structure and motif
but otherwise as various as their creators' imaginations. In the
following chapters, the skeins of other types of fantasies are

unwound and examined, each appealing to a slightly different type of reader, each with endless possibilities.

YAFE on Robert Jordan

Robert Jordan is one of the best fantasy writers of modern times. His writing is not only imaginative, enveloping, and powerful but easy to relate to, which not too many fantasy writers manage to pull off.

Jordan's characters are so incredibly vivid that the reader cannot help but find himself getting emotionally involved in the story. The protagonists strike a fire of sympathy and sometimes empathy in the reader while still being conspicuously imperfect. At times I find myself wanting to yell at them for their ignorance or even blatant stupidity. However, you cannot help rallying in their favor, especially when their imperfections take the story down an unexpected road. The evil characters—maybe not quite good would be a better description—also catch the reader in a frenzy of emotion with their actions. Not knowing how each thought or plan of the "Forsaken" will turn out keeps pages turning. Just as the good guys have their bad side, the bad guys have their good side. In most fantasy, antagonists are depicted as pure evil with no capability of emotion or sympathy from the rest of the characters. But Jordan's evil ones have their soft side, showing emotion, love, doubt, and any other feature you would expect to find in some average Joe walking down the street. The characters make the story readable and real.

Jordan's plot is unprecedented since Tolkien. In the first half of the first book, he manages to lay out a plot that stretches back thousands of years and will invariably run thousands of years into the future. Through the series, he continuously lays out the intricate history of his world and the thousands of other dimensions that mirror it. Epic tales of past ages pull together to create a world that exists above and beyond the covers of each book, still influencing the minds and actions of the several different cultures, each with conflicting beliefs and prejudices. Maybe the people he outlines are so vivid and rich in history because he models them after societies on Earth, but still the histories are so intricate and colorful that the reader is awestruck at their depth and precision.

—Eric Rice, 17

Recommended Reading

(* denotes title mentioned in text; other titles are additional)

Otherworld Foundations: Before We Heard of Tolkien

Eddison, E. R. *The Worm Ouroboros: A Romance.* (Orig. British pub. 1922.) New York: Dell, 1991, © 1926.

Morris, William. *The Wood Beyond the World.* (Orig. British pub. 1895.) Mineola, N.Y.: Dover, 1972.

———. *The Well at the World's End.* (Orig. British/U.S. pub. 1896.) New York: Ballantine, 1978 [out of print]; Stroud, U.K.: Alan Sutton, 1997.

Peake, Mervyn. *The Gormenghast Trilogy.* 3 vols. (Orig. British/U.S. pub. 1946.) New York: Overlook Press, single-volume edition 1995; separate volumes 1992.

Vol. 1: *Titus Groan.* 1992, 1995, © 1946.

Vol. 2: *Gormenghast.* 1992, 1995, © 1950.

Vol. 3: *Titus Alone.* 1992, 1995, © 1959.

English Inklings and Weird American Barbarians

De Camp, L. Sprague, and Fletcher Pratt. *The Complete Compleat Enchanter.* 1941; reprint, New York: Baen, 1992.

Howard, Robert E. *The Hour of the Dragon.* (Orig. pub. 1935–1936, 1950). New York: Ace, 1994.

Jordan, Robert. *The Conan Chronicles.* New York: Tor, 1995.

———. *Conan the Destroyer.* New York: Tor, 1991.

———. *Conan the Magnificent.* New York: Tor, 1991.

———. *Conan the Triumphant.* New York: Tor, 1991.

Leiber, Fritz. *The Swords of Lankhmar.* New York: Ace, 1986.

Moore, Sean A. *Conan the Hunter.* New York: Tor, 1994.

———. *Conan and the Grim Grey God.* New York: Tor, 1996.

———. *Conan and the Shaman's Curse.* New York: Tor, 1996.

Pratt, Fletcher. *The Well of the Unicorn.* New York: Ballantine/Del Rey, 1981, © 1948.

Williams, Charles. *War in Heaven.* (Orig. British pub. 1930.) Grand Rapids, Mich.: W. B. Eerdmans, 1981, © 1949.

J. R. R. Tolkien: Founder of Modern Heroic Fantasy

After the King: Stories in Honor of J. R. R. Tolkien. Ed. Martin H. Greenberg. New York: Tor, 1992.

Fonstad, Karen Wynn. *The Atlas of Middle-earth*. Boston: Houghton Mifflin, 1981.

Foster, Robert. *The Complete Guide to Middle-earth*. New York: Ballantine/Del Rey, 1990, © 1971.

Tolkien, J.R.R. *The Father Christmas Letters*. Ed. Baillie Tolkien. Boston: Houghton Mifflin, 1991, © 1976.

———. *The History of Middle-earth*. 12 vols. Ed. Christopher Tolkien. Boston: Houghton Mifflin.

Vol. 1: *The Book of Lost Tales*. Part 1. 1983.

Vol. 2: *The Book of Lost Tales*. Part 2. 1984.

Vol. 3: *The Lays of Beleriand*. 1985.

Vol. 4: *The Shaping of Middle-earth: The Quenta, the Ambarkanta, and the Annals*. 1986.

Vol. 5: *The Lost Road and Other Writings*. 1987.

Vol. 6: *The Return of the Shadow: The History of the Lord of the Rings*. Part 1. 1988.

Vol. 7: *The Treason of Isengard: The History of the Lord of the Rings*. Part 2. 1989.

Vol. 8: *The War of the Ring*. 1990.

Vol. 9: *Sauron Defeated*. 1992.

Vol. 10: *Morgoth's Ring: The Later Silmarillion*. Part 1. 1993.

Vol. 11: *The War of the Jewels: The Later Silmarillion*. Part 2. 1994.

Vol. 12: *The Peoples of Middle-earth*. 1996.

———. **The Hobbit; or, There and Back Again*. With illustrations by the author. (Orig. British pub. 1937.) Boston: Houghton Mifflin, 1988, © 1938.

———. *The Hobbit; or, There and Back Again*. Adapted by Charles Dixon with Sean Deming. Illus. by David Wenzel. New York: Eclipse Books/Ballantine, 1990. [Graphic novel.]

———. *The Letters of J. R. R. Tolkien*. Selected and ed. Humphrey Carpenter with the assistance of Christopher Tolkien. Boston: Houghton Mifflin, 1981.

———. **The Lord of the Rings*. 3 vols. (Orig. British pub. 1954.) Boston: Houghton Mifflin, 1988, © 1955; single-volume edition, 1988.

Vol. 1: *The Fellowship of the Ring*. 1988, © 1955.

Vol. 2: *The Two Towers*. 1988, © 1955.

Vol. 3: *The Return of the King*. 1988, © 1955.

———.**The Silmarillion*. Boston: Houghton Mifflin, 1983, © 1977.

———. *Smith of Wootton Major/Farmer Giles of Ham*. (Orig. British pubs. 1967, 1949.) New York: Ballantine/Del Rey, 1991.

———. *A Tolkien Reader*. New York: Ballantine/Del Rey, 1989, © 1966.

———. *Unfinished Tales*. Ed. Christopher Tolkien. Boston: Houghton Mifflin, 1980, 1982.

The Tolkien Legacy in America

Ursula K. Le Guin's Men and Women of Earthsea

Le Guin, Ursula K. *The Earthsea Quartet*. New York: Atheneum.
Vol. 1: *A Wizard of Earthsea*. 1991, © 1968.
Vol. 2: *The Tombs of Atuan*. 1985, © 1971.
Vol. 3: *The Farthest Shore*. 1985, © 1972.
Vol. 4: *Tehanu: The Last Book of Earthsea*. 1990.
———. *The Wind's Twelve Quarters: Seventeen Stories of Fantastic Adventure*. New York, HarperPaperbacks, 1995, © 1975.

The Magic Kingdoms of Terry Brooks: Responsibility and Choice

Brooks, Terry. *The Sword of Shannara* Trilogy. 3 vols. New York: Ballantine/Del Rey.
Vol. 1: *The Sword of Shannara*. Illustrated by The Brothers Hildebrandt. (Simultaneously published with Random House.) 1977.
Vol. 2: *The Elfstones of Shannara*. Illustrated by Darrell K. Sweet. 1982.
Vol. 3: *The Wishsong of Shannara*. Illustrated by Darrell K. Sweet. 1985.
———.*The Heritage of Shannara* Quartet. 4 vols. New York: Ballantine/Del Rey.
Vol. 1: *The Scions of Shannara*. 1990.
Vol. 2: *The Druid of Shannara*. 1991.
Vol. 3: *The Elf Queen of Shannara*. 1992.
Vol. 4: *The Talismans of Shannara*. 1993.
———.*Prequel: *The First King of Shannara*. New York: Ballantine/Del Rey, 1996.
———.*The Magic Kingdom of Landover* Series. 5 vols. New York: Ballantine/Del Rey.
Vol. 1: *Magic Kingdom for Sale—Sold!* 1986.
Vol. 2: *The Black Unicorn*. 1987.
Vol. 3: *Wizard at Large*. 1988.
Vol. 4: *The Tangle Box*. 1994.
Vol. 5: *Witches' Brew*. 1995.
———.*Hook*. Based on a screenplay by Jim V. Hart and Malia Scotch Marmo; screen story by Jim V. Hart and Nick Castle. New York: Fawcett Columbine, 1991.
———.*"Imaginary Friends." In *Once Upon a Time: A Treasury of Modern Fairy Tales*. Ed. Lester del Rey and Risa Kessler. New York: Ballantine/Del Rey, 1991.

————.*Running with the Demon.* New York: Ballantine/Del Rey, 1997.
Cole, Corey and Lori Cole. *Shannara: The Official Strategy Guide.* Rocklin, Calif.: Prima Publishing, 1996.

Ordinary Heroes: American Fantasy until the Millennium

Feminist Fantasists

Bradley, Marion Zimmer. **Hawkmistress! Darkover* Series. New York: DAW, 1982.
Hambly, Barbara. **The Sun Wolf* Trilogy. 3 vols. New York: Ballantine/Del Rey.
  Vol. 1: *The Ladies of Mandrigyn.* 1984.
  Vol. 2: *The Witches of Wenshar.* 1987.
  Vol. 3: *The Dark Hand of Magic.* 1990.
Lackey, Mercedes, and Piers Anthony. **If I Pay Thee Not in Gold.* New York: Baen, 1993.
Lackey, Mercedes, and Marion Zimmer Bradley. **Darkover: Rediscovery.* New York: DAW, 1993.
Lackey, Mercedes, Marion Zimmer Bradley, and Andre Norton. **Tiger Burning Bright.* New York: Avon, 1995.
Lackey, Mercedes, and C. J. Cherryh. **Reap the Whirlwind.* New York: Baen, 1989.
Lackey, Mercedes, and Andre Norton. **The Halfblood Chronicles.* 2+ vols. New York: Tor.
  Vol. 1: *The Elvenbane.* 1991.
  Vol. 2: *Elvenblood.* 1995.
Lackey, Mercedes. **Bardic Voices.* 4 vols. New York: Baen.
  Vol. 1: *The Lark and the Wren.* 1992.
  Vol. 2: *The Robin and the Kestrel.* 1993.
  Vol. 3: *The Eagle and the Nightingale.* 1995.
  Vol. 4: *Four and Twenty Blackbirds.* 1997
Lackey, Mercedes, and Josepha Sherman. **Bardic Choices.* New York: Baen.
  Vol. 1: *A Cast of Corbies.* 1994.
Lackey, Mercedes. **The Valdemar Sequence.* New York: DAW. *[In timeline order.]*
  The Mage Wars. Coauthor Larry Dixon. 3 vols.
    Vol. 1: *The Black Gryphon.* 1994.
    Vol. 2: *The White Gryphon.* 1995.
    Vol. 3: *The Silver Gryphon.* 1996.
  The Last Herald Mage Trilogy. 3 vols.
    Vol. 1: *Magic's Pawn.* 1989.
    Vol. 2: *Magic's Promise.* 1990.
    Vol. 3: *Magic's Price.* 1990.

Vows and Honor. 2 vols.
    Vol. 1: *Oathbound.* 1988.
    Vol. 2: *Oathbreakers.* 1989.
By the Sword. 1991.
The Heralds of Valdemar Trilogy. 3 vols.
    Vol. 1: *Arrows of the Queen.* 1987.
    Vol. 2: *Arrow's Flight.* 1987.
    Vol. 3: *Arrow's Fall.* 1988.
Mage Winds. 3 vols.
    Vol. 1: *Winds of Fate.* 1991.
    Vol. 2: *Winds of Change.* 1992.
    Vol. 3: *Winds of Fury.* 1993.
    Mage Storms. 3 vols.
    Vol. 1: *Storm Warning.* 1994.
    Vol. 2: *Storm Rising.* 1995.
    Vol. 3: *Storm Breaking.* 1996.
Owlflight. 1997.
Sword of Ice and Other Tales of Valdemar. Ed. Mercedes Lackey. 1997.
McKillip, Patricia A. *The Star-Bearer Trilogy.* 3 vols. New York: Ballantine/Del Rey.
    Vol. 1: *The Riddle-Master of Hed.* 1989, © 1976.
    Vol. 2: *Heir of Sea and Fire.* 1989, © 1977.
    Vol. 3: *Harpist in the Wind.* 1989, © 1979.
———. *The Cygnet* Series. 2 vols. New York: Ace.
    Vol. 1: *The Sorceress and the Cygnet.* 1991.
    Vol. 2: *The Cygnet and the Firebird.* 1993.
McKinley, Robin. *The Damar* Series. 2 vols, more forthcoming. New York: Greenwillow.
The Blue Sword. 1982.
Prequel: *The Hero and the Crown.* 1984.
Pierce, Tamora. *Song of the Lioness Quartet.* 4 vols. New York: Atheneum. Random House paperback set, 1997.
    Vol. 1: *Alanna: The First Adventure.* 1983.
    Vol. 2: *In the Hand of the Goddess.* 1984.
    Vol. 3: *The Woman Who Rides Like a Man.* 1986.
    Vol. 4: *Lioness Rampant.* 1988.
———. *The Immortals.* 4 vols. New York: Atheneum.
    Vol. 1: *Wild Magic.* 1992.
    Vol. 2: *Wolf-Speaker.* 1994.
    Vol. 3: *The Emperor Mage.* 1995.
    Vol. 4: *The Realms of the Gods.* 1996.

————. *Circle of Magic.* [2 vols. +.] New York: Scholastic.
   Vol. 1: *Sandry's Book.* 1997.
   Vol. 2: *Tris's Book.* 1998.
Smith, Sherwood. *The Crown and Court Duet.* 2 vols. San Diego: Harcourt Brace.
   Vol. 1: *Crown Duel.* 1997.
   Vol. 2: *Court Duel.* 1998.

The Epic Proportions of Heroic Fantasy

Alexander, Lloyd. *The Westmark Trilogy.* 3 vols. New York: Dutton.
   Vol. 1: *Westmark.* 1981.
   Vol. 2: *The Kestrel.* 1982.
   Vol. 3: *The Beggar Queen.* 1984.
Anthony, Piers. *Magic of Xanth* Series. 21 vols. Vols 1–9: New York: Ballantine/Del Rey. Vols. 10–15: New York: Avon. Vols. 16–21: New York: Tor.
   Vol. 1: *A Spell for Chameleon.* 1977.
   Vol. 2: *The Source of Magic.* 1979.
   Vol. 3: *Castle Roogna.* 1979.
   Vol. 4: *Centaur Aisle.* 1981.
   Vol. 5: *Ogre, Ogre.* 1982.
   Vol. 6: *Night Mare.* 1982.
   Vol. 7: *Dragon on a Pedestal.* 1983.
   Vol. 8: *Crewel Lye.* 1984.
   Vol. 9: *Golem in the Gears.* 1986.
   Vol. 10: *Vale of the Vole.* 1987.
   Vol. 11: *Heaven Cent.* 1988.
   Vol. 12: *Man from Mundania.* 1989.
   Vol. 13: *Isle of View.* 1990.
   Vol. 14: *Question Quest.* 1991.
   Vol. 15: *The Color of Her Panties.* 1992.
   Vol. 16: *Demons Don't Dream.* 1993.
   Vol. 17: *Harpy Thyme.* 1994.
   Vol. 18: *Geis of the Gargoyle.* 1995.
   Vol. 19: *Roc and a Hard Place.* 1995.
   Vol. 20: *Yon Ill Wind.* 1996.
   Vol. 21: *Faun and Games.* 1997.
Anthony, Piers, and Jody Lynn Nye. *Piers Anthony's Visual Guide to Xanth.* Illus. Todd Cameron Hamilton and James Clouse. New York: Avon, 1989.
Bemmann, Hans. *The Stone and the Flute.* Trans. Anthea Bell. (Orig. German pub. 1983.) New York: Viking, 1987.

Chetwin, Grace. *Child of the Air*. New York: Bradbury, 1991.

—. *The Chimes of Alyafaleyn*. New York: Bradbury, 1993.

—. *Tales of Gom in the Legends of Ulm*. 4 vols. Vol. 1: New York: Lothrop, Lee & Shepard. Vols. 2–4: New York: Bradbury.

Vol. 1: *Gom on Windy Mountain*. 1986.

Vol. 2: *The Riddle and the Rune*. 1987.

Vol. 3: *The Crystal Stair*. 1988.

Vol. 4: *The Starstone*. 1989.

Downer, Ann. *The Spellkey* Trilogy. 3 vols. New York: Atheneum.

Vol. 1: *The Spellkey*. 1987.

Vol. 2: *The Glass Salamander*. 1989.

Vol. 3: *The Books of the Keepers*. 1993.

Eddings, David. *The Belgariad*. 5 vols. New York: Ballantine/Del Rey.

Vol. 1: *Pawn of Prophecy*. 1982.

Vol. 2: *Queen of Sorcery*. 1982.

Vol. 3: *Magician's Gambit*. 1983.

Vol. 4: *Castle of Wizardry*. 1984.

Vol. 5: *Enchanter's End Game*. 1984.

—. *The Mallorean*. 5 vols. New York: Ballantine/Del Rey.

Vol. 1: *Guardians of the West*. 1987.

Vol. 2: *King of the Murgos*. 1988.

Vol. 3: *Demon Lord of Karanda*. 1988.

Vol. 4: *Sorceress of Darshiva*. 1989.

Vol. 5: *Seeress of Kell*. 1991.

—. *The Elenium*. 3 vols. New York: Ballantine/Del Rey.

Vol. 1: *The Diamond Throne*. 1989.

Vol. 2: *The Ruby Knight*. 1990.

Vol. 3: *The Sapphire Rose*. 1992.

—. *The Tamuli*. 3 vols. New York: Ballantine/Del Rey.

Vol. 1: *Domes of Fire*. 1993.

Vol. 2: *The Shining Ones*. 1993.

Vol. 3: *The Hidden City*. 1994.

—, and Leigh Eddings. *Prequels to *The Belgariad. 2 vols. New York: Ballantine/Del Rey.

Vol. 1: *Belgarath the Sorcerer*. 1995.

Vol. 2: *Polgara the Sorceress*. 1997.

Goodkind, Terry. *The Sword of Truth*. 4 vols. New York: Tor.

Vol. 1: *Wizard's First Rule*. 1994.

Vol. 2: *Stone of Tears*. 1995.

Vol. 3: *Blood of the Fold*. 1996.

Vol. 4: *Temple of the Winds*. 1997.

Jones, Diana Wynne. *Archer's Goon*. New York: Greenwillow, 1984.

—. *Castle in the Air*. New York: Greenwillow, 1992.

————. *The Dalemark Quartet*. 4 vols. Vols. 1–3: New York: Atheneum.
Vol. 4: New York: Greenwillow.
   Vol. 1: *Cart and Cwidder*. 1977, © 1975.
   Vol. 2: *Drowned Ammet*. 1978, © 1977.
   Vol. 3: Prequel: *The Spellcoats*. 1979.
   Vol. 4: *The Crown of Dalemark*. 1995.
————. *Homeward Bounders*. New York: Greenwillow, 1981.
————. *Howl's Moving Castle*. New York: Greenwillow, 1986.
————. *Sudden Wild Magic*. New York: Greenwillow, 1993.
Jordan, Robert. *The Wheel of Time Saga*. 7 vols. New York: Tor.
   Vol. 1: *The Eye of the World*. 1990.
   Vol. 2: *The Great Hunt*. 1990.
   Vol. 3: *The Dragon Reborn*. 1991.
   Vol. 4: *The Shadow Rising*. 1992.
   Vol. 5: *The Fires of Heaven*. 1993.
   Vol. 6: *Lord of Chaos*. 1994.
   Vol. 7: *A Crown of Swords*. 1996.
Jordan, Robert, and Teresa Patterson. *World of Robert Jordan's The Wheel of Time*. Illus. Todd Cameron Hamilton. New York: Tor, 1997.
Jordan, Sherryl. *Winter of Fire*. New York: Scholastic, 1993.
Kelleher, Victor. *Brother Night*. New York: Walker, 1991.
————. *The Red King*. New York: Dial, 1990.
Kerr, Katharine. *The Deverry* Series. 4 vols. New York: Doubleday.
   Vol. 1: *Daggerspell*. 1986.
   Vol. 2: *Darkspell*. 1987.
   Vol. 3: *The Bristling Wood*. 1989.
   Vol. 4: *The Dragon Reverant*. 1990.
————. *The Westlands* Series. 5 vols. Vols. 1–2: New York: Doubleday.
Vols. 3–5: New York: Bantam.
   Vol. 1: *A Time of Exile*. 1991.
   Vol. 2: *A Time of Omens*. 1992.
   Vol. 3: *Days of Blood and Fire*. 1993.
   Vol. 4: *Days of Air and Darkness*. 1994.
   Vol. 5: *Red Wyvern*. 1997.
Keyes, J. Gregory. *Chosen of the Changeling* Series. 2 vols. New York: Ballantine/Del Rey.
   Vol. 1: *The Waterborn*. 1996.
   Vol. 2: *The Blackgod*. 1997.
Kurtz, Katherine. *The Chronicles of Deryni*. 5 vols. New York: Ballantine/Del Rey.
   Vol. 1: *Deryni Rising*. 1970, 1976.
   Vol. 2: *Deryni Checkmate*. 1972, 1976.

Vol. 3: *High Deryni*. 1973, 1982.

Vol. 4: *Deryni Magic*. 1991.

Vol. 5: Prequel stories: *The Deryni Archives*. 1986.

―――. *The Legends of Camber of Culdi*. 3 vols. New York: Ballantine/ Del Rey.

Vol. 1. *Camber of Culdi*. 1976.

Vol. 2: *Saint Camber*. 1978.

Vol. 3: *Camber the Heretic*. 1980.

―――. *The Histories of King Kelson*. 3 vols. New York: Ballantine/Del Rey.

Vol. 1: *The Bishop's Heir*. 1984.

Vol. 2: *The King's Justice*. 1985.

Vol. 3: *The Quest for Saint Camber*. 1986.

―――. *The Heirs of Saint Camber*. 3 vols. New York: Ballantine/Del Rey.

Vol. 1: *The Harrowing of Gwynned*. 1989

Vol. 2: *King Javin's Year*. 1992.

Vol. 3: *The Bastard Prince*. 1994.

Lynn, Elizabeth A. *The Chronicles of Tornor*. 3 vols. New York: Ace.

Vol. 1: *Watchtower*. 1979.

Vol. 2: *The Dancers of Arun*. 1979.

Vol. 3: *The Northern Girl* 1980.

MacAvoy, R. A. *A Trio for Lute*. 3 vols. New York: Bantam.

Vol. 1: *Damiano*. 1983.

Vol. 2: *Damiano's Lute*. 1984.

Vol. 3: *Raphael*. 1984.

―――. *The Nazhuret Saga*. 3 vols. New York: Morrow.

Vol. 1: *The Lens of the World*. 1990.

Vol. 2: *King of the Dead*. 1991.

Vol. 3: *The Belly of the Wolf*. 1994.

Matas, Carol, and Perry Nodelman. *Minds* Series. 2 vols. New York: Simon & Schuster.

Vol. 1: *Of Two Minds*. 1995.

Vol. 2: *More Minds*. 1996.

Mayhar, Ardath. *Soul-Singer* Series. 2 vols. New York: Atheneum.

Vol. 1: *Soul-Singer of Tyrnos*. 1981.

Vol. 2: *Runes of the Lyre*. 1982.

Nix, Garth. *Sabriel*. New York: HarperCollins, 1996.

Pratchett, Terry. *Discworld* Series. 19 vols. Vols. 1–2: New York: St. Martin's. Vols. 3–12: New York: NAL/Penguin. Vols. 13–19: New York: HarperPrism.

Vol. 1: *The Colour of Magic*. 1983.

Vol. 2: *The Light Fantastic*. 1986.

Vol. 3: *Equal Rites*. 1987.

Vol. 4: *Mort*. 1987.
Vol. 5: *Sourcery*. 1988.
Vol. 6: *Wyrd Sisters*. 1988.
Vol. 7: *Pyramids*. 1989.
Vol. 8: *Guards! Guards!* 1989.
Vol. 9: *Eric*. 1990.
Vol. 10: *Moving Pictures*. 1990.
Vol. 11: *Reaper Man*. 1991.
Vol. 12: *Witches Abroad*. 1991.
Vol. 13: *Small Gods*. 1992.
Vol. 14: *Lords and Ladies*. 1994.
Vol. 15: *Soul Music*. 1995.
Vol. 16: *Men at Arms*. 1996.
Vol. 17: *Feet of Clay*. 1996.
Vol. 18: *Interesting Times*. 1997.
Vol. 19: *Maskerade*. 1997.

Shettle, Andrea. *Flute Song Magic*. New York: Avon, 1990.

Snyder, Zilpha Keatley. *Green Sky Trilogy*. 3 vols. New York: Atheneum.
Vol. 1: *Below the Root*. 1975.
Vol. 2: *And All Between*. 1976.
Vol. 3: *Until the Celebration*. 1977.

Tarr, Judith. *The Hounds of God Cycle*. 5 vols. Vol. 1: New York: Bluejay.
Vols. 2–3: New York: St. Martin's. Vols. 4–5: New York: Doubleday.
Vol. 1: *The Isle of Glass*. 1985.
Vol. 2: *The Golden Horn*. 1985.
Vol. 3: *The Hounds of God*. 1986.
Vol. 4: *Alamut*. 1989.
Vol. 5: *The Dagger and the Cross*. 1991.

———. *Avaryan Rising*. 5 vols. Vol. 1: New York: Bluejay. Vols. 2–5: New York: Tor.
Vol. 1: *The Hall of the Mountain King*. 1986.
Vol. 2: *The Lady of Han-Gilen*. 1987.
Vol. 3: *A Fall of Princes*. 1988.
Vol. 4: *Arrows of the Sun*. 1993.
Vol. 5: *Spear of Heaven*. 1994.

Turner, Megan Whelan. **The Thief*. New York: Greenwillow, 1996.

Voigt, Cynthia. **The Kingdom* Series. 3 vols. Vols. 1–2: New York: Atheneum. Vol 3: New York: Scholastic.
Vol. 1: *Jackaroo*. 1985.
Vol. 2: *On Fortune's Wheel*. 1990.
Vol. 3: *The Wings of a Falcon*. 1993.

Weis, Margaret, and Tracy Hickman. *The Death Gate Cycle*. 7 vols. New York: Bantam.

Vol. 1: *Dragon Wing*. 1990.
Vol. 2: *Elven Star*. 1990.
Vol. 3: *Fire Sea*. 1992.
Vol. 4: *Serpent Mage*. 1993.
Vol. 5: *The Hand of Chaos*. 1993.
Vol. 6: *Into the Labyrinth*. 1993.
Vol. 7: *The Seventh Gate*. 1994.
Williams, Tad. *Memory, Sorrow and Thorn Trilogy*. 3 vols. New York: DAW.
Vol. 1: *The Dragonbone Chair*. 1988.
Vol. 2: *Stone of Farewell*. 1990.
Vol. 3: *To Green Angel Tower*. 1993.
Zambreno, Mary Frances. **Jermyn* Series. 2 vols. San Diego: Harcourt Brace.
Vol. 1: *A Plague of Sorcerers*. 1991.
Vol. 2: *Journeyman Wizard*. 1994.

Selected Bibliography

Terry Brooks

Primary Sources

The Sword of Shannara Trilogy. 3 vols. New York: Ballantine/Del Rey.
Vol. 1: *The Sword of Shannara*. Illus. The Brothers Hildebrandt. (Simultaneously published with Random House.) 1977.
Vol. 2: *The Elfstones of Shannara*. Illus. Darrell K. Sweet. 1982.
Vol. 3: *The Wishsong of Shannara*. Illus. Darrell K. Sweet. 1985.
The Heritage of Shannara Quartet. 4 vols. New York: Ballantine/Del Rey.
Vol. 1: *The Scions of Shannara*. 1990.
Vol. 2: *The Druid of Shannara*. 1991.
Vol. 3: *The Elf Queen of Shannara*. 1992.
Vol. 4: *The Talismans of Shannara*. 1993.
Prequel: *The First King of Shannara*. New York: Ballantine/Del Rey, 1996.
The Magic Kingdom of Landover Series. 5 vols. New York: Ballantine/Del Rey.
Vol. 1: *Magic Kingdom for Sale—Sold!* 1986.
Vol. 2: *The Black Unicorn*. 1987.
Vol. 3: *Wizard at Large*. 1988.
Vol. 4: *The Tangle Box*. 1994.
Vol. 5: *Witches' Brew*. 1995.

Hook. Based on a screenplay by Jim V. Hart and Malia Scotch Marmo; screen story by Jim V. Hart and Nick Castle. New York: Fawcett Columbine, 1991.

"Imaginary Friends." In *Once Upon a Time: A Treasury of Modern Fairy Tales*. Ed. Lester del Rey and Risa Kessler. New York: Ballantine/ Del Rey, 1991.

Running with the Demon. New York: Ballantine/Del Rey, 1997.

Secondary Sources

Achiron, Marilyn, and Nick Gallo. "Laying Down the Law." *People* (10 May 1993): 53–54.

"Brooks, Terry." In *Something about the Author*. Vol. 60. Ed. Agnes Garrett and Helga P. McCue, 15. Detroit: Gale Research, 1990.

Francisco, Daniel. "An Interview with Terry Brooks." In Corey Cole and Lori Cole, *Shannara: The Official Strategy Guide*. Rocklin, Calif.: Prima Publishing, 1996, 169–79.

Herbert, Frank. "Some Arthur, Some Tolkien." *The New York Times Book Review* (10 April 1977): 15, 25.

Johnson, David P. "Terry Brooks." In *Authors and Artists for Young Adults*. Vol. 18. Ed. Thomas McMahon. Detroit: Gale Research, 1996, 33–38.

MacRae, Cathi Dunn. Interview with Terry Brooks. Boulder, Colorado, 7 May 1994.

Watson, Christine. *"The Sword of Shannara."* In *Survey of Modern Fantasy Literature*. Vol. 4. Ed. Frank N. Magill. Englewood Cliffs, N.J.: Salem Press, 1983, 1866–68.

Winters, Louise J. "Brooks, Terry." In *Twentieth Century Young Adult Writers*. Ed. Laura Standley Berger. Detroit: St. James Press, 1994, 80–81.

Otherworld Foundations: Before We Heard of Tolkien

Swinfen, Ann. *In Defence of Fantasy*. London: Routledge & Kegan Paul, 1984.

English Inklings and Weird American Barbarians

De Camp, L. Sprague. "The Miscast Barbarian: Robert E. Howard." In de Camp, *Literary Swordsmen and Sorcerers: The Makers of Heroic Fantasy*. Sauk City, Wis.: Arkham House, 1976, 135–77.

Hartwell, David G. "Dollars and Dragons: The Truth about Fantasy." *The New York Times Book Review* (29 April 1990): 1.

J. R. R. Tolkien: Founder of Modern Heroic Fantasy

Carpenter, Humphrey. *Tolkien: A Biography*. New York: Ballantine/Del Rey, 1978.

Collins, David R. *J. R. R. Tolkien: Master of Fantasy*. Minneapolis: Lerner, 1992.

De Camp, L. Sprague. "Merlin in Tweeds: J. R. R. Tolkien." In de Camp, *Literary Swordsmen and Sorcerers: The Makers of Heroic Fantasy*. Sauk City, Wis.: Arkham House, 1976, 215–51.

Lawler, Donald L. "Tolkien, John Ronald Reuel." In *Twentieth Century Science Fiction Writers*. 3d. ed. Ed. Noelle Watson and Paul E. Schellinger. Chicago: St. James Press, 1991, 798–801.

McKinley, Robin. "J. R. R. Tolkien." In *Writers for Children: Critical Studies of Major Authors Since the Seventeenth Century*. Ed. Jane Bingham. New York: Scribner's, 1988, 561–71.

Niemark, Anne E. *Myth Maker: J. R. R. Tolkien*. San Diego: Harcourt Brace, 1996.

Tolkien, J. R. R. "On Fairy-stories." In *Tree and Leaf*. London: Allen & Unwin, 1964.

The Tolkien Legacy in America

Egoff, Sheila A. "The New Fantasy." In Egoff, *Thursday's Child: Trends and Patterns in Contemporary Children's Literature*. Chicago: American Library Association, 1981.

Paxson, Diana. "The Tolkien Tradition." *Mythlore* 39 (Summer 1984): 23–27, 37.

Ursula K. Le Guin's Men and Women of Earthsea

Le Guin, Ursula K. "Dreams Must Explain Themselves." In *Language of the Night: Essays on Fantasy and Science Fiction*. New York: Putnam, 1979, 47–56.

———. "The Last Book of Earthsea." *Locus* (January 1990): 5.

Lenz, Millicent. "Ursula K. Le Guin's *The Tombs of Atuan:* Moving Toward Completion." In *The Phoenix Award of the Children's Literature Association, 1990–1994*. Ed. Alethea Helbig and Agnes Perkins. Lanham, Md.: Scarecrow Press, 1996, 93–99.

Welton, Ann. "Earthsea Revisited: *Tehanu* and Feminism." *Voice of Youth Advocates* (April 1991): 14–16, 18.

Feminist Fantasists

Altmann, Anna E. "Welding Brass Tits on the Armor: An Examination of the Quest Metaphor in Robin McKinley's *The Hero and* the Crown." *Children's Literature in Education* 23.3 (1992): 143–56.

Henderson, Helene. "Mercedes Lackey." In *Authors and Artists for Young Adults.* Vol. 13. Ed. Kevin S. Hile and E. A. Des Chenes. Detroit: Gale Research, 1994, 95–101.

MacRae, Cathi. "McKillip, Patricia A(nne)." In *Twentieth Century Science Fiction Writers.* 3d. ed. Ed. Noelle Watson and Paul E. Schellinger. Chicago: St. James Press, 1991, 546–48.

McKillip, Patricia A. "Moving Forward." *Locus* (August 1992): 5, 69.

McKinley, Robin. "Newbery Medal Acceptance." *Horn Book Magazine* (July/August, 1985): 395–405.

"McKinley, Robin." In *Authors and Artists for Young Adults.* Vol. 4. Ed. Agnes Garrett and Helga P. McCue. Detroit: Gale Research, 1990, 193–202.

Spivack, Charlotte. "Patricia McKillip." In *Merlin's Daughters: Contemporary Women Writers of Fantasy.* Westport, Conn.: Greenwood Press, 1987, 113–26.

Taylor, Rebecca, Gayle Keresey, and Margaret Miles. "Interview with Mercedes." *Voice of Youth Advocates* (October 1992): 213–17.

White, Donna R. "McKillip, Patricia A." In *Twentieth Century Young Adult Writers.* Ed. Laura Standley Berger. Detroit: St. James Press, 1994, 441–42.

Winters, Louise J. "Lackey, Mercedes R." In *Twentieth Century Young Adult Writers.* Ed. Laura Standley Berger. Detroit: St. James Press, 1994, 369–70.

The Epic Proportions of Heroic Fantasy

Cule, Michael. "Eddings, David." In *Twentieth Century Science Fiction Writers.* 3d. ed. Ed. Noelle Watson and Paul E. Schellinger. Chicago: St. James Press, 1991, 233–34.

D'Ammassa, Don. "Anthony, Piers." In *Twentieth Century Science Fiction Writers.* 3d. ed. Ed. Noelle Watson and Paul E. Schellinger. Chicago: St. James Press, 1991, 12–14.

3. Magic Realism:
Magic Here, There, and Everywhere

Uncovering magic in our everyday world, magic realism fantasies explore the inexplicable lurking beneath the surface. In its most simple form, magic realism happens right here on earth. R. A. MacAvoy's *Tea with the Black Dragon* is a realistic detective story, but detective Mayland Long is actually an ancient Chinese dragon in disguise. Such realistic tales with magical elements, recently labeled "contemporary fantasy," are discussed in this chapter under "Earthbound Magic."

A new type of magic realism has appeared with the recent popularity of fantasy role-playing games such as Dungeons and Dragons. Entire families of stories take place in worlds springing from games. Other stories concern fantasy gameplayers, ordinary young people who get so involved in the imagined world that fantasy infringes on reality. Because so many fantasy gamers are young adults, some were surveyed for this chapter's "Fantasy Gaming" section.

In the most familiar magic realism, travelers leave our "Primary World" for a "Secondary World," to use Tolkien's terms. A gateway usually marks the boundary between worlds, as in the following landmarks.

Gateway Magic: "There and Back Again"

The subtitle of Tolkien's *Hobbit,* "There and Back Again," aptly describes magic realism journeys. A sea voyage was the earliest route, in Jonathan Swift's English literary classic *Gulliver's*

Travels. Published in 1726 as political satire, this tale of a sailor shipwrecked amid miniature Lilliputians and other mythic folk is often adapted for children.

Still beloved in its delightful original language is *Alice's Adventures in Wonderland,* published in 1865 by Lewis Carroll, actually a British clergyman and mathematician named Charles Dodgson. Based on the real Alice Liddell, the fictional Alice follows a White Rabbit down a rabbit hole, where nothing is as it seems. Odd characters such as the Mad Hatter babble nonsense, and Alice herself expands and shrinks. In the 1871 sequel, *Through the Looking-Glass,* Alice again enters a fantasy land, this time striving to become queen, which is symbolic of growing up. Carroll's whimsical wordplay challenges the logic that controls our lives. The *Alice* books are masterpieces in which everyone recognizes his or her own transformation. They have inspired remakes from Disney and others since. An Australian aboriginal Alice appears in a 1992 picture book, *Alitji in Dreamland,* by Nancy Sheppard, and the original Alice is transported to a 1998 postmodern alternative English city of Manchester in Jeff Noon's *Automated Alice.*

The endless childhood of Peter Pan inspired a modern label for childlike adults. Introducing Peter in an 1892 novel, *The Little White Bird,* its Scottish author, Sir J. M. Barrie, produced *Peter Pan* as a play in 1904, then as a novel in 1911. When Peter Pan teaches three children to fly from their London nursery to Never-Never-Land, they need not grow older but must face the dreaded pirate Captain Hook. Despite the timeless appeal of escaping to another world to stop time, children must mature. Steven Spielberg's 1991 film *Hook* updates Peter as a burned-out lawyer, played by Robin Williams; the film was novelized by Terry Brooks (see chapter 2).

Barrie's contemporary, L. Frank Baum, who created magic realism's American prototype, is called "the founding father of American fantasy."[1] In *The Wizard of Oz,* ordinary Dorothy is whisked by a tornado from Kansas to Oz, where she encounters fantastical beings. On the way to the Emerald City to ask the wizard to send her home, Dorothy grows by confronting Oz's outlandish happenings. From 1900 until his death in 1919, Baum wrote 14 Oz books;

other authors continue to produce sequels—there are over 30 to date—which are still enjoyed by middle grade readers. Oz stays alive through endless screenings of the classic 1939 MGM film and by reincarnating into new forms, including a comics series and a prequel to Baum's Oz, the adult novel *Wicked: The Life and Times of the Wicked Witch of the West* by Gregory Maguire.

Oxford professor C. S. Lewis's renowned *Chronicles of Narnia* adds Christian allegory to fantasy adventure. It opened in 1950 when four children enter the world of Narnia through a wardrobe in *The Lion, the Witch, and the Wardrobe,* and was acclaimed as "a powerful novel that contains some of the most poignant and moving episodes in contemporary fantasy."[2] The series continued with six sequels in which the children's embroilment with magical creatures battling for control of Narnia mirrors their progress toward control of their own lives. In this fantasy for all ages, young readers may simply enjoy the adventure, though some critics claim they intuitively perceive its deeper layers (Tymn et al., 29). Never condescending, Lewis elegantly blends pagan and Christian myth with sensitivity for the human condition. The Narnia books may be the most widely read fantasies today; many more teen respondents to a fantasy survey had read Lewis than Tolkien.[3]

Four different young siblings slip into Alan Garner's *Elidor* while exploring a ruined church in an urban demolition area. When Elidor's dimension bleeds into theirs, the Watson children must fulfill a prophecy to restore its wasteland. Full of sibling rivalry and slang, *Elidor*'s immediacy appeals to younger YA readers despite its '60s British setting. Garner's pioneer use of physics in exchanges between worlds shows Elidor's events "reflected in some way, at some time" here.[4]

By contrast, Andre Norton's nearly 20 *Witch World* books place visitors from our world in its reality immediately, from which there is no return. An Ohio children's librarian, Norton began her *Witch World* series in 1963 with a six-volume sequence featuring Simon Tregarth. Evading modern earthly pursuers, Tregarth enters, through an Arthurian stone, "that existence in which his spirit . . . is at home,"[5] leading battles between a feudal matriarchal society of "white" witches and invaders in air ships.

Norton's "science fantasy," a blend of fantasy and science fiction, subordinates technology to magic. Mixing science fantasy and Mickey Spillane (Tymn et al., 153), further titles are loosely connected. Other authors' stories set in Witch World appear in two volumes of *Tales of the Witch World* (Tor, 1989, 1991). Norton, who also writes other magic realism, has declined in popularity with young adults.

The distinctive flavor of American magic realism was seasoned by "major new talent" Stephen R. Donaldson in the *Chronicles of Thomas Covenant the Unbeliever* (Tymn et al., 74). Deserted by his wife and child when he contracts leprosy, modern antihero Thomas is struck by a car, awakening in the Land without his leprosy. Throughout six long chronicles, published from 1977 to 1983, Thomas travels back and forth from home to otherworld, overcoming his cynicism to achieve healing of body and spirit.

Healing is often the point of an otherworld visit. In *The Neverending Story* by Michael Ende, a fat boy alienated from his father and schoolmates escapes into reading. The world Fantastica within his book is so real that Bastian literally enters it, becoming its savior and emerging to reconcile with his father. This 1979 German tale became a worldwide best-seller and film. In *The Dream of the Stone* by Christina Askounis, Sarah likewise soothes her grief for her dead parents, by using an Alice-inspired looking glass to save a world infected with earthly evil.

In Piers Anthony's *Virtual Mode,* suicidal teenager Colene's bleak reality changes when she falls in love with Darius, a king from another dimension whom she rescues from mugging. Like Thomas Covenant, Colene loses everything through disbelief when Darius returns home without her. Searching for him on a telepathic horse, Colene crosses 5,000 realities daily, braving dangers in each mode. When Colene reunites at last with Darius, her suicidal tendencies are gone. The series continues with *Fractal Mode* and *Chaos Mode.* In this magic realism for the '90s, Anthony bases Colene's depressive character on a composite of teens who have written to him. Moving among countless modes gives Anthony immense scope for the inventiveness that has won him throngs of teenaged fans; Colene's redemptive love story engages them further. YAFE Anthony fan Adam Chapin, 18, declares *Virtual Mode* Anthony's best work, having read it innumerable times.

Anthony also completed *Through the Ice,* an unfinished novel by Robert Kornwise, a Michigan youth who died in a car accident at 16. When Seth, a boy much like Robert, falls through an icy Michigan lake, he awakens on the magical Earth Plane 4, where he must battle evil threatening four linked earth planes. Did Robert Kornwise foresee his own death, keeping himself alive on another plane? Such is the power of magic realism.

In Terry Brooks's five-volume series *The Magic Kingdom of Landover,* lawyer Ben Holiday buys a magic kingdom from a Christmas catalog for $1 million, leaving his empty city life behind for the throne of Landover, which is entered through the Virginia mountains. There he finds healing for his grief over his dead wife through the challenges of ruling Landover, marriage with the sylph Willow, and the birth of their magically gifted daughter. This series is explored with the study of Terry Brooks in chapter 2.

When protagonists return from otherworlds to live more wholly here, their passage is powerfully symbolic for youth, who may find more "gateway" titles in this chapter's Recommended Reading. Magic realism also operates in myths in chapter 4 and time travel in chapter 7.

Many thoughtful voyages "there and back again" are made by Barbara Hambly, an author of adult fantasies embraced by teenagers searching, with her characters, for a place to belong.

Barbara Hambly: Bridging Two Worlds

Chronology: Barbara Hambly's Life and Works

1951   Barbara Joan Hambly born August 28 in San Diego, second daughter of Florence Elizabeth Hambly and Everett Edward Hambly Jr., a master sergeant in the marines.

1952   Family moves to naval base housing in China Lake, in the Mojave Desert.

Barbara Hambly
Photo by Kinky

1955   Family moves to Montclair, California; parents work for General Dynamics.

1956   Barbara begins composing fantasy tales.

1967   Family is transferred temporarily to New South Wales, Australia.

1969   Barbara graduates from Montclair High School.

1971   Begins a year abroad at University of Bordeaux in France.

1973   Receives bachelor's degree in medieval history from University of California–Riverside.

1975   Earns master's degree in history at UC–Riverside.

1977   Returns to UC–Riverside for teacher training. Begins first novel, *The Time of the Dark*.

1978   Achieves black belt in karate. Becomes publications coordinator for General Dynamics.

1981   Del Rey Books buys *The Time of the Dark* just as General Dynamics layoff occurs.

1982   *The Time of the Dark* (*Darwath* 1) is published. Suffers knee injury in karate.

1983   *The Walls of Air* (*Darwath* 2), *The Armies of Daylight* (*Darwath* 3), and *The Quirinal Hill Affair* are published. Retires from karate, moves to Ontario, California.

1984   *The Ladies of Mandrigyn* (*Sun Wolf* 1) is published.

1985   *Dragonsbane* named Best Book for Young Adults by American Library Association. Publishes first *Star Trek* novel, *Ishmael*. Writes television scripts. Moves to Venice, California.

1986   *The Silent Tower* (*Windrose* 1) is published.

1987   *The Witches of Wenshar* (*Sun Wolf* 2) is published. Buys a house in Los Angeles.

1988   Publishes *The Silicon Mage* (*Windrose* 2). *Those Who Hunt the Night* becomes ALA Best Book for Young Adults.

1989   *Beauty and the Beast* novelization is published. *Those Who Hunt the Night* wins Locus Horror Award.

1990   *The Dark Hand of Magic* (*Sun Wolf* 3) and *Song of Orpheus* (*Beauty/Beast* 2) are published.

1991   *The Rainbow Abyss* (*Sun-Cross* 1), *Star Trek* novel *Ghost-Walker,* and short story "Changeling" are published.

1992   Publishes *The Magicians of Night* (*Sun-Cross* 2). Awarded French Prix Verlanger for *Dragonsbane*.

1993   *Dog Wizard* (*Windrose* 3) is published.

1994   Publishes *Bride of the Rat God, Star Trek* novel *Cross-road,* short story "The Little Tailor and the Elves," and *Stranger at the Wedding (Windrose* 4), which is listed as ALA Best Book for Young Adults.

1995   Publishes *Star Wars* novel *Children of the Jedi* and vampire sequel *Traveling with the Dead.* Edits *Sisters of the Night* short-story anthology, including her "Madeleine."

1996   Publishes *Star Wars* novel *Planet of Twilight,* Sandman short story "Each Damp Thing," and *Mother of Winter (Darwath* 4).

1997   Publishes *A Free Man of Color.*

1998   Publishes *Icefalcon's Quest (Darwath* 4).

> I am fascinated by the diversity of humankind and human reactions to stress. I write what I like to read: how people handle different situations, how people get themselves into trouble and out again, how people grow up different and can still find love and friendship and help.
>
> I write about heroes rather than anti-heroes, about love rather than selfishness, about triumph and healing rather than existential despair.
>
> —Barbara Hambly, from personal interview

Since she was only four years old, Barbara Hambly has used other worlds as arenas for adventure stories about heroes with authentic human concerns. When her older sister Mary Ann could not sleep, little Barbara entertained her with stories she made, borrowing from Dr. Seuss, *The Jungle Books,* Sherlock Holmes, and such cartoon characters as Colonel Bleep and Q. T. Hush. Eventually the sisters evolved their own "vast, jungly morass of plot and character," says Barbara.[6] Many stories took place in her magical realm the Islands. Though the Islands never appear in her adult work, "for a writer," Barbara Hambly asserts, "nothing is ever wasted."

Born in San Diego in 1951, Barbara soon moved with her family to naval base housing in the Mojave Desert, where her father was a master sergeant in the marines. Just before Barbara began storytelling, the Hamblys, now including her younger brother, moved to Montclair, California. Both parents worked in aerodynamics at General Dynamics in Pomona.

Barbara continued to write in high school—stories about the Beatles, characters from the television spy show *The Man from U.N.C.L.E.,* and the brand-new *Star Trek.* Could she have guessed that she would grow up to publish *Star Trek* novels? As a teenager scribbling "fan writing," Barbara never showed her work to anyone. The year she was 16, her family was temporarily transplanted to Blaxland, a small town in the Blue Mountains of New South Wales, Australia. That first experience of another world on this planet awakened Barbara's abiding interest in travel, expanding the worlds in her stories.

Until graduating from Montclair High School in 1969, "I was socially inept and a laughingstock," she says, "with reason—I was a rather weird child and teenager—but even then I could write very well, and the English teachers praised and encouraged me. This doesn't help, I might add, when you're having obscenities written on your locker, strange stories circulated about you among your classmates, and are being picked on for no reason you can determine. But as I took refuge in my fantasies and continued writing, at least I got lots of practice."

During her college years at the University of California–Riverside, Barbara did not forsake her writing. She switched her major from English to medieval history, enjoying her junior year abroad at the University of Bordeaux in France. As soon as she earned her bachelor's degree in 1973, Barbara began her master's degree at UC–Riverside, which she received in 1975 after working as a teaching assistant. Yet her degree still did not lead to her goal of teaching college history, so she worked part-time as a clerk at Stop 'n' Go Market, as a model, and as a secretary.

As a graduate student in 1974, Barbara became so deeply involved in karate training that she stopped writing for four years. Just before achieving her black belt in 1978, Barbara returned to writing to find it "had changed radically." Now she wrote with a view toward publication. Having returned to UC–Riverside in 1977 for teacher training, Barbara was student-teaching high school social studies and reading when she began her first novel, *The Time of the Dark*. "I wrote the basic outline in three weeks, working night and day. By the end of that three weeks I knew that I could never be a teacher. The rest of the year I was miserable. I would have crying jags daily because I just . . . couldn't see any way out. Then I'd go home and write all night."[7]

But Barbara was in luck. California spending cuts "made it obvious that I wasn't going to get hired as a teacher, and my father got me a job at General Dynamics as coordinator of in-house publications, where I was able to finish *Time of the Dark*." One publisher rejected it, but Ballantine/Del Rey suggested she rework it as a trilogy. After Barbara sent her revision to Ballantine in 1981 with outlines of the rest of *The Darwath Trilogy,* she "signed the contract for the trilogy literally three days" before a layoff ended her General Dynamics job.

In 1982, the year her first novel was published, Barbara injured her knee ligaments during karate training. Having no health insurance, she failed to get treatment, which forced her retirement from karate. That training had been "absolutely invaluable for writing action adventure," she says, "simply because in our society, women frequently are not put under combat conditions, certainly not taught to think calmly under that kind of stress. It taught me more than I was comfortable knowing about my own aggressiveness; it taught me how groups of men and groups of women deal with fighting; it taught me about leadership and trusting one's instincts."

Back to part-time modeling and shelving library books, Barbara continued writing *The Darwath Trilogy,* her first work of magic realism, which moved from her native southern California to the fantasy world of Darwath. In 1983, between volume 2, *The Walls of Air,* and volume 3, *The Armies of Daylight,* she strayed beyond fantasy, writing *The Quirinal Hill Affair* (St. Martin's Press), a historical mystery set in ancient Rome. Reissued in paperback, its title became *Search the Seven Hills* (Ballantine, 1987).

After moving to Ontario, California, Barbara stayed entirely within an otherworld in her next fantasy, *The Ladies of Mandrigyn* (1984), in which mercenary soldier Sun Wolf trains a band of female warriors to free their menfolk from an evil wizard's slavery. The *Sun Wolf* series, "separate stories about the same folks in the same universe, which can be read independently of each other," also includes *The Witches of Wenshar* (1987) and *The Dark Hand of Magic* (1990), discussed in chapter 2.

Featuring a dragonslayer from her childhood tales, *Dragonsbane* became Barbara's first Best Book for Young Adults, a 1985 honor from the American Library Association. In chapter 6, her distinctive dragon Morkeleb is compared to other mind-merging dragons.

Since Barbara was still unable to make a living from royalties, she wrote television animation scripts for *Jayce and the Wheeled Warriors, Mask Force, She-Ra Princess of Power, Centurions,* and *Star Com.* It was "during the big boom in 'action-adventure' shows, most of which concerned vehicles sold as toys—in other words, the scripts were 22-minute commercials for the toys, interrupted by actual commercials for the toys," Barbara explains. Pursuing this animation work, she moved to Venice, California, the same year her first *Star Trek* novel, *Ishmael* (Pocket Books, 1985), was published. In a later relationship with television, Barbara wrote modern fairy tale novelizations *Beauty and the Beast* (1989) and *Song of Orpheus* (1990), based on scripts of the popular 1987–89 romantic TV series created by Ron Koslow. Here her otherworld is beneath New York City, unknown to those above, where labyrinthine underground caverns shelter the Tunnelfolk, misfits from our world. The "Beast" from the fairy tale is Vincent, a deformed lionlike man who falls in love with beautiful lawyer Catherine when he rescues her from a brutal attack. Through her wounds, she shares his deformity—but only briefly, until she heals. Here is Hambly's most realistic treatment of the mask of the inner self, beauty within the beast. The only magic is love.

Barbara now publishes one or two books each year and no longer works odd jobs. By 1987, she was able to buy a house in Los Angeles. Ten years later, she lives half-time there and half-time in New Orleans. She works on "whatever book I have the most 'story' for"; usually she has five or six book ideas layered in her mind, some more developed than others. She is as comfortable writing historical mysteries as she is writing fantasy and *Star Trek* science fiction.

Her second magic realism series, *The Windrose Chronicles,* began with a two-parter, *The Silent Tower* (1986) and *The Silicon*

Mage (1988); the third chronicle, *Dog Wizard* (1993), is a related stand-alone, as is the fourth, *Stranger at the Wedding* (1994), which became an ALA Best Book for Young Adults in 1995. *Sun-Cross,* her third magic realism series, is a two-parter containing *The Rainbow Abyss* (1991) and *The Magicians of Night* (1992). All three magic realism series, through *Darwath*'s fourth title, *Mother of Winter* (1996), are dissected later in this chapter.

In 1988, Barbara Hambly crossbred historical mystery with horror in *Those Who Hunt the Night* (Ballantine), an atmospheric vampire detective story of Edwardian London, a setting inspired by her early fondness for Sherlock Holmes. This ALA Best Book for Young Adults stands up to the best of the vampire genre. Its sequel *Traveling with the Dead* (Ballantine, 1995) moves across Europe as a British agent tracks vampires conspiring with Austrian spies on the brink of World War I. As a history scholar, she sees history as "enormous fun, an escape rather than a lesson." Another historical mystery, *Bride of the Rat God* (Ballantine, 1994), which is set in 1923 Hollywood, features a beautiful silent film star stalked by what Hambly describes as a "giant Manchurian rat-demon, which is only visible to her three Pekineses." Her most recent in the genre, *A Free Man of Color* (Ballantine, 1997), illuminates a shadowy era in the rocky history of American race relations when a dark-skinned Creole surgeon from Paris is suspected of murdering an octoroon beauty in 1830s New Orleans.

Star Trek novels are also a regular undertaking. Besides *Ishmael,* Hambly wrote *Ghostwalker* (Pocket Books, 1991), a "ghost story on board the *Enterprise,*" and *Crossroad* (Pocket, 1994), based on stories she wrote as a teenager about visitors from the future. She moved on to the *Star Wars* series with *Children of the Jedi* (Bantam, 1995) and *Planet of Twilight* (Bantam, 1997).

Hambly used her vampire expertise to edit a short story collection about female vampires with veteran compiler Martin H. Greenberg, *Sisters of the Night* (Warner, 1995), which included her own story "Madeleine." *VOYA* reviewer Donna Scanlon colorfully describes the story about a "cold-hearted consumer of sleek young men . . . cursed to hear the voices of her victims."[8]

Another rare Hambly short story is "Changeling," in Lester del Rey's *Once Upon a Time: A Treasury of Modern Fairy Tales*

(1991). Her ordinary reluctant hero, Brown Michael, reminiscent of John in *Dragonsbane*, finds a speechless two-year-old girl in a dragon's cave with two odd companions whom he soon realizes must come from another world. "The Little Tailor and the Elves," in Jane Yolen's anthology *Xanadu 2* (1994), recasts the fairy tale in a bleak modern city where Iris, the abused wife of an embittered tailor, makes an ancient pact with the elves that ultimately saves her. Yet even magic barely elevates Iris's narrow world. Hambly's most recent story, "Each Damp Thing," appears in *The Sandman Book of Dreams* (HarperPrism, 1996), in which many authors set tales in Neil Gaiman's *Sandman* comics world of the Endless. Hambly's story takes place in the Dreaming, where dead mortals such as the biblical Cain and Abel endlessly repeat the actions of their lives—including Cain's killing of Abel—under the watchful eye of the immortal named Dream. It is not for the fainthearted, as it reflects Hambly's Lovecraftian fondness for horrific monsters.

Now that she is a professional writer, Barbara Hambly explains that her daily routine

> depends largely on what stage of a book I'm in, and what's going on in my life that specific day. I try every day, when I get up, to pray, meditate, take a shower, feed the dogs, eat breakfast, and take a walk. I'll usually do shopping or errands in the morning as well, then have lunch and settle down for work. On first draft, I'll sometimes work as little as two hours a day, usually more like four, and take lots of naps. First draft is very tiring.
>
> Second draft—the actual heavy shovel-work of building a story—I'll work four to six hours a day. By the time I get to doing rewrites by hand, and inputting those into the computer, I'm working eight and sometimes ten hours a day, with breaks for meals and walks.

Part of Barbara's work also happens at about eight science fiction conventions each year. Sometimes she is guest of honor, but she also attends on her own, meeting colleagues and fans and soaking up new places and people that may become stories. When she is working on a historical mystery, she might visit its location for atmosphere and detail; in New Orleans she combed old maps and drawings to help her depict its antebellum period for *A Free Man of Color*.

Barbara Hambly's vivid descriptions of place and atmosphere feel real because travel brings her experiences of "snow and Gulf-coast tropical heat, European street smells, and truly startling plumbing arrangements. I was having trouble picturing the Wizards' College in *Dog Wizard* until I went to Telegraph Hill in San Francisco. When I was writing about the city of Mandrigyn, I pictured Venice, Italy."

When creating characters, Barbara Hambly relies on her intense curiosity and habit of "keeping an open mind to the people around me." Her astuteness in delineating character extends to herself. Here is her sketch of Barbara Hambly, perceived with acute honesty:

> Physically I am on the short side of average, and after a long, bitter, and daily struggle, of normal weight. I spent my life fat and still tend to think of myself that way.
>
> My eyes are blue and nearsighted behind round John Lennon glasses, my hair is very short and dishwater blond. I have a lot of old acne scars. I don't consider myself particularly pretty, but I'm not bad for forty plus. I have small hands and feet, and have trouble buying shoes and gloves; I tend to clump around in jeans and Birkenstock sandals. Because of my constant typing, my nails are short and unpainted. I don't stand out in a crowd unless I'm dressed up, but for business I do tend to be a bit of a clotheshorse. I've been told I have nice cheekbones. My voice is just below a soprano and naturally very loud, so I try to keep it as soft as possible.
>
> It's my instinct to back off and think for a day or two about anything I'm asked to do before saying yes or no; I don't trust other people to drive my car; I am both sentimental and cynical—not by turns but simultaneously, both rational and superstitious. I am a compulsive overeater. I have a terrible temper which I keep very tightly controlled for fear of hurting someone with it. I tend to get very attached to places I live, and I have a strong taste for the grotesque and the absurd: gargoyles, majolica-ware, British humor.

Beyond writing and traveling, Barbara Hambly has little time for her favorite hobbies of painting and sewing. She is famous for the inventive costumes she creates for SF conventions, described by her fellow fantasy writer Diana Paxson: "[T]here's the Renaissance mercenary, the Demon-Hunter, the pirate, the zaftig baroque masterpiece in silver and shell-pink, and her rendition of the Queen of Hell, which combines sexy and sinister."[9] But what she most enjoys doing is "simply spending time with a few close friends." She also relaxes with her Pekinese dogs, Nicholas and Kismet, "who are very dear to me."

Of course, reading has been not only a favorite lifelong activity but an influence in Barbara Hambly's writing. She mined Heinlein, Tolkien, and Lovecraft for her science fiction and fantasy writing, Mary Renault and Georgette Heyer for historical fiction, and Josephine Tey and Dorothy L. Sayers for her mysteries. Barbara Hambly sees her current reading as "idiosyncratic," including "George MacDonald Fraser, George Alec Effinger, Tony Hillerman, some but not all Tanith Lee, James Lee Burke, Tim Powers, and isolated works *Gone With the Wind, Tai-Pan,* Sutcliff's *Sword at Sunset,* Le Guin's *Earthsea* trilogy." In her 1996 introduction to *The Road to Madness,* a collection of H. P. Lovecraft stories, Hambly cited Lovecraft as "*the* major influence on my own writing." Having started reading Lovecraft at 16, she confesses: "Every year or so I go on a Lovecraft binge, devouring story after story the way a glutton sits in a corner devouring cookies. Then I associate with those persons of more elevated tastes and feel a little ashamed of myself. But I meet the eyes of other Lovecraft addicts, and we smile."[10] Hambly's love of lush language and her ability to project ordinary people—both characters and readers—into nightmare realities beyond our own must be Lovecraft inspired, but these elements are so much classier in her hands than in his.

The Magic Realism of Barbara Hambly

Of all the genres in which Barbara Hambly has written, she returns most often to magic realism, in fantasies that begin in our familiar world, move into an otherworld, and sometimes move back again. "I find the archetype of traveling from this universe to another fascinating," Hambly says, "and have done so since its great archetype *The Wizard of Oz.* It is also the theme of the Burroughs *Mars* series, another favorite."

Readers of her three magic realism series, *Darwath, The Wind-rose Chronicles,* and *Sun-Cross,* notice that although each visits a different universe, travel arrangements are the same, through a Gate Between Worlds, across the Void, a curtain separating universes. At the beginning of Hambly's first magic realism novel, *The Time of the Dark,* a wizard explains to an astonished Californian that "there exists an infinite number of parallel universes, meshed in the matrix of the Void."[11]

Says Hambly, "I have a mental image of the Cosmos as mentioned in the Void stories, but I feel it would bring any story to a dead halt if I stopped to explain it." Readers piece tantalizing hints of Hambly's Void together throughout her work. "I want to know more about how the Void looks and feels," complained YAFE Dylan Burns, age 12, desperate to find the sequel to *The Rainbow Abyss.* In this *Sun-Cross* series, even Jaldis, the only wizard who can find the Void, catches only "glimpses . . . of worlds whose natures . . . are incomprehensible to me: ships that whirled flashing between stars; clouds of terrible . . . power, drifting eternally in the Abyss."[12]

In the first Void story, Ingold, the only Darwath wizard who knows the Void, shows it to a visitor through a crystal: "like bubbles in shining solution, gold spheres were . . . circling one another in the slow patterns of an unknowable dance, . . . revealing stars, galaxies, ages—cosmic vistas of something that was neither space nor time."[13] Each sphere is a separate universe.

In *The Silent Tower,* the first *Windrose Chronicle,* the Void is a "black and endless hollow, an abyss that seemed to swallow time itself," evoking "hideous nightmare fear."[14] By the series' third volume, *Dog Wizard,* uncontrolled gate openings create roving energy fields, involving a physicist from yet another universe. Through this perilous avenue, "abominations" from other universes can enter. By the third Void series, a harmless trip has become toxic, from a world of magic to a world without. Rhion remembers little "except the terror, and the cold that drank at his life in a single, greedy draught" (*Rainbow,* 293).

With Hambly, readers explore the Void from one book to the next, speculating about our otherworld connections. Even her

Sun Wolf series, set entirely in its own world, mentions the Hole Between Worlds. Facing unimaginable dangers, Void travelers survive by tapping those stress reactions that fascinate Hambly.

The Darwath Series

In the complex *Darwath Trilogy,* Hambly introduces the themes and character types that continually entrance her. In the opening novel, *The Time of the Dark,* Gil Patterson is a 24-year-old Ph.D. candidate in medieval history at UCLA, dreaming vividly about a city under attack in a world much like the past she studies. One night Gil awakes to find a figure from her dreams sitting at her kitchen table, a shabby old man in a homespun robe, who introduces himself as the wizard Ingold. He has crossed into Gil's world to ask her to shelter the baby Prince Altir.

When Ingold brings the baby to Gil through a brilliant curtain in the desert, biker Rudy Solis is an accidental witness. A vicious creature following Ingold sends them all back through the Void to hazardous Darwath, where monsters devour people alive. These alien Dark Ones have hidden underground since their invasion in the "Time Before," 3,000 years ago. Forced to stay in Darwath to keep the Dark from following them home, Gil becomes a warrior, and Rudy falls in love with the prince's widowed mother, Alde, as his mageborn talents awaken. Taking refuge in the massive Keep of Dare, constructed in the Time Before to withstand the Dark, survivors suffer a power struggle between the prince's regent, the wizards, and the church. Says *Library Journal:* "Heart-stopping adventures" in *The Time of the Dark* "enthrall the reader, as newcomer Hambly spins an unusually effective sword-and-sorcery fantasy.[15]

In the second volume, *The Walls of Air,* Ingold and his student Rudy fruitlessly journey to the ruined Wizard's City of Quo, seeking a way to defeat the Dark. While they are gone, researcher Gil combs the Keep's depths for clues to how its creators once held back the Dark. *Library Journal* names the Dark as "the most evil creations since Stephen Donaldson's Lord Foul, and the brisk action and atmosphere of ever-present menace keeps the reader deeply involved."[16]

In the final volume of the trilogy, *The Armies of Daylight,* Ingold himself is carried off by the Dark during a nightmare raid of their nests. Tension builds until the trilogy's triumvirate, Rudy, Gil, and Ingold, finally confront the Dark, each other, and their inner selves. Choosing to stay in Darwath to pursue their new callings, Gil pairs off with Ingold, and Rudy gets his Alde, as in a satisfying Shakespeare play. "The story moves to a grimly plausible climax with the same intelligent characterization, sound storytelling, and creative use of magic that distinguished . . . the first two volumes of the series," says *Booklist.*[17]

Thirteen years after completing the trilogy, Hambly returned to the Keep of Dare in *Mother of Winter* to pick up its story five years after the Dark Ones are vanquished. Ice storms are raging, and a fungus called slunch is devouring every living thing in the land. Ingold and Gil search for the source of this destruction in the south, leaving Rudy as the only wizard in the Keep, where factional rivals react to these ancient unknown magical attacks, somehow centered in ice mages who serve the Mother of Winter. *VOYA* notes that "action is sustained to the very end with a cast of believable, engaging characters. Hambly's writing is excellent; her imagery brings the ancient maze-like Keep and its residents to life."[18] Hambly's Darwath has become a classic otherworld, honored by artist Wayne Douglas Barlowe with a painting of the unspeakable Dark One in his *Barlowe's Guide to Fantasy* (HarperCollins, 1996). The fifth *Darwath, Icefalcon's Quest,* was published in 1998.

YAFEs on *The Darwath Series*

Though I had trouble understanding the motivations of the characters at the beginning, my sympathy for them grew as the trilogy progressed. I liked Hambly's meticulous descriptions of how magic works. *The Armies of Daylight* is one of the very best fantasy books I have ever read, because it was so intense, it wrapped me up completely. It was very suspenseful when the protagonists got into situations which seemed impossible to get out of—it wasn't predictable, like many other fantasies. Those unexpected turns of the plot are the major reason I'll continue reading Hambly.

—Naomi Perera, 16

Hambly's originality is refreshing. She didn't follow any of the normal fantasy patterns. The thing I enjoyed most in the entire *Darwath Trilogy* was the intelligence and being of the Dark. It wasn't the everyday magical enemy. It was a more vast intelligence serving their lifestyle that simply clashed and represented evil in our world. I found Ms. Hambly's writing style very intriguing and beautiful. Her descriptions were vivid, characters strong, and story magnificent. She has become the only rival to my favorite writer, Anne McCaffrey.

—Sara McCorkendale, 17

The Time of the Dark

The Dark reminded me of bedtime stories, of fearing the darkness under my bed or in my closet. I wish Hambly had provided more solid description. I never knew exactly what the Dark was, or where exactly the setting was, or exactly what the people were doing and why. Still, I liked the thrilling parts when characters are in a tight fix. Gil and Rudy had courage and faith; they adapted to the otherworld.

—Melissa Tolve, 17

The Windrose Chronicles

Hambly intricately weaves thematic threads from *The Darwath Trilogy* into *The Windrose Chronicles,* controlling the three-volume loom with breathlessly suspenseful pacing. In *The Silent Tower* our world is again Hambly's own southern California, where 26-year-old computer programmer Joanna Sheraton prefers machines to people. Working late in the deserted systems complex, Joanna is knocked unconscious by a dark robed figure. She awakens in a stone chamber, where two men rescue her, explaining that her unknown captor carried her through the Void to the Empire of Ferryth, which is on the brink of industrial revolution. With straggly beard, earrings, and tawdry beads hanging over an unkempt gown, her older rescuer, Antryg Windrose, swears he is a powerful mage. He cannot send Joanna home because such magic would alert other wizards to his whereabouts, unknown since his escape from the Silent Tower. Behind his cracked spectacles, Antryg's eyes glitter with madness. How can Joanna trust his absurd claims?

Joanna never trusts men as gorgeous as her other rescuer, young warrior Caris, who accuses Antryg of kidnapping his grandfather, the Archmage Salteris. Stranded with these squabbling strangers, Joanna tramps a wintry countryside afflicted with "abominations," devouring monsters slipping through an open Void gate. Antryg speculates that the dead Darkmage Suraklin, the only one besides himself who could operate the Gate, has resurrected within the Archmage Salteris's body, capturing Joanna when using her company computer's energy. Only Joanna's computer expertise can stop Suraklin from taking ultimate power.

Readers are swept through a labyrinth of plot as crafty as the Darkmage, playing detective with the characters, constantly shifting perceptions about whether Antryg can be trusted and about Suraklin's scheme. By the time they chase Suraklin across the Void to California, Joanna has fallen in love with Antryg, only to face his treachery. The Darkmage lives within her beloved Antryg, not Salteris, and Joanna must send him back to Ferryth for execution. *Library Journal* credits Hambly with demonstrating "once more her skill at building worlds rich in magic, atmosphere, and inhabitants.[19]

In a brilliant opening line, the sequel, *The Silicon Mage,* reverses Joanna's conclusions: "The worst thing about knowing that Gary Fairchild had been dead for a month was seeing him every day at work."[20] The Darkmage inhabits not Antryg but her old boyfriend Gary. Joanna must destroy his computer programs and return to Ferryth to stop Antryg's execution. *Booklist* calls *The Silicon Mage* an "intelligent, literate, and generally superior fantasy" that "develops some extremely original concepts."[21]

After the Dead God, a physicist Void expert from another universe, becomes Antryg's unlikely savior, Joanna and Antryg live happily ever after in California, until Joanna is kidnapped by another robed figure in *Dog Wizard,* the first book using the series name *The Windrose Chronicles.* Forced to track Joanna to Ferryth, where he is a wanted man, Antryg is waylaid by the Council of Wizards, who demand his help to close a Gate letting abominations into their Citadel. Since Antryg is condemned, he undergoes painful spells that nullify his powers.

Worse, someone is trying to murder Antryg, and he can find no trace of Joanna. Despite the Dead God's stabilizing energy with computer scanners, the Citadel is propelled into the Void, where it will implode within hours. Just when there seems no way out, our intrepid duo makes it back to L.A., where Antryg's last line proves he will never be free of Ferryth. "Extremely well written, *Dog Wizard* is packed with adventure, mystery, and love," says *VOYA*. It is "a story that all young adults will enjoy."[22]

In *Stranger at the Wedding,* a stand-alone Ferryth sequel without Antryg and Joanna, female wizard Kyra the Red is promoted from her minor status in *Dog Wizard*. Estranged from her family by her study at the Citadel of Wizards, Kyra returns home when a dream foretells her younger sister Alix's death on her wedding night. Weathering family disapproval, Kyra solves the mystery of the curse on her sister, with a typical Hambly twist and the triumph of love at the end. The "final pages have all the tension and action of a good thriller," says *Publishers Weekly*. "Kyra herself is a heroine in the Jane Eyre tradition, plucky, sharp-tongued, and iconoclastic; and like her prototype she finds herself increasingly drawn to a man who is outwardly attractive but nonetheless compelling."[23]

YAFEs on *The Silent Tower*

It was too confusing. I didn't understand it.
—Raymond Drummond, 15

It was pretty exciting all the way through. You wanted to find out who the evil dark mage was, and when you thought you knew, the story changed on you, telling you otherwise. It's almost a detective story. It's up there, one of my favorites.
—Melissa Tolve, 17

Sun-Cross

Instead of beginning in our world and moving elsewhere, Hambly's two-part *Sun-Cross* begins with *The Rainbow Abyss,* entirely within the Forty Civilized Realms, where wizards are persecuted.

According to *VOYA*, it is "just the sort of meticulously constructed, historically and magically reasonable world that [fans] have come to expect."[24] Since old wizard Jaldis the Blind's eyes and tongue were torn out, he sees through magic spectacles, speaking through a rosewood sound chamber. Jaldis is obsessed with voices from a Dark Well into the Void that he has opened but never explored, voices begging him to visit another universe to restore its lost magic. His apprentice, Rhion, must leave his lover, Tally, and their children to accompany Jaldis into the abyss, their only guide a beacon shaped like a sun-cross.

The second *Sun-Cross* volume, *The Magicians of Night,* opens as battered Rhion awakens to face Paul Von Rath, a wizard in a world without magic. Von Rath explains that his colleague Eric perished when pulling Rhion into his world, and Jaldis never arrived. The Dark Well has vanished; only the two dead wizards could construct it. Rhion is alone in an alien world where his magic may not work, with no way to return home. He has not heard of this land, Nazi Germany.

Rhion agrees to help harness magic to defeat Germany's enemies until he discovers Von Rath using death camp prisoners as sacrifices; Rhion becomes a hostage forced to advise his evil captors, Hitler's Occult Bureau. The sun-cross symbol of light that led Rhion through the Void is reversed on their uniforms, turning toward darkness—the swastika, of course. As mad Von Rath becomes "Satan in uniform" (*Magicians,* 331), two Americans, prostitute Sara and secret agent Tom Saltwood, become Rhion's unlikely accomplices against the Nazis.

In an author's note, Hambly apologizes for trivializing the Nazi Holocaust as a setting for fantasy. Yet her historian's sensibilities and Rhion's otherworld view expose the Nazis as "darkness masquerading as triumphant light" (*Magicians,* 214) in a unique contribution to Holocaust literature. This magic realism tale, which feels like time travel, is comparable to another Holocaust time fantasy, Jane Yolen's *The Devil's Arithmetic,* discussed in chapter 7. "Most notable," says *Booklist,* is *Magicians'* "vivid reconstruction of ordinary daily life in World War II Germany and of 1940s occultism. Certain to find readers among Hambly's many fans, this novel may also have a broader appeal to the readers of historical fantasy in general."[25]

YAFEs on *The Rainbow Abyss*

It was hard to get through, but I kept going because of Hambly's cool ideas.

—Dylan Burns, 12

Her style was better than usual, not so ponderous, but I would recommend it only to a few older readers.

—Sarah Luna, 17

I couldn't put it down. It is in the top group of fantasy that I've read.

—Vanessa Bowler, 17

The Void Connection: Themes between Worlds

In all the Void stories, otherworlds are held up as mirrors to ours; travelers between universes learn much about their own worlds. In the *Darwath* series, Gil and Rudy attain self-realization only outside their familiar world, where they develop new skills: hermit scholar Gil becomes a warrior, and "punk airbrush jockey" Rudy becomes a mage (*Walls,* 135). Coping with life-or-death decisions, they draw from inner resources. Refusing a chance to go home, they reject the aimless materialism of California life.

With scholarly discipline, Gil juxtaposes two worlds to reconstruct Darwath's past. Its religion, so like Christianity in the Middle Ages, seems "weirdly familiar, a confusing mirror to her medieval studies . . . oppressing her with the sense of dealing on two planes of reality."[26] Darwath also uses the same zodiac signs, "another unexplained transfer . . . across the Void" (*Walls,* 122). Such transfers between worlds allow Hambly's characters to forge their power.

In her *Windrose Chronicles,* Hambly makes more ambiguous judgments of the alignment between worlds. Instead of staying in the world of magic like Gil and Rudy, Antryg and Joanna move back and forth from Ferryth to California, one of them always in an alien world. When Joanna observes weary child laborers on their way to the Ferryth flax mills, she is taken aback, having expected something "more medieval" in this magical realm (*Tower,* 175). Breaking medieval fantasy conventions, Hambly uses Ferryth's exploitation of man for machines as commentary on our practice of doing so. Joanna sees Ferryth's "world, working to become what hers suddenly seemed to be—colorless, alienated, so impersonal that she herself could disappear and it would be days before her closest friend . . . knew she was even gone" (178).

Barbara Hambly constantly examines power's uses for both good and evil. Suraklin tells Antryg, "You know in your heart that there is nothing we would not do—*nothing*—to realize our power. We give up everything for it—our lovers, our parents, our homes . . . the children we might otherwise bear, the people we might otherwise be."[27] Hambly's wizards choose either corruption, with actual physical rotting for Suraklin in *Windrose* and Altiokis in her *Sun Wolf* alternate world fantasy, or service to others. Rhion sacrifices himself to stop the Nazis, as does Antryg to stop Suraklin, and Ingold to stop the Dark, while evil mages use human psychic energy to feed their power. The Council of Wizards in both *Darwath* and *Windrose* controls magic's temptations. Ingold confesses, "Wizards are not nice people. . . . Most of us are proud as Satan. . . . That's the reason for the Council. Something must exist to counterbalance the effects of the knowledge that you can, in fact, alter the paths of the universe" (*Walls,* 84).

In our magicless world, technology holds power. When looking through the rainbow abyss in the novel of the same name, Jaldis sees flying boats with metal wings and other "magic things without magic. . . . Things that can be used by anyone, for good or ill, . . . without the training or restraint of wizardry" (*Rainbow,* 93). So Hambly ties magic securely to the laws of physics. In *Sun-Cross*, Sara says, "What the hell do you think magic is supposed to be, if not the action of thought waves on the material world?" (*Magicians,* 251). Says Ingold in *Darwath*: "[W]hat makes magic possible [is] a change in the ways the laws of physics operate" (*Time,* 45).

Computer wizards in our world will be fascinated by connections between computers and magic in *The Windrose Chronicles.*

Joanna comments to Antryg: "You say magic is predicated on visualization and hope. With a computer, that's graphics and statistical projection. . . . But to write a series of programs that complex, you'd need . . . a programmer and a mage working together" (*Tower*, 320)—exactly what Suraklin does with Gary, programming a computer for his own immortality. Joanna declares:

> "a computer doesn't give a damn whether a thing is supposed to be able to exist or not . . ."
> "Rather like wizards," Antryg mused, "or madmen. Are all computers insane?" (*Silicon*, 284)

In all Hambly's fantasies, magic is a discipline revealing the nature of being. In *Darwath*, Rudy realizes that if he doesn't use the power he feels within, "nothing will mean anything. . . . It's the center of everything" (*Time*, 191). As Rudy struggles to make his new spells work, Ingold counsels, "The strength of your spells is the strength of your soul. . . . As you grow, your spells will grow also" (*Walls*, 201). To Antryg in *The Windrose Chronicles*, "Hope, and magic, both involve the casting forward of the soul. In a way, both magic and hope are a kind of madness" (*Tower*, 184). In summary, "Magic isn't a science . . . nor an art. . . . It's life itself" (*Silicon*, 240).

In *Sun-Cross*, Rhion studies wizardry as "the interweavings of all things in the physical world, the metaphysical, and the strange shadowland of ghosts . . . that lay between them—learning how . . . no alteration of the fabric of the world could be made without somehow affecting the rest of the universe" (*Rainbow*, 74). To Rhion, "magic was not something one did; it was something you were, ingrained in the deepest marrow of the soul" (75). Is Hambly suggesting that there is little spiritual meaning in our world, with magic missing?

From world to world, Hambly's concept of how magic works is consistent. In both Darwath and Ferryth, master-spells pass from Archmage to successor on the Archmage's death. Magic can be crippled in both worlds, by the Rune of the Chain in Darwath and by the Sigil of Darkness in Ferryth. Wizardry and organized religion stand opposed, through two severe shaven-headed female bishops, one in each world, and their Witchfinders (directly recalling our Inquisition), who serve the Straight God in Darwath and the Sole God in Ferryth. Similar patterns prevail in the Forty Realms.

The working of magic is an isolating practice; power sets one apart. So Hambly's lonely wizards seek support in human relationships. Hambly's fellow writer Diana Paxson points out the abiding Hambly theme of "ex-loners learning how to be friends," suggesting that Hambly's own experience among her peers at school prepared her to empathize with other loners (Paxson 1988). Hambly's misfits find each other—hence her popularity with teenagers, who often see themselves as outsiders. Her wizards are attracted to independent women from our world. Both Gil in *Darwath* and Joanna in *Windrose* don't expect to find male partners; there is literally no man in the world for them. But as their self-concepts are enhanced in otherworlds, they are drawn to the wizards with whom they work. Loving a wizard is a challenge, for wizards often sacrifice personal relationships. But Hambly plausibly brings together those who are often misunderstood, in mage/nonmage romances: Gil and Ingold, Rudy and Alde, Joanna and Antryg, Rhion and Tally, and beyond magic realism, Jenny Waynest and John Aversin in *Dragonsbane* and Starhawk and Sun Wolf in that series.

Hambly's formidable powers of description render even minor characters memorable. Her monsters are as gruesome as any in horror stories. Gil slashes the Dark, "dousing them both in a stream of foul and gritty black water that gushed from the wound. She saw ... crustaceous pincers and the long, sudden slash of a spined tail, coiling like a whip and thicker than a man's forearm" (*Walls*, 69). When Antryg and Joanna encounter the Dead God, "a tsunami of stench struck them first, overwhelming. Even the brief glimpse Joanna got of the thing was heart-shaking, a slobbering half-melted travesty of a face whose fangs, she realized, were broken-off ribs thrusting out from the corners of the rotting jaw. Bone showed where the flesh of two of the arms was falling off" (*Silicon*, 196).

Such descriptions are so grittily realistic that readers believe in them as Rudy believes Ingold, who makes "anything seem possible, even feasible" (*Time*, 237). Hambly's words skewer character: Caris was "handsome with the Nordic gorgeousness of a prince of fairy tales, save for a straight scar about an inch and a half long that marked a cheekbone straight out of a TV commercial for designer jeans" (*Tower*, 138). Doused with tangible sensation and atmosphere, readers feel the weather. Word wizard Hambly enjoys unfamiliar terms: *mephitic, phthalo, fulvid, purpuric, persiflage*—heaven for language lovers but heavy going for less competent readers.

Two symbols are inseparable from Hambly's evocative style. Mazes appear everywhere. Mazes in the Keep of Dare hide the secrets of the Time Before the Dark. Gil navigates the mazes of Darwath's lost history as well as mazelike riddles of the present crisis. And "between the two mazes of present and past lay a third maze, . . . a maze of memory" (*Walls*, 124), inherited memories of previous life in the Keep. Mazes of illusion protect the Wizards' City of Quo. In *Windrose*, Antryg maps the mazes in the vaults below the Citadel. Hambly's fantasy realms contain mazelike ley lines. Her image of the cosmos is a maze, as are her intricate plots, their mysteries leading readers through twists and turns and to dead ends. Flawlessly integrated into her plots, Hambly's mazes create riveting suspense.

Also flooding Hambly's work is imagery of light. Good and evil fantasy themes naturally call forth light and dark; Hambly's light is triumphant, stressing hope and optimism. When the Dark bang on the gate of Darwath's Keep, its defenders rush forward, "the bobbing of the torches and lamps in their hands like the storming of fireflies on a summer night" (*Walls*, 22). Antryg Windrose rarely appears without light glinting: "Dim daylight flicked along one spectacle rim, picked out the fracture in the glass and the facet of an earring" (*Silicon*, 155). When Tom Saltwood looks at the night sky through Rhion's magic Spiracle, he sees hints of Hambly's entire cosmos: "for a split second . . . half a galaxy of brightness, of tiny pinlights infinitely far away, seemed caught within that loop, an alternate firmament that had nothing to do with the one overhead" (*Magicians*, 289). At their best, Barbara Hambly's works shimmer with her vision of endless worlds spinning through the Void.

Though Hambly's plots are strong and action packed, plot-oriented YA readers may find her style muddling. YAFE Sam Walter, 15, a voracious fan of plot-heavy Piers Anthony and David Eddings, struggled to read Hambly, rarely getting beyond a few pages. This confusion is reflected in some of the YAFE comments and is rarely taken into account in critics' praise. Hambly's style appeals most to older girls who demand depth with adventure. Young adult readers are definite in their responses to Hambly's writing, feeling either affinity or little attraction at all. When Barbara Hambly does strike a chord in YA readers, it resounds deeply.

Earthbound Magic

People have often wondered if unseen forces in our mundane world are magic. Stories of mythical creatures, ghosts, and monsters embody our hopes and fears of the unknown. Earthbound magic also probes our inner motivations, revealing secrets of the spirit.

An author of "vast importance . . . to the history of fantasy" (Searles et al., 91), Edith Nesbit wrote in turn-of-the-century Britain about children encountering magic in their everyday lives. In *Five Children and It,* a grumpy psammead (sand fairy) grants wishes that come with hilarious consequences. Nesbit's gentle warning to be careful what you wish for is wreathed in such reassuring reality that her popularity has endured for generations. Nesbit was also one of the first to follow consistent rules of fantasy, unlike the madcap whims of her predecessors, such as Lewis Carroll (92).

Another British originator of earthbound fantasy was Oscar Wilde, whose wit lightened exposure of the soul. In 1891, *The Picture of Dorian Gray* showed its subject aging horribly while Dorian Gray himself squandered eternal youth in corruption, Peter Pan gone awry.

Naturalist W. H. Hudson made prophetic commentary on our disregard for nature in *Green Mansions,* a best-selling romance in

America from 1916 to 1923. After falling in love with a Venezuelan adventurer, primitive Rima tragically loses her magic jungle paradise. In *Lost Horizon,* published in 1933, James Hilton also questions modern progress. Those who want the secret of long life in Shangri-La, a Tibetan lamasery in the highest Himalaya, must forsake the outside world. And it is only in the Sahara Desert, stranded by a plane crash, that a pilot learns the truths of the universe from the small otherworldly traveler in *The Little Prince.* This illustrated 1943 French fable by Antoine Saint-Exupéry is still beloved by readers of all ages.

These few classics gave root to recent novels in which magic deepens life experience. For her first novel, *Tea with the Black Dragon,* R. A. MacAvoy won the John W. Campbell Best New Writer Award in 1984. This "charming little novel—part fantasy, part love story, part detective thriller,"[28] is counted among critic David Pringle's "Hundred Best" fantasies. In modern California, Asian Mayland Long helps Martha Macnamara find her missing daughter, who is involved in a computer scandal. But Long is no ordinary detective—he can master any language overnight and has astounding physical strength. An ancient Chinese dragon in disguise, he seeks understanding of humanity, which he continues to explore by investigating murder in *Twisting the Rope.*

Healing is paramount in a brutally realistic fantasy, Elizabeth Ann Scarborough's 1989 Nebula winner, *The Healer's War.* Lieutenant Kitty McCulley, an American nurse in the Vietnam War, receives an amulet from a dying Vietnamese holy man that enables her to see colored auras around living things. As she learns to interpret them, Kitty not only understands the bewildering human conflicts around her but eventually heals with her hands, saving her own life and others. Based on Scarborough's own Vietnam nursing experiences, Kitty's are as horrifying as any true account. Through Kitty, the amulet transmits spiritual power into the real world, thereby relieving human suffering and redeeming the spirit in what *Booklist* calls a "powerful, soulstirring . . . antiwar novel."[29]

Two respected YA novelists mix fantasy with realism to challenge young readers to rethink their own realities. In his complex masterpiece *Fade,* Robert Cormier illustrates our abuse of power in the ability of an adolescent boy to "fade," or become invisible. Convincing us that Paul truly fades, Cormier forces us to reshape reality. In a lighter vein, in Julian F. Thompson's *Herb Seasoning,* high school student Herbie samples careers from crime to public service by spinning a giant roulette wheel, then speeding off to try them in a magic Upwardlimobile.

Alongside more traditional and popular heroic or epic fantasy, earthbound stories of magic all around us are proliferating and have acquired a recent label, "contemporary fantasy." Declares *Publishers Weekly* in a 1997 update of the state of fantasy: "[C]ontemporary fantasy remains an area full of interesting experimentation and unusual approaches. Where traditional fantasy thrives on familiarity, the contemporary variety derives its energy from the unexpected, strange, and different." It is typified by a new series begun by Terry Brooks in *Running with the Demon,* "more like Stephen King than Tolkien,"[30] in which a teenaged girl in a small Illinois town battles the intrusion of demons with the help of an elf (see chapter 2). Other titles may be found in this chapter's Recommended Reading.

YAFEs on Earthbound Magic

MacAvoy—*Tea with the Black Dragon*

If you're tired of elves, fairies, and assorted ghouls, here is a refreshing break. Though it is solidly anchored in reality, it is very mysterious.

—Ben Cantrick, 16

It's enthralling. The incomparable mix of a modern world combined with old magics, along with original and intriguing characters, makes this book one of the most unusual and enjoyable fantasies I have ever read.

—Naomi Perera, 16

This book is beautiful and possible. It makes you think about your own morals. Are they what will hurt or heal you?

—Sarah Luna, 17

Thompson—*Herb Seasoning*

As you read a story of wonderful fun, it reveals ultimate good as the struggle to be willing to be involved in the world.

—Sarah Luna, 17

Fantasy Gaming

Since 1974, when Dungeons and Dragons was designed by Gary Gygax and Dave Arneson for TSR, Inc., role-playing games have become inextricably tied to fantasy literature. Blazing a trail through the intricacies of this "RPG" phenomenon, game creator Rick Swan's *Complete Guide to Role-Playing Games* reviews 166 games available in 1990. Indexed by subject, they include espionage, horror, and science fiction. Some, such as Marvel Superheroes (TSR, 1984), are based on comic books. Bullwinkle and Rocky (TSR, 1988) and Star Trek (FASA Corp., 1983) began as television shows, whereas Teenage Mutant Ninja Turtles (Palladium Books, 1985) is most famous as a movie. Some are original, such as Macho Women with Guns (Blacksburg Tactical Research Center, 1989), a funny game about Amazons.

Book Tie-ins to Game Worlds

Many games are set in literary worlds. The humorous Paranoia (West End Games, 1987) was inspired by both *Brave New World* and *1984*. Call of Cthulhu (Chaosium, Inc., 1989) brings H. P. Lovecraft's creatures to life; Conan (TSR, 1985) resurrects Robert E. Howard's barbarian. Thieves' World (Chaosium, 1981) is set in Robert Asprin's Sanctuary, whereas Pendragon (Chaosium, 1985) is Arthurian, allowing players to aspire to the Round Table. Shannara (Legend Entertainment, 1995) is a computer game based on the otherworld of Terry Brooks (see chapter 2).

Nearly one-quarter of all role-playing games are classified as fantasy. Which came first, the book or the game, the chicken or the egg? Games themselves are often presented as books, enormous manuals detailing every aspect of setting, characters, and rules of play.

Although Wendy and Richard Pini's *ElfQuest* graphic novels predated the related game, the two most well-known game-related novel series, DRAGONLANCE and FORGOTTEN REALMS, are both spin-offs from Advanced Dungeons and Dragons (TSR, Inc., 1979). Five years after the original Dungeons and Dragons was created, the advanced version appeared with more complicated rules, spawning many settings and "adventure module" supplements. DRAG-ONLANCE adventures were converted into novels in 1984 by Margaret Weis and Tracy Hickman. Their first series, *Dragonlance Chronicles,* was astoundingly successful, opening the game world to a more general public and remaining the touchstone for future game-to-novel conversions. DRAGONLANCE has "rich characters, vivid locales, and . . . [a] detailed story line . . . as charming as a fairy tale,"[31] according to game reviewer Rick Swan.

The *Chronicles* maintain a taut balance between reluctant hero Tanis Half-Elven, his elf and human sides conflicting, and anti-hero wizard Raistlin, torn by desires for power. With a band of companions, they fight to save their way of life in Krynn from threatening corruption. The three paperbacks *Dragons of Autumn Twilight, Dragons of Winter Night,* and *Dragons of Spring Dawning* were reprinted in a collectors' hardcover. In its introduction, authors Weis and Hickman reveal that "the most important part of the DRAGONLANCE Saga for us has been its characters and their relationships with one another."[32]

The consensus of the YAFE group was that along with great character development, Weis and Hickman provide "perfect balance between action and intrigue," earning their place as best of the many authors penning the 13 DRAGONLANCE series available through 1994. Six out of seven YAFE readers of the *Chronicles* gave it top ratings. However, Weis and Hickman "fell down a bit" on their only other DRAGONLANCE trilogy, *Legends.* Four YAFEs enjoyed it, but two others had identical reactions to each volume. For the latter, *Time of the Twins* was just "okay," *War of the Twins* was disliked, and the third, *Test of the Twins,* redeemed the series with a high rating.

Of the other 11 DRAGONLANCE series, each written by as many as six authors, only some attracted YAFE readers, who were generally unimpressed. With five readers, the *Heroes* trilogy was most widely read and received mixed reviews from "bad" to "excellent."

FORGOTTEN REALMS, the "setting of choice for experienced players" of Advanced Dungeons and Dragons, is "sprawling" in both games and novels (Swan, 27–28). Through 1994 it had spawned 11 novel series by many authors, R. A. Salvatore clearly outstanding among them. His three original paperback series were such best-sellers that his publisher, TSR, issued their first hardcover, Salvatore's *The Legacy,* in 1992.

Among YAFEs, Salvatore fans are legion. The group teases enthusiastic Dungeon Master Robin Deeter, 15, for considering Salvatore "a god," though Robin counters that he would have read his "boring-sounding" *Cleric Quintet* if he really thought that (not one YAFE read it). Salvatore's two trilogies, *Icewind Dale* and *Dark Elf,* were each awarded top marks by seven YAFEs. The Dark Elf Drizzt, who as a man of honor does not fit in with his evil people, is at the core of both trilogies. Exiled from other elves, in *Icewind Dale* Drizzt struggles to make his home in a harsh northern land of tundra amid distrusting humans, barbarians, an evil mage, and myriad monsters from goblins to yetis. *Dark Elf* is a prequel, explaining how Drizzt came to be exiled from his underground city.

Salvatore's work urges YA readers to venture into other works of FORGOTTEN REALMS. Yet the only series by other authors that YAFEs found superb was *The Finder's Stone Trilogy* by Kate Novak and Jeff Grubb. The few YAFEs sampling *Moonshae, Maztica,* and *Harpers* series found them uninspiring. Some series were not even attempted. Sam Walter points out that many such tie-ins are published to keep fans going and are not always worth much beyond escapist entertainment. To keep such fans stocked with this confusing wealth of material, DRAGONLANCE and FORGOTTEN REALMS series, current through 1994, are listed in this chapter's Recommended Reading. Those who order these books should note that their publisher, TSR, merged with Wizards of the Coast in 1997, moving from Wisconsin to Seattle.

The computer role-playing game The Bard's Tale (Electronic Arts) captured hot author Mercedes Lackey to write series books with different coauthors. In the first, *Castle of Deception,* written with Josepha Sherman, bardling apprentice Kevin searches for excitement beyond his Master Bard's lessons, rescuing a damsel in distress who fools him. In its sequel *The Chaos Gate,* shared again with Josepha Sherman, Kevin is a full bard keeping a Dark Elf from a trap. Twenty years later, another bardling, Gawaine, also chafes at the bit of his Master Bard, in *Fortress of Frost and Fire,* coauthored with Ru Emerson. Lackey displays her usual sympathy for adolescent angst as well as playfulness with fantasy conventions. *VOYA* included *Castle of Deception* in their Best Fantasy 1993 list and called *Fortress of Frost and Fire* "well-paced, lively, entertaining reading."[33] *Prison of Souls,* written with Mark Shepherd, was unavailable at this writing.

All such tie-in novels may be read without reference to associated games. Of 14 gaming survey respondents, only one had never played a role-playing game, only 3 did not read novel tie-ins at all, and 5 read novels referring to games they never played. All but one gamer who read connected novels found they enhanced playing; Peter Boonekamp, 16, felt it "hard to play creatively" once he had read the books. Nine respondents enjoyed novels apart from games. Ashley Burns "read the books long before I played the games and loved them."

While publishers target the game audience with tie-in novels, often separately shelved in bookstores, they are careful not to limit a book's appeal to gamers only. An editor of Viking Penguin's Roc imprint purposely gave his game tie-in *Earthdawn* "the look of a big fantasy novel" to attract more general fantasy readers.[34] In fact, it is undesirable to have too close an attachment between games and novels. Rick Swan negatively reviews the game Darksword Adventures (Bantam Spectra, 1988), created by the ubiquitous Weis and Hickman, because it demands too much familiarity with the novels. It even looks like the fourth installment of the novel series, like "a role-playing game in the guise of a mass-market paperback" (Swan, 62).

Librarians and teachers trying to keep up with the literature related to fantasy gaming must follow the lead of teen gameplayers. Collect game publisher catalogs, such as Wizards of the Coast,

which also feature tie-in books; read gaming reviews in *Dragon*
magazine; visit your local gaming shop; be a guest observer—or
player—at gaming sessions. Most importantly, consult your own
YA gamers, who would be thrilled to mark checklists of titles they
deem essential for informed game-world visitors.

YAFEs on Book Tie-ins to Game Worlds

DRAGONLANCE

I found a piece of me fitting into each character's characteristics: distrust, pity, sadness, energy, joking, love. *Dragons of
Autumn Twilight* was a very very very very very good book,
with enough battle scenes to keep me addicted and enough
love to keep me believing the humanity of the characters.
The underlying mystery theme made me flip through the
pages. The humor kept me from getting too emotional. And
the companions' successes filled me with such hope that I
want to read on.

—Melissa Tolve, 17

FORGOTTEN REALMS

R. A. Salvatore

He makes you care about the characters.

—Dylan Burns, 12

Characters are the way people are in real life—even if they
are elves.

—Ian Kelly, 15

I like Salvatore's dwarves.

—Ashley Burns, 15

I really, really like him.

—Erik Hansen, 14

He's above average, but not innovative.

—Sarah Luna, 17

I give Salvatore an A−. Though he develops characters well
at the beginning, he stops development cold for action. Then

there's too much action, not enough intrigue—you expect the
next killing.

—Sam Walter, 15

The Finder's Stone Trilogy

I loved the writers' style and pace. It really kept me on my
toes. I couldn't put any of the three books down and couldn't
wait to get my hands on the next one in the series. Read it
unless you have a death wish.

—Ashley Burns, 15

The Bard's Tale

The Castle of Deception is my favorite in the game series
because of its very creative ideas.

—Jesse Coffelt, 15

Gameplayer Adventures

Obviously, many teenagers are avid participants in "the world's
most fascinating hobby" of role-playing games (Swan, 2). Within
Fantasy Fanatics, there are at least three separate gaming groups
that play a variety of games, including regular or Advanced Dungeons and Dragons, GURPS, Rifts, and Vampire. All these groups
have exclusively teen membership. Three survey respondents
outside Fantasy Fanatics play 17 different games among them,
two in groups with adults.

What do players do in these sessions? Each takes the role of a
player-character, or PC, such as an elf or thief, as outlined in
game manuals. Many-sided dice determine characters' attributes,
such as strength and intelligence. Dice also decide outcomes, such
as who wins in combat. One referee, called a Dungeon Master in
D&D, is familiar with complex rules and plans an adventure for
the characters to join as a team. If players achieve the goal, such
as finding a ring in a cave, all are winners. Depending on the obsta-
cles PCs must surmount and the choices they make, the game
may be brief or may evolve through many sessions. Always, the
referee controls the scenario and interprets the rules. Manuals
merely offer guidelines; there is room for imagination and chance

to change outcomes. The fun is in cooperation rather than competition.

"Role-playing," writes Swan, "has a lot more in common with novels than it does with games. Just as a good novel takes readers to places they've never imagined and enables them to experience incredible adventures, . . . so does a good role-playing game. . . . [It is] an improvised novel in which all the participants serve as authors" (Swan, 3). Not coincidentally, many gamers write their own fantasy stories; gaming groups contain a high number of creative writers.

Since games and novels interlock, the emergence of a fantasy gameplayer subgenre is not surprising. A 1981 Best Book for Young Adults, *Mazes and Monsters* by Rona Jaffe was the earliest, fictionalizing a news story about a disturbed college student who disappeared after confusing fantasy role-playing with reality. During the '70s role-playing craze among youths, psychologists warned of the dangers of losing touch with reality that such games might provoke.

In 1985 a true crime account studied *The Dungeon Master: The Disappearance of James Dallas Egbert III*. Texas private investigator William Dear wrote of his search for Dallas, who had been missing from his Michigan State University campus since 1979. Connecting "genius" Dallas's vanishing with his obsession for a Dungeons and Dragons game played "live" in tunnels beneath the campus, Dear attended gaming sessions himself. At that time, *Parade* magazine called D&D "the hottest craze on college campuses since streaking," which attracted students whose only shared characteristic was "a higher-than-average IQ."[35] Though controversy over psychological harm in RPGs has faded, YA readers still enjoy *Dungeon Master*'s unraveling of a riveting missing-person search. Dear's book split the opinions of three YAFEs, which ran the gamut from excellent to poor. Young fantasy readers are not guaranteed to find any realistic book about games appealing.

In *A Map of Nowhere*, British YA author Gillian Cross used role-playing games to explore other games people play with ethics. When playing Jezebel, a game based on biblical concepts, with a brother and sister from a religious family, Nick must find his own sense of right and wrong, both in the game and in actual dealings with others. Though critics found Cross's work thought provoking, three YAFEs were united in strong dislike for the book. Gaming was a device on which to hang a morality tale, they felt; they were disappointed to find no "real" fantasy element.

Inevitably, fantasy authors responded to the gaming craze by fulfilling players' fantasies. "Imagine beginning a campaign in a fantasy game and suddenly finding yourself not just acting out the parts of characters but actually becoming the characters in body and mind," writes Jehnie Burns, 17, in her review of Joel Rosenberg's *Guardians of the Flame* series. With *The Sleeping Dragon* in 1983, Rosenberg began his paperback series about seven college students who actually enter the realm of their role-playing game. Stranded there in *The Sword and the Chain* and *The Silver Crown,* they help its citizens overcome slavery. Readers responded less enthusiastically to each succeeding volume, however. The series seemed to run out of steam; no YAFE read the last four titles, *The Heir Apparent, The Warrior Lives, The Road to Ehvenor,* and *The Road Home.*

Fantasy gameplayers do not necessarily like to read stories about gamers. In a survey of 14 YAFEs, 13 of whom play RPGs, only 6 enjoyed reading about them. Of those six, most liked stories of gamers confusing fantasy with reality, but four disliked stories in which involvement in a game is a way to cope with real problems. Five of the six disliked books in which there is only psychological escape, not actual entry into alternate universes. All insisted that gamers must enter the game world and enjoy the sensation that such worlds can really come alive. Melissa Tolve experienced "total letdown" when Morris never shrank into a tiny warrior in Elisabeth Mace's *Under Siege.* Readers were split as to whether they liked connections between gamers' real personalities and those of their role-playing characters.

Recent young adult novels address these preferences, forging compelling connections between players and the worlds they enter. In Australian Gillian Rubinstein's two-parter, *Space Demons* and *Skymaze,* players enter computer game worlds. At first, players see themselves on-screen in the Skymaze. After the computer game ends, a three-dimensional maze opens in the sky above players when they are in actual crises. Rubinstein aligns real conflicts within and among four players with their experiences in the maze. Triggering each person's worst fears, the maze holds solutions to their problems at its hidden core. Merging fantasy and reality, Rubinstein combines fine character study with gripping adventure.

With computer games and virtual reality so popular, more fantasy and science fiction plots make such games real. Yet one of the most haunting YA gaming novels features an old, handcrafted game, Albion's Dream, in Roger Norman's book of the same name. Unearthed by 12-year-old Edward in his uncle's house, the meticulously drawn game board, dice, and cards come with a warning: they are capable of great harm. But Edward, like his uncle and father before him, cannot resist playing, especially when he notices that the Hangman card looks just like his disagreeable headmaster, Tyson. As Edward and his friend Hadley play, they realize that the game board landscape is the Wessex countryside near Edward's home, that its cards' mythic characters connect to actual people, and that when harm befalls a game character it does so in real life as well. In a twist on gameplayers entering another world, Norman's game world infringes upon ours; its events affect our reality. In an atmosphere redolent with ancient forces of enchantment and dread, the game plays to its chilling conclusion. Unknowable mysteries are part of the world we know in *Albion's Dream*. Other YAFE recommendations for gameplayer reading are listed in this chapter's Recommended Reading.

YAFEs on Gameplayer Adventures

Rosenberg—*The Sleeping Dragon*

This masterpiece rivals my favorite Terry Brooks fantasy.
                                                    —Dylan Burns, 12

I was intrigued by how people changed into their player-characters.
                                                    —Melissa Tolve, 17

I appreciated dilemmas between their real characters and their alternate-world characters as well as amusing references to the real world.

—Jehnie Burns, 17

Norman—*Albion's Dream*

My brother Dylan and I were entranced by this book. Just because the author lives in Greece, is he too far away to write a sequel?

—Ashley Burns, 15

Recommended Reading

(* denotes title mentioned in text; other titles are additional)

Gateway Magic: "There and Back Again"

Anthony, Piers. **Mode* Series. 3 vols. New York: Putnam's.
  Vol. 1: *Virtual Mode.* 1991.
  Vol. 2: *Fractal Mode.* 1992.
  Vol. 3: *Chaos Mode.* 1994.
Anthony, Piers, and Robert Kornwise. **Through the Ice.* Lancaster, Penn.: Underwood-Miller, 1989; reprint, New York: Baen, 1993.
Askounis, Christina. **The Dream of the Stone.* New York: Farrar, Straus, & Giroux, 1993.
Barrie, J.M. **Peter Pan.* (Orig. British title *Peter and Wendy,* 1904.) Illus. F. D. Bedford. Everyman's Library of Children's Classics. New York: Knopf, 1992.
Baum, L. Frank. **The Wizard of Oz.* (Orig. title *The Wonderful Wizard of Oz,* 1900.) Illus. W. W. Denslow. Books of Wonder. New York: Morrow, 1987.
Brooks, Terry. **Magic Kingdom of Landover* Series. 5 vols. New York: Ballantine/Del Rey.
  Vol. 1: *Magic Kingdom for Sale—Sold!* 1986.
  Vol. 2: *The Black Unicorn.* 1987.
  Vol. 3: *Wizard at Large.* 1988.
  Vol. 4: *The Tangle Box.* 1994.
  Vol. 5: *Witches' Brew.* 1995.
Carroll, Lewis. **Alice's Adventures in Wonderland.* (Orig. British pub. 1865.) Illus. John Tenniel. Books of Wonder. New York: Morrow, 1992.

————. *Through the Looking Glass.* (Orig. British pub. 1871.) Illus. John Tenniel. Books of Wonder. New York: Morrow, 1993.

Charnas, Suzy McKee. *The Kingdom of Kevin Malone.* San Diego: Harcourt Brace Jovanovich, 1993.

Chetwin, Grace. *Out of the Dark World.* New York: Lothrop, Lee & Shepard, 1985.

Crew, Gary. *Strange Objects.* New York: Simon & Schuster, 1993.

Donaldson, Stephen R. *The Chronicles of Thomas Covenant the Unbeliever.* 3 vols. New York: Henry Holt.

Vol. 1: *Lord Foul's Bane.* 1977.

Vol. 2: *The Illearth War.* 1978.

Vol. 3: *The Power That Preserves.* 1979.

————. *The Second Chronicles of Thomas Covenant.* 3 vols. New York: Henry Holt.

Vol. 1: *The Wounded Land.* 1981.

Vol. 2: *The One Tree.* 1983.

Vol. 3: *White Gold Wielder.* 1983.

Duane, Diane. *The Wizard Sequence.* 3 vols. New York: Delacorte.

Vol. 1: *So You Want to Be a Wizard.* 1983.

Vol. 2: *Deep Wizardry.* 1985.

Vol. 3: *High Wizardry.* 1990.

Ende, Michael. *The Neverending Story.* (Orig. German pub. 1979.) Trans. Ralph Manheim. Illus. Roswitha Quadflieg. New York: Doubleday, 1983; hardcover reprint, New York: Dutton, 1997.

Gaiman, Neil. *Neverwhere.* New York: Avon, 1997.

Garner, Alan. *Elidor.* (Orig. British pub. 1965.) New York: Philomel, 1979.

Hambly, Barbara. *Darwath* Series. 5 vols. New York: Ballantine/Del Rey.

Vol. 1: *The Time of the Dark.* 1982.

Vol. 2: *The Walls of Air.* 1983.

Vol. 3: *The Armies of Daylight.* 1983.

Vol. 4: *Mother of Winter.* 1996.

Vol. 5: *Icefalcon's Quest.* 1998.

————. *Sun-Cross* Series. 2 vols. New York: Ballantine/Del Rey.

Vol. 1: *The Rainbow Abyss.* 1991.

Vol. 2: *The Magicians of Night.* 1992.

————. *The Windrose Chronicles.* 4 vols. New York: Ballantine/Del Rey.

Vol. 1: *The Silent Tower.* 1986.

Vol. 2: *The Silicon Mage.* 1988.

Vol. 3: *Dog Wizard.* 1993.

Vol. 4: *Stranger at the Wedding.* 1994.

Hilgartner, Beth. *Colors in the Dreamweaver's Loom.* Boston: Houghton Mifflin, 1989.

————. *The Feast of the Trickster*. Boston: Houghton Mifflin, 1991.

Le Guin, Ursula. *The Beginning Place*. New York: Harper & Row, 1980.

Lewis, C.S. *The Chronicles of Narnia*. 7 vols. (Orig. British pub. 1951.) Illus. Pauline Baynes. New York: HarperCollins, ©1956, 1994.
Vol. 1: *The Lion, the Witch, and the Wardrobe*.
Vol. 2: *Prince Caspian*.
Vol. 3: *Voyage of the Dawn Treader*.
Vol. 4: *The Silver Chair*.
Vol. 5: *The Horse and His Boy*.
Vol. 6: *The Magician's Nephew*.
Vol. 7: *The Last Battle*.

Maguire, Gregory. *Wicked: The Life and Times of the Wicked Witch of the West*. New York: Regan/HarperCollins, 1995.

Noon, Jeff. *Automated Alice*. New York: Crown, 1996.

Norton, Andre. *Witch World: Simon Tregarth Sequence*. 6 vols. Vols 1–5: New York: Ace. Vol. 6: New York: DAW.
Vol. 1: *Witch World*. 1986, ©1963.
Vol. 2: *Web of the Witch World*. 1986, ©1964.
Vol. 3: *Three Against the Witch World*. 1986, ©1965.
Vol. 4: *Warlock of the Witch World*. 1986, ©1967.
Vol. 5: *Sorceress of the Witch World*. 1986, ©1968.
Vol. 6: *Spell of the Witch World*. 1972.

Sheppard, Nancy, adapter and translator. *Alitji in Dreamland*. Illus. Donna Leslie. Berkeley, Calif.: Tricycle Press, 1992.

Swift, Jonathan. *Gulliver's Travels into Several Remote Nations of the World*. (Orig. British pub. 1726.) Everyman's Library. New York: Knopf, 1991.

Earthbound Magic

Aiken, Joan. *The Cockatrice Boys*. New York: Tor, 1996.

Brooks, Terry. *Running with the Demon*. New York: Ballantine, 1997.

Charnas, Suzy McKee. *Sorcery Hall Trilogy*. 3 vols. Vol. 1: Boston: Houghton Mifflin. Vol. 2–3: New York: Bantam.
Vol. 1: *The Bronze King*. 1985.
Vol. 2: *The Silver Glove*. 1988.
Vol. 3: *The Golden Thread*. 1989.

Cormier, Robert. *Fade*. New York: Delacorte, 1988.

Dalton, Annie. *Out of the Ordinary*. New York: HarperCollins, 1990.

De Saint-Exupéry, Antoine. *The Little Prince*. (Orig. French pub 1943.) Trans. Katherine Woods. Illus. by author. New York: Harcourt

Brace Jovanovich, 1943; paperback reprint ed., San Diego: Harcourt Brace Jovanovich, 1982.

Furlong, Monica. *Juniper* Series. 2 vols. New York: Knopf.
    Prequel: *Juniper*. 1991, ©1990.
    Wise Child. 1987.

Gaiman, Neil, and Terry Pratchett. *Good Omens: The Nice and Accurate Prophecies of Agnes Nutter, Witch*. New York: Workman, 1990.

Gilmore, Kate. *Enter Three Witches*. Boston: Houghton Mifflin, 1991.

Goldstein, Lisa. *The Red Magician*. New York: Tor, 1982; 1st hardcover ed., New York: Tor, 1993.

Hilton, James. **Lost Horizon*. New York: Morrow, 1933; reprint ed., Cutchogue, N.Y.: Buccaneer Books, 1983; paperback reprint ed., New York: Pocket Books, 1981.

Hudson, W. H. **Green Mansions*. (Orig. British pub. 1893.) New York: Putnam, 1904; reprint ed., Cutchogue, N.Y.: Buccaneer Books, 1982; paperback reprint ed., New York: Dover Publications, 1989.

Lackey, Mercedes. *Sacred Ground*. New York: Tor, 1994.

MacAvoy, R. A. **Black Dragon* Series. New York: Bantam.
    Vol. 1: *Tea with the Black Dragon*. 1983.
    Vol. 2: *Twisting the Rope*. 1986.

Nesbit, E(dith). **The Five Children and It*. (Orig. British pub. 1902.) Cutchogue, N.Y.: Buccaneer Books, ©1905, 1981; paperback reprint ed., New York: Scholastic, 1988.

Pratchett, Terry. *The Bromeliad*. 3 vols. New York: Delacorte.
    Vol. 1: *Truckers*. 1990.
    Vol. 2: *Diggers*. 1991.
    Vol. 3: *Wings*. 1991.

Scarborough, Elizabeth Ann. **The Healer's War*. New York: Doubleday, 1988.

Shetterly, Will. *Dogland*. New York: Tor, 1997.

Springer, Nancy. *The Hex Witch of Seldom*. New York: Baen, 1988.

Thompson, Julian F. **Herb Seasoning*. New York: Scholastic, 1990.

Wells, Rosemary. *Through the Hidden Door*. New York: Dial, 1987.

Wilde, Oscar. **The Picture of Dorian Gray*. (Orig. British pub. 1891.) Modern Library. New York: Random House, 1992.

Willard, Nancy. *Things Invisible to See*. New York: Knopf, 1984.

Fantasy Gaming: Book Tie-ins to Game Worlds

DRAGONLANCE **Novels.** Lake Geneva, Wis.: TSR, Inc.

Chronicles Trilogy. Weis, Margaret, and Tracy Hickman.
    Vol. 1: *Dragons of Autumn Twilight*. 1984.

Vol. 2: *Dragons of Winter Night.* 1985.

Vol. 3: *Dragons of Spring Dawning.* 1985.

Legends Trilogy. (Sequel to *Chronicles.*) Weis, Margaret, and Tracy Hickman.

Vol. 1: *Time of the Twins.* 1986.

Vol. 2: *War of the Twins.* 1986.

Vol. 3: *Test of the Twins.* 1986.

Tales Trilogy. (Anytime after *Chronicles* and *Legends.*) Anthology.

Vol. 1: *The Magic of Krynn.* 1987.

Vol. 2: *Kender, Gully Dwarves, and Gnomes.* 1987.

Vol. 3: *Love and War.* 1987.

Tales II Trilogy. (Anytime after *Chronicles* and *Legends.*) Anthology.

Vol. 1: *The Reign of Istar.* 1992.

Vol. 2: *The Cataclysm.* 1992.

Vol. 3: *The War of the Lance.* 1992.

Heroes Trilogy. (Anytime after *Chronicles* and *Legends.*)

Vol. 1: *The Legend of Huma.* Knaak, Richard A. 1988.

Vol. 2: *Stormblade.* Berberick, Nancy Varian. 1988.

Vol. 3: *Weasel's Luck.* Williams, Michael. 1988.

Heroes II Trilogy. (Anytime after *Chronicles* and *Legends.*)

Vol. 1: *Kaz, the Minotaur.* Knaak, Richard A. 1990.

Vol. 2: *The Gates of Thorbardin.* Parkinson, Dan. 1990.

Vol. 3: *Galen Beknighted.* Williams, Michael. 1990.

Preludes Trilogy. (Prequel to *Chronicles.*)

Vol. 1: *Darkness and Light.* Thompson, Paul B., and Tonya R. Carter. 1989.

Vol. 2: *Kendermore.* Kirchoff, Mary. 1989.

Vol. 3: *Brothers Majere.* Stein, Kevin. 1990.

Preludes II Trilogy. (Prequel to *Chronicles.*)

Vol. 1: *Riverwind, the Plainsman.* Thompson, Paul B., and Tonya R. Carter. 1990.

Vol. 2: *Flint, the King.* Kirchoff, Mary, and Douglas Niles. 1990.

Vol. 3: *Tanis, the Shadow Years.* Siegal, Barbara, and Scott Siegal. 1990.

The Meetings Sextet. (Prequel to *Preludes* 1 and 2.)

Vol. 1: *Kindred Spirits.* Anthony, Mark, and Ellen Porath. 1991.

Vol. 2: *Wanderlust.* Kirchoff, Mary, and Steve Winter. 1991.

Vol. 3: *Dark Heart.* Daniell, Tina. 1992.

Vol. 4: *Oath and the Measure.* Williams, Michael. 1992.

Vol. 5: *Steel and Stone.* Porath, Ellen. 1992.

Vol. 6: *The Companions.* Daniell, Tina. 1992.

The Elven Nations Trilogy. (Prehistory).

Vol. 1: *Firstborn.* Thompson, Paul B., and Tonya R. Carter. 1991.

Vol. 2: *The Kinslayer Wars*. Niles, Douglas. 1991.
Vol. 3: *The Qualinesti*. Thompson, Paul B., and Tonya R. Carter. 1991.
The Dwarven Nations Trilogy (Prehistory). Parkinson, Dan.
    Vol. 1: *Covenant of the Forge*. 1993.
    Vol. 2: *Hammer and Axe*. 1993.
    Vol. 3: *The Swordsheath Scroll*. 1994.
The Villains Series. (Anytime after *Chronicles* and *Legends*).
    Vol. 1: *Before the Mask*. Williams, Michael and Teri Williams. 1993.
    Vol. 2: *The Black Wing*. Kirchoff, Mary. 1993.
    Vol. 3: *Emperor of Ansalon*. Niles, Douglas. 1993.
    Vol. 4: *Hederick the Theocrat*. Severson, Ellen Dodge. 1994.
    Vol. 5: *Lord Toede*. Grubb, Jeff. 1994.
    Vol. 6: *The Dark Queen*. Williams, Michael and Teri Williams. 1994.
Hardcover Anthology. (Anytime after *Chronicles* and *Legends*.)
    The Second Generation. Weis, Margaret, and Tracy Hickman. 1994.
The Defenders of Magic Trilogy (Prehistory). Kirchoff, Mary.
    Vol. 1: *Night of the Eye*. 1994.
    Vol. 2: *The Medusa Plague*. 1994.
    Vol. 3: *The Seventh Sentinel*. 1995.

FORGOTTEN REALMS **Novels.** Lake Geneva, Wis.: TSR, Inc.

The Moonshae Trilogy. Niles, Douglas.
    Vol. 1: *Darkwalker on Moonshae*. 1987.
    Vol. 2: *Black Wizards*. 1988.
    Vol. 3: *Darkwell*. 1989.
The Druidhome Trilogy. (Sequel to *Moonshae Trilogy*.) Niles, Douglas.
    Vol. 1: *Prophet of Moonshae*. 1992.
    Vol. 2: *The Coral Kingdom*. 1992.
    Vol. 3: *The Druid Queen*. 1993.
Icewind Dale Trilogy. Salvatore, R. A.
    Vol. 1: *The Crystal Shard*. 1988.
    Vol. 2: *Streams of Silver*. 1989.
    Vol. 3: *The Halfling's Gem*. 1990.
The Legacy. (Sequel to *Icewind Dale Trilogy*.) Salvatore, R. A. 1992.
Starless Night. (Sequel to *The Legacy*.) Salvatore, R. A. 1993.
Siege of Darkness. (Sequel to *Starless Night*.) Salvatore, R. A. 1994.
The Dark Elf Trilogy. (Prequel to *Icewind Dale Trilogy*.) Salvatore, R. A.
    Vol. 1: *Homeland*. 1990.
    Vol. 2: *Exile*. 1990.
    Vol. 3: *Sojourn*. 1991.
The Finder's Stone Trilogy. Novak, Kate, and Jeff Grubb.

Vol. 1: *Azure Bonds.* 1988.
Vol. 2: *The Wyvern's Spur.* 1990.
Vol. 3: *Song of the Saurials.* 1991.
The Avatar Trilogy. Awlinson, Richard.
Vol. 1: *Shadowdale.* 1989.
Vol. 2: *Tantras.* 1989.
Vol. 3. *Waterdeep.* 1989.
Prince of Lies. (Sequel to *Avatar Trilogy.*) Lowder, James. 1993.
The Empires Trilogy.
Vol. 1: *Horselords.* Cook, David. 1990.
Vol. 2: *Dragonwall.* Denning, Troy. 1990.
Vol. 3: *Crusade.* Lowder, James. 1991.
The Maztica Trilogy. Niles, Douglas.
Vol. 1: *Ironhelm.* 1990.
Vol. 2: *Viperhand.* 1990.
Vol. 3: *Feathered Dragon.* 1991.
The Cleric Quintet. Salvatore, R. A.
Vol. 1: *Canticle.* 1991.
Vol. 2: *In Sylvan Shadows.* 1992.
Vol. 3: *Night Masks.* 1992.
Vol. 4: *The Fallen Fortress.*1993.
Vol. 5: *The Chaos Curse.* 1994.
The Harpers Series.
Vol. 1: *The Parched Sea.* Denning, Troy. 1991.
Vol. 2: *Elfshadow.* Cunningham, Elaine. 1991.
Vol. 3: *Red Magic.* Rabe, Jean. 1991.
Vol. 4: *The Night Parade.* Ciencin, Scott. 1992.
Vol. 5: *The Ring of Winter.* Lowder, James. 1992.
Vol. 6: *Crypt of the Shadowking.* Anthony, Mark. 1993.
Vol. 7: *Soldiers of Ice.* Cook, David. 1993.
Vol. 8: *Elfsong.* (Sequel to *Elfshadow.*) Cunningham, Elaine. 1994.
The Superharpers Series. Greenwood, Ed.
Vol. 1: *Spellfire.* 1988.
Vol. 2: *Crown of Fire.* 1994.
The Twilight Giants Trilogy. Denning, Troy.
Vol. 1: *The Ogre's Pact.* 1994.
Vol. 2: *The Giant Among Us.* 1995.
Vol. 3: *The Titan of Twilight.* 1995.

THE BARD'S TALE Novels

Lackey, Mercedes, and Josepha Sherman. *Castle of Deception.* New York: Baen, 1992.

———. *The Chaos Gate. New York: Baen, 1994.

Lackey, Mercedes, and Ru Emerson. *Fortress of Frost and Fire. New York: Baen, 1993.

Lackey, Mercedes, and Mark Shepherd. Prison of Souls. New York: Baen, 1993.

KING'S QUEST

Mills Craig. The Floating Castle. New York: Boulevard Books, 1995.

MAGIC: THE GATHERING

Distant Planes: An Anthology. Ed. Kathy Ice. New York: HarperPrism, 1996.

Gameplayer Adventures

Anderson, Kevin. The Gamearth Trilogy. 3 vols. New York: Signet.
Vol. 1: Gamearth. 1989.
Vol. 2: Gameplay. 1989.
Vol. 3: Game's End. 1990.

Anthony, Piers. Killobyte. New York: Putnam's, 1993.

Beagle, Peter. The Folk of the Air. New York: Ballantine, 1987.

Carpenter, Christopher. The Twilight Realm. New York: Putnam's, 1986.

Cross, Gillian. *A Map of Nowhere. New York: Holiday House, 1989.

Dear, William. *The Dungeon Master: The Disappearance of James Dallas Egbert III. Boston: Houghton Mifflin, 1984.

Jaffe, Rona. *Mazes and Monsters. New York: Delacorte, 1981.

Mace, Elisabeth. *Under Siege. New York: Orchard, 1990.

Norman, Roger. *Albion's Dream. New York: Delacorte, 1992.

Posner, Richard. Sparrow's Flight. New York: M. Evans & Co., 1988.

Rosenberg, Joel. *Guardians of the Flame Series. 7 vols. Vols. 1–6: New York: NAL/Dutton. Vol. 7: New York: Penguin.
Vol. 1: The Sleeping Dragon. 1986, ©1983.
Vol. 2: The Sword and the Chain. 1987, ©1984.
Vol. 3: The Silver Crown. 1985.
Vol. 4: The Heir Apparent. 1987.
Vol. 5: The Warrior Lives. 1990, ©1988.
Vol. 6: The Road to Ehvenor. 1991.
Vol. 7: The Road Home. 1995.

Rubinstein, Gillian. Beyond the Labyrinth. New York: Orchard, 1990.

———. *Space Demons. New York: Dial, 1988.

———. *Skymaze. New York: Orchard, 1991.

Vande Velde, Vivian. User Unfriendly. San Diego: Harcourt Brace Jovanovich, 1991.

Selected Bibliography

(Notations: "C3", etc., refers to chapter in which title is discussed.)

Barbara Hambly

Primary Sources

Beauty and the Beast Series. 2 vols. New York: Avon.
  Vol. 1: *Beauty and the Beast* (C3). 1989.
  Vol. 2: *Song of Orpheus* (C3). 1990.
Darwath Series. 5 vols. New York: Ballantine/Del Rey.
  Vol. 1: *The Time of the Dark* (C3). 1982.
  Vol. 2: *The Walls of Air* (C3). 1983.
  Vol. 3: *The Armies of Daylight* (C3). 1983.
  Vol. 4: *Mother of Winter* (C3). 1996.
  Vol. 5: *Icefalcon's Quest.* 1998.
Dragonsbane (C6). New York: Ballantine/Del Rey, 1985.
Short Stories:
"Changeling," in *Once Upon a Time: A Treasury of Modern Fairy Tales* (C3). Ed. Lester del Rey and Risa Kessler. New York: Ballantine/Del Rey, 1991.
"Each Damp Thing," in *The Sandman Book of Dreams* (C3). Ed. Neil Gaiman and Ed Kramer. New York: HarperPrism, 1996.
"The Little Tailor and the Elves." In *Xanadu 2* (C3). Ed. Jane Yolen. New York: Tor, 1994, 1996.
Sun-Cross Series. 2 vols. New York: Ballantine/Del Rey.
  Vol. 1: *The Rainbow Abyss* (C3). 1991.
  Vol. 2: *The Magicians of Night* (C3). 1992.
Sun Wolf Trilogy. 3 vols. New York: Ballantine/Del Rey.
  Vol. 1: *The Ladies of Mandrigyn* (C2). 1984.
  Vol. 2: *The Witches of Wenshar* (C2). 1987.
  Vol. 3: *The Dark Hand of Magic* (C2). 1990.
The Windrose Chronicles. 4 vols. New York: Ballantine/Del Rey.
  Vol. 1: *The Silent Tower* (C3). 1986.
  Vol. 2: *The Silicon Mage* (C3). 1988.
  Vol. 3: *Dog Wizard* (C3). 1993.
  Vol. 4: *Stranger at the Wedding* (C3). 1994.

Secondary Sources

Hambly, Barbara. "Barbara Hambly: Saved by the Ax." *Locus* (June 1986): 27, 39–40.
MacRae, Cathi Dunn. Interview with Barbara Hambly. Los Angeles, California, 15 March 1993.

Paxson, Diana L. "What a Piece of Work: An Appreciation of Barbara Hambly." Washington, D.C.: Disclave Convention Program, 1988, n.p.

The Magic Realism of Barbara Hambly

MacRae, Cathi Dunn. "The Young Adult Perplex." *Wilson Library Bulletin* (March 1990): 106–7, 134–35.

———. "The Young Adult Perplex." *Wilson Library Bulletin* (March 1994): 124–25.

Swan, Rick. *The Complete Guide to Role-Playing Games.* New York: St. Martin's, 1990.

4. Myth: Dreams
of the Soul's Adventure

What Is Myth?

Webster's College Dictionary defines myth as traditional stories of gods and heroes that attempt to explain cultural customs or natural phenomena. Yet the dictionary says nothing of myth's fascination. Stirring adventures of Greek gods and heroes have enchanted children of all ages for 3,000 years. Human response to myth is consistent, but perceptions change with the times.

Thomas Bulfinch of Boston devoted his life to retelling myths from classical sources worldwide, making them accessible to popular audiences. We still use his 1855–1863 *Bulfinch's Mythology*. In *The Golden Bough*, Scottish anthropologist James G. Frazer astounded 1890 readers with his revelation that "the customs and superstitions of civilized society were in many ways comparable to the beliefs and practices of primitive peoples."[1] Yet a 1939 textbook scoffed at mythology's "mistaken and superstitious attempts to satisfy the curiosity of primitive and unenlightened peoples, to unveil the mysteries of existence."[2] By the 1950s, anthropologists, theologians, philosophers, linguists, psychologists, and literary critics argued endless theories about mythology's significance. One reasonable definition of mythology emerged: "a complex of stories, some no doubt fact, and some fantasy—which, for various reasons, human beings regard as demonstrations of the inner meaning of the universe and of human life."[3]

Why do people make myths? Since Sigmund Freud and Carl Jung were trailblazers in psychology, we have looked to expanded understanding of the human mind for explanations. In 1955, folk-lorist Stith Thompson reflected this awareness: "[C]ertain psychological compulsions . . . impel people to tell tales of particular kinds. Dreams, fears, and stresses—it is from these that come the gods, the heroes, and the tales about them."[4]

Joseph Campbell revolutionized our concept of myth by comparing world mythologies. "Why is mythology everywhere the same?" asked Campbell,[5] deftly drawing similar Eskimo, Hindu, and European myths together. In his masterwork *The Hero with a Thousand Faces,* Campbell offers many arresting definitions. Myths are:

- Spontaneous productions of the psyche. (4)
- The depersonalized dream; dream is the depersonalized myth. (19)
- The wonderful story of the soul's high adventure. (22)

To Campbell, there is one main myth: the monomyth, the hero's great adventure. Every hero undertakes a journey alone, a quest through challenging trials to find himself and the secrets of the universe. His journey mirrors our own path from birth through life to death and eternal life. The formula for this monomyth, says Campbell, appears in tribal coming-of-age ceremonies, when the candidate separates from childhood surroundings, is initiated into adult secrets, and returns as a member of adult society (Campbell 1968, 30). Today we replace the tribal shaman with the psychologist, whose "role is precisely that of the Wise Old Man of the myths . . . [to] assist the hero through the trials and terrors of the weird adventure" (Campbell 1968, 9).

No wonder myths and hero tales have such appeal for youth! When Joseph Campbell's 1988 PBS television series *The Power of Myth* aired just after Campbell's death, teenagers were among the millions captivated by his dialogue with journalist Bill Moyers. One girl from my Baltimore library group spent her summer between high school and college deeply involved with the series and its companion book, identifying her personal transition into adulthood.

When Moyers asked why Campbell's college lectures overflowed with students, Campbell replied, "Young people just grab this stuff. Mythology teaches you what's behind literature and the arts, it teaches you about your own life. It's a great, exciting, life-nourishing subject."[6] Since our "demythologized" society robs youth of rituals, youth need to "become members . . . of the community"; young people "make them up themselves. . . . These kids have their own gangs and their own initiations and their own morality. . . . But they're dangerous because . . . they have not been initiated into our society" (Campbell 1988, 9).

We hang on to an outdated myth in which humanity masters the universe, declares Campbell, and we must find a new myth to unite all cultures and religions, one that will bring us back into "accord with nature" before we destroy it (Campbell 1988, 40–41). Could that new myth evolve through contemporary fantasy literature? In ancient oral tradition, bards kept myth alive by memory. Now the printed word allows variations to be exchanged among many. Today's novelists rarely retell old stories faithfully. Instead they extract classic motifs, refashioning them to their own tastes and visions, breathing new life into enduring themes. Campbell's monomyth reappears constantly; fresh twists from each writer's consciousness regenerate the reader.

Hungry for new myths, youths react fervently when ancient Greek child murderess Medea is recast as a gifted healer betrayed by shallow Jason in H. M. Hoover's young adult novel *The Dawn Palace,* voted a top book of 1988 by teens in Baltimore's Youth-to-Youth book conference. Teenagers relate to Orpheus's enthralling music when Cynthia Voigt transforms him into a rock musician *Orfe.* Moses's exodus is humanized in *Escape from Egypt,* Sonia Levitin's 1995 ALA Best Book for Young Adults; readers see the story through the eyes of a Hebrew slave and an Egyptian girl who fall in love. Inspired by C. S. Lewis, Japanese writer Noriko Ogiwara converts her culture's philosophies into mythic fantasy in *Dragon Sword and Wind Child.* Patricia Wrightson imports Australian aboriginal myth into modern life in mysterious *Balyet* and other lyrical novels for young adults.

Teenagers also enjoy adult novels that re-create mythology in today's terms. They are terrified when an archaeologist on a Mexican dig contemplates sacrificing her own daughter to appease a ghostly Mayan priestess in Pat Murphy's *The Falling Woman*. They welcome Orson Scott Card's brilliant parable of pioneer American life in his *Tales of Alvin Maker* series, an alternate history in which George Washington is beheaded, folk magic protects settlers against Indians, and a psychic boy battles dark powers; its first volume, *Seventh Son*, was a 1987 ALA Best Book for Young Adults. Joseph Bruchac, a Native American storyteller of the Abenaki tribe, converts pre-Columbian northeastern Indian tribal myth into a superb coming-of-age trilogy, starting with the 1994 ALA Best Book *Dawn Land* and continuing through *Long River* (a final volume is forthcoming). A 1984 Best Book, *On a Pale Horse*, opens Piers Anthony's *Incarnations of Immortality* series, a teen favorite in which mythological forces are personified as Death, Fate, and Time.

In 1949, author John Myers Myers shipwrecked a Chicago man in an otherworld to explore every myth and literary allusion from Circe to King Arthur, from the Alamo to the Mad Hatter, in the fantasy classic *Silverlock*. Along similar, more profound lines, Robert Holdstock won international recognition with the 1985 World Fantasy Award and local appreciation with Spokane, Washington, teens' Golden Pen Award for *Mythago Wood*, an astonishing evocation of myth's essence. In three square miles of English primeval forest, mystical energies alter time and space so that all the mythic figures in the isle's history walk together. Living at the edge of Ryhope Wood just after World War II, George Huxley and his sons Christian and Steven become obsessed with its impenetrable secrets, discovering their ability to manifest mythical forms from their own minds. Breathing mythagos of such heroes as Robin Hood, King Arthur, and an Ice Age boar-beast emerge from unconscious memories, archetypes that psychologist Jung described as coming from our collective unconscious and that Campbell defined as "common ideas of myth" (Campbell 1988, 60). When all three Huxleys fall in love with beautiful mythago Guiwenneth of the Green, "the idealized version of the Celtic princess,"[7] their own inexorable legend unfolds as they track each other through endless sinister woods. Awestruck with the power of the mind's creations, no reader of *Mythago Wood* will consider myth a harmless story. Mature teen readers cannot resist this potent mix of science fantasy, suspense, and horror.

In its sequel, *Lavondyss*, teenaged Tallis, sister of pilot Harry Keeton, who disappeared in the first volume, makes her own foray into the wood in a tale as "eerie, beautiful, and frightening as nature itself ... or an unforgettable dream," according to *Locus*.[8] Another youth entangled in the wood awaits rescue in the third volume, *The Hollowing,* which resonates with "Holdstock's mythic lore and exquisite characterization and prose."[9] *Gate of Ivory, Gate of Horn,* a new volume in *The Mythago Cycle,* was published in late 1997. Says Holdstock, "All my work is concerned with evolution, and with the persistence of memory, the continued presence—genetically, spiritually, passionately—of all of life in all of mankind."[10]

Study of mythic modern novels could fill volumes; readers may find more suggestions in this chapter's Recommended Reading. This chapter focuses on Jane Yolen, whose life and writing embodies holistic understanding of myth and folklore from all cultures.

Mythmaking

In our media-influenced universe, young people steeped in comic superheroes and commercial slogans miss references to ancient myth. Jane Yolen believes that without "the myths, fairy tales, fantasies and folklore that are their proper legacy,"[11] children speak "a barren language ... that accurately reflects their equally barren minds." Her eloquent essays in *Touch Magic* show how mythology fills a "basic developmental need":

- To appreciate literature, we must know the archetypes on which it is based.
- To get along with others, we must understand how our culture's values relate to theirs.

- To process our own experiences, we must compare them to those in stories.
- To build our own belief systems, we must find their roots. (*Touch Magic*, 15–20)

Myth comes not from the people, asserts storyteller Yolen, but "from the teacher, the shaman and visionary as the giver and interpreter of myth. . . . The tale teller . . . holds culture in the mouth."[12]

In our global village, storytellers mix many cultural traditions. As a "new mythmaker"[13] who composes stories from mythic elements, Jane Yolen calls herself "empress of thieves."[14] She takes "characters like gargoyles off Parisian churches, the *ki-lin* (or unicorn) from China, swords in stones from the Celts, landscapes from the Taino people."[15] Like quiltmakers who save scraps from old clothes to shape into new patchwork patterns, Jane Yolen fashions new tales from old.

Jane Yolen: "Empress of Thieves"

Chronology: Jane Yolen's Life and Works

1939   Jane Hyatt Yolen born February 11 in New York City, first child of Isabelle Berlin Yolen, social worker, and Will Hyatt Yolen, author and journalist in public relations.

1940   Lives in Hollywood, California, where her father works for Warner Brothers.

1944   Lives in Virginia with grandparents when father is in England during World War II.

1945   Returns to New York City to attend elementary school.

1952   Moves to Westport, Connecticut, to attend high school.

1956   Graduates from Staples High School in Westport.

1957   As a student at Smith College, wins awards for first published poetry and journalism.

Jane Yolen
David Stemple

1960   Graduates from Smith College in Massachusetts with a B.A. in English; moves to New York City to become a writer, working for several magazines.

1961   Becomes assistant editor at Gold Medal Books.

1962   Marries David Wilber Stemple, photographer and computer scientist, on September 2; becomes associate editor at Rutledge Books.

1963   Publishes first children's poetry book, *See This Little Line?*, and first juvenile nonfiction, *Pirates in Petticoats;* becomes assistant juvenile editor at Alfred A. Knopf Publishers.

1964   Publishes first juvenile fiction, *The Witch Who Wasn't.*

1965   Leaves publishing to become full-time writer; travels to Europe and the Middle East.

1966   Moves to Conway, Massachusetts; daughter Heidi Elisabet born July 1.

1967   Musical play *Robin Hood* produced in Boston.

1968   Son Adam Douglas born April 30; *The Emperor and the Kite* becomes Caldecott Honor Book for Ed Young's illustrations and one of the *New York Times*'s Best Books of the Year.

1969   Moves to Bolton, Massachusetts, near Boston.

1970   Son Jason Frederic born May 21.

1971   Moves to Phoenix Farm in Hatfield, Massachusetts.

1972   Attends Democratic National Convention in Miami as Massachusetts delegate.

1973   Publishes advice in *Writing Books for Children,* revised as *Guide to Writing for Children.*

1974   Publishes first children's fairy tales, *The Girl Who Cried Flowers and Other Tales,* an American Library Association Notable Book, National Book Award finalist, and Golden Kite Award winner; joins board of directors of Society of Children's Book Writers.

1976   Receives master's of education degree from University of Massachusetts; begins first of seven years as chairman of the board of library trustees in Hatfield.

1978   Edits first anthology, *Shape Shifters;* wins Christopher Medal for *The Seeing Stick.*

1979   Begins first of five years as lecturer in education at Smith College in Massachusetts.

1980   Wins honorary doctor of law degree from Our Lady of the Elms College in Massachusetts for having a writing career "true to her primary source of inspiration—folk culture."

1981   Publishes first young adult novel, *The Gift of Sarah Barker,* an ALA Best Book for Young Adults, and book of essays, *Touch Magic: Fantasy, Faerie and Folklore in the Literature of Childhood.*

1982   *Dragon's Blood* (*Pit Dragon* 1) wins Parents' Choice Award and is one of American Library Association's Best Books for Young Adults; *The Gift of Sarah Barker* is selected as a *School Library Journal* Best Book for Young Adults.

1983   *Dragon's Blood* wins Children's Choice Award; *Tales of Wonder,* first adult collection, is published.

1984   *Heart's Blood* (*Pit Dragon* 2) is selected as Best Book for Young Adults by *School Library Journal* and American Library Association; publishes first adult novel, *Cards of Grief,* and the young adult novel *The Stone Silenus,* which wins a Parents' Choice Award.

1985   CBS Storybreak presents *Dragon's Blood* as a television movie.

1986   Publishes young adult novel *Children of the Wolf* and adult story collection *Merlin's Booke;* begins term as president of Science Fiction Writers of America; wins Daedelus Award for "a body of work—fantasy and short fiction."

1987   Publishes *A Sending of Dragons* (*Pit Dragon* 3).

1988   Publishes *Sister Light, Sister Dark; The Devil's Arithmetic* wins Parents' Choice Silver Seal Award, Jewish Book Council Award, and Association of Jewish Libraries Award; wins Kerlan Award for "singular achievements in children's literature" and World Fantasy Award for *Favorite Folktales from Around the World;* John Schoenherr's *Owl Moon* illustrations win Caldecott Medal; becomes editor in chief of Jane Yolen Books.

1989   Publishes *White Jenna, The Faery Flag,* and *Guide to Writing for Children;* makes long visit to Scotland.

1990   Publishes *The Dragon's Boy.*

1992   Publishes children's autobiography, *A Letter from Phoenix Farm;* wins Regina Medal for body of work; wins Smith College Medal; spends six months in St. Andrew's, Scotland.

1993   *Briar Rose* becomes ALA Best Book for Young Adults; publishes *Here There Be Dragons;* wins Distinguished Alumna Mythopoeic Society Award.

1994   Publishes *Here There Be Unicorns.*

1995   Publishes *The Wild Hunt* and edits *Camelot;* becomes grandmother.

1996   Publishes first two volumes of *The Young Merlin Trilogy, Passager* and *Hobby;* collects own stories in *Here There Be Witches* and *Here There Be Angels.*

1997   Combines *Sister Light, Sister Dark* and *White Jenna* in trade paperback *The Books of Great Alta; Merlin* completes *The Young Merlin Trilogy;* story collection *Twelve Impossible Things Before Breakfast* is published.

> It is all true.
> It is not true.
> The more I tell you,
> The more I shall lie.
> What is story but jesting Pilate's cry?
> I am not paid to tell you the truth.
> —Jane Yolen, from "The Storyteller," in
> *Dragonfield and Other Stories*

As a storyteller, Yolen calls herself a liar and a thief. Her "lies" embroider the truth of story she knows inside, added to stolen bits of others' tales. It is her legacy; Jane Yolen comes from "a family of storytellers. My great-grandfather told stories in the inn that he owned in a little Russian village. My mother and father and all my aunts and uncles were wonderful spinners of tales."[16]

When Jane Yolen was born in New York City on February 11, 1939, her father, Will, was embarking on a career writing nonfiction and public relations material. As a small boy, he emigrated from a town in Russia near Kiev. By his daughter's first year, he was working in California as a publicist for Warner Brothers. Jane remembers nothing of Hollywood but does recall Hampton Roads, Virginia, where she, her mother, Isabelle, and her baby brother, Steve, lived with her grandparents during World War II while her father headed a secret radio broadcasting service in England. Jane "played in the same back acre my mother . . . had played in; I climbed the same trees" ("Route," 143). Her first experience of loss intensifies her Virginia memories, for her beloved grandfather died of a sudden heart attack.

When the war was over, Jane's family reunited in New York City. Since both parents read aloud to her, Jane knew how to read before she started school. Her mother, who created crossword puzzles, shifted Jane among several schools, searching for the best. Finishing her first-grade reading overnight, Jane skipped into second grade at P.S. 93 at 93rd Street and Columbus Avenue, where she earned gold stars in reading and writing and "wrote the school musical, lyrics *and* music, in which everyone was some kind of vegetable," Jane recalls. "I played the lead carrot. Our finale was a salad."[17]

At camp in Maine at age seven, Jane heard "the first *great* story I was ever told." With her back to the fire on a chilly summer night, the storyteller

> was ringed with an aura of flame. . . . She began . . . the story of a mighty hero named Perseus who sought the Gorgon's head. And when the teller came to the point where he had slain Medusa and held up her head, I could have sworn—sworn, mind you, on my mother's heart—that I saw snakes curling and uncurling around her wrist. . . . It was Story. It turned me to stone as surely as Medusa's gaze stared down the wicked king. I could not have moved at that moment had my young life depended upon it.[18]

Jane must have longed to emulate that storyteller's spell casting. Books were also a passion: Stevenson's *Treasure Island* and Andrew Lang fairy tales in all colors were among "endless books" she read "while curled up on the living room windowseat that overlooked Central Park West" ("Route," 143).

Jane enjoyed a stimulating childhood in New York City, much safer then than it is today. She rode the subway all day for just one nickel and played fantasy games about King Arthur and Robin Hood in Central Park. She took classes for eight years at Balanchine's famous ballet school. In seventh grade at Hunter, a school for gifted girls, her alto voice landed her the role of Hansel in *Hansel and Gretel*. She indulged her penchant for poetry by converting her eighth-grade social studies exam to rhyme, a habit she later followed for term papers. Jane also wrote two books at Hunter: a nonfiction account of pirates, which seeded her first published book, and her still-unpublished 17-page novel about Western pioneers. Her storytelling interest blossomed during summers at a Quaker camp in Vermont.[19]

Such talents were encouraged after Jane moved at 13 to Westport, Connecticut, "a hotbed of writers and artists" (*A&A*, 234). Busy Jane not only wrote for the school newspaper but sang in a touring choir, took piano lessons, joined jazz, Spanish, and Latin clubs, captained the girls' basketball team, and learned to ride Lipizzaner show horses from Austria. Valued for her "ability to tell funny stories," Jane ran with both "the intellectual and the fast social crowd." Hidden from friends was Jane's "secret, alien, meditative, poetic side," supported by "the greatest influence on me in high school, . . . my cousin-in-law Honey Knopp." The home of peace activist Honey became a haven for Jane, who loved the folk songs she learned at hootenannies (sing-alongs) there. Such interests, which branded her a "beatnik" or "left-winger," were better kept secret by a '50s teenager (*A&A*, 235). Adding dimension to Jane's Jewish heritage, she attended Mass with her Catholic best friend, Stella. After graduation from Staples High School in Westport in 1956, a summer volunteering at an American Friends Service Committee work camp in Ohio fueled Jane's Quaker instincts (*Major Authors*, 2529). All these spiritual influences later found their way into Jane's books.

Jane's writing developed during her years at Smith College, the prestigious Massachusetts women's school. Enamored of both poetry and journalism, Jane won Smith's journalism prize as well as all its poetry prizes, publishing her poems in student literary magazines. Between junior and senior years, her first poem appeared in a "real" poetry magazine. But she couldn't resist making up parts of her newspaper stories, which became more fictional than factual. Eventually Jane realized that the poet and storyteller in her swamped the journalist (*A&A*, 236).

After graduating from Smith in 1960 with a degree in English, Jane moved to New York City "to find out if I can be a writer." From a summer internship doing research at *This Week* magazine, she moved to a job in the production department of *Saturday Review,* helping to lay out magazine pages. Becoming the seventh person fired by its difficult manager in two years, Jane "spent the first few months of 1961 trying to make a living as a freelance writer." Her father gave her a start, hiring her for "very low" pay to help research and write his book, *The Young Sportsman's Guide to Kite Flying.* She also wrote "short, pithy bios for Cleveland Amory's *Celebrity Register*," where her first puns appeared in print, later to be seen in the children's stories she was beginning to write. But funds were short, and she was "living in a . . . skylit studio apartment in the attic of a three-story house on Commerce Street in Greenwich Village, next to the Cherry Lane Theater" (*A&A*, 236). So Jane got a job as manuscript reader of "bang-bang-shoot-'em-up" paperbacks at Gold Medal Books. On her 22nd birthday, Jane received a marvelous gift from McKay Publishers, a contract for her first children's books, a rhymed concept book, *See This Little Line?*, and the nonfiction *Pirates in Petticoats*. To learn more about children's publishing, Jane began working with "the physical process of putting a book together" at Rutledge Press, a children's book packager.[20]

At a wild housewarming party in her New York apartment with three roommates and the famous Irish singing group the Clancy Brothers and Tommy Makem, Jane met the man she would marry. Unable to squeeze through the crowded doorway, a "handsome mustached young man" climbed through the window to kiss Jane "on the nape of the neck" and introduce himself as David Stemple (*A&A*, 237). They married in 1962. With her first two books published in 1963, Jane began three years as assistant juvenile editor at Alfred A. Knopf Publishers, where her own writing flourished as she met successful authors.

During Jane's last year at Knopf, she saved her entire salary for a trip overseas. In their Volkswagen camper, she and David traveled in Europe and the Middle East for nearly a year. Jane wrote "when we were camping, when we worked on a kibbutz in Israel, when we slept in an olive grove in Greece, when we snorkeled in the Red Sea, when we joined grape pickers in France" (Gallo, 226) and "got pregnant . . . on a town common outside of Paris!" (Roginski, 225). The day after they landed back home, when Jane was eight months pregnant, her agent sold three of her books. Two of them, *The Emperor and the Kite* (a 1968 Caldecott Honor Book featuring Ed Young's intricate paper-cut illustrations and a *New York Times* Best Book of the Year) and *The Minstrel and the Mountain,* went to editor Ann Beneduce at World Publishing, beginning a relationship that would last through many years and many books (Roginski, 225).

When David became a computer science professor at the University of Massachusetts, they bought a house in Conway, welcoming their first child, Heidi, in July 1966. Two more babies arrived at two-year intervals, Adam in 1968 and Jason in 1970. Jane wrote while her children napped; her musical *Robin Hood* was produced in Boston in 1967. In 1971, the Stemples moved into a 14-room farmhouse, Phoenix Farm, in Hatfield, Massachusetts, where Jane has enjoyed walking along the Connecticut River ever since. The farm appeared as Fe-Fi-Fo-Farm in her picture book *The Giants' Farm* (Seabury, 1977), illustrated with sturdy grinning giants by Tomie dePaola.

Throughout the 1970s, Jane Yolen deepened her involvement in children's literature, eventually teaching it at Smith College. As demand grew for her speeches, she wrote *Guide to Writing for Children,* which contains advice on writing all types of books and getting published as well as heartfelt philosophies behind her work. Revisiting such favorite childhood characters and authors as Nancy Drew, Uncle Wiggly, T. H. White, Rudyard Kipling, and Louisa May Alcott, Yolen analyzes which ones "stood the test of the ages—my age as well as theirs." As an adult, she found new favorites, including Natalie Babbitt, Lloyd Alexander, Patricia McKillip, and Maurice Sendak. As they do, she learned to tell children's stories "to the child inside" her.[21]

In 1974, Jane Yolen's first collection of composed fairy tales, *The Girl Who Cried Flowers and Other Tales,* won the most acclaim she had yet earned: It became an American Library Association Notable Book and a National Book Award finalist and won the Golden Kite and other awards. The same year, Yolen published her first novel-length fairy tale for all ages, *The Magic Three of Solatia,* in which she explores her conviction that magic has consequences as three magic wishes connect four stories. Her reputation for seamless literary fairy tales led to her editing *Shape-Shifters* in 1978, the first of many anthologies of stories by other writers.

Yolen assumed leadership in literary organizations, joining the board of directors of the Society of Children's Book Writers, becoming chairman of the board of library trustees in her Hatfield public library, and starting a monthly writers' workshop at her library, which lasted for over 20 years. Meanwhile she attended the 1972 Democratic National Convention in Miami as a Massachusetts delegate, earned a master of education degree from the University of Massachusetts in 1976, and won an honorary law degree from Our Lady of the Elms College in 1980. In 1986, she began two years as president of the Science Fiction Writers of America.

"It was in the 1980s that I was discovered!" asserts Jane Yolen, by adults as well as children (*A&A*, 240). Her stories were in demand for such adult publications as *Isaac Asimov's SF Magazine* and for many anthologies. Yolen's 70th book, *Tales of Wonder*, published in 1983, was her first collection compiled for adults. The following year, her science fantasy *Cards of Grief* was her first adult novel. In *Merlin's Booke* she interpreted legends surrounding King Arthur. Companion novels *Sister Light, Sister Dark* and *White Jenna*, together called *The Books of Great Alta*, explored the relation between myth and story in a community of warrior women. These adult works are analyzed later in this chapter; *Merlin's Booke* is discussed with Arthurian fiction in chapter 5.

As her children became teenagers, Jane Yolen ventured into young adult fiction. Since writing her nonfiction *Simple Gifts: The Story of the Shakers* (Viking) in 1976, she had wanted to tell a personal narrative about a follower of this strict religion that isolates men from women. When her daughter, Heidi, turned 14, Jane wondered "how, in a Shaker community, you could keep the boys away from a girl like Heidi or keep Heidi away from the boys. I imagined a Romeo and Juliet story within the Shaker setting" (*A&A*, 240). That story became *The Gift of Sarah Barker* (Viking, 1981), a young adult novel set in the mid-1800s, in which Sarah, her looks and personality borrowed from Heidi, falls in love with Abel and is not allowed to get anywhere near him (*Guide*, 19). The novel was named a Best Book for Young Adults by both *School Library Journal* and the American Library Association.

Yolen's older son, Adam, inspired young dragon breeder Jakkin in her young adult science fantasy *The Pit Dragon Trilogy*, which began as a short story, "Cockfight," became a novel, *Dragon's Blood,* and kept its grip on Yolen until it had filled two more books. Parts of the trilogy won both the Parents' Choice and Children's Choice Awards and were named Best Books for Young Adults by both ALA and *SLJ;* the trilogy is examined with other dragon books in chapter 6.

Yolen's next YA novel, *The Stone Silenus,* is magic realism, a Parents' Choice winner in which a teenaged girl, again patterned after Heidi, imagines her dead father returned as a faun; the work is described with books on mythical creatures in chapter 6. *Children of the Wolf* (Viking, 1986), a realistic novel based on fact from 1920s India, is narrated by 14-year-old Mohandas, who brings two feral children raised by wolves to an orphanage to be civilized. In yet another YA genre, a Jewish girl from the present time travels to a Nazi concentration camp in *The Devil's Arithmetic,* which won several awards and is discussed with time travel books in chapter 7.

Meanwhile, Jane Yolen remembered her original audience, introducing two children's series during the 1980s. *Commander Toad* (Coward), sparked by her small son Adam's fear of going upstairs,[22] follows the comic science fiction adventures of frogs and toads on the spaceship *Star Warts.* The *Piggins* series (Harcourt) features a charming mystery-solving pig butler who serves a family of foxes. The '80s also brought Jane Yolen a number of major awards: the 1986 Daedelus Award for "a body of work—fantasy and short fiction"; the Kerlan Award for "singular achievements in children's literature"; the World Fantasy Award for her compilation *Favorite Folktales from Around the World;* and the Caldecott Medal for *Owl Moon,* illustrated by John Schoenherr and inspired by the nighttime owling treks of Jane's husband, David, with little Heidi. The last three awards arrived in 1988, when Harcourt Brace Jovanovich launched Jane Yolen Books, an imprint publishing young adult fantasy books edited by Jane Yolen.

Yolen's '90s decade opened with the Catholic Library Association's Regina Medal and the Smith College Medal. Her middle grade novel *The Dragon's Boy* appears with Arthurian legends in chapter 5. Yolen's strong interest in the Arthurian myth also manifested in her editing of stories by such authors as Anne McCaffrey and Terry Pratchett in 1995's *Camelot: A Collection of Original Arthurian Stories.* For readers ages 7 to 10, Yolen wrote the *Young Merlin Trilogy; Passager* and *Hobby* were published in 1996, *Merlin* in 1997.

Yolen's Jewish heritage led her to profound exploration of the resounding effects of the Nazi Holocaust on the generations that followed it. Having begun that literary witness for young readers in 1988 through time travel in *The Devil's Arithmetic,* her vision developed five years later into the most significant adult novel of her career, *Briar Rose.* Through fearless innovations in story structure, Yolen weaves a modern young American woman's childhood remembrances of her Polish grandmother Gemma's vivid retellings of the "Sleeping Beauty" fairy tale into a search for Gemma's true identity after her death. Following clues revealed in Gemma's own rewording of the fairy tale, her granddaughter Becca journeys to Poland to uncover hidden horrors that Gemma endured during the war. When Becca finally learns the truth that Gemma could never speak, she is able to face her own future and heal her grief. Nowhere has any other writer succeeded so brilliantly in demonstrating the power of story to translate and transform lives. Older YA readers are mesmerized by the tragic beauty and ultimate healing hope in the haunting *Briar Rose,* which was both a Mythopoeic Society Award winner and an ALA Best Book for Young Adults in 1993. Soon after, Yolen used another fairy tale character, the demon imp from "Rumpelstiltskin," to portray the evil of a pogrom in the Jewish ghetto in her ancestral homeland, the Ukraine. This short story "Granny Rumple" appears in the adult fairy tale collection *Black Thorn, White Rose* (Morrow, 1994), edited by Ellen Datlow and Terri Windling.

Elegant illustrated volumes of Yolen's YA fantasy stories, 1993's *Here There Be Dragons* and 1994's *Here There Be Unicorns,* are described in the dragon and unicorn sections of chapter 6. The beautiful oversize series, illustrated on heavy coated stock in black and white by David Wilgus, continued in 1996 with *Here There Be Witches* and *Here There Be Angels.* Yet another collection of Yolen's own fairy tale retellings and composed literary tales, *Twelve Impossible Things Before Breakfast: Stories,* appeared in 1997.

Jane Yolen's three children have grown up to collaborate on books with their mother. Yolen sends story drafts back and forth to her daughter, Heidi E.Y. Stemple over the Internet. Mother and daughter coauthored three short stories for magazines and a Random House anthology, *Great Writers and Their Great Kids,* as well as a children's book, *Meet the Monsters* (Walker, 1996). Heidi, the mother of Yolen's first grandchild, Maddison Jane Piatt, born in 1995, lives in Atlanta, having given up her career as a private detective.

Musician Adam Stemple arranged music for his mother's *Lullaby Songbook* (Harcourt, 1986), *Lap-Time Song and Play Book* (Harcourt, 1989), and for *Hark! A Christmas Sampler* (Putnam, 1991), which also contains Adam's original tunes. Playing guitar, keyboards, and mandolin in a band called Boiled in Lead, Adam composed Celtic and Middle Eastern–influenced rock music for the band's album *Antler Dance* (Omni Records). Boiled in Lead leaves its Minneapolis base to tour nationally, members sometimes sleeping on Yolen's farmhouse floor. Adam also collaborated on an unusual CD with author Steven Brust, whose novel *The Gypsy* (Tor, 1992), coauthored with Megan Lindhold, can be read on computer disk or played as a music CD, Adam's music accompanying Brust's lyrics.

As a Colorado college student, Jason Stemple took photographs for his mother's autobiography for children, *A Letter from Phoenix Farm.* Fans of all ages will appreciate pictures of her sprawling 1896 farmhouse jammed with books. She calls her two-room attic office the Aerie. In its writing room, Yolen begins each day at six o'clock, still wearing her nightgown. In the editing room, she spends her time on the phone "helping other people turn their stories into books."[23] Jason's camera captures his mother with a huge pile of mail at the post office, including letters from young readers, which she always answers. He shows her storytelling, signing autographs, writing music, poring over page proofs with her editor and over a story draft with her husband,

and singing with her family on a holiday when everyone comes together.

Living in rugged Crested Butte, Colorado, Jason skis, mountain bikes, and hikes with his dog, Misty, while pursuing a freelance photography career. His surroundings provide ample inspiration for further collaborations with his mother; her children's poems about water team with Jason's stunning nature photographs in *Water Music* (Boyds Mills Press, 1995).

Jane Yolen leaves Phoenix Farm for conferences, speaking engagements, and regular long stays in Scotland. She and her husband, who traces his Scottish heritage to the Douglas clan, "have loved Scotland ever since our first visit there, in the early 1980s, when we walked the Highland hills, strolled by misty dark lochs, and explored the stone brochs and the standing stones on Orkney. There is . . . still much magic left there."[24] In 1992, she transported her work to "a beautiful stone turn-of-the-century house named Wayside" in St. Andrews, Fife, an ancient seacoast town. There she read more books "in six months than I had in the past six years," from Ruth Rendell mysteries and George Mackay Brown poetry to Scottish history. Though she finished writing "five picture books, six short stories, four essays, and innumerable poems" during that time, only one story and a few poems were about Scotland, since she usually writes "about Place long after I have left."[25] When her husband retires, she plans to spend more time in Scotland.

Jane Yolen continues to add to her astounding body of 200 works of all kinds for all ages, read around the world in many languages. She also bakes bread, performs folk music, rides horses, dances, camps, skis, fences, and spoils her baby granddaughter.

Heart's Blood: A Conduit for Stories

Jane Yolen is candid about her writing. "I look back at some of my early writing with a mixture of amusement and despair. . . . It . . . seems . . . incredibly amateurish or at least unformed. Or uninformed. The thing about being a writer is that one has a chance to get better. We revise not only our stories but, in a sense, our abilities, our lives. . . . [W]riting is the kind of work where you can grow older and grow up into your potential" (*Unicorns*, 103). She sees room for improvement. "I think my strengths are inventiveness, story, and style. My weakest link is characterization. I tend to take people at face value in life, never looking for that dark underside. . . . I also wish I could plot more intricately. I love to read murder mysteries. . . . But I can't write them because I am not a good chess player. I can't think two or three moves ahead" (Roginski, 230). Meticulously revising her work, Yolen takes pride in her "books as representatives of my labors and my particular gifts. . . . Long after I am gone, my books will live. A child showed me this in a letter. He wrote, 'Your stories will live forever. I hope you live to ninety-nine or a hundred, but who cares!' " (Roginski, 233).

Jane Yolen sees her "most significant contribution to literature for children" as her fairy tales (*A&A*, 238), for which she has been called "America's Hans Christian Andersen."[26] Other stories are difficult to categorize. "I tell a story," Yolen declares, "then someone else decides how it should be packaged—for children or adults. That is a blurry line in many of my works" (*A&A*, 237). Age or genre distinctions limit Yolen's inclusive art, which interprets the great human story.

"Storytelling is a personal art that makes public what is private and makes private what is public. By choosing this or that story to tell, I reveal much about myself," says Yolen (*Folktales*, 13). Stories help her work out her own relationships. "Many of my stories are about a girl trying to please her father. That's me. But my father didn't know. He never really read anything that I'd written. . . . He felt they were not 'real' books because they were kids' books," so he never got Jane's messages (*A&A*, 238). Jane embraced his interests as International Kite Flying Champion by helping with his book about kites, then wrote kite nonfiction of her own, *World on a String*. Dedicated to her father, her Caldecott Honor book *The Emperor and the Kite* features a tiny Chinese princess, unnoticed until she saves her imprisoned emperor father by sending him food and an escape rope on a flying kite. Then he allows her to rule the kingdom beside him, fulfilling Jane's vain wish.

In another Ed Young picture book, *The Girl Who Loved the Wind,* Jane's father is represented by a wealthy Persian merchant who protects his daughter Danina in a house with a walled garden beside the sea. When the wind whispers that things change, Danina cannot resist the call of truth, escaping across the sea on her cape, billowed by the wind. "It is in a very real way the story of my life, for my own father was extremely protective," confesses Yolen (*Guide,* 60). The same wind that lifted her father's kites carried Danina/Jane to a new life with her husband; she dedicated this book to David Stemple.

Thirteen years later, a kite reappeared in "Dragonfield," whose hero, says Yolen, "knows himself not to be a hero, and the audience knows him not to be a hero, and yet he is a hero despite it all."[27] Handsome, muscle-bound Lancot ("Yes, his name is supposed to remind you of Lancelot") has no intention of ridding an island of the dragon Aredd. Only the tenacity of the healer's daughter Tansy—and his love for her—make Lancot shimmy up the rope of a dragon kite to stuff blistering dragonsbane into Aredd's mouth. Fascinatingly, Tansy repeats the strategy used by the princess in *The Emperor and the Kite,* hanging a rope and basket from a kite (Yolen stealing from herself!). This classic hero tale challenges readers to grow along with Lancot as he "seeks himself, seeks to mature, so that when he comes into his powers, he uses them for others, not himself."[28] The title story in a 1985 paperback collection, "Dragonfield" also appears in *Here There Be Dragons.*

Two stories eight years apart helped Jane Yolen cope with her mother's death. The day she learned her mother had incurable cancer, Yolen began writing her picture book *The Bird of Time,* in which miller's son Pieter finds a magic bird that can slow, speed, or stop time. After reading the manuscript, Jane's mother commented, " 'Intimations of mortality, eh?'. . . And I knew at once that she knew she was dying," confesses Yolen. "The story was a bridge between us" (*A&A,* 239–40). Isabelle Yolen did not live to see *The Bird of Time* published and dedicated to her. Only after her death did Jane realize that her book was about her desire to stop time, to save her mother. But Jane's mourning was not finished. Eight years later, she read aloud her new story, "The Boy Who Sang for Death," from *Dream Weaver*. When she reached the line "Any gift I have I would give to get my mother back," Jane began to sob, her grief emerging "out loud. Stories do give us permission to have feelings; not only do they give permission to the author, but they also give it to the reader. Stories help people, heal people" (*A&A,* 240).

"We humans *are* story," declares Yolen. "We define ourselves by story, we give ourselves guidelines, we record our histories and mysteries and our relationships—to one another, to our gods, to the world. No other creature on Earth is a storyteller. Over the years I have come to terms with the fact that my one great gift is to be the conduit for stories."[29] Transmitting them becomes "the most potent kind of magic, . . . for they catch a glimpse of the soul beneath the skin. Touch magic. Pass it on" (*Touch Magic,* 57). That saying is Yolen's mantra. She describes this life-giving exchange: "Storytelling, like any other form of mouth-to-mouth resuscitation, needs two people for the experience. So does writing, which I have often described as a private act between two consenting individuals: storyteller and story listener, or story writer and story reader. Breath giver, breath taker" ("Wood," 7).

Story's "code," Yolen explains, "can be read on many levels. The child reads it on one, the adult on another. . . . My husband reads it differently than my father. And I read it another way still. . . . But a child, more open than the adult, is more changed by that reading. . . . What slips in . . . shapes the man or woman into which that child will grow. Story is one of the most serious intruders into the heart." Between writer and child, "there is a literary Eucharist: heart to heart, body to body, blood to blood. The writer is parent to all children who read what he or she writes" (*Touch Magic,* 26–27). Strong imagery indeed.

Where in this process is the young adult reader, eagerly forming his or her own interpretations? Yolen explains that a performing storyteller "can tell, just by the faces, when she has hit *the* story for a particular person. And that is because the listener is immobilized, paralyzed by hearing his or her own particular truth being spoken aloud" (*Touch Magic,* 54). A young woman in one of

Yolen's workshops found *her* story in "The Face in the Cloth" from *The Faery Flag*. A princess who wears her dead mother's portrait sewn into her clothes is unable to prosper until she replaces it with her own picture, struggling to "pull free of her famous mother's image and . . . live her own life" ("Wood," 6)—a powerful realization to Yolen's listener.

Any of Jane Yolen's stories might so resonate with young adult readers, who could begin searching for *the* story in *Tales of Wonder*, Yolen's first adult collection. Among 30 eclectic, vibrant tales are examples of most Yolen story types, from a Cinderella variant to a contemporary take on the classic myth of Icarus. Shorter early versions of her novels are here: "Cockfight" evolved into *Dragon's Blood*, "Wild Goose and Gander" is book 4 of *The Magic Three of Solatia*, "In the Hall of Grief" and "Cards of Grief" merged into the novel *Cards of Grief*, and "Sister Light, Sister Dark" seeded the novel of that title. Picture books' texts appear as short stories, including "The Bird of Time" and "The Girl Who Loved the Wind." Stories from collections edited by Yolen are easier to locate here; her crafty Communist Russian Baba Yaga in "Boris Chernovsky's Hands" otherwise appears only in the paperback *Hecate's Cauldron*. Several tales illustrate favorite Yolen themes. "Old Herald" unnervingly satirizes our attitudes toward art, as a dying blind artist, revered as a god, is helped by lifelong servant Critics to paint his final canvas with tubes threaded through veins into his heart: "Truly great art is lifeblood spilled upon the canvas."[30] In "Names," the daughter of a Nazi death camp survivor starves herself to mirror her mother's torture. This piercing piece is echoed later in Yolen's Holocaust novels *The Devil's Arithmetic* and *Briar Rose*.

Critics applauded Yolen's foray into adult literature. "Universal themes come to life in Yolen's lucid prose and linger glowing in memory. . . . [Yolen] pierces the armor of adult sophistication to touch the heart of childlike wonder in us all," raved *Publisher's Weekly*.[31] *SF and Fantasy Review* called for "two kinds of readers" to "learn from or take delight in *Tales of Wonder* . . . the first . . . who considers Yolen a writer of children's stories and hence, perhaps not deserving of adult attention," and "the second . . .

who thinks . . . that interesting art folk tales no longer are being created." This "splendid collection . . . should remind readers of how much they really enjoy stories."[32]

Three stories in *The Faery Flag: Stories and Poems of Fantasy and the Supernatural* address youth's central concern, coming of age. "Words of Power" takes place in a society "based loosely on Native American cliff dwellers" (Interview). At 15, Late Blossoming Flower is angry when her womanhood is so tardy. Impatient with lessons on adult disciplines and skills, Flower prefers to be with irreverent old Laughing Man. When her flow begins, her sudden power of Shaping changes Laughing Man, by mistake, into a butterfly; now Flower understands why she must learn control. Yolen writes about such rituals because "we have no real rites of passage in American society today. Teens dictate that passage for themselves now with the prom, the first car, the first date/ kiss/making love, instead of the older, wiser adult society having trials to welcome them in" (Interview). Different cultures in her stories underline this transformation's universality. In "The Foxwife," Japanese student Jiro is isolated on an island until he rids himself of anger much like Flower's. Shapeshifting again reveals Jiro's growth when he accepts a wife who changes into a fox. *The Faery Flag*'s title story involves another such passage in a fairy-human marriage in Scotland. *The Faery Flag* also includes a light-hearted revision of "Little Red Riding Hood," "The Three Little Pigs," and "Peter and the Wolf," as the retired wolves explain their side of the stories in "Happy Dens, or, A Day in the Old Wolves' Home." A critic found it "remarkable . . . that Yolen seems equally at home in all these varied voices and settings. . . . These stories resonate with deeply felt emotions of love, hatred, wonder, terror, and a particular haunting quality which is Yolen's own."[33]

Ritual is also a hallmark of Yolen's first adult science fantasy, *Cards of Grief*. Written during her "long grieving period" when Yolen's father lived his last years with her, ravaged by Parkinson's disease,[34] it is set on L'Lal'lor, Planet of the Grievers. Their matriarchal culture is based on ritualized grief that is so pervasive that no one laughs or shows emotion. At 13, peasant Lina-Lania's talent for composing grief poetry is noticed by a prince, who makes her Queen's Griever, soon a legend called Gray Wanderer, or Linni. Unknown to these artists of grief, their world is being studied from a space lab by scientists from Earth. Against all rules, anthropologist Aaron Spenser falls in love with Linni, and she bears his child. After serving a five-year sentence for cultural contamination, Aaron joins Linni, now an old woman, since 10 years pass on the planet for each space station year. Aaron's laughter changes her world forever.

With its complex structure of the lab's taped transcripts in varied voices and its stately elegiac style, *Cards of Grief* is demanding to read. Intense scrutiny of art and culture questions our basic beliefs, as love transforms this planet more fearful of change than of death. Like clouds scuttling across the sun, shifting light and dark moods intrigue the reader. Yolen calls the novel her "manifesto" (*A&A,* 236). Critics call it "bittersweet . . . gentle, poetic,"[35] or "a poignant love story and a well-felt story of first contact,"[36] or "lyrical, . . . unusual, . . . engrossing and unpredictable."[37] A 1984 original paperback, the novel is difficult to locate in libraries and may be too experimental for many teenaged readers.

More accessible are two works demonstrating how story shapes life. "The tales that I write are my dreams just as folk tales are the collective dreams of society," writes Yolen ("Mythmakers," 494). *Dream Weaver,* illustrated by Michael Hague and packaged as a children's book, speaks to all ages. In seven stories within a story, a blind old woman cajoles passersby into parting with a penny for a dream. For payment received, she selects threads from her basket to weave a dream, actually a story she "sees" fits each customer perfectly. For a worried young widow with a little boy, she weaves "The Tree's Wife," in which a wealthy widow refuses greedy suitors by marrying a tree, his birch grove protecting her from attacking villagers. The widow hearing this tale knows her husband's people will take her in. As these flawless tales flow, readers enjoy working out how dreams symbolize people's lives.

"Every memorable story," writes Yolen, "is about the working through evil in order to come at last to the light" (*Touch Magic,* 72). Her adult novels *Sister Light, Sister Dark* and *White Jenna,* recently published together as *The Books of Great Alta,* are breathtaking revelations of light and dark. Reporting the same story in different forms, their structure reveals how myth entwines with human experience to create reality.

In the Dales, a culture that devalues females, unmarried women rescue baby girls left to die and foster them in 17 walled Hames, refuges for women who worship the goddess Alta. Unknown to surrounding villages, Alta's women have a secret. During coming-of-age rituals, each girl gazes into a mirror to call forth her dark sister, her mirror image or alter ego. Thereafter, at moonrise, dark sisters come to share their other halves' lives, doubling each Hame's population. Enjoying disciplined, fulfilling lives, Hames women await an event professed by Alta: a white babe with black eyes, made of dark and light, will be born to three mothers. Thrice orphaned, she will make the bull, the bear, the cat, and the hound bow down. The coming of this White One, the Anna, marks both beginning and end. After losing three mothers, white-haired baby Jenna is raised communally at Selden Hame. Everyone notices her exceptional talents, but Jenna scoffs at rumors of her destiny as White One. Befriending exiled Prince Carum, Jenna kills a man to save him, appalled to learn her victim is the Hound, from Alta's prophecy. Proclaimed as the Anna at only 13, Jenna's unsettling fate must involve saving Hames destroyed by usurper King Kalas.

These events are related in separate sections of the text. "The Myth" contains Alta's symbolic pronouncements, while "The Legend" makes past events as reliable as gossip. "The Tale" is an unadorned folk fragment, while "The Parable" makes a moralistic point. "The Ballad" celebrates the Anna's heroics, while "The Song" can be a lullaby or other folk remnant of Jenna's culture. (Yolen provides music at the end of the book.) "The History" attempts to reconstruct dead Dales culture through evidence from a pompous historian in furious disagreement with folklorist Magon, whom he calls a fool. All these commentaries interweave with "The Story," the action centering around Jenna. It is fascinating to trace each diverging interpretation from Jenna's story; Yolen reveals her hand when reviled folklorist Magon proves more accurate than the historian, who shuns all mystical elements, dismissing dark sisters as hocus-pocus. With wry wit,

Yolen mines the humor in these variations, allowing the reader to select the version he or she prefers. She is in such control of her material that what might in less capable hands be intrusive to the story's flow enhances it instead; Jenna's narrative is so entrancing that it never loses momentum.

At the end of the first volume, Jenna enters womanhood by calling her dark sister, Skada, from the mirror. Uncomfortable meeting her other half, Jenna must accept two parts of her whole. Skada greets her: "I am you. And what you keep yourself from being."[38] Only when Jenna descends into the underworld to meet Alta herself in *White Jenna* does she understand her role as the Anna. Immortal Alta says Jenna must "bring light and dark together," not only overcoming Kalas's evil to restore the throne to Carum but also reuniting men and women.[39] Fulfilling the prophecy, Jenna and Carum become lovers. All ends in graceful symmetry as variants of Jenna's tale merge into a shimmering tapestry of textured threads. This definitive work crowns Yolen's storytelling mission, relating truth to myth. "The reader may want to know which strand of the story to trust—the narrative, the myth, the legend, the history," says Yolen. "They are all equally trustworthy and equally untrustworthy. Just like the real world" (Interview).

Many see *The Books of Great Alta* as her finest work. *Locus* critic Tom Whitmore declared them, "as a whole, . . . one of my favorite books of the decade. Yolen has done a marvelous job of balancing here: light and dark, history and folklore, cracks at academia and brilliant storytelling all interwoven to make a tale as complex and beautiful as the most intricately braided hair."[40] (He refers to Alta's black-and-white braids.) Only sophisticated readers will grasp Yolen's concept. Though her devoted teenaged fans enjoy the novels, appreciation varies according to experience. Some YAFEs skipped variants to get back to "the Story"; others found comparisons intriguing. Baltimore teens named *Sister Light, Sister Dark* a Youth-to-Youth Book. More YAFE comments on Yolen's work may be found in chapters 6 and 7.

Her latest unclassifiable picture book, *The Wild Hunt*, ventures into mythic landscapes, reenacting the potent pagan myth of the Horned Man and the White Goddess. Like *The Books of Great*

Alta, it infuses mythic power into real life through structure. Chapters come in triads: a straight narrative of a boy alone in a house with a white cat and a book containing the Wild Hunt story, a "sort of" chapter in the same house in a parallel world, and an "almost" chapter about the hunt itself. In this creepy tale, the reader, represented by the boy, may consent or refuse to give myth dimension in our world. With deceptively simple language, Yolen probes our fears and dreams in symbolic layers that peel indefinitely, like the pungent onion of the world.

Recommended Reading

(* denotes title mentioned in text; other titles are additional)

What Is Myth?

Mythic Novels and Stories

AFRICAN-AMERICAN MYTH
Hamilton, Virginia. *The Magical Adventures of Pretty Pearl.* New York: Harper & Row, 1983.

ASIAN MYTH
Alexander, Lloyd. *The Remarkable Journey of Prince Jen.* New York: Dutton, 1991.

Kipling, Rudyard. *Kipling's Fantasy Stories.* Presented by John Brunner. New York: Tor, 1992.

Ogiwara, Noriko. **Dragon Sword and Wind Child.* Trans. Cathy Hirano. New York: Farrar, Straus, & Giroux, 1993.

AUSTRALIAN ABORIGINAL MYTH
Wrightson, Patricia. **Balyet.* New York: Margaret K. McElderry Books, 1989.

BRITISH/CELTIC MYTH
Gardner, John. *Grendel.* New York: Knopf, 1971.

Hendry, Frances Mary. *Quest for a Maid.* New York: Farrar, Straus, & Giroux, 1990, 1992.

Holdstock, Robert. **The Mythago Cycle.* 4 vols.

    Vol. 1: *Mythago Wood.* New York: Arbor House, 1985.

    Vol. 2: *Lavondyss.* New York: Morrow, 1989.

    Vol. 3: *The Hollowing.* New York: Penguin/ROC, 1994.

    Vol. 4: *Gate of Ivory, Gate of Horn.* New York: ROC, 1997.

Holt, Tom. *Who's Afraid of Beowulf?* New York: St. Martin's, 1989.

Classical Myth

BIBLICAL MYTH

Levitin, Sonia. *Escape from Egypt*. Boston: Little Brown, 1994.

GREEK MYTH

Alcock, Vivien. *Singer to the Sea God*. New York: Delacorte, 1993.

Bradley, Marion Zimmer. *The Firebrand*. New York: Simon & Schuster, 1987.

Bradshaw, Gillian. *Beyond the North Wind*. New York: Greenwillow, 1993.

Hoover, H. M. *The Dawn Palace: The Story of Medea*. New York: Dutton, 1988.

Johnston, Norma. *Pride of Lions*. New York: Atheneum, 1979.

———. *Strangers Dark and Gold*. New York: Atheneum, 1975.

McCaughrean, Geraldine. *Greek Myths*. Illus. Emma Chichester Clark. New York: McElderry/Simon & Schuster, 1993.

McLaren, Clemence. *Inside the Walls of Troy*. New York: Atheneum/Simon & Schuster, 1996.

Orgel, Doris. *Ariadne, Awake!* Illus. Barry Moser. New York: Viking, 1994.

Purtill, Richard. *Enchantment at Delphi*. San Diego: Harcourt Brace Jovanovich, 1986.

Renault, Mary. *The King Must Die*. New York: Pantheon, 1958.

Sequel: *The Bull from the Sea*. New York: Pantheon, 1962.

Sutcliff, Rosemary. *Black Ships Before Troy: The Story of the Iliad*. Illus. Alan Lee. New York: Delacorte, 1993.

———. *The Wanderings of Odysseus: The Story of the Odyssey*. Illus. Alan Lee. New York: Delacorte, 1996.

Voigt, Cynthia. *Orfe*. New York: Atheneum, 1992.

SCANDINAVIAN MYTH

James, J. Alison. *Runa*. New York: Atheneum, 1993.

Jones, Diana Wynne. *Eight Days of Luke*. New York: Greenwillow, 1988, © 1975.

Paxson, Diana L. *The Wolf and the Raven*. New York: Morrow, 1993.

WORLD MYTH

Anthony, Piers. *Incarnations of Immortality* Series. 7 vols. Vols. 1–5: New York: Ballantine/Del Rey. Vols. 6–7: New York: Morrow.

Vol. 1: *On a Pale Horse*. 1983.

Vol. 2: *Bearing an Hourglass*. 1984.

Vol. 3: *With a Tangled Skein*. 1985.

Vol. 4: *Wielding a Red Sword*. 1986.

Vol. 5: *Being a Green Mother*. 1987.

Vol. 6: *For Love of Evil*. 1988.

Vol. 7: *And Eternity*. 1990.

Cotterell, Arthur. *The Macmillan Illustrated Encyclopedia of Myths and Legends*. New York: Macmillan, 1989, 1996.

Hamilton, Virginia. *In the Beginning: Creation Stories from Around the World*. Illus. Barry Moser. San Diego: Harcourt Brace Jovanovich, 1988.

McCaughrean, Geraldine. *The Golden Hoard: Myths and Legends of the World*. Illus. Bee Willey. New York: McElderry/Simon & Schuster, 1996.

Myers, John Myers. **Silverlock*. New York: Dutton, 1949; Cutchogue, N.Y.: Buccaneer Books, reprint 1993.

Philip, Neil. *The Illustrated Book of Myths: Tales and Legends of the World*. Illus. Nilesh Mistry. New York: Dorling Kindersley, 1995.

NATIVE AMERICAN MYTH

Bruchac, Joseph. **Dawn Land Trilogy*. 3 vols. Golden, Colo.: Fulcrum.
   Vol. 1: *Dawn Land*. 1993.
   Vol. 2: *Long River*. 1995.
   Vol. 3: Forthcoming.

Card, Orson Scott. *Tales of Alvin Maker* Series. 4 vols. New York: Tor.
   Vol. 1: **Seventh Son*. 1987.
   Vol. 2: *Red Prophet*. 1988.
   Vol. 3: *Prentice Alvin*. 1989.
   Vol. 4: *Alvin Journeyman*. 1995.

MacGregor, Rob. Hopi Series. 2 vols. New York: Simon & Schuster.
   Vol. 1: *Prophecy Rock*. 1995.
   Vol. 2: *Hawk Moon*. 1996.

Murphy, Pat. **The Falling Woman*. New York: Tor, 1986.

Wangerin, Walter, Jr. *The Crying for a Vision*. New York: Simon & Schuster, 1994.

RUSSIAN MYTH

Price, Susan. *Ghost* Series. New York: Farrar, Straus, & Giroux.
   Vol. 1: *The Ghost Drum*. 1987.
   Vol. 2: *Ghost Song*. 1992.
   Vol. 3: *Ghost Dance*. 1995.

Mythmaking

Jane Yolen—Heart's Blood: A Conduit for Stories

MYTHIC NOVELS AND STORIES BY JANE YOLEN

(See Yolen Selected Bibliography for other titles and chapter notations.)

*The Books of Great Alta. 2 vols. New York: Tor.
   Vol. 1: *Sister Light, Sister Dark*. 1988.
   Vol. 2: *White Jenna*. 1989.
   Also published in single volume *The Books of Great Alta*. 1997.

Cards of Grief. New York: Ace, 1984.
Dragonfield and Other Stories. New York: Ace, 1985.
Dream Weaver. Illus. Michael Hague. New York: Philomel, 1989, © 1979.
The Faery Flag: Stories and Poems of Fantasy and the Supernatural. New York: Orchard, 1989.
Here There Be . . . Sequence. 4 vols. Illus. David Wilgus. San Diego: Harcourt Brace.

Here There Be Dragons. 1993.
Here There Be Unicorns. 1994.
Here There Be Witches. 1996.
Here There Be Angels. 1996.

Tales of Wonder. New York: Schocken Books, 1983.
Twelve Impossible Things Before Breakfast: Stories. San Diego: Harcourt Brace, 1997.
The Wild Hunt. San Diego: Harcourt Brace, 1995.

STORY ANTHOLOGIES EDITED BY JANE YOLEN

Camelot: A Collection of Original Arthurian Stories. Illus. Winslow Pels. New York: Philomel, 1995.
Dragons & Dreams. Ed. Jane Yolen, Martin H. Greenberg, and Charles G. Waugh. New York: Harper & Row, 1986.
Favorite Folktales from Around the World. New York: Pantheon, 1988.
Shape Shifters: Fantasy and Science Fiction Tales about Humans Who Can Change Their Shapes. New York: Seabury Press/Clarion, 1978.
Things That Go Bump in the Night: A Collection of Original Stories. Ed. Jane Yolen and Martin H. Greenberg. New York: Harper & Row, 1989.
Vampires: A Collection of Original Stories. Ed. Jane Yolen and Martin H. Greenberg. New York: HarperCollins, 1991.
Werewolves: A Collection of Original Stories. Ed. Jane Yolen and Martin H. Greenberg. New York: Harper & Row, 1988.
Xanadu. New York: Tor, 1993.
Xanadu 2. New York: Tor, 1994.
Xanadu 3. New York: Tor, 1995.

Selected Bibliography

(Notations: "C4", etc., refers to chapter in which title is discussed.)

Jane Yolen

Primary Sources

The Bird of Time (C4). Illus. Mercer Mayer. New York: Thomas Y. Crowell, 1971.

The Books of Great Alta. 2 vols. New York: Tor.
   Vol. 1: *Sister Light, Sister Dark* (C4). 1988.
   Vol. 2: *White Jenna* (C4). 1989.
   Also published in single volume *The Books of Great Alta.* 1997.
Briar Rose (C4). *The Fairy Tale Series.* New York: Tor, 1992.
Cards of Grief (C4). New York: Ace, 1984.
"The Creative Process: The Route to Story." *The New Advocate* (Summer 1991): 143–49.
The Devil's Arithmetic (C7). New York: Viking, 1988.
The Dragon's Boy (C5). New York: HarperCollins, 1990.
Dragonfield and Other Stories (C4). New York: Ace, 1985.
Dream Weaver (C4). Illus. Michael Hague. New York: Philomel, 1989, © 1979.
The Emperor and the Kite (C4). Illus. Ed Young. New York: World Publishing, 1967.
"An Empress of Thieves." *The Horn Book Magazine* (November/December 1994): 702–5.
The Faery Flag: Stories and Poems of Fantasy and the Supernatural (C4). New York: Orchard, 1989.
The Girl Who Cried Flowers and Other Tales (C4). Illus. David Palladini. New York: Thomas Y. Crowell, 1974.
The Girl Who Loved the Wind (C4). Pictures by Ed Young. New York: Thomas Y. Crowell, 1972.
Guide to Writing for Children (C4). Boston: The Writer, Inc., 1989.
Here There Be . . . Sequence. 4 vols. Illus. David Wilgus. San Diego: Harcourt Brace.
   Here There Be Dragons (C4, C6). 1993.
   Here There Be Unicorns (C6). 1994.
   Here There Be Witches (C4). 1996.
   Here There Be Angels (C4). 1996.
"Jane Yolen." In *Speaking for Ourselves: Autobiographical Sketches by Notable Authors of Books for Young Adults.* Ed. Donald R. Gallo. Urbana, Ill.: National Council of Teachers of English, 1990, 225–27.
A Letter from Phoenix Farm (C4). Photographs by Jason Stemple. Katonah, N.Y.: Richard C. Owen Publishers, 1992.
The Magic Three of Solatia (C4). New York: Harper & Row, 1974.
Merlin's Booke (C5). Illus. Thomas Canty. Minneapolis: SteelDragon Press, 1986.
"The Modern Mythmakers." *Language Arts* (May 1976): 491–95.
Neptune Rising: Song & Tales of the Undersea Folk (C6). New York: Philomel, 1982.
Owl Moon (C4). Illus. John Schoenherr. New York: Putnam/Philomel, 1987.

The Pit Dragon Trilogy. 3 vols. New York: Delacorte.
  Vol. 1: *Dragon's Blood* (C6). 1982.
  Vol. 2: *Heart's Blood* (C6). 1984.
  Vol. 3: *A Sending of Dragons* (C6). 1987.
The Stone Silenus (C6). New York: Philomel, 1984.
Tales of Wonder (C4). New York: Schocken Books, 1983.
Touch Magic: Fantasy, Faerie, and Folklore in the Literature of Childhood (C4). New York: Philomel, 1981.
Twelve Impossible Things Before Breakfast: Stories (C4). San Diego: Harcourt Brace, 1997.
Water Music (C4). Photographs by Jason Stemple. Honesdale, Penn.: Wordsong/Boyds Mills Press, 1995.
The Wild Hunt (C4). Illus. Francisco Mora. San Diego: Harcourt Brace, 1995.
"The Wood Between the Worlds." *Mythlore* 41 (Winter-Spring 1985): 5–7.

Secondary Sources

Greenlaw, M. Jean. "Yolen, Jane." In *Twentieth Century Science Fiction Writers*, 3d ed. Ed. Noelle Watson and Paul E. Schellinger. Detroit: St. James Press, 1991, 897–99.
"An Interview with Jane Yolen." *Mythlore* 47 (Autumn 1986): 34–36.
"Jane Yolen." In *Authors and Artists for Young Adults*. Vol. 4. Ed. Agnes Garrett and Helga P. McCue. Detroit: Gale Research, 1990, 229–41.
MacRae, Cathi Dunn. Interview with Jane Yolen. St. Andrew's, Fife, Scotland, 29 April 1992.
Miller, Etta. "Yolen, Jane." In *Twentieth Century Young Adult Writers*. Ed. Laura Standley Berger. Detroit: St. James Press, 1994, 725–29.
Roginski, Jim. "Jane Yolen Interview." In *Behind the Covers: Interviews with Authors and Illustrators of Books for Children and Young Adults*. Englewood, Colo.: Libraries Unlimited, 1985, 224–35.
"Yolen, Jane." *Major Authors and Illustrators for Children and Young Adults*. 6 vols. Ed. Joyce Nakamura and Laurie Collier. Detroit: Gale Research, 1992, 2525–30.

MYTH: DREAMS OF THE SOUL'S ADVENTURE

Bulfinch, Thomas. *Bulfinch's Mythology*. New York: The Modern Library, 1993, 1855–63.
Campbell, Joseph. *The Hero with a Thousand Faces*. 2nd ed. Princeton, N.J.: Princeton University Press, 1968.
———. *The Power of Myth*. With Bill Moyers. Ed. Betty Sue Flowers. New York: Doubleday/Anchor, 1991, © 1988.

5. Legends:
The Shaping of Heroes

Related to myths that explain the way the world works, legends preserve human heroes through the ages until they grow larger than life. What might have begun as historical fact becomes glorified legend. Keeping our culture's British heritage strong are two of our most enduring legends, King Arthur and Robin Hood, one royal, one a commoner, both centuries old. The familiar stories everyone knows about them prove that legendary heroes live forever.

The Celtic Roots of King Arthur

Long before his land was called England by Anglo-Saxon conquerors, a leader who may have been Arthur was a Celtic hero in Britain. The popular misconception of Arthur as King of England distorts the vibrant Celtic tradition from which he sprang. It is likely that Arthur was actually Welsh. In central Europe since 800 B.C., Celtic ancestors of the Welsh, Scots, and Irish reached the British Isles by the Iron Age. Tall and fair, Celts were cattle herders and warriors, renowned for courage, honor, and zest for life. Under egalitarian law, women equaled men as "provocative protagonists, able in both love and war."[1] In refined Celtic arts, intricate circular knot designs ornamented jewelry, fabrics, furnishings, and buildings. Celtic religion compares to Native Americans', Druids acting as shamans interpreting nature's relation to people.

For the first four centuries A.D., Celts in Britain were influenced by organized, patriarchal Roman occupation. After the Romans left in 383, Celts enjoyed a brief resurgence as the Britons of Arthur's era, but Anglo-Saxon invasions from what is now Germany and Scandinavia absorbed them by 600. Today, the few who speak the Celtic languages of Gaelic, Welsh, or Breton are isolated on rocky coasts of Wales, Scotland, Ireland, Brittany in France, and Nova Scotia in Canada. Yet we still feel Celtic influence; their festivals of Beltain, Samhain, and Winter Solstice merged with our May Day, Halloween, and Christmas. Celtic traditions have enjoyed a recent revival due to the feminist appeal of their independent women and goddess and to their spiritual connection to nature, which many in our industrial world long to regain.

Celtic mythology flourishes in contemporary novels as exciting history, heroic fantasy, or a powerful spirit reaching into our times. That the Celtic essence remains alive in story is only fitting, for storytelling formed the heart of Celtic life. Bards were rewarded the highest respect as seers, Druids, or counselors to kings. Recording tribal feats in story and song, bards were admired for prowess and power with words, regardless of whether poetic imagery embroidered reality. Borders between Celtic history and mythology are indistinct, their "conscious mythic history" as convoluted as a Celtic knot (C. Matthews, 2). The "misty Celtic past of has been and never was" is ripe for modern writers' interpretations.[2]

Early Irish and Welsh literature preserves Celtic origins. The twelfth-century *Book of Invasions* chronicles the arrival of six successive races in Ireland, beginning with the biblical Noah's granddaughter. Using this mythic history as a resource, Morgan Llywelyn breathes life into Irish heroes in novels such as *Finn Mac Cool,* named for the third-century leader of the Fir Bolg, the third race of invaders. The primitive Fir Bolg were overcome by the Tuatha De Danaan, the most mystical and mysterious early Celtic tribe. In a shimmering novel embodying Celtic reverence for story in its title, *Bard,* Llywelyn reveals the psychic powers of the Tuatha De Danaan, who inspired myths of the faerie realm by seeming to vanish into the earth when defeated by Gael invaders from Iberia. An invader who falls in love with Danaan princess Shinann, Llywelyn's bard Amergin crafts "the epic poem of his race" to tell his Celtic people "the entire truth of themselves."[3] His *Song of Amergin* survives from "the oldest known western European poet" (*Bard,* 461).

Recently Llywelyn adapted her 1980 best-seller *Lion of Ireland* into slender YA novel format; *Brian Boru: Emperor of the Irish* dilutes none of this tenth-century king's vigor. In her 1982 ALA Best Book for Young Adults, *The Horse Goddess,* Llywelyn examines the roots of the real Druids, Celtic intellectuals, through Cernunnos the Shapechanger. This man who changes into the beast Horned God was precursor of the Green Man, Robin Hood, and even the werewolves of today's horror fiction. Llywelyn makes him real. She says, "My novels are an exploration of the thesis that myth is history; history distorted by the imaginations of centuries of storytellers and propagandists until truth is hidden beneath a cloak of fiction. But I believe the truth is still there, the seed at the heart of the tale."[4] Once hooked on Llywelyn's incisive character studies in meticulous historical settings, young adult readers will follow her thick adult novels through richly reimagined Irish history.

In her *Keltiad* trilogy, *The Tale of Aeron,* science fantasist Patricia Kennealy propels the compelling Tuatha De Danaan into outer space rather than to earthly faerie mounds, creating a Keltic monarchy on another planet. Dedicated to her husband, rock music legend Jim Morrison, Kennealy's trilogy is listed in this chapter's Recommended Reading with other novels of Irish legend.

Welsh legend is preserved in *The Mabinogion,* 11 tales derived from ancient oral sources and recorded around 1225. It begins with the four branches of the *Mabinogi,* lively tales of heroes with godlike powers who visit the underworld, change into beasts, and battle supernatural monsters, including talking severed heads. Other tales include five that mention King Arthur. The *Mabinogion* reflects Celtic spirituality: regeneration recurs with changing seasons, powerful women embody earth's fertility, and men journey to the underworld to find the cauldron of rebirth, in which dead warriors are dipped to rekindle life. Wildly unrealistic and sometimes cryptic and confusing, *Mabinogion* tales benefit from modern retellings. Evangeline Walton lyrically retells the four branches in a quartet of novels: *The Prince of Annwn, The Children of Llyr, The Song of Rhiannon,* and *The Island of the Mighty,* which together weave a fable about ecological destruction of the earth.

The Mabinogion inspired Lloyd Alexander's *Chronicles of Prydain,* fondly recalled by young adults from middle grade reading. In five volumes starting with *The Book of Three,* impetuous assistant pig-keeper Taran quests with heroes and villains from Welsh myth to win knowledge of himself and the nature of good and evil. Winning the Newbery Medal in 1969 for the final volume, *The High King,* Alexander produced "true classics of the genre, . . . characterized by magic, humor, and warmth."[5] Says Alexander, "I used the imaginary kingdom not as a sentimental fairyland, but as an opening wedge to express . . . some very hard truths."[6]

Embedded in the earth around us, Welsh myths naturally import into modern life. In Alan Garner's landmark novel *The Owl Service,* winner of Britain's 1967 Carnegie Medal, a tragic love triangle from the *Mabinogion*'s fourth branch, "Math Son of Mathonwy," replays among three teenagers. Alison, her new stepbrother, Roger, and their parents are vacationing in Wales. When Alison and housekeeper's son Gwyn find a dusty set of dinner plates with an owl design—the owl service—in the attic, odd events are set in motion. As the atmosphere grows menacing, Gwyn connects their troubles with a legend surrounding the Stone of Gronw in their valley, through which Lleu speared Gronw for stealing his wife, Bloudeuwedd, a goddess made of flowers. In a mesmerizing climax, jealousy rekindles as the three young people become entangled in forces as old as fate.

Alan Garner fuses human relationships into legend "to force from the two together the power of pity and terror,"[7] says a reviewer. Myth lives in his work, believes Garner, as "a recycling of energy. Myth is a very condensed form of experience. . . . It has passed through unknown individual subconsciouses, until it has become almost pure energy. [Writing] is a way for me to tap that energy."[8] Published as a young adult book, *The Owl Service* has been criticized as too difficult for many YA readers, who may not be familiar with the myths Garner uses. But Garner is concerned with subconscious recognition of mythic truths; "as long as young readers sense the power of the myths," says one critic, "it is not crucial for them to know the original sources."[9] Teenagers respond to Garner because he does not patronize them. Written in the '60s and '70s, his YA novels remain guideposts of mythic fantasy (*Elidor* is discussed in chapter 3, as are his Alderley Edge tales later in this chapter). "I am read with far greater passion, intelligence, and commitment by young people than by adults," Garner remarks. "Is that strange?"[10]

Louise Lawrence captures Bloudeuwedd's sinister, hypnotic power in another YA novel, *Earth Witch*. As vibrant Bronwen Davis, the goddess claims blood sacrifice from a modern Welsh community in return for bringing spring. Scandalizing neighbors by moving in with his bewitching older lover, Bronwen, teenaged Owen responds to forces too potent to resist, as inescapable as Bronwen's aging with winter's approach. Bloudeuwedd has even reincarnated in America, in Nancy Garden's *Fours Crossing* trilogy.

The "first appearance in Celtic prose" of King Arthur himself is in the *Mabinogion* tale "How Culhwch Won Olwen" (Gantz, 11). To win Olwen's hand, Arthur's cousin Culhwch performs a whopping 39 impossible tasks set by her fierce giant father, who must die when his daughter marries. Arthur and his men assist Culhwch in obtaining the required items, from the tusk of a boar to the blood of a hag, during outrageously exaggerated adventures. Though Arthur is not much of a personality in this bizarre tale, over 200 members of his court are listed in one run-on sentence! "The Dream of Rhonabwy," just as curious, is a later tale in which Arthur immovably plays chess while an interminable succession of messengers reports on the progress of battles raging nearby. All action occurs offstage, and minutely detailed outfits worn by messengers seem more important than the slaughter. Arthurian scholars suggest the story may be an allegory of events during Arthur's reign.[11] The other three *Mabinogi* tales of Arthur are Welsh romances, similar to the French. In the stories, which feature exploits of heroes Owain, Peredur, and Gereint, Arthur's court functions as mere backdrop. How did this shadowy Celtic Arthur become the vigorous immortal legend we all know?

YAFEs on Celtic Legend in Fiction

Garner—*The Owl Service*

Based on a Welsh legend I didn't recognize, this unique, imaginative book seemed like a surreal puppet show. The oddities in the writing style and symbolism combine to make it difficult but rewarding to read. It makes you think.

—Anne Pizzi, 15

Lawrence—*The Earth Witch*

Starting slowly, the mystery quickly picked up and drew me in; it was so realistic that it seemed the "powerful Druid goes crazy" idea could really happen.

—Dylan Burns, 14

Walton—*The Prince of Annwn*

It has the feel of a myth or legend, one I don't know. It was terribly pessimistic—unlike most fantasy, there was nothing strangely appealing about the evil, it just made me uncomfortable. It was definitely too dark and intense.

—Midian Crosby, 17

The Once, Future, and Living Legend of King Arthur

When the American Library Association exhibit "The Many Realms of King Arthur" visited our library in Colorado, teenagers enthusiastically attended accompanying events. As YAFEs planned a discussion of novels about Arthur, our Fantasy Fanatics group doubled in size, with teens eager to share his legend. School booktalks revealed that even "reluctant" readers knew the story. Teen audiences named its principal characters Guinevere, Lancelot, and Merlin, and its Camelot setting in Britain. They listed objects associated with Arthur: the Round Table, the Holy

Grail, and Excalibur. Some knew scandals involving Arthur: his sister Morgan's incest, his son Mordred's betrayal, his wife Guinevere's infidelity. Where had they heard of Arthur? In a television cartoon series, computer games, comics, the movies *Camelot, The Sword in the Stone,* or *Monty Python and the Holy Grail,* and even books or children's stories.

These YA audiences were proof that Arthur's legend still lives, transmitted by the media today as it once was by oral tradition. Asked when King Arthur lived, however, most teens were stumped, guessing "the Middle Ages." This common misconception of Arthur's time is a fascinating clue about how legend develops. The actual existence of King Arthur is one of our most baffling historical mysteries. Historians agree on few facts about Arthur, though he probably lived in the late fifth and early sixth centuries. Fifteen hundred years later, our image of Arthur is based more on legends created in intervening ages than on the historical figure he may have been.

Facts about Arthur are scarce because he lived in the Dark Ages, when few could read or write. Even the monks who kept the only written records did not define fact the way we do. For political and personal motives, they glorified some rulers and ignored others, filling gaps between their rare sources with their own creative interpretations. As Catherine M. Andronik explains in *Quest for a King: Searching for the Real King Arthur,* the only account written within living memory of Arthur was by cantankerous monk Gildas, consumed with ranting against his enemies. Gildas never mentions Arthur by name yet records battles of his own Celtic Britons against invading Saxon barbarians. Three hundred years later, Gildas's battles can be matched with those listed by another monk, Nennius, who names Arthur as the military commander—not a king—who held back the Saxons for 20 years of peace.

Arthur's upgrade to king took another 300 years, occurring in Geoffrey of Monmouth's 1136 *History of the Kings of Britain;* the story adds details that cling to Arthur's story. As Britain sinks into chaos from Saxon invasions and civil war, enchanter Merlin arranges Arthur's birth at Tintagel to Uther Pendragon and

Ygerna (Igraine). When Uther dies, Arthur becomes king at age 15 and is given a magic sword, Caliburn. Meanwhile Merlin builds the huge monument Stonehenge, a clear example of Geoffrey's fancy, since archaeology dates Stonehenge's origins to around 2000 B.C. Trouncing the Saxons, Arthur reigns in peace until Mordred betrays and mortally wounds him. Geoffrey leaves Arthur's fate open by having him carried off to the Isle of Avalon—a fate that is the basis for our hope that this visionary king might return. Geoffrey also began a practice most subsequent tellers of Arthur's tale followed; he moved the hero from the sixth century to his own time, the twelfth. Since spelling was fluid at the time, he used many variations of each character's name, and writers today still choose from different spellings. By portraying his Celtic forbears as virtuous and Anglo-Saxons as villains, Welsh Geoffrey created a "myth fantasy of a defeated people,"[12] the basis of every Arthurian tale since.

Thanks to Geoffrey's "historical fiction,"[13] the Arthurian myth was in full swing. Only 20 years later, Jersey poet Wace, declaring that "the tales of Arthur are not all lies nor all true,"[14] felt free to add the Round Table to the story. By 1170, the French poet Chrétien de Troyes popularized Arthur's tale in medieval romances. He names knights such as Lancelot for the first time, introducing the concept of chivalry and Camelot.

When Sir Thomas Malory wrote *Le Morte D'Arthur* (*The Death of Arthur*) in 1470, he unified a vast body of Arthurian stories into one coherent account. His publisher, printing press inventor William Caxton, arranged Malory's 506 chapters into 21 books totaling nearly 800 pages in reprint today. When published in 1485, Malory's book became the first best-seller, an Arthur blockbuster that did not have to be laboriously copied by hand. English professor Tom Napierkowski sees *Le Morte D'Arthur* as the "defining moment" in Arthurian literature, a "seminal work of English prose," perhaps the first novel written in the English language.[15] Writing of heroes while imprisoned for violent crimes, Malory developed dozens of characters surrounding Arthur, who brings on his kingdom's doom through his tragic flaw of loving his wife and best friend more than his country and thereby allowing their adultery to destroy it. Malory's masterful development of this theme, says Napierkowski, contributes to the legend's endurance. Malory also set Arthur's court in his own High Middle Ages, knights in shining armor and turreted castles replacing historical Arthur's coarse leather-clad warriors and crude hill forts.

Medieval images 1,000 years beyond Arthur's actual time persist today through many modern retellings of Malory, from John Steinbeck's and T. H. White's to Walt Disney's. Children still read Howard Pyle, the first great American illustrator, who added stylized black-and-white drawings to four volumes of rousing adventures compiled from Malory between 1903 and 1910, *The Story of King Arthur and His Knights*. In 1917, Pyle's art student N. C. Wyeth reissued poet Sidney Lanier's 1880 version of Malory, *The Boy's King Arthur*, with expressive color paintings. Like Malory, in 1953 Roger Lancelyn Green combined existing retellings to achieve a fluid whole in *King Arthur and His Knights of the Round Table*. Green meshes Malory with Geoffrey of Monmouth, the fourteenth-century Middle English poem *Sir Gawain and the Green Knight*, *The Mabinogion*, French and German medieval romances, and later folk legends about Arthur and his knights sleeping forever under a hill. From 1979 to 1981, historical novelist Rosemary Sutcliff also meshed sources for what critic Raymond H. Thompson terms "the finest" retelling in three short novels, *The Sword and the Circle, The Light Beyond the Forest,* and *The Road to Camlann* (a 1983 ALA Best Book), "which combine a keen sensitivity to the spirit of the legend with a simple yet elegant prose style."[16] Modernizing archaic language, Green and Sutcliff avoid what Thompson deplores in children's versions, laundering "all traces of sexual immorality . . . crucial . . . to the meaning of certain key events," robbing "the legend of much of its power" (13).

Removing medieval overlay by reconstructing Celtic stories, Joy Chant achieves striking coherence in *The High Kings: Arthur's Celtic Ancestors*. Chant blends insight into extravagant Celtic character and customs with lavishly illustrated tales of Arthur's predecessors, such as Brutus, Leir, and Vortigern, culminating with Arthur's entrance onto the stage. These rediscovered Celtic roots place the current legend in perspective. According to Celtic scholar John Wright, Romans forced "cultural amnesia" upon Celtic peoples in Britain. When "divine female figures Matrona and the Morrigan were driven underground," they transformed into medieval witch Morgan le Fay.[17] What Christians saw as sinful infidelity in Guinevere's affair with Lancelot was once acceptable for Celtic queens, as free to choose lovers as kings were. The mythical land of Avalon began as Celtic underworld Annwn. The Holy Grail became the cup Jesus used at the Last Supper but also the Welsh cauldron of rebirth; its medieval seeker Percival was once the Welshman Peredur. The Tuatha De Danaan tribe slept under a hill long before Arthur's knights did. After the last stand of Arthur's Celtic Britons, Anglo-Saxon invaders stole the Celtic hero myth as surely as they stole the land. Even America is not immune to political use of Arthurian myth, for President Kennedy called for a rebirth of Camelot during his 1960s term.

In recent years, "Arthurian myth-making has gone mad," declare researchers Phillips and Keatman (3). Modern pilgrims descend upon England's Glastonbury in search of the Isle of Avalon, Arthurian societies gather enthusiasts, Internet Web sites abound, and theories about his origins grow ever wilder; he might come from outer space or Atlantis. Archaeologists cannot keep up with the hundreds of sites in England, Wales, Scotland, and Brittany that claim, "King Arthur slept here." Serious scholars continually unearth new theories about the historic Arthur. Three of the most intriguing propositions stem from the same idea, that Arthur is not named in history because Arthur was a title meaning "high king" or "supreme ruler," not a personal name. Young adults with an instinct for probing the historical mystery may follow suspenseful, well-reasoned clues leading to three different conclusions and three different names for Arthur in Geoffrey Ashe's *The Discovery of King Arthur* (1985), Phillips and Keatman's *King Arthur: The True Story* (1994), and Frank D. Reno's *The Historic King Arthur: Authenticating the Celtic Hero of Post-Roman Britain* (1996). Most accessible is Andronik's *Quest for a King*, a 1990 ALA Best Book for Young Adults, which concisely gathers historical evidence and folklore to help readers investigate the places and characters associated with Arthur.

Disagreeing about the real Arthur, experts harmonize about what Napierkowski calls "the extraordinary resilience of Arthurian legend." Why does it still sing for us?

- Andronik quotes an early 1900s historian: "We need not believe that . . . legends are records of facts; but the existence of those legends is a very great fact" (109).
- Phillips and Keatman: "The very lack of historical information concerning the man who was Arthur . . . has made him . . . free to become many things to many people" (161).
- Geoffrey Ashe: "To diagnose the spell of his legend we must ask what is . . . the active ingredient in all versions. I would define it as the . . . promise which is not truly lost" (190).
- John Matthews: In "a constellation around the central star that was Arthur, we may see a dream being worked out, . . . the encapsulated desire of an age that even in its most violent moments consistently sought to reach upward . . . and touch the hand of God."[18]
- Jane Yolen: "I have always thought that Arthur was the Greatest Story Ever Told . . . though I see different reasons each time I work with it. . . . It is the continuing power of that story to enchant us again and again that has *really* moved me. Each time I read an account of Arthur I hope . . . I desire . . . I fear . . . I grieve."[19]

People in the 1,500 years since Arthur have rewritten his story to suit themselves. In our current chaotic moment, Arthur tugs forcefully at our hopes and fears.

Arthur Alive in Contemporary Fiction

In *The Return from Avalon,* Raymond H. Thompson surveys 200 novels and stories of Arthur written between 1882 and 1983. Arthurian fiction continues to multiply. Borrowing some of Thompson's categories to organize endless variations, we see

Arthur's legend from every point of view, though rarely from his own. Speaking as a true Celt in Parke Godwin's *Firelord,* Arthur objects to others stealing his story:

> A king should write his own story, especially a Briton. We are a race of musical liars, and who you are may depend on who's singing your song. . . . I want to write of us the way we were before some pedant petrifies us in an epic and substitutes his current ideal for ours. As for poets and bards, let one of *them* redecorate your life and you'll never be able to find any of it again.[20]

Arthur in Historical Novels

Struggling to identify the enigmatic king, historical novelists portray a more authentic Arthur than ever before. Few misplace him in Malory's Middle Ages anymore, setting him accurately instead in post-Roman Celtic Britain around the turn of the sixth century. Forsaking the romance popular through the first half of our century, recent novelists explore the man behind the legend, probing psychological motivations while drawing realistic details of life in those remote times. Upon foundations of facts, novelists test legend's authenticity.

Few writers surpass Rosemary Sutcliff's re-creation of Arthur. Her affinity for Dark Ages Britain was inspired by childhood readings of "Rudyard Kipling's three wonderful Romano-British stories in *Puck of Pook's Hill,*" she says.[21] Committed to realism, Sutcliff leaves out the love potion in *Tristan and Iseult,* her version of the tragic love triangle between Arthur's warrior Tristan, King Marc of Cornwall, and Marc's wife, Iseult. Her Arthur is Artos, appearing without artifice in *The Lantern Bearers,* winner of the 1960 Carnegie Medal. Fictional narrator Aquila, young British commander of a Roman legion, cannot abandon his homeland when Roman troops withdraw, so he joins Celtic warlord Ambrosius, often called the last Roman Briton, to keep the Saxons out. Watching Ambrosius's nephew Artos grow into a charismatic leader, Aquila bridges the fading Roman age to Arthur's, where "we stand at sunset . . . to carry what light we can forward into the darkness and the wind."[22] Readers experience palpably how one age builds foundations for the next, as this YA novel does for its adult sequel *Sword at Sunset,* "one of the most admired historical novels about Arthur" (Thompson, 47). After Ambrosius dies, Artos becomes "the Sacred King" who must "die for the life of the people."[23] A caring leader burdened with the ironic necessity of fighting for peace, Sutcliff's Artos emerges from remote legend as thoroughly real. His courageous self-sacrifice brings "tears to the eyes" (Thompson, 48).

Most historical novels see Arthur through others' eyes. One of the most famous is Mary Stewart's *Merlin Trilogy,* all best-sellers when published in the 1970s. Due to magician Merlin's supernatural qualities, Stewart's trilogy is not entirely comfortable in Thompson's historical category; more accurately, like its source, Geoffrey of Monmouth, it "is a blend of history and fantasy, myth and faery tale" (Tymn et al., 158). Declares critic Charlotte Spivack, "Mary Stewart's unique achievement is the humanization of Merlin"[24] and the rational explanation of fantastic elements. In *The Crystal Cave,* Merlin is born illegitimately to Welsh princess Niniane. He has a reputation as devil's spawn because his mother refuses to name his father, who teenaged Merlin discovers is exiled Ambrosius. After helping his father win his throne from usurper Vortigern, Merlin, by a feat of engineering, moves a huge standing stone from Ireland to Stonehenge to mark Ambrosius's grave. Merlin's Sight of future events is sent unbidden by a god, so Stewart leaves "only his inner power as seer to set him apart" (Spivack, 101). *The Crystal Cave* ends as Merlin helps the new king, his uncle Uther Pendragon, to conceive baby Arthur secretly at Tintagel with Ygraine, compelled by a vision of a king uniting Britain. Throughout the rest of the trilogy, Merlin is Arthur's counselor, the intuitive side to the practical king. *The Hollow Hills* spans Arthur's childhood until he removes the sword from the stone and is seduced by his unknown half sister, Morgause. In *The Last Enchantment,* Stewart frees Merlin's apprentice, Nimue, from legendary betrayal of her teacher and lover; Merlin voluntarily enters enchanted sleep in his crystal cave.

Transforming the enchanter into a god-driven human, Stewart herself is enchanted by the British landscape, as vivid and moody a character as her people. Long, descriptive passages are not to every reader's taste. Though young adults enjoy the tale of Merlin's boyhood in *The Crystal Cave,* a 1970 ALA Best Book for Young Adults, they may lose interest in succeeding volumes (see YAFE comments). Teenagers may also have difficulty responding to "introspective narrator" Merlin, whose account, admits Spivack, "inevitably lacks drama. What comes through in a powerful way is the supple, sensitive, meditative mind of the enchanter set against the dark background of fifth century Britain" (Spivack, 110). After her trilogy, Stewart explored the story of Arthur's bastard son, Mordred, in *The Wicked Day,* making this eternal villain entirely sympathetic but unable to escape the real villain of fate, which forces him to bring about his beloved father's destruction.

Mordred is a more ambivalent figure as Elizabeth E. Wein's compelling Medraut in *The Winter Prince.* Abused by his cruel mother, Morgause, Medraut carries both physical scars and wounds on his soul. Choosing the healing arts over Morgause's destructive poisons, he escapes her to present himself at his father, Artos's, court. Winning trust with his integrity and skill, Medraut accepts Artos's intolerable assignment: to heal and protect Artos's frail but legitimate younger son, Lleu, whom Artos then declares his heir. Bitterly betrayed by Artos and still vulnerable to his mother's manipulations, Medraut wages a fierce internal battle for his own soul. The outcome after Medraut kidnaps Lleu is not certain until readers tear through the final pages. Wein chooses the same Alderley Edge setting as Alan Garner, needing no further magic than Welsh lore; Lleu's namesake is *Mabinogion* hero Lleu Llaw Gyffes. Critics applauded Wein's "believable and lifelike" new perspective[25] in this "mesmerizing, splendidly imagined" first novel.[26]

Guinevere, Arthur's queen, who betrayed him in adultery with his most trusted warrior, Lancelot, is usually blamed for the downfall of the realm. Portraying her as foolish and self-indulgent, traditional male writers rarely understood her. Feminism has made novelists more sympathetic. In a trilogy telling "the human story" that "could have planted the seed from which the legend grew,"[27] Persia Woolley reimagines Guinevere as a spirited Celtic queen. In

Child of the Northern Spring, Guinevere recounts her childhood as a tomboy raised by her widowed father, King Leodegrance, in rugged Rheged. In an arranged marriage, Guinevere competently corules with Arthur. Though a Celtic queen was permitted lovers, throughout the second volume, *Queen of the Summer Stars,* Guinevere and Lancelot deny physical expression of their love through loyalty to Arthur. Woolley convincingly depicts Guinevere as devoted to both men; Arthur is a driven leader wounded by unwitting incest with his half sister, Morgause, and Lancelot is giving and spiritual. Had Arthur been more emotionally available to Guinevere, Woolley suggests, she might not have turned to Lancelot. When Morgause announces Arthur's incest by introducing Mordred as Arthur's son, shocked Guinevere feels betrayed by Arthur's secrecy. Blaming Arthur's problems on Igraine's lack of mothering, childless Guinevere fosters Mordred herself. Though Woolley's interpretation seems logical to the modern mind, Guinevere's ready grasp of psychology may strain credulity. In the final volume, *Guinevere: The Legend in Autumn,* Gwen looks back on events leading to her charge of treason.

Acknowledging debts to Parke Godwin, Marion Zimmer Bradley, Mary Stewart, and historian Geoffrey Ashe, Woolley clarifies the clash of Roman, Celtic, Anglo-Saxon, and Pictish cultures. Her Arthur is dedicated to religious freedom among peoples of all backgrounds. She "provides a genuine sense of a changing society caught between paganism and Christianity," says *Booklist,* while "Gwen comes alive . . . as a likable, compassionate, witty, and strong-willed young woman."[28] The first two volumes of the trilogy were ALA Best Books for Young Adults in 1987 and 1991.

Arthur in Heroic Fantasy

According to Thompson, heroic fantasy is the most popular Arthurian fiction category (114). Rich in period detail, it can be confused with historical fiction but focuses on the legendary hero instead of the historic figure and may or may not contain magic.

Giant among such works is Parke Godwin's *Firelord.* To "stretch an elastic legend over the bone of historical fact," Godwin boldly revises the story, claiming that "it should have happened this way, it could have, and perhaps it did" (*Firelord,* acknowledgments). Merlin is a subconscious aspect of Arthur, forecasting in dreams his destiny as sacrificial god-king. No longer Arthur's incestuous sister, Morgana is one of the Prydn, primitive nomads mistaken for Faerie folk. As his beloved first wife before he becomes king, Morgana teaches him the natural ways of his true people. But Arthur must tear himself from Morgana to lead the Britons, who displace her people and inevitably earn their son Modred's enmity. Carrying Morgana's love with him, Arthur becomes a compassionate ruler who understands his diverse peoples, choosing Guenevere to rule beside him. As strong as Woolley's Celtic queen, Guenevere, Arthur's equal and best friend, betrays him not with Lancelot—an affair Arthur silently tolerates—but through murderous jealousy of Morgana.

Godwin's fallible, witty, empathetic visionary is the heroic embodiment of the dreams his sacrifice bought. Thompson declares Godwin's Arthur "one of the most vigorous and attractive characterizations" in "one of the most exuberant and enjoyable stories in all Arthurian literature" (128, 132). Arthur came alive for Godwin as he wrote a scene in which the king, trapped by "duty and fate," sweeps a little boy at play into his arms to celebrate "the beauty of life, a beauty that encompasses joy and sadness, honor and betrayal, and accepts them all." In that moment, Godwin's story became "universal, old as the cave and fresh as tomorrow. Now I could write Arthur because I was writing me. And you."[29]

In his sequel, *Beloved Exile,* Guenevere struggles to hold the throne after Arthur's death. In a realm riddled by treachery, Guenevere is sold into slavery to Angles who have no idea who she is. Ten years with her fair-minded master, Gunnar, teaches "Gwenda" the democratic laws of these Germanic invaders, now called English, causing her to reconsider her old philosophy of rule. When freed, she tries to bring feuding inhabitants of Britain together with the will of the common people. Godwin's complex Guenevere has a genius for government and personal evolution; she is a stalwart survivor in literature at last, which elevates her to heroine status.

Third in Godwin's series is *The Last Rainbow,* which makes the legendary St. Patrick as real as Arthur. Set just before Arthur's time around 429 A.D., it does not seem to be part of the same story as the earlier volumes, until Godwin makes a brash but satisfying connection between Patrick (called Padrec) and Arthur at the very end. Guenevere's grandfather, Prince Marchudd, and Arthur's predecessor, Ambrosius, make brief appearances throughout, but Godwin stuns readers with the revelation that Padrec's primitive tribal Prydn wife, Dorelei, is an ancestor of Morgana, who mothers traitor Modred in *Firelord*. Here Godwin makes a compelling case for legend's roots in history.

Recent heroic fantasy has roots in what Thompson labels "ironic" fantasy, in which the gap between Arthur's "high-minded ideals" and disappointing human results is exploited for its comedy (139). Its earliest example is Mark Twain's *A Connecticut Yankee in King Arthur's Court*. Twain's Yankee, Hank Morgan, time travels from 1879 to Arthur's time in 528, miscast as the Middle Ages. With his knowledge of science and technology, Hank achieves power over Arthur's childlike, superstitious people. Yet Hank is callous and uncaring; Twain's pungent satire shows that humans' character has not progressed with their machines. Twain's cynicism is bitter, his Arthur a shadowy nonentity, his political agenda opaque to us today. When it was published in 1889, British critics were offended that Twain trampled their legend, but we see Twain's regret that human error sullied its purity. Few teens will settle for such a bleak view.

The next great ironic fantasy was *The Once and Future King*, published as three separate volumes starting in 1938 with *The Sword in the Stone*, which became an animated Disney film. The revised complete edition added a fourth book in 1958, inspiring the musical *Camelot*. It made a fortune for its brilliant British author, T. H. White, a falconer and pacifist who exiled himself from World War II in Ireland while writing about Arthur. Using Malory as a model, White gave the legend his own stamp as wise, witty narrator. In the first and most charming book, *The Sword in the Stone,* the wizard Merlyn is Arthur's childhood tutor, who shapeshifts him into the animal world to learn the universe's secrets. Since Merlyn lives backward in time and knows modern references, White makes caustic commentary on the timeless sub-

ject of human nature in his alternate world where historical timing does not matter. Robin Hood appears with other heroes
beyond history, and the reader, introduced to Sir Ector's castle in
today's ruins, is invited to imagine how it once appeared full of
life. When Arthur tells his life story to page boy Tom on the eve of
his last battle, we know the boy grows up to be Malory himself.

T. H. White's alternately hilarious and poignant view still
delights and moves readers. Critics pronounce it a "singular classic of Arthurian fantasy" that "evokes a range of emotions rarely
found, from the joy of a boy's carefree energy to the massive sorrow of a thwarted ideal" (Tymn et al., 174). YAFE Naomi Perera,
17, reveals its timeless appeal to young adult readers:

> The theme that struck me the most powerfully was how people,
> dreams, ideals all grow old and decay yet still somehow perse-
> vere. T. H. White has taken this sad legend, fraught with
> human foibles and the collapse of greatness, and made it quietly
> uplifting, showing that to have hoped is a triumph in itself. At
> the end of the book, this idea comes as a revelation, and . . .
> when the aging Arthur goes to his final battle, one is left with a
> feeling of bittersweet peace. I don't know how to put into words
> how deeply this book has impressed me. It will always remain on
> my shelf.

T. H. White meant his tale to have a fifth part, *The Book of
Merlyn,* in which adult Arthur returns to the animal world with
Merlyn to learn why man must "find an antidote to war," as
White noted during his wartime Irish exile.[30] His publisher would
not accept this conclusion, believing Merlyn's preaching of
White's own anger at humanity's error of war to be a flaw. *The
Book of Merlyn* was not published until 1977, 13 years after
White's death, and remains a dark book without that "uplifting"
quality that so touches White's readers, like Naomi.

In her 1982 best-seller *The Mists of Avalon,* Marion Zimmer
Bradley irrevocably alters our perception of the myth. In this
"pervasively feminine fantasy," says Spivack, Bradley "revisions
one of the most powerfully masculine legends of all time from the
viewpoint of its major female characters" (160–61). Interwoven
perspectives of four women give new insights into Arthur's

tragedy: Arthur's mother, Igraine, her pagan priestess sister, Viviane, Arthur's pious Christian queen, Gwenhwyfar, and Morgaine, in the dominant role as Arthur's half sister, mother of his son, Mordred, and heir to her aunt Viviane's position as high priestess of Avalon. In this intensely spiritual novel, the pivotal conflict is "between what Bradley calls 'the cauldron and the cross' " (Spivack, 150): the old pagan religion of the Goddess and emerging patriarchal Christianity.

From her sacred Isle of Avalon, Viviane engineers Arthur's birth to her sister Igraine, and then Mordred's birth to her niece Morgaine and to Arthur, to ensure that Britain's ruler will be sympathetic to the Goddess. But the new force of Christianity is beyond the priestess's power to control. Though Arthur became king through the pagan ritual of the Great Marriage between himself as king stag and Morgaine as earth mother, the Christian taboo against incest undermines their son, Mordred. "Fanatically, mindlessly Christian" Gwenhwyfar sways her husband to convert his Goddess-pledged sword, Excalibur, to the Christian God, a betrayal that Morgaine, torn between love for her brother and devotion to her Goddess, must avenge.[31]

Bradley uses variant names of legendary figures to delineate different characters, often in triangles. Sorceress Morgan le Fay splits into Lady of the Lake Viviane, sympathetic but driven Morgaine, and her lusty aunt Morgause, the Orkney queen who fosters Mordred. Aspects of Viviane appear in two other priestesses, Mordred's lover, Niniane, and Merlin's betrayer, Nimue. Enacting Avalon's religion in the outside world is the Merlin, not a name but the title of head Druid and bard Taliesin, and his successor, Kevin, the only ones who see that the Goddess must merge with strengthening Christian beliefs to keep her influence. Bradley boldly reinvents Kevin the Merlin as a gifted musician, deformed by childhood injury and made vulnerable through physical suffering and human need for a woman's love, for Morgaine and then for Nimue, who both betray him. In two other triangles, three women love Lancelet: Morgaine, Gwenhwyfar, and Elaine, none ever truly winning this tormented perfection seeker caught in another triangle, with Gwenhwyfar and Arthur. In a daring departure, Bradley's Arthur invites Lancelet to share his bed with Gwenhwyfar in a moving, loving triad; Lancelet's seed may create the heir Arthur needs. It is not adultery but rival religions that tear Arthur's realm asunder.

As Arthur's world inexorably bows to Christian dominance, Avalon retreats into mists, though Kevin knows "Avalon will always be there for all men to find, if they seek the way" (*Mists*, 470), as converts to the Goddess religion, including Bradley herself, do today. Her Holy Grail embraces both religions; when it appears in a vision, some see it as Jesus's chalice, some as the Holy Cup of Avalon, demonstrating one God but fragmenting Arthur's court as his companions rush off on solo quests. At last Morgaine realizes her Goddess is reborn in the Virgin Mary. Meshing mythic elements from ancient Welsh to modern feminist consciousness, the inner conflicts of Bradley's fascinating cast mirror their spiritual dilemmas.

Widely read, *The Mists of Avalon* resonates for '90s readers like no other Arthurian interpretation. Since female characters embody archetypal aspects of the Goddess, says Spivack, the experience of reading it becomes profoundly spiritual; it "addresses the woman reader as the goddess incarnate" (161). Outnumbering men, women in a Colorado book discussion emotionally expressed enthusiasm for Bradley's book. One woman found it overwhelmingly powerful to read while she was pregnant, birthing her awareness of her natural earth mother role. Another woman gave the book to her 11-year-old daughter to demonstrate what emerging womanhood meant. The group agreed that Bradley answered issues unresolved in other Arthur interpretations, illuminating eternal conflicts of male and female, passion and reason, illusion and reality, bringing myth into our lives today. Women's fantasy critic Thelma J. Shinn explains this phenomenon: "Bradley retells the Arthurian story to let the face of the Goddess be seen again and to return women to their equally important role in human life, despite the denigration of that role historically and spiritually in the centuries since Arthur."[32]

"Something fateful happened," says YAFE Allison Barrett, 15, in her article "Women in the Arthurian Legend: A Growing

Trend in Fantasy Literature," when she encountered *The Mists of Avalon* during the summer before seventh grade.[33] Unable to find strong female characters with whom to identify, Allison had been left cold by Arthurian legend but became "entranced" with Bradley's "extraordinary story" with women at its core and males who "were not exactly hero material." A "devoted *Mists of Avalon* junkie," Allison discounted other writers' interpretations, especially of "religious hypocrite" Gwenhwyfar, until she found Parke Godwin. Opposing portraits of Guenevere, Godwin's splendid political genius and Bradley's weak, shallow zealot, remake the myth for modern consciousness. Allison agrees that Godwin stands with Bradley head and shoulders above other Arthur inventors. Twelve years after *Mists of Avalon,* Bradley wrote a prequel, *The Forest House,* about the early Goddess religion, followed in 1997 by *Lady of Avalon,* which links the two previous books by covering the establishment of priestesses and Druids on the Isle of Avalon and the childhood of Viviane, Lady of the Lake, who becomes such a force in *Mists.*

When T. A. Barron realized that only Mary Stewart had explored the enigmatic Merlin's youth, he filled the gap with *The Lost Years of Merlin,* a 1997 ALA Best Book for Young Adults that heralds a projected quintet. Barron's young Merlin is unknown because he really did disappear; he washed ashore in Wales with no name, becoming Emrys until he could discover who he was. On the underwater isle of Fincayra, a bridge between Earth and the spirit world from Celtic mythology, Emrys encounters legendary beings who teach him the great truth of himself, his power, and his connection to the natural world. Says *VOYA:* "What is truly interesting in this fantasy is Barron's treatment of power—how one uses or abuses it; how it can take control regardless of one's good intentions. . . . The climactic ending offers a twist to seeking one's identity and heritage."[34] In Book 2, *The Seven Songs of Merlin,* Merlin takes the hero's journey to the spirit otherworld through the power of his wizard grandfather, Tuatha's, Songs of Wisdom. Book 3 will be titled *The Fires of Merlin.*

Since Bradley cites *Prince Valiant* as youthful inspiration, comics must not be overlooked. *Prince Valiant, in the Days of King*

Arthur was born in 1937 in Sunday newspapers; the comic, which continues to this day, outlived its creator, Harold R. Foster, who died in 1982. Arthur's comic strip knight Val lives in a romanticized medieval era full of historic but unmagical detail. According to H. Alan Stewart in "King Arthur in the Comics," three recent comics provide "a gateway into the richness of the legend for many readers, especially young ones." P. Craig Russell's *Parsifal* adapts Wagner's opera in "the finest comics treatment of the Grail Quest." Arthur returns in the year 3000 with a "punk futuristic look" in Mike W. Barr's *Camelot 3000* series. In Matt Wagner's *Mage*, Kevin Matchstick is the current incarnation of "Eternal Hero" Arthur in "impressionistic and murky" artwork accompanied by "ironic humor with the expected heroism and thrills."[35] The series has been reprinted in bound volumes.

Arthur in Mythic Fantasy

The timeless tale of Arthur lends itself well to the most inventive type of fantasy, untied to time or place, in which "the contradictory nature of humanity itself" is expressed "in terms of an eternal conflict between good and evil" (Thompson, 6). Though most mythic fantasies revive Arthurian characters beyond his historical time, one of the most lyrical keeps the traditional setting. Invoking moods of light and dark in an antiheroic tragedy in which three complex narrators struggle and fail to uphold their ideals, *Hawk of May,* a 1980 ALA Best Book for Young Adults, opens Gillian Bradshaw's trilogy in sensitive Gwalchmai's voice. Usually called Gawain in the legend, the boy escapes the evil sorcery of his mother, Morgawse, to pledge to the light during mystical training in the Blessed Isles. Proving himself to Arthur, Gwalchmai forges spiritual integrity. *Kingdom of Summer* is narrated by farmer's son Rhys, who joins Gwalchmai on a quest. *In Winter's Shadow* closes the trilogy with another strong Gwynhwyfar, whose practicality holds the realm together while Arthur is away fighting. "Exquisitely written, with a controlled blend of fantasy and historical detail," (Spivack, 139), Bradshaw's intricate shades of gray inspire readers to examine their own colors.

Jane Yolen's "luminous contribution to the Arthurian canon"[36] is *Merlin's Booke,* in which she trains her lens on multiple facets of the mysterious "shape-changer, Druid high priest, wizard *extraordinaire,* counselor to kings," Merlin.[37] In poetry and short stories, Yolen's multitude of Merlins wink at readers through many eyes in many mirrors, from his birth as an imp humanized by Brother Blaise's blessing through his living death, imprisonment in the Whitethorn Wood. Quoted passages from Geoffrey of Monmouth and Malory are points from which Yolen takes off, borrowing alchemy from Merlin's own wand, as unsettling as "the Gwynhfar," a mewling albino babe introduced by a cynical bard remaking the past to "call it truth" (*Merlin's,* 71), as sprightly as another Guenevere disguised as a boy who tricks Merlin by lifting the sword from the stone with butter. In another incarnation she is Gwyneth, forging Excalibur herself on an Isle of Women until Merlin takes her to be Arthur's bride in "Evian Steel." In "The Dragon's Boy," later expanded to a middle grade novel, Merlin masquerades as a dragon to teach young Artos wisdom. In the final "Epitaph," an archaeologist announces the discovery of Merlin's tomb at a press conference, where Yolen wittily exposes the legend's commercialization.

Praising Yolen's respect for the legend contrasted to its "dumbing down" in popular versions, Judith L. Kellogg finds *Merlin's Booke* has "diverse, even paradoxical versions" that reflect "the disruptions . . . of this Merlin's twentieth century creation."[38] For "the first trilogy of short stories and poems ever written," Jane Yolen plans two more volumes exploring Guinevere and Arthur. Each book's centerpiece will be set on the Isle of Women. "In *Guinevere's Booke,*" forecasts Yolen, "I will show the coming of Guinevere to the island. . . . In *Arthur's Booke,* I plan to skip years and show what happens when Arthur, dying from his wounds, is brought ashore." Yolen's Guinevere, she promises, will be concerned with "the very personal," while Arthur will be "different from the Arthurs that have been limned before me."[39]

Enchanted underground forever, Merlin is a natural choice for rebirth in other times and places. Peter Dickinson lets him sleep in *Merlin Dreams,* dreamily illustrated by Alan Lee to match 10 tales fashioned from the mage's musings. With the aura and setting of traditional fairy tales, each contains a fresh twist of each hero's choice, in "a dense, rich book" in which readers "are given the shapes of ideas, shimmers of insight, left on the edge of understanding, as if they were dreaming, too."[40] Baltimore youth made *Merlin Dreams* a Youth-to-Youth Book.

C. S. Lewis woke Merlin from his 1,500-year sleep in *That Hideous Strength,* the third novel in his 1940s adult space trilogy. Merlin assists Arthur's twentieth-century descendant Dr. Ransom in a cosmic struggle between science and souls. In this gripping, deeply spiritual science fantasy, angel-like interplanetary beings become part of Lewis's profound Christianity. Challenged to confront their own ethical convictions, young adults may read this volume alone or be drawn to its companions, *Out of the Silent Planet* and *Perelandra.* Healer Deepak Chopra brings Merlin and Mordred to modern England to demonstrate New Age spirituality in *The Return of Merlin;* its message overburdens the fiction format, unlike Lewis's classic.

In 1960, Alan Garner led British young adult novelists in Merlin's reach into our time with his Alderley Edge books *The Weirdstone of Brisingamen* and *The Moon of Gomrath.* Visiting a farm in modern Cheshire, Susan and Colin are swept into a local legend of knights sleeping under a hill, arousing trolls, elves, dwarves, and wizards from Welsh lore in a new struggle between light and dark. Though Arthur's name is never mentioned, the wizard Cadellin seems to be Merlin, as is Merriman in Susan Cooper's influential 1970s quintet T*he Dark Is Rising.* Merriman mentors Will Stanton, a modern English boy who is actually an Old One, upholding the Light from chaotic Dark forces. Crackling with tension, Cooper's "five . . . wild entrancing" books are models for YA mythic fantasy that have rare "sustained power."[41]

American writers also revive suspended characters. A "master of satiric fantasy unique in American letters,"[42] Robert Nathan makes Merlin and Nimue part of an ever-living cast of historical and legendary characters who coexist with us in *The Elixir.* In this transcendent 1971 novel, an American professor vacationing in

England falls in love with Nimue in her current form, experiencing and defining both history and legend anew. For younger readers, the ancient Horn of Merlin alters reality in *The Merlin Effect* by T. A. Barron, creating a whirlpool off Baja California near a sunken Spanish galleon. As in companion volumes *Heartlight* and *The Ancient One* (see chapter 7), intrepid young heroine Kate solves *Effect*'s mystery beyond time, inspiring Barron to begin writing his own Merlin quintet. The Grail quest comes to America in Sanders Anne Laubenthal's *Excalibur,* in which a Pendragon descendant in modern Alabama presides over a clash between good and evil that "expands the imagination and leaves the reader breathless but delighted from the effort" (Tymn et al., 107). The Grail confers immortality in the supernatural thriller *The Forever King;* in nail-biting suspense, authors Molly Cochran and Warren Murphy toss the cup among Arthur, reborn as a 10-year-old Chicago boy; his protectors, ancient Merlin and Galahad, the latter reincarnated as an alcoholic ex-FBI agent; and 4,000-year-old Saladin.

In three complex fantasies by Canadian authors, the Arthurian cast plays in new realms. Three worlds interlock in Welwyn Wilton Katz's intriguing YA novel *The Third Magic,* with teenaged Morgan transported from modern Cornwall to otherworld Nwm and then Celtic Britain, as Morgan le Fay. In *The Fionavar Tapestry* by Tolkien scholar Guy Gavriel Kay, contemporary Toronto college students enter Fionavar's otherworld to play roles including Guinevere, Arthur, and Lancelot. This dense trilogy was cited by *Booklist* as a Fantasy Highlight of the '80s and by David Pringle as one of his "Hundred Best" modern fantasies; Kay's "ingenuity, and . . . loving care . . . has rarely been matched by anyone since [Tolkien] himself," he says.[43] Topping this distinguished Canadian list is *The Lyre of Orpheus,* a 1989 best-seller by eminent novelist Robertson Davies. In this stand-alone conclusion of his *Cornish Trilogy,* members of a university arts foundation reenact Arthur's love triangle when funding the completion of a nineteenth-century Arthurian opera by a gifted student composer, discovering that "if we are true to the great myth, we can give it what form we choose."[44] Davies's witty, allusion-rich novel is a delightful modern classic.

Mythic Arthurian fantasy envelops many genres. In science fiction, its characters are clones on a spaceship in C. J. Cherryh's *Port Eternity*, or thrust into star kingdom Keltia in Patricia Kennealy's *Tales of Arthur*, which takes place 1,500 years earlier than her other Keltic trilogy. Now known as Kennealy-Morrison, she has a new novel, *Blackmantle*, a prequel to the entire *Keltiad*. Winifred Bryher's futurist *Visa for Avalon* never mentions Arthur or lets readers see the mythic land that may be the only safe haven in a world overthrown by the right-wing "Movement" in this tense, powerful fable. Avalon is also a quest for tenth-century English monk Rumon and his unrequited lover, Merewyn, believed to be Arthur's last descendant in Anya Seton's compelling historical novel *Avalon*. In *Castle Dor*, the site of Tristan and Iseult's original tale, "a senseless repetition of one of the saddest love stories in the world" occurs in the 1800s in this romantic novel completed by Daphne Du Maurier from Sir Arthur Quiller-Couch's manuscript.[45] Arthur has even infiltrated a spy thriller; the discovery of the site of his most famous battle heats up the cold war between Russia, America, and Britain in *Our Man in Camelot* by Anthony Price. In Phyllis Ann Karr's murder mystery *Idylls of the Queen*, Sir Kay plays detective.

Anthologies are a treasure trove for Arthur enthusiasts. Mike Ashley collects unpublished new and unavailable traditional tales in *The Pendragon Chronicles;* his informative introductions, character list, and bibliography of Arthurian fiction set in context stories and excerpts by authors including John Steinbeck, Vera Chapman, and Andre Norton. *The Camelot Chronicles* contains "The Quiet Monk," Jane Yolen's tale of Lancelot wandering for centuries in search of Guenivere's grave. Other Ashley anthologies are listed in this chapter's Recommended Reading. In 1995, Jane Yolen edited *Camelot: A Collection of Original Arthurian Stories*, which contains the short-story version of Anne McCaffrey's new historical novel, *Black Horses for the King*, and Diana L. Paxson's "Wild Man," which features a primitive Merlin.

Arthur's appearance in every type of modern literature reflects repeated stabs at the truth of our most pervasive Western myth.

As the professor muses in Nathan's *Elixir,* "What actually occurs is history, and what one likes to remember is legend, and . . . there is a vast difference between the two. For history is the record . . . of man's mistakes; and legend is the well-worn oft-told tale of his glories. . . . The truth lies somewhere in between, and one is no more honest than the other, but one is dearer. And the further off in time, the softer it glows" (116).

Young Adult Response to Arthurian Legend

Young adults who enjoy Arthurian literature may resist interpretations that tamper with cherished versions of the legend. Favorites are as individual as readers, but whatever adaptation a YA reader adopts, its challengers are passionately refuted. Myth is both universal and personal; young adults concerned with choosing their own codes have difficulty accepting multiple views. Shades of gray are hard to see for youth, who often focus on black and white, but teenagers who explore variations ultimately find this self-stretching exercise valuable. Bradley's *Mists of Avalon* gathers the most fervent young fans—and enemies—though Parke Godwin often wins respect from Bradley converts. The following YAFE comments demonstrate readers' commitments to particular versions of Arthurian legend.

YAFEs' Best and Worst of Arthur

Allison Barrett, 16

BEST: Bradley—*The Mists of Avalon*

This darksome female side of the classic Arthurian myth is the best book I have ever read. Morgaine was brilliant, devoted, and angry. I loved her so much, I wished I could be her. Bradley ruined other tellings of the myth for me, except for Parke Godwin's, the only one to compare with it.

WORST: Woolley—*Child of the Northern Spring*

I hated it—Woolley obviously read *The Mists of Avalon,* lifted Morgaine, and changed her name to Guinevere.

Ashley Burns, 16

BEST: Bradley—*The Mists of Avalon*/Godwin—*Firelord*

It's hard to decide between Godwin and Bradley. *Firelord* is so beautifully written, and I love what Godwin does with Arthur. Godwin is god. *The Mists of Avalon* has tangible characters, magic, adventure, true love, eternal longing, scandal, and despair. But be warned: everyone who reads it loathes Guinevere forevermore.

WORST: Stewart—*The Crystal Cave*

Though Merlin was an interesting character, the overly descriptive writing style bored me. There are much better versions of the story.

Ben Cameron, 16

BEST: Bradley—*The Mists of Avalon*

It is the most beautiful portrayal of human nature and mysticism I've ever read.

WORST: White—*The Once and Future King*

It went from overly juvenile to overly morbid.

Nathan Doyle, 16

BEST: Godwin—*Firelord*

I really liked the way he stuck to his own time line, adding parts of real history.

WORST: Bradley—*The Mists of Avalon*

Arthur was never developed—how can you forget the main character in his own legend? Gwenhwyfar was shallow and Lancelet was a creep. Though the goddess religion was interesting, I didn't like any of the characters.

Brian Dunning, 13

BEST: Cooper—*The Dark Is Rising* Quintet

It had really good three-dimensional characters and an interesting plot, and it flowed at a perfect pace—one of the best fantasies I've ever read.

WORST: Stewart—*Merlin Trilogy* except *The Crystal Cave*

The trilogy kept slowing down more and more until it was dead on its feet. The characters were boring and the plot predictable.

Jessica Lundie, 11

BEST: Cooper—*The Dark Is Rising* Quintet

Even though it was slow moving, it kept you interested.

WORST: Barron—*The Merlin Effect*

I didn't like the character development. It was not as good as *The Ancient One*.

Anne Pizzi, 16

BEST: Stewart—*The Crystal Cave* (but not the rest of the series)

I read it at age 11, the best introduction to Arthurian legend I could have had.

WORST: Woolley—Guinevere series

I couldn't accept the way she just changed Guinevere into a pagan without following the traditional legend. I didn't like her character, but others were interesting.

YAFEs on Arthur

Bradley—*The Mists of Avalon*

Waiting since fourth grade, I read it in seventh grade and found it the most fabulous and magical women's book.
—Midian Crosby, 17

Though it was a good story, it lost my interest because it was too long and detailed, and I already knew what was going to happen.
—Melissa Tolve, 16

Bradshaw—*Hawk of May*

This beautifully written book gave the traditional characters a whole new twist. Though I liked the series overall, the later books were weaker. In *Kingdom of Summer* I kept asking, "Gwalchmai, why don't you just ditch this stupid girl?"

—Dylan Burns, 14

Cooper—*The Dark Is Rising* Quintet

Wonderfully, vividly descriptive and realistic, symbolism everywhere.

—Ashley Burns, 16

Dickinson—*Merlin Dreams*

From inside his trap, Merlin is reviewing his life, dreaming a story for each idea where lessons are learned—kind of dream therapy. Characters have individuality; the many female heroes impressed me coming from a male author. I enjoyed how Merlin's ponderings connected stories, the smooth writing style, and really good pictures for older people.

—Midian Crosby, 17

Godwin—*Firelord*

I loved the Morgana he created, but I identified most with Arthur himself because he was trying to be great but was never quite sure how. Unlike other tellings of the legend, this version was not a clear struggle but was as murky as Arthur's struggle between his selves. Godwin's greatest strength is his development of this complex Arthur.

—Allison Barrett, 16

Godwin—*Beloved Exile*

It isn't often done, explaining what happened to Guenevere after Arthur died—or bringing good Saxons into the story. It wasn't a purist interpretation, but again, murky as Guenevere's discovery of herself. Parke Godwin is neat.

—Allison Barrett, 16

Kay—*The Fionavar Tapestry*

Reincarnated Jennifer/Gwenivere possesses qualities that I would like to have: with grace she survives the horrible experience of being raped by a god and manages to find love in a hopeless situation. Kay is adept at using certain emotionally charged phrases repetitively to emphasize important themes and imagery. There are echoes of so many things and so many different levels from which meaning can be taken, with shadings of classical fantasy themes. This book lends itself well to being reread.

—Maria Taylor, 15

Kennealy—*The Hawk's Grey Feather* (*Tales of Arthur* I)

The concept of the Kelts having left Earth is interesting. I enjoyed the realistic passage of time and the changing presentation of space—everything seems huge to the innocent, and small to the great. Taliesin's third-person limited perspective was well done; as a bard/Druid he sees very deeply.

—Ben Cameron, 16

Lawhead—*Arthur*

The friendship ran so strong between Gwenhwyvar and Arthur. I enjoyed the pace and descriptions. Only a few books are better than this.

—Robin Deeter, 16

Rice—*The Last Pendragon*

This excellent historical novel about Bedwyr returning to Britain 11 years after Arthur's death to fulfill Arthur's dying wish that his sword be thrown into the lake had no magic but a fast pace and just enough detail. I identified with Arthur's grandson Irion, trying to live down his father, Medraut's, betrayal of Arthur.

—Jesse Coffelt, 18

Stewart—*The Crystal Cave*

Though it was a little slow, it gave a taste of what Merlin's childhood was like and seemed as if it really happened. It was a gripping story.

—Sam Walter, 15

Sutcliff—*Sword at Sunset*

I read this historical novel on the Arthur legend after reading fantasy, amazed it could be done so well without a fantastic slant. It makes the legend feel tangible, as though it could have really happened.

—Ben Cameron, 16

Wein—*The Winter Prince*

I liked Arthur's daughter Goewin, who reminded me of Bradley's Morgaine. With the flavor of a Greek tragedy, the line between good and evil was a narrow one. The strongest part of the book was the slow description of Medraut's downward spiral, but Wein reformed him for the too-neat ending, which didn't fit with the rest of the book.

—Allison Barrett, 16

White—*The Once and Future King*

I loved the whimsical writing style in the first part, in which Wart learns lessons from the animals, which seemed remarkably true and entertaining. The rest of the book was much more depressing.

—Ashley Burns, 16

Though it gave an eloquent description of Arthur's boyhood and is really a classic, it's too meandering without enough plot to fill the pages.

—Allison Barrett, 16

Robin Hood: Common Man against Injustice

Six hundred years after Arthur tried to stem the Saxon tide, Saxons invoked his name for justice when Normans invaded from France. Norman rule brought the code of knightly chivalry, so often mistaken for Arthur's, but rode roughshod over Saxon law, which protected commoners' rights. A yeoman farmer challenging Norman authority might have become outlaw Robin Hood. Like Arthur, Robin Hood may or may not have been a real person, but what he stood for, the common people rising up against tyranny, lives in legend.

Like Arthur's, Robin Hood's deeds were not recorded during his lifetime; he may be a composite of several outlaws, from common yeoman to disinherited earl. His story appears in ballads written in the fifteenth and sixteenth centuries; like Malory, the anonymous author of the long poem "A Gest of Robyn Hode" combined earlier legends everyone knew. *The Merry Adventures of Robin Hood,* written and illustrated in 1883 by Howard Pyle (who also retold the King Arthur legend) is the classic retelling, still enjoyed by young readers. Pyle admitted making "good sober folks of real history . . . frisk and caper" in his "land of Fancy."[46]

When Robin McKinley began her outstanding new version of Robin Hood in *The Outlaws of Sherwood,* she believed Howard Pyle's story was "simply . . . the *truth* about Robin Hood."[47] She was horrified to discover that Robin's longbow was not used until 150 years after King Richard the Lion-Hearted's 1189–1199 reign, that Robin appears in three other kings' reigns, that the Sheriff of Nottingham never administered Sherwood Forest, and that Robin himself, if he existed, may have had another hideout altogether. How does Barnsdale sound in place of Sherwood? Historical Robin Hood, as McKinley explains in her afterword, probably did not live until around 1260, and the details of his story took hundreds of years to adhere to his name. In 1377 he entered literature in *Piers Ploughman* but was not portrayed as stealing from the rich to give to the poor until 1500, when Maid Marian also made her first appearance. Not until 1819 did Robin represent Saxons against Normans, in Sir Walter Scott's *Ivanhoe.*

After McKinley read historian James C. Holt's thesis that "the tales of Robin Hood have always reflected what the teller and the audience needed him to be at the time of the telling," she knew there was room for her Robin (*Outlaws,* 282). Though Robin Hood represents honorable resistance to abusive power, Holt's "quiverful of possible Robin Hoods" lived in a violent age;[48] the real Robin was probably a brutal, desperate man. But our "fancy," says Holt, makes "heroes of outlaws" (190), an image borrowed by Jesse James and Billy the Kid.

McKinley's Robin Hood is a forester in hiding since killing a man in self-defense, his Saxon people persecuted by the Norman Sheriff's cruel policies. Marian is no longer Maid but Robin's best friend and unacknowledged sweetheart, a spirited Saxon-Norman noblewoman who insists that reluctant Robin become a rallying point for other disenchanted Saxons. Robin is a second-rate archer; Marian wins the archery contest. McKinley convincingly describes how Robin and familiar companions Much the Miller, Will Scarlet, Little John, and some 30 others create an outdoor haven, waylaying rich travelers to redistribute wealth to the poor. Her mission, though, is exploring women's place in a man's world, as in her other books (see chapter 2). The iron grip of Norman lords over Saxon people is mirrored in men's hold over women, and McKinley's Marian will have none of it. Resisting her father's efforts to marry her to a Norman lord and Robin's determination to keep her out of outlaw business, Marian is "equal to anything the boys might do, equal as if she gave it no thought; she did what she chose" (*Outlaws*, 203).

Though an able leader of his displaced crew, Robin is anxious, moody, and resistant to Marian's perception that people must make someone their hero. Though Robin's outlaw career lasts only a year and a half, until King Richard returns to order Robin's bedraggled survivors to join his next Holy Land Crusade, legend is already born. At the Nottingham Fair, an old lady swears that Robin is an old god returned to save England from the Normans. Only Marian sees that such notions are necessary to Robin's survival. People need Robin to be a champion archer, so Marian disguises herself as a man to be mistaken for him. Only when she is wounded does Robin realize what she has done for him. At last, Robin and Marian declare their love, which releases Marian from her "dangerous and lonely business of the burnishing of a legend" (*Outlaws*, 216).

McKinley's independent medieval women are forced into male disguise. Will Scarlet's sister Cecily joins Robin's band as Cecil, escaping her father's decree to marry a Norman lord. Cecily's case mirrors Marian's: she has grown up idolizing Marian, sharing her distaste for skirts and feminine roles, resisting a forced marriage, learning male skills, and falling in love with a proud man, Little John, who resists that love. McKinley depicts the strivings of strong women like Marian and Cecily as utterly natural, untied to any era or philosophy, making readers believe that such women have always existed, long before feminism.

Though *The Outlaws of Sherwood* was a 1988 ALA Best Book for Young Adults and a Youth-to-Youth Book, critics disagreed on McKinley's effectiveness. A pointered *Kirkus* review noted characters' "charmingly ironic 20th-century self-awareness" in an "entrancing . . . dramatic" tale that "should be delighting readers for years to come."[49] Though *Booklist* applauded "the sensitive nonmacho Robin" as "a hero for our times," it found "McKinley's world . . . unconvincing," even "tedious," and her story "poorly plotted."[50] *School Library Journal* declared that McKinley's "wish to raise her characters' political and feminist consciousness do[es] not work."[51] For most YAFEs it did work; see their comments at the end of this section.

Typically daring, Parke Godwin revises Robin Hood to his taste in his vibrant adult novel *Sherwood*. A hundred years earlier than his usual twelfth century, during bitter Norman-Saxon conflict at the time of William the Conqueror's 1066 invasion, Godwin's Robin, named Edward Aelredson, fights William beside his father, Aelred, Thane of Denby. Inheriting his lands, Edward protests harsh Norman punishment that blinds his tenant for poaching the king's deer. For this challenge, the Sheriff of Nottingham forfeits Edward's lands; as outlaw Robin, Edward flees to Sherwood.

Godwin's teeming society reveals his keen understanding of the elements that forged British culture. Celtic Britons, survivors of Arthur's time, are represented by Robin's Welsh slave Will Scatloch, loyal but unable to make Robin see why he must buy his freedom. Saxon Robin is tied heart and soul to his lost land, while the Norman Sheriff's loyalty is to King William, for the power that spells the only survival he knows. Attuned to subtleties of human nature, Godwin adds dimension to the legend: Marian as newlywed wife of an outlaw is forced into service at the court of William's shrewd queen, Matilda, where she meets Ralf Fitz-Gerald, the Sheriff of Nottingham, who falls in love with her. That villain becomes Robin's worthy opponent, then his ally when Ralf and Robin join forces against a treacherous Saxon; both love the same woman, and both must serve the same king. Robin's purpose broadens when he learns to read his own English and the Normans' Frankish. "To have any place in this changed new world, . . . he must be able to read the law";[52] when Robin saves a rare manuscript of *The Anglo-Saxon Chronicle,* he preserves his people's traditions. Robin's help in the revolt against William earns the king's pardon and the return of his lands. But Robin's peaceful life is shattered again eight years later when he makes another stand against William's merciless policies in *Robin and the King,* transforming from outlaw to lawyer. Godwin's richly realized Robin and his times are truly three dimensional.

In her young adult novel *The Forestwife,* Theresa Tomlinson uses her hometown lore from Robin's possible Sheffield birthplace to revive a local hero who fled to Barnsdale when unjustly accused of killing his stepfather. Tomlinson's hero is never called Robin Hood; he is Robert, son of healer forestwife Agnes. Refugee Robert is a wild, reckless devotee of absent King Richard until converted to charitable ways by his mother and Marian, Agnes's orphaned ward, who inherits her forestwife role, helping people torn from their homes by a cruel lord to build a hidden woodland community. Though Robert and Marian fall in love, forestwife Marian can never marry. Yet together they provide for the poor in Robin Hood's typical manner and represent spirits of nature the Green Man and Lady on Mayday. Noting Robin Hood's association with Mayday customs, Tomlinson pleasingly connects the legend with ancient powers of the land, which helped keep it alive.

Jennifer Roberson expertly threads many aspects of the legend together in her *Lady of the Forest,* a 1994 ALA Best Book for Young Adults. In an adult novel as vast as Bradley's *Mists of Avalon,* Marian FitzWalter occupies center stage. Orphaned daughter of a knight killed in the Lionheart's Crusades, Marian is at the mercy of ruthless William deLacey, Sheriff of Nottingham, determined to marry her by force if necessary. Robin is Robert of Locksley, heir to the powerful Earl of Huntington, who returns from crusading emotionally scarred from brutal slaughter and Turkish imprisonment and in a "shell-shocked" state. In this thrilling romance, Marian and Robert become passionate lovers who are each other's only hope. Suspense heightens as the Sheriff stalks Marian and Robert stalks his inner demons.

After Will Scarlet abducts Marian to escape hanging, Robert rescues her in Sherwood, meeting the already existing band of outlaws, led by Adam Bell (one of Robin Hood's possible historical identities). Robert becomes Robin Hood by asking for the outlaws' aid in recovering taxes stolen by scheming Prince John; Robin will send the money to ransom imprisoned King Richard. When his father refuses to allow marriage to Marian, who is assumed despoiled by outlaws, Robin disinherits himself. It is Marian's unjust loss of honor that gives her courage to defy the Sheriff. Meanwhile, outlaw minstrel Alan of the Dales composes a ballad revering the hero he recognizes, for "legend's name was Robin."[53] Roberson's compelling characters, intensely scrutinized, tie up dangling ends of the legend while they engage our sympathy—or outrage.

Arthur's natural democratic successor, Robin Hood reincarnates repeatedly, from Errol Flynn's 1938 film *Adventures of Robin Hood* to Kevin Costner's uninspired avenger with his unmerry men in the 1991 movie *Robin Hood: Prince of Thieves*. Literature abounds with cameo appearances of this champion of the oppressed, from Shakespeare's *As You Like It* to White's *Once and Future King,* Holdstock's *Mythago Wood,* Myers's *Silverlock,* Nathan's *Elixir,* and countless others. In Cynthia Voigt's YA fantasy *Jackaroo,* set in the medieval Kingdom, the idea of a masked righter of wrongs is so embedded in popular lore that several people independently don the robes of Jackaroo, including a young innkeeper's daughter. R. A. Salvatore's new *Crimson Shadow* series, named for another outlaw who symbolizes the people's rebellion, also borrows from Arthurian legend, as is obvious in its first volume's title, *The Sword of Bedwyr*.

Will new myths grasp our consciousness as tenaciously as Arthur and Robin have?

YAFEs on Robin Hood

Godwin—*Sherwood*

This unique telling of the Robin Hood story is one of the best because of its historical accuracy, the realism of the circumstances, and the quirks of its characters.

—Ashley Burns, 16

McKinley—*The Outlaws of Sherwood*

It was unremarkable, the only book by Robin McKinley (who is, in my opinion, a goddess) that I did not adore immediately.

—Ashley Burns, 16

The book is packed with unique ideas and wonderful characters. The idea of Marian as a better archer than Robin seems almost shocking, until you find that this Robin is not the fabled man of steel, defender of the poor, but a man with many shortcomings.

—Nathan Doyle, 16

In McKinley's compelling style, the recognizable elements of the legend are combined with an entirely believable, fresh perspective.

—Deirdre Kambic, 16

McKinley's wonderful storytelling skills make this the best retelling I have ever read, my introduction to Robin McKinley. I loved every other book of hers too; only *The Door in the Hedge* was better.

—Anne Pizzi, 14

Roberson—*Lady of the Forest*

This evocative retelling reawakens interest even in those bored with the legend because it shows heroes as normal people forced to extremes, each with different motives and morals.

—Ashley Burns, 16

As characters from the original story all got tied into it in strange ways, the book kept my interest all the way through.

—Pixy Dougherty, 14

Roberson took the legend as a backbone so she could develop motivations for characters and devise plot elaborations, for those who have the folly to read it for the plot. I found it tedious when a writer with such style had characters so obsessed with lust for Marian and power. Though some characters seem clichéd and corny, I would recommend this book to someone willing to see the Robin Hood tales trampled and almost fitted back together.

—Anne Pizzi, 14

Recommended Reading

(* denotes title mentioned in text; other titles are additional)

The Celtic Roots of King Arthur

Alexander, Lloyd. *The Chronicles of Prydain*. 5 vols. New York: Holt.
  Vol. 1: *The Book of Three*. 1964.
  Vol. 2: *The Black Cauldron*. 1965.
  Vol. 3: *The Castle of Llyr*. 1966.
  Vol. 4: *Taran Wanderer*. 1967.
  Vol. 5: *The High King*. 1968.
Garden, Nancy. *Fours Crossing* Series. 3 vols. New York: Farrar, Straus
  & Giroux.
  Vol. 1: *Fours Crossing*. 1981.
  Vol. 2: *Watersmeet*. 1983.
  Vol. 3: *The Door Between*. 1987.
Garner, Alan. *The Owl Service*. New York: Henry Z. Walck, 1968.
Kennealy, Patricia. *The Keltiad: The Tale of Aeron*. 3 vols. New York:
  New American Library.
  Vol. 1: *The Copper Crown*. 1986.
  Vol. 2: *The Throne of Scone*. 1987.
  Vol. 3: *The Silver Branch*. 1991.
Lawrence, Louise. *The Earth Witch*. New York: Harper & Row, 1981.
Llywelyn, Morgan. *Bard: The Odyssey of the Irish*. Boston: Houghton
  Mifflin, 1984.
———. *Brian Boru: Emperor of the Irish*. New York: Tor, 1995.
———. *Finn Mac Cool*. New York: Tor, 1994.
———. *The Horse Goddess*. Boston: Houghton Mifflin, 1982.
———. *The Lion of Ireland: The Legend of Brian Boru*. Boston:
  Houghton Mifflin, 1980.
———. *Red Branch*. New York: Morrow, 1989.
———. *Strongbow: The Story of Richard and Aoife*. New York: Tor,
  1996.
The Mabinogion. Trans. and intro. Jeffrey Gantz. New York: Penguin,
  1976.
McGowen, Tom. *Shadow of Fomor*. New York: Dutton/Lodestar, 1990.
O'Shea, Pat. *The Hounds of the Morrigan*. New York: Holiday House,
  1986.
Paxson, Diana L., and Adrienne Martine-Barnes. *The Adventures of
  Fionn mac Cumhal*. 3 vols. New York: Morrow/Avon.
  Vol. 1: *Master of Earth and Water*. 1993.
  Vol. 2: *The Shield Between the Worlds*. 1995.

Vol. 3: *Sword of Fire and Shadow*. 1995.
Paxson, Diana L. *The Serpent's Tooth*. New York: Avon, 1991.
Tenny, Dixie. *Call the Darkness Down*. New York: Atheneum, 1984.
Thomas, Gwyn, and Kevin Crossley-Holland. *Tales from the Mabinogion*. Illus. Margaret Jones. Woodstock, N.Y.: The Overlook Press, 1985.
Walton, Evangeline. *The Mabinogion Tetralogy*. 4 vols. New York: Macmillan, © 1936, 1970–1972.
   Vol. 1: *The Prince of Annwn*. 1992.
   Vol. 2: *The Children of Llyr*. 1992.
   Vol. 3: *The Song of Rhiannon*. 1992.
   Vol. 4: *Island of the Mighty*. 1993.

The Once, Future, and Living Legend of King Arthur

Retellings

Chant, Joy. *The High Kings: Arthur's Celtic Ancestors*. Illus. George Sharp. New York: Bantam, 1983.
Green, Roger Lancelyn. *King Arthur and His Knights of the Round Table*. Illus. Aubrey Beardsley. New York: Knopf, 1993, © 1953.
Hodges, Margaret, and Margery Evernden. *Of Swords and Sorcerers: The Adventures of King Arthur and His Knights*. Woodcuts by David Frampton. New York: Scribner's/Macmillan, 1993.
Lanier, Sidney, ed. *The Boy's King Arthur: Sir Thomas Malory's History of King Arthur and His Knights of the Round Table*. Illus. N. C. Wyeth. New York: Scribner's, 1989, © 1917.
Malory, Sir Thomas. *Le Morte D'Arthur*. New York: Random House, 1993, 1485, © 1879.
Matthews, Caitlín and John. *The Arthurian Book of Days*. New York: Macmillan, 1990.
Morpurgo, Michael. *Arthur: High King of Britain*. Illus. Michael Foreman. San Diego: Harcourt Brace, 1995.
Paterson, Katherine. *Parzival: The Quest of the Grail Knight*. New York: Lodestar, 1997.
Pyle, Howard. *The Story of King Arthur and His Knights*. 4 vols. New York: Scribner, 1993, © 1903.
Sutcliff, Rosemary. *King Arthur Series*. 3 vols. New York: Dutton.
   Vol. 1: *The Sword and the Circle: King Arthur and the Knights of the Round Table*. 1981.
   Vol. 2: *The Light Beyond the Forest: The Quest for the Holy Grail*. 1979.
   Vol. 3: *The Road to Camlann: The Death of King Arthur*. 1981.
———. *Tristan and Iseult*. New York: Dutton, 1971.

Search for the Historical Arthur

Andronik, Catherine M. *Quest for a King: Searching for the Real King Arthur*. New York: Atheneum, 1989.

Ashe, Geoffrey. *The Discovery of King Arthur*. New York: Henry Holt, 1985.

Phillips, Graham, and Martin Keatman. *King Arthur: The True Story*. North Pomfret, Vt.: Trafalgar Square, 1994.

The Quest for Arthur's Britain. Ed. Geoffrey Ashe. Chicago: Academy Chicago Publishers, 1988, © 1968.

Reno, Frank D. *The Historic King Arthur: Authenticating the Celtic Hero of Post-Roman Britain*. Jefferson, N.C.: McFarland, 1996.

Arthur in Historical Novels

Cornwell, Bernard. Arthur Trilogy. New York: St. Martin's.

    Vol. 1: *The Winter King*. 1996.

    Vol. 2: *Enemy of God*. 1997.

    Vol. 3: Forthcoming.

Jones, Courtway. *The Story of Dragon's Heirs*. 3 vols. New York: Pocket.

    Vol. 1: *In the Shadow of the Oak King*. 1991.

    Vol. 2: *The Witch of the North*. 1994.

    Vol. 3: *A Prince in Camelot*. 1995.

McCaffrey, Anne. *Black Horses for the King*. San Diego: Harcourt Brace, 1996.

McKenzie, Nancy. Guinevere Series. 2 vols. New York: Ballantine.

    Vol. 1: *The Child Queen*. 1994.

    Vol. 2: *The High Queen*. 1995.

Rice, Robert. *The Last Pendragon*. New York: Walker, 1991.

Stewart, Mary. *The Merlin Trilogy*. 3 vols. New York: Morrow.

    Vol. 1: *The Crystal Cave*. 1970.

    Vol. 2: *The Hollow Hills*. 1973.

    Vol. 3: *The Last Enchantment*. 1979.

——. *The Wicked Day*. New York: Morrow, 1983.

——. *The Prince and the Pilgrim*. New York: Morrow, 1996.

Sutcliff, Rosemary. *The Lantern Bearers*. New York: Henry Z. Walck, 1959.

——. *Sword at Sunset*. New York: Coward McCann, 1963.

Wein, Elizabeth E. *The Winter Prince*. New York: Atheneum, 1993.

Whyte, Jack. *The Camulod Chronicles*. 4 vols. New York: Tor.

    Vol. 1: *The Skystone*. 1996.

    Vol. 2: *The Singing Sword*. 1996.

    Vol. 3: *The Eagles' Brood*. 1997.

    Vol. 4: *The Saxon Shore*. Forthcoming.

Wolf, Joan. *The Road to Avalon*. New York: New American Library, 1988.

Woolley, Persia. *Guinevere Series. 3 vols. New York: Simon & Schuster.
Vol. 1: *Child of the Northern Spring*. 1987.
Vol. 2: *Queen of the Summer Stars*. 1990.
Vol. 3: *Guinevere: The Legend in Autumn*. 1991.

Arthur in Heroic Fantasy

Attanasio, A. A. Arthor Trilogy. New York: HarperPrism.
Vol. 1: *The Dragon and the Unicorn*. 1996.
Vol. 2: *The Eagle and the Sword*. 1997.
Vol. 3: *The Wolf and the Crown*. 1998.

Barron, T.A. *The Lost Years of Merlin* Quintet. New York: Philomel.
Vol. 1: *The Lost Years of Merlin*. 1996.
Vol. 2: *The Seven Songs of Merlin*. 1997.
Vol. 3: *The Fires of Merlin*. Forthcoming.

Berry, James R. *Magicians of Erianne*. New York: Harper & Row, 1988.

Bradley, Marion Zimmer. *Avalon Series. 3 vols. Prequels: New York: Viking. *Mists:* New York: Knopf.
Prequel: *The Forest House*. 1994.
Prequel: *Lady of Avalon*. 1997.
The Mists of Avalon. 1982.

Chapman, Vera. *The Three Damosels Trilogy*. 3 vols. New York: Avon.
Vol. 1: *The Green Knight*. 1978, © 1975.
Vol. 2: *The King's Damosel*. 1976.
Vol. 3: *King Arthur's Daughter*. 1978.

Godwin, Parke. *Firelord* Series. 3 vols. Vol. 1: New York: Doubleday.
Vols. 2–3: New York: Bantam.
Vol. 1: *Firelord*. 1980.
Vol. 2: *Beloved Exile*. 1984.
Vol. 3: *The Last Rainbow*. 1985.

Goldberg, Todd, and C. Horak, R. Norwood, and D. Markestein. *The Prince Valiant Companion*. Mountain Home, Tenn.: Manuscript Press, 1992.

Jones, Mary J. *Avalon*. Tallahassee, Fla.: Naiad Press, 1991.

Lawhead, Stephen R. *The Pendragon Cycle*. 5 vols. New York: Avon.
Vol. 1: *Taliesin*. 1987.
Vol. 2: *Merlin*. 1988.
Vol. 3: *Arthur*. 1989.
Vol. 4: *Pendragon*. 1994.
Vol. 5: *Grail*. 1997.

Newman, Sharan. Guinevere Series. 3 vols. New York: St. Martin's.
Vol. 1: *Guinevere*. 1981; Tor, 1996.

Vol. 2: *The Chessboard Queen.* 1983.

Vol. 3: *Guinevere Evermore.* 1985.

Paxson, Diana L. *The White Raven.* New York: Morrow, 1988.

Sampson, Fay. *Daughter of Tintagel* Series. 5 vol. omnibus edition. North Pomfret, Vt.: Trafalgar Square, 1995, © 1989–1992.

Vol. 1: *Wise Woman's Telling.* 1989.

Vol. 2: *White Nun's Telling.* 1989.

Vol. 3: *Black Smith's Telling.* 1990.

Vol. 4: *Taliesin's Telling.* 1991.

Vol. 5: *Herself.* 1992.

Springer, Nancy. *I Am Mordred: A Tale of Camelot.* New York: Philomel, 1998.

Steinbeck, John. *The Acts of King Arthur and His Noble Knights from the Winchester Manuscripts of Thomas Malory and Other Sources.* New York: Farrar, Straus, & Giroux, 1993, © 1976.

Twain, Mark. **A Connecticut Yankee in King Arthur's Court.* New York: W. W. Norton, 1982, 1889.

Wagner, Matt. **Mage: The Hero Discovered.* 3 vols. Ed. Kate Reynolds. Virginia Beach, Va.: Comico Comics/Donning Company, 1987–1989.

White, T.H. **The Once and Future King.* New York: Putnam's, 1958, 1965, © 1939; Ace, 1996.

———. **The Book of Merlyn.* Austin: University of Texas Press, 1977.

Arthur in Mythic Fantasy

Fantasy Novels

Barron, T.A. **The Merlin Effect.* New York: Philomel, 1994.

Bradshaw, Gillian. **Hawk of May* Trilogy. 3 vols. New York: Simon & Schuster.

Vol. 1: *Hawk of May.* 1980.

Vol. 2: *Kingdom of Summer.* 1981.

Vol. 3: *In Winter's Shadow.* 1982.

Chopra, Deepak. **The Return of Merlin.* New York: Harmony Books, 1995.

Cochran, Molly, and Warren Murphy. Arthur Blessing Trilogy. New York: Tor.

Vol. 1: **The Forever King.* 1992.

Vol. 2: *The Broken Sword.* 1997.

Vol. 3: Forthcoming.

Cooper, Susan. **The Dark is Rising Sequence.* 5 vols. Vol. 1: New York: Harcourt, Brace & World. Vols. 2–5: New York: Atheneum.

Vol. 1: *Over Sea, Under Stone.* 1966.

Vol. 2: *The Dark Is Rising.* 1973.

Vol. 3: *Greenwitch.* 1974.

Vol. 4: *The Grey King.* 1975.

Vol. 5: *Silver on the Tree.* 1977.

Crompton, Anne Eliot. *Merlin's Harp.* New York: Penguin/ROC, 1997.

Curry, Jane Louise. *The Sleepers.* New York: Harcourt, Brace & World, 1968.

Davies, Robertson. **Lyre of Orpheus.* New York: Viking Penguin, 1990.

Dickinson, Peter. *The Weathermonger.* Vol. 3 of *The Changes Trilogy.* New York: Delacorte, 1986, © 1969.

———. **Merlin Dreams.* Illus. Alan Lee. New York: Delacorte, 1988.

Garner, Alan. **Tales of Alderley.* 2 vols.

Vol. 1: *The Weirdstone of Brisingamen.* New York: Henry Z. Walck, 1963, © 1960.

Vol. 2: *The Moon of Gomrath.* London: Collins, 1963.

Katz, Welwyn Wilton. **The Third Magic.* New York: Margaret K. McElderry, 1989.

Kay, Guy Gavriel. **The Fionavar Tapestry.* 3 vols. New York: Arbor House.

Vol. 1: *The Summer Tree.* 1985.

Vol. 2: *The Wandering Fire.* 1986.

Vol. 3: *The Darkest Road.* 1986.

Laubenthal, Sanders Anne. **Excalibur.* New York: Ballantine, 1978.

Lewis, C. S. **That Hideous Strength: A Modern Fairy-tale for Grownups.* Vol. 3 of *The Space Trilogy.* New York: Macmillan, 1990, © 1946.

Mayne, William. *Earthfasts.* New York: Dutton, 1967.

Nathan, Robert. **The Elixir.* New York: Knopf, 1971.

Norton, Andre. *Here Abide Monsters.* New York: Atheneum, 1973.

———. *Steel Magic.* New York: Archway, 1978.

Yolen, Jane. **The Dragon's Boy.* New York: HarperCollins, 1990.

———. **Merlin's Booke.* Minneapolis: SteelDragon Press, 1986.

Mythic Arthur in Genres beyond Fantasy

Bryher, [Winifred]. **A Visa for Avalon.* New York: Harcourt, Brace and World, 1965.

Chadwick, Elizabeth. *First Knight.* Story by Lorne Cameron, David Hoselton, and William Nicholson. Screenplay by William Nicholson. New York: Pocket, 1995.

Cherryh, C. J. **Port Eternity.* New York: DAW, 1982.

Karr, Phyllis Ann. **Idylls of the Queen.* New York: Ace, 1982.

Kennealy-Morrison, Patricia. **The Keltiad: Prequel. Blackmantle.* New York: HarperPrism, 1997.

————. *The Keltiad: The Tales of Arthur.* 3 vols. Vols. 1–2: New York: Penguin/Roc. Vol. 3: New York: HarperCollins.
Vol. 1: *The Hawk's Gray Feather.* 1990.
Vol. 2: *The Oak Above the Kings.* 1994.
Vol. 3: *The Hedge of Mist.* 1996.
Norton, Andre. *Merlin's Mirror.* New York: DAW, 1975.
Price, Anthony. *Our Man in Camelot.* New York: Warner, 1988, © 1975.
Quiller-Couch, Arthur, and Daphne Du Maurier. *Castle Dor.* New York: Doubleday, 1961.
Service, Pamela F. Arthur Series. 2 vols. New York: Ballantine.
Vol. 1: *Winter of Magic's Return.* 1985.
Vol. 2: *Tomorrow's Magic.* 1987.
Seton, Anya. *Avalon.* Boston: Houghton Mifflin, 1965.

Arthurian Short-Story Collections

Camelot: A Collection of Original Arthurian Stories. Ed. Jane Yolen. Illus. Winslow Pels. New York: Philomel, 1995.
The Camelot Chronicles: Heroic Adventures from the Time of King Arthur. Ed. Mike Ashley. New York: Carroll & Graf, 1992.
The Chronicles of the Holy Grail: The Ultimate Quest from the Age of Arthurian Legend. Ed. Mike Ashley. New York: Carroll & Graf, 1996.
Excalibur. Ed. Richard Gilliam, Martin H. Greenberg, and Edward E. Kramer. New York: Warner, 1995.
Invitation to Camelot. Ed. Parke Godwin. New York: Ace, 1988.
The Merlin Chronicles. Ed. Mike Ashley. New York: Carroll & Graf, 1995.
The Pendragon Chronicles: Heroic Fantasy from the Time of King Arthur. Ed. Mike Ashley. New York: Peter Bedrick Books, 1990.

Robin Hood: Common Man against Injustice

Friesner, Esther. *The Sherwood Game.* New York: Baen, 1995.
Godwin, Parke. *Sherwood* series. 2 vols. New York: Morrow.
Vol. 1: *Sherwood.* 1991.
Vol. 2: *Robin and the King.* 1993.
Holt, James C. *Robin Hood.* New York: Thames and Hudson, 1982.
McKinley, Robin. *The Outlaws of Sherwood.* New York: Greenwillow, 1988.
Morpurgo, Michael. *Robin of Sherwood.* Illus. Michael Foreman. San Diego: Harcourt Brace, 1996.
Pyle, Howard. *The Merry Adventures of Robin Hood.* New York: Scribner's, 1946, © 1883.

Roberson, Jennifer. *Lady of the Forest*. New York: Kensington Publishing/Zebra Books, 1992.

Salvatore, R. A. *The Sword of Bedwyr*. New York: Warner, 1995.

Tomlinson, Theresa. *The Forestwife*. New York: Orchard, 1995.

Voigt, Cynthia. *Jackaroo*. Vol. 1 of *Kingdom* Series. New York: Atheneum, 1985.

Selected Bibliography

(Note: For fiction, see starred titles in Recommended Reading)

Secondary Sources

The Once, Future, and Living Legend of King Arthur

The Arthurian Encyclopedia. Ed. Norris J. Lacy. New York: Garland, 1986. Paperback edition: New York: Peter Bedrick Books, 1987.

Coghlan, Ronan. *The Illustrated Encyclopedia of Arthurian Legends*. Rockport, Mass.: Element Books, 1993.

Matthews, Caitlín. *The Celtic Tradition*. Rockport, Mass.: Element Books, 1995.

———. *The Elements of the Celtic Tradition*. Shaftesbury, Dorset, U.K.: Element Books, 1989.

Matthews, John. *The Arthurian Tradition*. Rockport, Mass.: Element Books, 1994.

———. *The Elements of the Grail Tradition*. Shaftesbury, Dorset, U.K.: Element Books, 1990.

The New Arthurian Encyclopedia. Ed. Norris J. Lacy, Geoffrey Ashe, Sandra N. Ihle, Marianne E. Kalinke, and Raymond H. Thompson. New York: Garland, 1991.

Thompson, Raymond H. *The Return from Avalon: A Study of Arthurian Legend in Modern Fiction*. Westport, Conn.: Greenwood Press, 1985.

Search for the Historical Arthur

Andronik, Catherine M. *Quest for a King: Searching for the Real King Arthur*. New York: Atheneum, 1989.

Ashe, Geoffrey. *The Discovery of King Arthur*. New York: Henry Holt, 1985.

Phillips, Graham, and Martin Keatman. *King Arthur: The True Story*. North Pomfret, Vt.: Trafalgar Square, 1994.

The Quest for Arthur's Britain. Ed. Geoffrey Ashe. Chicago: Academy Chicago Publishers, 1988, © 1968.

Reno, Frank D. *The Historic King Arthur: Authenticating the Celtic Hero of Post-Roman Britain*. Jefferson, N.C.: McFarland, 1996.

Robin Hood: Common Man against Injustice

Holt, James C. *Robin Hood*. New York: Thames & Hudson, 1982.

6. A Magic Bestiary

People have looked to animals for lessons in living since at least 500 B.C., when Aesop's fables provided morals-of-the-story. In folktales of all cultures, animals exaggerate human characteristics; we call ourselves "quiet as a mouse" or "sly fox."

Even realistic animal tales are fantasy, for we cannot know animals' realities. We imagine their speech and thoughts through sounds, actions, or psychic communication. And we really let our fantasies run wild with mythical dragons, unicorns, and mixes of human and beast, such as mermaids.

Psychic Beasts

Once all story animals were anthropomorphic, with human characteristics. Favorite childhood stories teach gentle lessons in behavior through talking animals in clothes, such as Frances, the badger who eats bread and jam.

Classic animal tales live long. *The Jungle Book,* made into a Disney movie, began in the 1890s when its author, Rudyard Kipling, traveled to India, where he created Mowgli, the boy raised by wolves, and Rikki-Tikki-Tavi, the mongoose. Like Aesop's fables, Kipling's humorous *Just So Stories,* which include "How the Rhinoceros Got His Skin," reveal human character. In late 1800s Georgia, Joel Chandler Harris adopted the African-American voice of Uncle Remus to spin tales of Brer Rabbit, a cunning trickster based on Anansi the Spider from African folktales. Kipling and Uncle Remus so charmingly displayed human nature that modern authors still write stories in their styles.

In 1908, Scottish author Kenneth Grahame created enduring talking animals in *Wind in the Willows,* which depicts the English countryside adventures of bachelors Mole, Water Rat, Badger, and Toad. Dim-sighted Mole was Grahame's tribute to his four-year-old son, Alastair, nearly blind from birth.[1] Animals also imitated people in George Orwell's fable *Animal Farm,* a 1945 satire warning of the dangers of totalitarianism just after Hitler's defeat.

The first realistic animal fantasy was *Bambi,* by Hungarian journalist Felix Salten, published in 1928. Overshadowed by the sentimental Disney film, the original book is a sensitive study of a deer's natural life. Joy and fear are basic expressions for Bambi and his forest companions; death is part of life. Salten's respect for animals' experience was revolutionary.

Bambi set the stage for Richard Adams's contemporary classic *Watership Down,* in which English rabbits make an epic quest for a new home when their burrow is destroyed by real estate developers. Building their culture on myth and prophecy, Adams engages readers with the credibility of this underground rabbit world and carries the story to a suspenseful climax. Humans are the villains; our sympathies are firmly with the rabbits. A 1974 best-seller and ALA Best Book for Young Adults, *Watership Down* continues to win fervent fans. Endless imitators follow its animal fantasy conventions, which include

- Language and communication with other species
- A nonanthropomorphic culture
- Legends and lore explaining their origins
- A visionary leader who predicts danger and urges the group toward change
- A conviction that animals are more highly evolved than brutal humans
- A struggle for survival with some force, often human, which threatens their way of life

Watership Down is such a prototype that few animal fantasies escape comparison, though the genre has developed beyond imitation and appeals to animal lovers aware of vital links among species. When I introduce a new animal fantasy to Fantasy Fanatics, they chorus, "A *Watership Down* of _____!" (Fill in featured creature.) Here are fine *Watership Down*s of:

- Ants—*A Rustle in the Grass* by Robin Hawdon
- Badgers—*The Cold Moons* by Aeron Clement
- Foxes—*The Foxes of Firstdark* by Garry Kilworth
- Horses—*The Heavenly Horse from the Outermost West* and *Piper at the Gate* by Mary Stanton
- Moles—*Duncton Wood* and other Duncton books by William Horwood
- Pigs and boars—*The Pig Plantagenet* and *Castle Crespin* by Allen Andrews
- Roaches—*The Collectors* by Robert Carter

The most popular animal fantasy since *Watership Down* is the *Redwall* series, begun in the late 1980s by Brian Jacques and now numbering ten volumes (see this chapter's Recommended Reading). Though published for children, *Redwall* appeals to a broad age range, from advanced readers of eight to adults. Since the first volume, in which a vermin army led by rat Cluny the Scourge invades a peaceful community of mice, good and evil have clashed in the lovely countryside of Mossflower. A British comedian and radio personality, Jacques embellishes his animals with lively wit and character in swashbuckling adventures effortlessly digested by YAFEs.

YAFEs on *Redwall*

Redwall is one of my very favorites. I love the characters, the believable way it's told with humor, and the detailed setting.
—Katherine Doherty, 15

It is very lifelike, with characters who fit actual people's images.
—Linda Reling, 14

Brian Jacques is creative, imaginative, and cool. The animals
were real for me. I felt that I was part of the story.

—Aron Kelly, 12

It will probably be a classic years from now.

—Galadriel Wills, 13

In generous starred reviews, critics agree. Unable to resist
Jacques's delightful and rascally creatures, Gene LaFaille declares, "Long live the Redwallers!"[2] The series's first volume was
a 1989 ALA Best Book for Young Adults.

Recent animal fantasies show new cooperation between animals and humans. In Richard Ford's ALA 1982 Best Book *Quest
for the Faradawn,* a human baby raised by badgers becomes savior of the world all species share. James Gurney's gorgeously
illustrated *Dinotopia,* a 1993 ALA Best Book, reveals a utopia
where people and dinosaurs live in harmony. In Dennis Hamley's
exquisite *Hare's Choice,* children write about a dead hare found
by a classmate, winning eternity for the hare, who meets famous
animals in the afterlife. What a critic calls "strange and fascinating" is seen by YAFE creative writer Galadriel Wills as inspiring
reading for writing students.[3]

Cats with Consciousness

Of all creatures in the magic bestiary, cats inspire some of the
finest animal fantasy. No matter how well we know cats, their
mystique intrigues us. Once objects of worship or persecution,
cats with such names as Snowball or Prudence live in our homes.
Yet in "The Naming of Cats," T. S. Eliot reminds us that their
true names stay hidden:

When you notice a cat in profound meditation,
    The reason, I tell you, is always the same:
His mind is engaged in a rapt contemplation
    Of the thought, of the thought, of the thought of his name:
        His ineffable effable

Effanineffable
Deep and inscrutable singular Name.[4]

Magicians need names to cast spells, so cats stay powerful as long as their names are secret.

The Wild Cats of Clare Bell

What lurks behind cats' unfathomable gazes? In the fascinating Ratha series, Clare Bell interprets cat culture on peopleless Earth twenty-five million years ago. Ratha is one of the Named, a clan of thinking, speaking wild cats, who herd horses and deer. In *Ratha's Creature,* clan life is threatened by Un-Named raiders, who the clan believes cannot speak because they have no intelligent light in their eyes and no names, the essence of clan identity.

During a forest fire, gutsy yearling Ratha watches the powerful burning "creature" who sends her clan fleeing in terror. With great ingenuity, Ratha discovers how to make the creature give warmth, how to feed it with twigs and carry its nurslings on green sticks. Yet when she presents the creature to her clan, Ratha is banished, and her creature drowns in the river.

Forced to live with the Un-Named, Ratha learns from a ginger male she calls Bonechewer that not all Un-Named are without eye light. Among them, she senses "a life far older than that of the clan, a life far deeper, and in a strange way, far wiser."[5]

Having mated with Bonechewer, Ratha is distressed when their cubs' eyes are bereft of light. As she quarrels violently with Bonechewer about abandoning them, eldest cub Thistle-chaser steps between her parents. Enraged, Ratha bites her brutally, and Bonechewer drives Ratha away. Rediscovering her creature, Ratha uses it to kill her clan's tyrant and subdue the Un-Named, killing even Bonechewer. New leader Ratha renames her clan the People of the Red Tongue.

Second in the series, *Clan Ground* is a sobering study of abusive power. Ratha unwisely allows Un-Named newcomer Shongshar to join her Firekeepers. Isolating the Red Tongue in a cave where all "crouch in obedience to this new power,"[6] Shongshar drives Ratha out. Only by destroying everything can Ratha reclaim what is left of her clan. Her lesson: "The veneration of fire had thrust her people into debasement and . . . savagery, . . . but it also fed a hunger of the spirit, a need that could neither be ignored or denied" (*Ground*, 240).

With new allies the treelings, lemurlike animals proficient with their paws, Ratha's clan expands capabilities beyond those of either species alone. This society of cats and treelings advances in *Ratha and Thistle-chaser*. Forced by drought to move near the sea, they meet Newt, a lone, lame cat who swims with sea creatures. Admiring Newt's independence, Ratha's old teacher Thakur shows her leg exercises and language. Newt suffers seizures from terrifying dreams about Dreambiter, who tore her leg, and Thakur realizes Newt is Ratha's abandoned cub, Thistle-chaser.

In a heart-stopping climax, Newt ambushes the tormenting Dreambiter/Ratha. After that brutal mother-daughter battle, Ratha realizes she was wrong about her cubs' eyes. As Thakur says, "The thing we call the light in our eyes is more than just that. . . . we must learn to see it in whatever form it takes."[7] With such acceptance, Ratha's clan is on the road to true civilization. In the last volume, *Ratha's Challenge*, Ratha must confront the Dreambiter inside herself in order to exorcise it from her daughter. Then Thistle can use her special gifts to bridge understanding between Ratha's clan and a strange tribe of cats who communicate from within.

Clare Bell so forcefully conveys her sentient cats' perspective that their struggle for control of their world seems credible. As a professional engineer enthralled by evolution, Bell traces how culture develops, challenging readers to study ours. ALA librarians echoed teens' appreciation in their comments on Bell by listing the first and third volumes as Best Books for Young Adults in 1983 and 1991.

Clare Bell left Ratha's ancient times for future feline evolution in *Tomorrow's Sphinx*, ambitiously combining naturalist studies, science fiction, fantasy, and time travel to postulate profound mind links between humans and beasts. In a world abandoned by people after ecological catastrophe, wild cheetahs roam the Nile

Valley. Like Bell's other wild cats, they are sentient beings governed by legend, language, and law, and their names set them apart from animals like lions, who don't "have the wit or need to give each other names."[8]

Because her black coat is no camouflage against sand, abandoned cub Kichebo finds hunting hopeless. Shunned by her bright-pelted kind, Kichebo lives in a "strange stone forest" (*Sphinx*, 94)—ruins of human civilization—which awakens puzzling images from another time. When a "sinister one-eyed bird" falls from the sky (*Sphinx*, 79), Kichebo rescues a small furless creature from inside it. Though it smells like prey and stands oddly on two legs, its eyes reveal a mind as gifted as the cheetahs'. When it communicates its name, Menk, Kichebo adopts the human cub, fiercely protecting it from other cheetahs.

Another black cheetah comes to Kichebo in "a dream that walked with his legs, that touched with his whiskers, and saw with his eyes" (*Sphinx*, 115). Long ago he was sacred Kheknemt, companion to the young Egyptian pharaoh Tutankhamen. Connecting to Kheknemt's consciousness, Kichebo experiences his life with Tut. In their cult based on psychic links between humans and cats, Tut and Kheknemt achieved complete empathy, until Tut fell from an assassin's spear. Kichebo recognizes her similar link with Menk.

When Menk's people return to re-create the human-cheetah link of their ancestors, they expect Kichebo to forsake her world for theirs, far beyond the stars. How can humans impose that upon her? In an age when animal-rights activists ask us to share our planet respectfully with other creatures, Clare Bell's message is timely.

Young adults report confusion with Bell's genre-mixing. Having followed Ratha avidly, YAFE Domenica Mirarchi, 14, assumed *Tomorrow's Sphinx* was the third volume in the trilogy, minus Ratha, but became bored with long hunting scenes. Some YAFEs found it "weird"; its dense plotting and structure demands sophisticated readers.

In her first adult novel, *The Jaguar Princess*, Bell continues animal/human exchanges with shapeshifting woman/jaguar Mixcatl, who brings peace to the Aztec empire. A critic describes it as "*The Cat People* merged with the Aztec codices and a soupçon of Scarlett O'Hara."[9]

YAFEs ON THE WILD CATS OF CLARE BELL

Ratha Books

I reread the Ratha books often because I like how Bell connects cats to primitive people. Both use power for good or bad.

—Katherine Doherty, 15

Bell's cats warn us not to disturb or change indigenous life forms.

—Vanessa Bowler, 16

The Ratha books are my favorite animal fantasies because they are very tense and dramatic, showing how tyranny spreads and is removed in society.

—Ben Cantrick, 16

Tomorrow's Sphinx

This original, poweful, and captivating book is interesting to many age groups.

—Deirdre Kambic, 15

A Cacophony of Cats

Unlike Bell's wild cats, the cats of *Tailchaser's Song* by Tad Williams are domestic, living without furless M'an in a forest society of clans, the Folk. When several cats mysteriously disappear, young ginger tom Fritti Tailchaser, joined by his kitten admirer Pouncequick, solemn orphan Roofshadow, and roving, raving Eatbugs, searches for Hushpad. At an enormous mound that emanates menace, they are captured by huge cat Clawguards, then dragged through twisting tunnels where slaving Folk diggers are brutalized by Nazi-like guards. Deep in the mound's core, they face Lord Hearteater, a grotesque bloated cat reclining atop a writhing pile of maimed animals, which he devours alive. After mustering all his cunning and courage to destroy this cat concentration camp, Fritti finally finds Hushpad in a lighthouse; now the snug pet of M'an, Hushpad is so removed that her bond with Fritti cannot survive. A wiser Fritti returns to his true friends.

Also known for his epic fantasy trilogy *Memory, Sorrow, and Thorn* (DAW, 1988–1992), Williams spins a vigorous tale rich in the elements of animal fantasy and propelled by spirited cat characters who rarely stray from feline to human motivations. As in the Ratha books, the legends of Fritti's Folk guide their fates, and Common Singing connects them with other species. In their civil war, good and evil manifest in natural or unnatural behavior. Cannibalistic oppressor Lord Hearteater abuses psychic power, while Fritti's natural instinct leads him to victory.

Published around the same time, *Tailchaser* and *Ratha* have notable similarities. Both feature nonconforming natural leaders, though Tailchaser is more affable than the prickly Ratha. Both concern the abuse of power by decadent rulers. Their cat clans are defined by Naming. Williams's three cat names, one known only within each cat, must be borrowed from poet T. S. Eliot. While Bell's evolutionary concerns outweigh Williams's standard quest, both *Ratha* and *Tailchaser* are significant cat fantasies, attracting the same readers.

Cat fanciers will also savor the short stories in four paperback *Catfantastic* collections. Science fiction and fantasy authors from Andre Norton to Mercedes Lackey echo each other's themes in fresh ways. Each volume features a Clare Bell story, such as "Damcat," in which a bobcat saves a huge dam from destruction. In volumes 2 and 3, Bell's ship's cats use magic to win wars for human friends; one beats the *Bismarck* in World War II, and one stops a 1767 Tahitian feud. Other entertaining cat anthologies appear in this chapter's Recommended Reading.

Paul Gallico's heartwarming 1950 classic *The Abandoned* is worth rediscovering. When a boy becomes a big white tomcat, he owes his survival to tough but sweet tabby Jennie. The Catswold race also shapeshifts from human to cat in *The Catswold Portal* by Shirley Rousseau Murphy. Drifting between being artist Braden West's pet cat and his human lover, Melissa discovers her Catswold identity in the Netherworld below their California garden. Could our own cats be Catswold? In *The Cats of Seroster* by Robert Westall, enormous 30-pound golden cats called the Miw psychically control the fates of medieval French people. Westall also created the remarkable *Blitzcat,* which features a deaf female cat who searches for her beloved missing soldier through World War II England and France, even flying in a bomber.

Perhaps the most touching cat-human link is between Nemrod and his Roman Catholic bishop in *Magnifi-Cat,* a 1972 small masterpiece by Carolyn and Edmund Sheehan. With wit and pathos, Nemrod's story unfolds between his lifesaving mission on Earth and his arrival in Heaven as a saint. When Nemrod wins his wings, there is not a dry eye among readers convinced that cats are our most rewarding animal companions.

YAFEs on *Tailchaser's Song*

The description of cat life puts you in their shoes [pawprints?].

—Ben Cantrick, 16

Ratha fans will also like *Tailchaser,* which would even attract nonfantasy readers who simply like cats.

—Vanessa Bowler, 16

Mythical Creatures

Believing in the special powers of familiar animals, we also invent mythical beasts. We combine aspects of ourselves with animals, "exaggerating or distorting" them. When "fact and fantasy have been fused in such a way . . . the being takes on a life of its own and has its own reality," says Malcolm South, editor of *Mythical and Fabulous Creatures.*[10]

According to the beautifully illustrated *Magical Beasts,* such fancies began in our early hunter-gatherer days. During intimate coexistence with animals, we gave godlike attributes to such great beasts as the cave bear, considered our animal master. Celtic Britain's animal master was a stag, and the Greeks believed people descended from great beasts.[11] By the Middle Ages, a huge array of imaginary creatures was portrayed in art and literature with symbolic meanings everyone understood; such works often illuminated the story of Christ.

South classifies more than 140 types of fabulous creatures, from familiar dragons and unicorns to obscure human-animal composites, such as hideous harpies, with vultures' bodies and women's faces. These creatures appeal to us because they "reflect something meaningful about human experience, and engage our emotions in a powerful way" (xx).

Modern writers place mythical beasts in surroundings beyond their classic homes. Patricia McKillip's *Forgotten Beasts of Eld* are a legendary falcon, lion, cat, swan, dragon, and talking boar who live atop Eld Mountain with the female wizard Sybel, who controls them telepathically. Isolated from people until Lord Coren brings the baby heir of Eldewold for her to hide from danger, Sybel feels her first love for baby Tam and for Coren, who becomes her husband. When political power struggles threaten that love, Sybel tries to control love with magic. Only when Sybel frees the beasts does love win over power in this passionate, brooding tale.

Another inventive group of rare species is studied by veterinary students in *The Magic and the Healing* by Nick O'Donohoe, a 1995 ALA Best Book for Young Adults. Crossing the border from Virginia to the alternate world of Crossroads, the students treat unicorns, fauns, and treacherous werewolves. Crossroads magic heals human disease, and vet student B.J. has been diagnosed with fatal Huntington's Chorea. But when civil war threatens this haven for misfits, the students weigh the risks of their healing mission. As people mingle with fantastical creatures and medicine mixes with magic, animal-loving readers will find their assumptions about all species challenged. Crossroads adventures continue in O'Donohoe's *Under the Healing Sun.*

Myth master Jane Yolen channels healing through another faun in *The Stone Silenus.* Since her famous poet father died,

Melissa has been consumed by grief. As she recites his poetry, in which he took a faun's identity, a boy suddenly appears beside her on the beach, looking just like photographs of Melissa's father as a youth. Could her wishing have called "his own mythic image"?[12] Yolen explores her favorite turf, that between myth and reality, keeping both readers and Melissa teetering on that fine line between the two.

Charles Finney's 1935 classic mixing of mythical beasts and humans is *The Circus of Dr. Lao,* in which the circus hits an Arizona town with animals more unusual than expected. Other books in which humans and creatures intermingle are recommended in this chapter's Recommended Reading.

Creatures of the Sea

We have always populated the unpredictable waters of our planet with supernatural sea creatures. Ancient Greeks and Romans watched for irresistible sirens to dash their ships upon rocks. European sailors were terrified of tentacled sea monsters; explorer Henry Hudson reported mermaid sightings. In the 1840s, P. T. Barnum fooled gullible people by exhibiting monkey skeletons attached to fish as mermaids.[13] Though scientists have classified mermaids as manatees, and sea monsters as giant squid, mythic sea creatures still mesmerize us. Tales from seawashed Scotland and Ireland swarm with selkies, kelpies, and merfolk who interact with humans.

The recent Disney movie *The Little Mermaid* is based on a story by Danish tale spinner Hans Christian Andersen, who wrote in 1835 of tragic consequences of love between a mermaid and a man. Jane Yolen updates such myths in *Neptune Rising: Songs and Tales of the Undersea Folk.* In "Sule Skerry," a cynical teenaged girl evacuated from London to Scotland for safety during World War II has a disturbing encounter with the Great Selchie, a seal who becomes a man. Like Andersen's mermaid tale without Disney's happy ending, Yolen's "Undine" makes readers keenly feel a prince's empty promises to a mermaid. To become his lover, she transforms her fish tail to legs, which "bit like knife points into her waist."[14] The sad tale of Undine, first recorded in

1811 by a German baron, has also been bewitchingly refashioned by Mary Pope Osborne in *Haunted Waters*. Though she loves her husband, Lord Huldbrand, Undine is compelled to swim at midnight to hear the fish sing, terrified she will be dragged "into that other world. Forever."[15]

The moody sea also affects lonely Peri, daughter of a drowned fisherman and a mourning mother, who blames the sea for her misfortunes in Patricia McKillip's evocative novel *The Changeling Sea*. Peri helps the magician Lyo cope with a sea-dragon, which is somehow related to the king's two sons exchanged at birth, one born to the queen, one to a sea-woman. McKillip binds Peri's love to Lyo's magic, restoring their world by connecting sea and land. Four YAFEs agree with the critic who found McKillip's tale "like the sea, . . . constantly moving and changing. . . . [T]he secrets it reveals captivate the reader until the final page."[16]

Australian Ruth Park brings seapeople into modern life in her remarkable novel *My Sister Sif*. When teenaged sisters Riko and Sif return to the island of their birth, tiny Rongo in the Epiphanies of the Pacific, readers meet their merwoman mother, Matira, splashing with her tail in the ocean. Sif's fiancé, Henry, an American marine biologist, learns that seapeople's tails are manufactured swimming aids for a human race adapted to ocean life. Rongo's dazzling airlocked underwater city is one of many near islands around the world. Park's scientific explanations convince us of this secret undersea reality, where Sif's love for Henry rebuilds the polluted earth of our near future. Park sees her young readers as "the generation that woke up" to heal a dying world. Other tales of human entanglement with sea creatures, which reflect growing consciousness of our effect on the environment, are listed in this chapter's Recommended Reading.

Dragons: Our Favorite Fearsome Creature

In virtually every culture around the world, the dragon is the supreme mythical beast. A multitude of multicultural dragons are awesomely pictured by artist Wayne Anderson in *Dragons: Truth, Myth, and Legend* by David Passes, and in large pop-ups in *Greg Hildebrandt's Book of Three-Dimensional Dragons*. They include:

- Vritra, burst by a god to form the sea in the creation story from 1200 B.C. India
- Midgard, a Norse dragon who sleeps in the sea, encircling the whole world
- Nine-headed Hydra, who grew a new head whenever Greek hero Hercules cut one off
- The African Amphisbaena, one head on each end
- The piasa, with a man's face and long tail, worshipped by Algonquin Native Americans
- Benevolent Chinese dragons, who control the weather and bring good luck

Many other types of dragons are cataloged in *Dragons and Unicorns: A Natural History.* Anyone could describe our European dragon: between 20 and 200 feet long and scaly, with a spiny back and long, snaky tail. He flies with batlike wings, breathes fire, and has chronic bad breath. His blood burns or poisons; his glaring eyes hypnotize. He's mean and greedy, hoards treasure in a cave, and enjoys a tasty morsel of maiden for breakfast. Wherever there are dragons, there are dragonslayers. In the eighth-century epic poem *Beowulf,* the hero slays the Fire-drake. By the Middle Ages, the dragon embodied Satan himself, and hordes of dragon-slaying saints went after him, the most famous being Saint George.

If dragons are merely mythical, why have they gripped us so relentlessly for thousands of years? *Tailchaser's Song* author Tad Williams thinks dragons are "everything we fear and wonder about and worship—everything we don't quite understand—given powerful, fiery flesh."[17] Author Peter Dickinson believes dragons captivate us because they actually did exist, as he convinces us in his marvelous book *The Flight of Dragons.* His theory hinges on evolution; species survive if they develop what they need. Birds' ancestors were dinosaurs whose ability to fly saved them from extinction. Dragons are logical descendants of dinosaurs—and dragons fly. The flight of such massive beasts seems impossible, until Peter Dickinson explains that their mass was mostly hollow cavities for storing the hydrogen gas that propelled them. To say more would spoil the elegance of Dickinson's logic, enhanced by the detailed diagrams and lush color artwork of Wayne Anderson. Dragons' life cycle was so precarious that they became extinct soon after their greatest enemy, man, arrived on the scene. Dragons live in literature because, says Dickinson, they "continued to evolve in folk-memory. . . . memory became myth."[18]

In 1898, a new kind of dragon emerged in *The Reluctant Dragon* by Kenneth Grahame (who later wrote *The Wind in the Willows*). After a boy befriends his local dragon, who would rather be writing poetry than "rampaging and skirmishing,"[19] he prevents his townspeople's typical dragon-slaying reaction. Grahame's reluctant dragon became "first in a long lineage of peaceful dragons in children's stories, . . . affable, cute, misunderstood, but always nonthreatening creatures more like overgrown puppies."[20]

Gordon Dickson's *The Dragon and the George* "turns the St. George legend inside out" (Evans, 52). In an experiment gone awry, history professor Jim Eckert is astrally projected from his Minnesota university to another world inside the body of young dragon Gorbash. With good-natured humor, "endearing and memorable" characters from our time romp through many "thoroughly delightful" adventures in a feudal society too intriguing to leave (Tymn et al., 73). Since 1976, Jim the Dragon Knight has starred in seven volumes.

The classic ferocious dragon isn't dead yet. Both C. S. Lewis and J. R. R. Tolkien introduced memorable traditional dragons, including Tolkien's Smaug in *The Hobbit*. In 1968, a pillaging dragon appeared in Ursula K. Le Guin's *Wizard of Earthsea* (see chapter 2), but the same year a unique new dragon was born in Anne McCaffrey's *Dragonflight*.

McCaffrey's dragons are telepathic, sharing an intimate mind-to-mind bond with the few humans who can communicate with them. Colonists from Earth on the planet Pern, elite dragonriders and their dragon companions guard their world from deadly threats. When McCaffrey created these human/dragon pairs, she was influenced by her own bond with her beloved horse and was fed up with books about human isolation. " 'That's why the dragons are telepathic,' " she says; " 'their riders are never alone. Further, the dragon never criticizes: he adores his rider no matter what he does or is.' "[21]

Never dreaming that her dragon stories would attract a cult following, McCaffrey produced *Dragonflight*'s sequel, *Dragonquest*, before she was asked by a publisher to create a young female dragon friend for young adults. Hence, Menolly appears in the popular YA trilogy *Dragonsong, Dragonsinger,* and *Dragondrums*. Meanwhile, McCaffrey completed her adult series with *The White Dragon*. At this writing, six more Pern books add to the original two trilogies. The latest title novella of a story collection, *The Girl Who Heard Dragons,* finally recaptures an earlier mood lost in some recent Pern tales. "Characters who were rich in nuance became the cardboard versions of themselves, lacking the originality of detail that made them so well-loved in the first books. The later books are more devoted to science than to storytelling,"[22] claims a critic.

Anne McCaffrey would be disgruntled to find herself in a book about fantasy. She considers her writing science fiction due to her scientific "dragonology," including the fact that her dragons do not actually fly. She explains, "[D]ragons have too much mass for their wing-span. They levitate, using wings for guidance, braking, and self-deception."[23] McCaffrey has even studied physics—and Pern is a planet, a science fiction setting.

The Dragons of Jane Yolen and Barbara Hambly

McCaffrey's dragons have inspired other dragon makers, especially Jane Yolen's popular *Pit Dragon Trilogy* set on the planet Austar IV, where people bet on dragon fights in the Pits. In *Dragon's Blood,* Jakkin at 15 is a bondboy on Master Sarkkhan's dragon farm. Hoping to buy his freedom, Jakkin steals a dragon hatchling to train secretly for fighting, with his healer friend Akki as confederate. The young red dragon's ability to communicate telepathically with Jakkin in shimmering rainbow thoughts brings victory in his first fight. With winnings to buy freedom, Jakkin wants Akki as his bride, but she leaves without explanation.

In the second volume, *Heart's Blood,* whose title reflects his dragon's new name, Jakkin is raising her hatchlings when he must rescue Akki from rebels against Austar's government. During the revolt, Heart's Blood is killed, but Jakkin, Akki, and the five hatchlings are closely bonded by sheltering inside the dragon's egg chamber. In *A Sending of Dragons,* Jakkin, Akki, and the growing hatchlings hide from the rebels in an underground community, shocked to find these primitive cave people using psychic abilities to abuse dragons.

Human/dragon telepathy is Yolen's obvious link with McCaffrey, but Yolen also explores its ethics. Vivid descriptions crescendo by the last volume, contrasting oblique, intrusive human communication with dragons' direct style. Jakkin and Akki must balance psychic connection with personal boundaries. Jane Yolen was forced to "kill off" Heart's Blood. "I tried not to do it, but Jakkin had to leave his mother to grow up, and Heart's Blood, by becoming a mother, had become—symbolically—Jakkin's mother. My daughter was furious with me and wouldn't speak to me for days." She describes how Jakkin and Akki change after their symbolic rebirth in Heart's Blood's egg chamber and their year on the run: they are "interdependent and at one with the world . . . , and they have been forced out of their child-lives, cut off from everything they had grown up believing and 'knowing.' "[24] Now they must "become vegetarians," says Yolen, and fight "against the immorality of the stews and pits. Two teenagers can't change the world on their own, so I send Jakkin and Akki back to the [dragon] nursery at the end of Book 3, to change what they *can* change—their own home."

Until writing her first young adult novel, *Dragon's Blood,* Jane Yolen was known for composing literary fantasy and fairy tales (see chapter 4). Her own teenaged children modeled Austar's characters.

> "Jakkin is based on my middle child, Adam, who is a creative musician, intense, very critical of himself, always making moral judgments on others as well. He even looks like Jakkin. And Akki is definitely Heidi—strong-willed, inventive, outspoken. My youngest son, Jason, the animal compleatist, is also a bit of Jakkin.

When I wrote the first book of the trilogy—never expecting to write any others—I found that halfway through I loved Jakkin and Akki and hated their penal colony world. . . . My main characters [could] work to change the moral tone of their world, . . . so the one book grew to three. . . . The Austar saga seems to be continuing . . . in the possibility of a movie [it became a CBS Storybreak movie in 1985] and a series of comic books leading to the movie. . . . I am also working on a short story about how Jakkin comes to the Nursery after his father dies.

Yolen has not yet decided if she will write a fourth Austar novel, set 15 years later.

This accessible series has wide appeal, from the youngest YA readers to the most sophisticated who take Yolen's dragons to heart in comments following. *VOYA* found *Dragon's Blood* "a thoroughly delightful fantasy" in an "imaginary world . . . within the realm of possibility."[25] *School Library Journal* declared that "the telepathic gentle giants of Pern might meet their match in Yolen's fierce fighters."[26] Also reminded of McCaffrey, another *VOYA* reviewer saw the trilogy as "absorbing and powerful, rich in the fantastic and yet with the essential realism necessary to draw the reader into a world of rainbow-colored telepathic communication and dragons."[27] The first two volumes were both named ALA Best Books for Young Adults. *Dragon's Blood* won the International Reading Association's Children's Choice Award, as well as the Parents' Choice Award. *School Library Journal* also named *Heart's Blood* a Best Book.

Though Jane Yolen's pit dragons are her most popular, she also writes about other types of dragons. In *The Dragon's Boy,* young King Arthur is Artos, who takes lessons in wisdom from a dragon who is not what he seems (see chapter 5). In *Here There Be Dragons,* a handsome collection of Jane Yolen's dragon tales and poems, illustrated with dreamlike scenes by David Wilgus, "The Dragon's Boy" appears in its original short form. Yolen reveals that while she wrote the story, she was taking care of her dying father, whom she never seemed to please. Seeing her father asleep, so ill and weak, she realized, "The dragon has no teeth";[28] a fictional father brought understanding of her own. Such personal introductions enhance Yolen's other dragon viewpoints in this collection, from a twist on the St. George legend and a Chinese dragon to "Cockfight," the story that inspired Austar's dragons. Yolen describes her school visit to a whole class of sixth-grade students all dressed like Jakkin, with bondbags around their necks. Yolen's collection of others' dragon tales, *Dragons and Dreams,* is listed with other dragon anthologies in this chapter's Recommended Reading.

YAFEs on Jane Yolen's *Pit Dragon Trilogy*

The idea that dragons have telepathic links with humans is extraordinary, with dragonsight, where things are seen and felt in colors.

—Sara McCorkendale, 15

I love dragons' communication in abstract designs focused on colors. Dragon liked jokes, too, so they would have been fun. For the story, the style, the nice images—I can read it and read it and still love this series.

—Katherine Doherty, 15

There is a very strong, important message about refusing to conform, standing up for one's beliefs, and not destroying the land we share with animals.

—Jehnie Burns, 17

Another human-dragon link is stunningly portrayed in Barbara Hambly's *Dragonsbane,* an ALA Best Book of 1986. Morkeleb the Black Dragon seems to be a traditional scourge to humankind. But Lord John Aversin, called dragonsbane since reluctantly killing a golden dragon to protect his fading Winterlands people, is not your typical dragonslayer. Scruffy John is more interested in studying his crumbling books, constructing engineering experiments, and indulging his mischievous sense of humor than in being a hero. His plain mistress, Jenny Waynest, torn between her limited magical abilities and her devotion to John and their sons, is not your typical healer. This 30-something couple is waylaid by young Gareth, who, bedazzled by ballads proclaiming John's heroism, begs John to slay the dragon terrorizing his father's kingdom. Ultimately, Jenny alone must face the dragon Morkeleb and her own temptations toward power. Looking into his silver eyes, Jenny recognizes "a mage like herself. It was an alien intelligence, clean and cutting as a sliver of black glass. . . . [T]he singing in her mind was like a voice speaking to her in words she almost understood."[29] In tense wrestling with the dragon's ancient consciousness, Jenny finds the very source of magic. Hambly's strengths (see chapter 3) are all here: vibrant characterization of a strong woman, rich atmosphere and language, heart-stopping intrigue, compelling conflict between love and power, and insistence that good and evil are gray areas governed by human choices. Her dragon twists traditional conventions. As Morkeleb's psychic connection with Jenny awakens her magic, it also opens Morkeleb to human love.

A starred *Booklist* review cites the "new dimensions" Hambly gives to a "classic . . . quest to slay a dragon" in "a superior blend of the conventional and the unexpected."[30] *VOYA* sees Hambly's novel "extolling the power, serenity, and triumph of womanhood."[31] YAFE opinions at the end of this section include a rare male reader of Hambly.

Nowadays, our favorite mythical monster is usually reluctant. Though often maintaining hoarding and plundering habits, dragons can be coaxed into beneficial relationships with special people. This chapter's Recommended Reading contains Patricia C. Wrede's rollicking send-ups of fairy-tale dragons and superb series by Laurence Yep, R. A. MacAvoy, Shirley Rousseau Murphy, and others.

YAFEs on Barbara Hambly's *Dragonsbane*

It was nice having a middle-aged, not-drop-dead-gorgeous character in this rich, creative story.

—Allison Barrett, 15

I stayed really interested in this original story.
—Raymond Drummond, 14

I enjoyed descriptions that painted pictures in my mind. I finished it in one sitting.
—Vanessa Bowler, 16

I liked Hambly's poetic images and felt Jenny was very real. However, I found some parts confusing.
—Melissa Tolve, 16

I was not too enthused by Hambly's style of writing.
—Alisa Kotmair, 15

Unicorns: Believing in Beauty

The two most popular mythical beasts may endure because together, they symbolize both our deepest hopes and our deepest fears. If dragons provoke our fear of awesome power, then unicorns inspire our love of pure beauty. We imagine that the unicorn fills "one of the most basic human needs of all: the need to believe in an ideal."[32] So writes James Cross Giblin in *The Truth About Unicorns,* a pictorial introduction to unicorn legend.

We know the unicorns prancing on beach towels, mugs, and greeting cards, who glow like white horses, only smaller and more delicate, with silky, goatlike beards. Their hooves are cloven, or split. A single spiral horn is centered on their foreheads. Unicorn storybooks tell us those horns heal illness and purify water, and that unicorns live wild and free, tamed only by young virgins. Unicorns find maidens so irresistible that they lay their heads in girls' laps, and so are caught with golden bridles.

But do you also know that people once believed in unicorns? The Greek traveler Ctesias was the first Westerner to describe unicorns, in 398 B.C., "wild asses" in India with single horns striped white, crimson, and black (Giblin, 8). Over 2,000 years earlier, the Chinese referred to a "ki-lin," with a multicolored coat, a deer's body, an ox's tail, a wolf's head, and a horse's hooves,[33] that gave written language to the Chinese emperor. Another ki-lin on a special mission foretold the birth of the great philosopher Confucius.

Marco Polo, an early explorer of Europe and Asia, may have mistaken a rhinoceros for a unicorn. In the Middle Ages, unicorn horns were worth 10 times their weight in gold. If placed near poisoned food, these horns became beaded with sweat. Powdered horn was sold as a cure-all medicine. How could such horns exist? Most probably came from the narwhal, a small whale with a single tusk, which swam in cold northern waters until hunted to near extinction. Such "sea unicorns" were considered a type of land unicorns. Unicorns' inclusion in the Bible and in bestiaries, or encyclopedias of animals, also lent credence to their existence.

In medieval art, unicorns often symbolized Christ. The most famous unicorn appears in a series of seven tapestries of a unicorn hunt; dating from 1500 Brussels, the tapestries now reside in New York's Cloisters Museum. Though the unicorn is killed, it resurrects in "The Unicorn in Captivity," the last tapestry. Even King Arthur (more legend than real himself—see chapter 5) met a unicorn, on a remote Scottish island, which gave him the vision of peace that inspired his philosophy (*Magical Beasts,* 119–22). Arthur also dreamed of dragons.

With the scientific era, belief in unicorns waned until dealt "a death blow" by French zoologist Cuvier in 1827, who proved that no single horn could grow from the divided skull of cloven-hoofed animals (Giblin, 87). Interest revived in the 1930s, when an American doctor transplanted a calf's horn buds to the center of his skull, where they joined to form one horn. As recently as 1985, a circus tried to pass off four goats with transplanted horns as unicorns, until animal-rights activists protested (Giblin, 94).

Fake unicorns are unnecessary as long as unicorns live in literature. The authority on "one of the most beautiful legends in the world," Odell Shepard writes in *The Lore of the Unicorn,* "[W]hether there is or is not an actual unicorn, . . . he cannot possibly be as fascinating . . . as the things men have dreamed and thought and written about him."[34] *A Book of Unicorns* gathers some of these writings with large color prints of unicorns through the ages. In a charming field guide, *Dragons and Unicorns: A Natural History,* naturalist Paul Johnsgard and his daughter Karin treat these mythical beasts as if they were real, discussing their evolution, life histories, and conservation, as well as tips for benevolent hunters.

As one catches only fleeting glimpses of unicorns in the wild, so they flit through classic literature. Shakespeare merely alludes to unicorns, and "The Brave Little Tailor," by the Brothers Grimm, captures one easily. Lewis Carroll introduces a unicorn to Alice in *Through the Looking-Glass.* In his 1940 fable "The Unicorn in the Garden," James Thurber pokes fun at modern "reality" when a shrewish wife tries to send her husband to the "booby-hatch" for seeing a unicorn.[35] A year later, Dorothy Lathrop wrote an illustrated children's book, *The Colt from Moon Mountain,* in which a little girl befriends a "colt" with a nub of a horn—a unicorn, of course. The first major unicorn character for older readers was Jewel, best friend of King Tirian in *The Last Battle,* the final volume of C. S. Lewis's *Chronicles of Narnia,* published in 1956. Soon after, T. H. White, in *The Once and Future King,* wrote "one of the saddest scenes in literature," according to Jane Yolen,[36] in which a unicorn hunt ends brutally.

The Last Unicorn by Peter S. Beagle, which in 1968 became the first major unicorn novel, is now a modern classic for all ages. Influenced especially by Finney's *Circus of Dr. Lao,* Peter Beagle at age 23 elegantly explored the conflict between the free-spirited, life-preserving unicorn and possessive, destructive humans. Living alone in an enchanted forest, a unicorn fears she is the only one left of her kind, so she sets out on a quest to find others. Joined by Molly Grue and Schmendrick the magician, she encounters the Red Bull, who controls her with fearsome power until Schmendrick changes her into a woman, Lady Amalthea. As a lady, she attracts the love of Prince Lír, whose father helped the Red Bull imprison the other unicorns in the sea. Lady Amalthea must return to unicorn form to save her fellows and herself, but she can never be like other unicorns after knowing mortal shape. In Schmendrick's words, Beagle gently mocks the heroic quest: "The hero has to make a prophecy come true, and the villain is the one who has to stop him. . . . We are in a fairy tale, and must go where it goes."[37]

Beagle's unicorn, which is immortal, "possessing that oldest, wildest grace" (Beagle, 3), becomes "weary of human beings . . .

bending under the heaviness of knowing their names" (Beagle, 81). Capturing its elusive charisma, Beagle concludes that the unicorn "can never belong to anything mortal enough to want her" (Beagle, 204). *The Last Unicorn* is landmark fantasy literature because it defines our impossible longing for the wondrous unicorn.

Beagle's definitive work influenced all unicorn stories that followed. Michael Bishop's *Unicorn Mountain,* for example, is an unusual contemporary adult novel in which AIDS mirrors an epidemic among unicorns, who come from an alternate reality through a Colorado cave. This powerful tale of love, redemption, and healing in a rural American community will haunt mature YA readers. In a violent, polluted world like ours magnified, Noah's Ark is re-created in Barbara Cohen's *Unicorns in the Rain,* in which depressed young Nikki helps preserve unicorns and hope. This 1980 ALA Best Book for Young Adults deeply affected its YAFE readers.

Tanith Lee's *Black Unicorn* made two "Best" lists for young adults in 1992, ALA's and *VOYA*'s, and won the raves of many reviewers. After breathing life into a black unicorn from another world, sorceress's daughter Tanaquil must help it return home in this "stylish, humorous fantasy" that reflects Lee's "boundless imagination" and "lush and highly visual style."[38] The series continues with *Gold Unicorn* and *Red Unicorn.* Lee's title must not be confused with *The Black Unicorn* by Terry Brooks, second in his *Magic Kingdom of Landover* series (see chapter 2). As Beagle's unicorns are trapped in the sea, so all white unicorns are locked in Landover's books of magic; their spirit roams separately as a black unicorn. They must reunite to bring Landover's magic to life again. Unicorns appear in unbelieving worlds like Chicago, for "there has to be *some* belief in the magic . . . for any world to survive."[39]

A delightful variety of unicorns cavort in two anthologies. *The Unicorn Treasury* editor Bruce Coville summarizes unicorn lore before presenting stories and poems from fine authors including Patricia Wrede and Jane Yolen. The volume also contains excerpts from two trailblazing YA unicorn novels, C. S. Lewis's *The Last Battle* and Madeleine L'Engle's *A Swiftly Tilting Planet.* Jane Yolen's illustrated collection of her own unicorn tales and poems, *Here There Be Unicorns,* is a lush treat. One poem comes from Yolen's unicorn-obsessed college days. Her tales' settings range from medieval to modern. "Unicorn Tapestry" imagines the famous tapestries forming from the needle of Princess Marian, who unstitches a golden halter to save a real unicorn from the hunt. In "The Healing Horn," Yolen's own children discover a unicorn horn in their Scottish family home. Other unicorn books are listed in this chapter's Recommended Reading.

YAFEs on Unicorns

Beagle—*The Last Unicorn*

I was completely enthralled by this perfect, beautiful book, the very best fantasy I've read.

—Malinda Dunckley, 14

It's a perfect classic, with wonderful writing style and a lot of feeling—humor, excitement, sorrow, loss. The characters are so alive as they talk about what will happen next in the fairy tale, and about what is real and what is not.

—Midian Crosby, 16

Cohen—*Unicorns in the Rain*

It was very compelling, convincing me to believe the unbelievable.

—Malinda Dunckley, 14

Nikki was lost, exactly the way I feel. I was left with a feeling of hope in this story, which didn't let you go until the very end.

—Sarah Luna, 18

Meredith Ann Pierce:
"The Silver in My Blood"

Chronology: Meredith Ann Pierce's Life and Works

1958   Meredith Ann Pierce born July 5 in Seattle, second child of Jo Ann Bell Pierce, a professor of agriculture, and Frank N. Pierce, a professor of advertising.

Meredith Ann Pierce
Jo Ann Bell Pierce

1967   At age nine, begins what will become her novel *Birth of the Firebringer.*

1973   At age 14, wins first prize in national creative writing contest for story "The Snail."

1976   Earns high school diploma from A. Quinn Jones Adult Education Center in Florida.

1978   Earns B.A. in English, with minor in classical studies, from University of Florida.

1979   Wins Graduate Teaching Assistant Award to teach composition at University of Florida.

1980   With *The Darkangel* manuscript as thesis, receives M.A. from University of Florida.

1982   Publishes first novel, *The Darkangel,* which wins many citations: ALA Best Books for Young Adults 1982 and its

Best of the Best Books 1970–1982, *New York Times* Notable Children's Book, and Parents' Choice Award Superbook.

1983   Wins Children's Book Award from International Reading Association for *The Darkangel*.

1984   *A Gathering of Gargoyles (Darkangel* 2); teaches creative writing; becomes Jane Tinkham Broughton Fellow in writing for children at Bread Loaf Writers' Conference in Vermont.

1985   *Birth of the Firebringer (Firebringer* 1); *The Woman Who Loved Reindeer* becomes ALA Best Book for Young Adults and wins Parents' Choice Award for Literature.

1986   Wins California Young Reader Medal for *The Darkangel* and New York Public Library Books for the Teen Age citation for *The Woman Who Loved Reindeer*.

1987   Becomes library assistant at Alachua County Library in Gainesville and wins a Florida State Individual Artist Fellowship Special Award for Children's Literature.

1988   Children's picture book *Where the Wild Geese Go,* illustrated by Jamichael Henterly.

1989   Novella "Rampion" appears in Andre Norton's *Four from the Witch World;* novelette "Icerose" published in *Jabberwocky* magazine.

1990   *The Pearl of the Soul of the World (Darkangel* 3); *The Darkangel* is placed among *Booklist* Best Books of the Decade 1980–1989.

1991   *The Pearl of the Soul of the World* is listed as ALA Best Book for Young Adults.

1992   *Dark Moon (Firebringer* 2); earns master of library science degree at Florida State University.

1993   New York Public Library Books for the Teen Age citation
        for *Dark Moon;* moves into solar-powered home in
        Florida's Micanopy woods.

1996   *Son of the Summer Stars (Firebringer 3).*

> Between the covers of every book, there is a dream. I, the writer,
> dream the story, and write it down, and each time a reader
> opens the book, that story is dreamed again.
> —Meredith Ann Pierce, from "The Queen of the Night," in *The*
> *New Advocate*

To Meredith Ann Pierce, who created an unforgettable band of
unicorns in her *Firebringer Trilogy,* "dreaming and storytelling
are connected. . . . When I sit down to write, I enter a state that is
very like dreaming. I become still, relaxed. I lose all track of my
surroundings and of the passage of time."[40]

Two recurring dreams forged Meredith Ann Pierce's awareness
as a fantasy writer. Until she was eight years old, Meredith
dreamed of a tall, beautiful woman with "long black hair that
falls in waves . . . wearing a long, dark blue gown and slippers of
silver," always walking away from her ("Queen," 225). When
Meredith was a little older, another dream began, in which a herd
of "Horses of Umbr," in impossibly brilliant colors like "sparks of
fire" ("Queen," 226), thundered across a plain. As the dream
repeated, it lasted longer, until Meredith leapt onto a horse's back
to gallop toward a precipice. She always woke before hurtling over
the edge, though finally managed to stay in her dream until her
horse jumped. Landing safely beside a palace, Meredith recognized its owner, the beautiful "Queen of the Night" from her
other dream. The Queen held out a choice of two gifts: a burning
sword or a pearl of light. But Meredith wanted neither, desiring
instead "one of the silver rings twined in her hair" ("Queen,"
227). The Queen walked away as before. On a surreal horse chase,
Meredith pursued her, grabbing the silver ring only to see it vanish in her hand. Yet Meredith knew it had "only melted, transformed, transfused itself into me somehow. . . . I can feel the sil-

ver in my blood, and in a rush like hot wind, it sweeps up my arm, passing over my heart and through me with a force that turns my head" ("Queen," 228).

That silver in Meredith's blood is her gift to readers: her transformation of dream to story. This dreaming child was born in Seattle on July 5, 1958; her dream Horses of Umbr are Fourth of July fireworks, "the great celestial celebration on my birthday eve" that she knew "must be all for me" ("Queen," 228).

Meredith's father was an advertising copy and layout specialist, and her mother became a newspaper reporter and editor of agricultural publications. Since they often read aloud to her and took her to the library, Meredith began reading by age three.[41] She loved fairy tales, myths, and fantasy, including "Felix Salten's *Bambi,* Anna Sewell's *Black Beauty, The Jungle Books* by Rudyard Kipling, Lloyd Alexander's *Chronicles of Prydain,* and most everything by Madeleine L'Engle, Andre Norton, and Arthur C. Clarke."[42] When Meredith read, she entered "the same dreamlike state" she would later experience when writing ("Queen," 221). Reading along with records of Lewis Carroll's *Alice in Wonderland,* it became "my religion," she says, "wired into my psyche. I can't distinguish between my own mythology and early influences like *Alice* . . . or the movie *The Wizard of Oz* (*SATA* 67, 161). Fascinated by how reading reconstructs in her writing, Meredith knows that "what you read in childhood affects you far below the conscious level."[43]

By age four, Meredith practiced for later stories by acting out "role-playing games . . . before role-playing games were invented" (*SATA* 67, 160). With her brother Drew, who was two years older, Meredith invented her "earliest imaginary life . . . called 'Hansel and Gretel and the Magic Trailer.' " When little sister Alison and baby brother Matthew were old enough, they joined the cast as Buzzy and Buzz. In shades of *The Wizard of Oz,* the four were "asleep in their bunk bed one night . . . when a tornado ripped off the wall of their house and snatched their sturdy bed high into the air. Colliding with a passenger jet, the bed (somehow) acquired a jet engine. . . . The bed, thus metamorphosed into the Magic Trailer, zoomed unstoppably all over the earth, carrying the hapless children on adventures"; in real life, the Pierce family moved from California to Illinois.

By the time they moved to Texas, when Meredith was nine, the four had graduated to "The Jungle Game. I was the mysterious black panther Shah, who had ruby-red eyes and wore a red ruby on a chain about his neck. Drew was a wise bear named Scar. Allison and Matthew were a pair of leopards. Mostly we hunted, fought off . . . a large sea serpent, . . . and escaped from . . . natural disasters. . . . [We] typed out many chapters of the immortal saga, complete with illustrations." The four were also a family of witches, then "Slaves in India," homeless beggars wrapped in bedsheets. Other characters in these dramas, which "absorbed us for years at a time," came from collections of dolls, stuffed animals, and models.

Needing gryphons and dragons for "The Unicorn Game," Meredith "began writing and directing plays, roaming the block to round up semi-willing victims" to perform dragon wars for yawning parents.[44] As a rainstorm brewed in Austin, Texas, when Meredith was still nine, she stayed indoors with Drew to write the first line of what would become *Birth of the Firebringer:* "Storm-clouds were building in the east." Three unicorn colts, Jan, Tek, and Dagg, "are startled by the sudden appearance of Jan's father, Korr, the prince of the unicorns." Though Drew soon abandoned the story, Meredith persisted with "The Last of the Unicorns" from fourth through eighth grades, carrying it around everywhere. When her family moved to Florida after eighth grade, Meredith put her unicorn story away, never dreaming it would emerge when she grew up.

In ninth grade, Meredith encountered the first of several mentors who would champion her writing. Her teacher Ms. Frances Watkins submitted "The Snail"—a story Meredith "tossed off for an English assignment"—to a national creative writing contest. Both were surprised when the sponsors, *Scholastic Magazine* and Hallmark Cards, awarded her first prize, though the story was never published. Meredith sees Ms. Watkins as "one of the early facilitators of my career," allowing her to "sit in the back room during class . . . and write stories. This was heaven to me."

So much reading and writing made school easy for Meredith, who felt no need to be popular. Though writing was "the most important thing in my life," Meredith's parents treated it as "one of those obsessive little hobbies; 'Why would you rather be writing a novel than doing something else normal?' " (*SATA* 67, 161). Meredith dropped out of high school, graduating in 1976 with a diploma from an adult education center. A CLEP test allowed her to skip freshman year and enter the University of Florida as a sophomore. There she met her second mentor, Joy Anderson, a children's writer and professor who "helped me channel my out-of-control imagination into coherent storylines and hone my writing style" (*Sixth Book*, 225). Anderson taught Meredith about writing as a career, imparting practical skills on preparing a manuscript for publication. She also gave Meredith "very precise suggestions and comments that would leave the solution up to me," increasing Meredith's confidence in her writing (*SATA* 67, 161).

After earning her bachelor's degree in English with a minor in classical studies in 1978, Meredith won a Graduate Teaching Assistant Award, which paid her to teach composition to freshmen at her own university until 1980. When Joy Anderson became ill, Meredith taught Anderson's classes with "the finest method of teaching creative writing I've ever encountered." Students read published authors and critiqued each other's work respectfully and anonymously, while their instructor, Ms. Pierce, wrote extensive comments and held personal conferences.

Using the unpublished manuscript of *The Darkangel* as her master's thesis, Meredith earned her M.A. in 1980, and then took a year off to write. Thanks to Anderson's coaching, she knew *The Darkangel,* an atmospheric novel about a vampire on the moon, "was marketable. What surprised me was how quickly it was accepted." After one rejection, Meredith submitted her manuscript to six publishers at once, and "Melanie Kroupa of Atlantic Monthly Press accepted [it] right away." Only 24 years old in 1982, Meredith Ann Pierce became a published author. *The Darkangel* won glowing reviews and several awards.

To support herself, Meredith still worked at a Gainesville bookstore and continued to teach writing. In 1984, *The Darkangel*'s sequel, *A Gathering of Gargoyles,* was published. The same year, Meredith used the first five chapters of *The Woman Who Loved Reindeer,* about a supernatural trangl who shapeshifts from man to reindeer, to win the Jane Tinkham Broughton Fellowship. The award paid her tuition, room, and board for two weeks that summer at the prestigious Bread Loaf Writers Conference in Vermont. There Meredith met her third mentor, acclaimed author Nancy Willard, to whom she dedicated the completed *Reindeer* novel. Willard helped Meredith shape the "mythic nature" of her main character, Caribou, by asking "all the right questions." For Meredith, it "was a very great pleasure" to work with Willard, "a marvelously unique writer, with brilliant creative power that flows directly from the unconscious. Had she been born a few hundred years ago, she would have been a great shaman or a witch. In today's world, she's turned out to be a poet and fiction writer."

At Bread Loaf, Meredith also rejuvenated her unicorn story, pulled "out of mothballs" four years before, after sending *The Darkangel* to publishers. Sitting atop a vibrating washing machine on another "violently rainy afternoon" 13 years after she wrote its first sentence, she rewrote that line with few changes: "Stormclouds were rolling in out of the southeast." A year later, both *Birth of the Firebringer* and *The Woman Who Loved Reindeer* appeared from different publishers. *Reindeer* became an ALA Best Book for Young Adults and won other citations.

Unfortunately, when Meredith's *Firebringer* editor left Macmillan publishers, her book faced imminent "remainderhood," going out of print with remaining copies sold at a reduced price. Fortunately, Meredith won a $5,000 Florida Individual Artist Fellowship Special Award for her picture book manuscript of *Where the Wild Geese Go* and used most of the money to purchase leftover copies of *Birth of the Firebringer.* At this writing, Meredith's storage boxes are the only source for an unused hardcover copy. The publication of its sequel, *Dark Moon,* in 1992 by Little, Brown did not alter the first volume's fate. The trilogy's conclusion, *The Son of Summer Stars,* appeared in 1996; all three volumes may become available in paperback.

Where the Wild Geese Go, illustrated by Jamichael Henterly, was published in 1988, its wintry landscape reminiscent of *Reindeer*. Little Truzjka is an absentminded dreamer who searches for wild geese to soothe her sick grandmother, encountering several magical helpers on her journey, which ends when she wakes in her own bed after being very ill. Did she travel only in dreams? Truzjka still holds "a pearl from the sea of memory," a crystal globe in which her berry woman's image speaks: "Like dreams, I am real."[45] It reminds us of the pearl held by young Meredith's dream Queen of the Night, and also of *The Pearl of the Soul of the World,* the concluding 1990 volume of the *Darkangel Trilogy.* A reviewer found Pierce's picture book "rich, evocative, and image-filled," recommending it for teens as well as children.[46]

In 1989, Meredith produced two short works, the novelette "Icerose" for *Jabberwocky* magazine and the novella "Rampion," published in *Four from the Witch World.* Meredith was honored when Andre Norton, one of her favorite authors, asked her to contribute a story set in her famous otherworld. In her afterword to "Rampion," Meredith remembers herself in fifth grade, checking Norton's books "out of the library by the stack, and devouring them. '*This* is the kind of stories I want to write,' I recall thinking."[47] "Rampion" is set on Witch World's remote island of Ulys, where young Alys feels stuck forever unmarried, since her father lost his fortune. Her only friend, Sif, disappeared into the sea long ago, and Alys feels threatened when mysterious seasinger Gyrec comes looking for her. Just when Alys finds a way to escape the island, "Rampion" ends. Eventually the story may continue with Alys's discovery of a gate out of Witch World.

Meredith Ann Pierce plans continuations of both the *Darkangel* and *Firebringer* trilogies, as well as *Reindeer*'s growth beyond its single volume. But first she must finish an illustrated tale about woodland wisewoman Brown Hannah and rewrite a long adult fantasy novel. Not confined to fiction, Pierce has published a scholarly study of the mythological character Lilith in *Mythlore,* several essays on her creative process, and an article about book-talking science fiction, all listed under "Secondary Sources" in this chapter's Selected Bibliography.

Meredith Ann Pierce also has another entire career. In 1987 she began working as a library assistant at Alachua County Library in Gainesville, and by 1992 had earned a master of library science degree from Florida State University. Working full-time at the public library, she finds her two jobs complementary. "It's a wonderful job working with books and readers, and one I don't have to take home with me." The writing she then does at home "is not . . . taxing and draining, it's very renewing."[48] Since her library schedule varies, Pierce "seizes whatever time becomes available to write," from library lunch breaks and evenings to "nice chunks of . . . five and six hours" on days off. She carries her portable Macintosh computer everywhere, and her family prevents her from becoming "savagely grouchy" by leaving her alone to write.

Meredith Ann Pierce also enjoys music through listening, singing, composition, and playing piano. In 1988 she began taking harp lessons, and now owns a lovely 30-string Celestial Wind folk harp by local maker John Chambers, made of black walnut with claw feet and standing 45 inches high. Avid reading supports other interests: picture book collecting, languages, anthropology, folklore, and poetry. She still reads a great deal of fantasy and science fiction, mentioning Stephen Donaldson, William Gibson, Anne Rice's *Mayfair Witches* series and Gurney's *Dinotopia* as recent "grand" reading. She also enjoys theater, movies, and videos.

One great love was "nifty catchild Pygmalion (Kitty for short)," tended for "seventeen of the happiest years of my life" until the cat's death. It took a while for Meredith to "look back on our time together without bursting into sobs," but Kitty still "abides with me in spirit daily."

Since 1993, Meredith has put her belief in ecological responsibility into action by moving into a solar-powered house, in Florida's Micanopy woods. Using fluorescent lighting, no air conditioning, a propane refrigerator, a composting toilet, and food from her own garden and fishpond, Meredith finds "a serene and satisfying life" with her housemate.

In her late teens, Meredith's awareness of dreams and symbols drew her to the Tarot. She owns several decks, and loves to "lay the cards out" for herself and her friends. Though some believe Tarot is fortune-telling and others insist that the cards have "mystical power," Meredith believes instead that their images and patterns "jog the reader's intuition into realizations and associations he or she might not otherwise have made." The cards' meaning comes from within us, "bringing to consciousness our own interior landscape." Readers familiar with Tarot may notice that its High Priestess card, which represents dreams, intuition, and secrets, resembles Meredith's dream Queen of the Night. Though Meredith discovered Tarot long after her Queen dreams, she agrees that "dreams and Tarot unquestionably draw from the same archetypes." Along with the Moon and the Star, Meredith considers the High Priestess her special personal card.

Thus ends Meredith Ann Pierce's "Queen of the Night" essay: "And every story and every dream is a silver ring, that hangs in the hair of the Queen of the Night. We catch it; we hold it; we experience it until it's over, and then it's gone. Except it *isn't* gone. It's *in* us" ("Queen," 228). Few who experience the silver in her stories will ever shake them from their blood.

Unicorn Firebringers

Since *Birth of the Firebringer* began as Meredith Ann Pierce transformed from child to teenager, it has resonated with readers experiencing the same transition. Jan the unicorn princeling must resolve his conflict with his father, come to terms with his own fiery nature, recognize his destiny, and learn the way his world works. These are teenagers' most pressing concerns.

Pierce's unicorn culture has its own mythology. Just as humans are the last to occupy biblical creation, unicorns' Alma, Mother-of-All, "took from the cycling moon some of its shining stuff to fashion their hooves and horns and make them dancers. So the last-born and best-beloved of Alma call themselves also the moon's children."[49] Unicorns have been exiled for 400 years, since treacherous wyverns stole their home in the Hallow Hills. The pure water of their sacred pool has turned bitter. Each year, when the wyverns hibernate, unicorn initiates make the long trek home to drink of the sacred pool, which brings visions of their futures. A prophecy foretells the coming of the Firebringer, a black unicorn who will restore them to the Hallow Hills.

High-spirited sable brown Jan worries that he will never earn the approval of his stern father, Korr, the unicorn prince. The only initiate who fails to see his destiny at the pool, despairing Jan is lured into the cave of the deadly three-headed wyvern, mistress of fire. Struggling to resist her hypnotic spell, Jan is stung by the wyvern's poisoned tail, then burned on the forehead when he overturns her firebowl. Lying near death, he attains his vision at last, seeing the entire universe of all creatures as linked and himself as the fabled Firebringer. On this spirit journey, his guide is the Red Mare Jah-lila, who as seer lives apart from his Ring but has accompanied Jan all along, the secret narrator of the story. Jan's vision reveals that because unicorns separated themselves from other beings, their legend has grown false. To restore their home, the Firebringer must salvage the truth within their ideals of beauty and purity.

Pierce's flowing style reinforces the legend that drives the story, integrating dreams and action in poetic words wielded with perfect brush strokes. Her description of pale snaky wyverns is as shudderingly mesmerizing as they are, while vivid unicorn characters shimmer. She choreographs battles with gryphons and wyverns as graceful, lethal ballets.

Young adults drawn to this lyrical initiation story will savor its enlightening spiritual element and address questions they wonder about but rarely discuss. Meredith Ann Pierce reports that this book inspires letters from her youngest fans, "gifted fourth graders," though mostly older readers catch its deeper message.

Critics were complimentary: "The untangling of the satisfying plot and Pierce's ability to foster belief in her unicorns ... are enhanced by her stately use of language and the sense of their history and culture which she creates and sustains," says *School Library Journal*.[50] While appreciating Jan's "strong appeal for many young people as ... a dramatic hero" and "wonderful rhythm and sweeping images," *Booklist* found the language "sometimes overheightened and awkwardly archaic."[51] In response to such criticism of her language, Pierce retorts, "Should I dumb it down?"

(*SATA* 67, 162). She revels in her hobby of language, unearthing archaic terms, respelling familiar words, as in *vampyre* and *lyon*, or indulging in "pure invention" to create names that "just sound right," heightening the feeling of a world apart in her stories.

As usual in a trilogy's middle book, *Dark Moon* poses questions that won't be resolved until the final volume. It exchanges the uplifting aura of *Birth of the Firebringer* for a gloomy, unsettling mood, fitting the test Jan must undergo to be worthy of his destiny. Jan's coat has turned black, the crescent burn scar on his forehead marking him as Firebringer. No longer a frisky colt, he chooses Jah-lila's daughter Tek for his mate. Their joy together is short lived, for Jan is seized by a gryphon and dropped into a stormy sea. Washing ashore without memory in the foreign City of Fire, Jan is found by two-footers, humans who hail him as a rare horned da. Though idolized as Moonbrow for his marking, Jan is as much a slave as their hornless daya, or horses, with whom he is stabled. Breaking out to explore the city, he sees how fire, unknown to the unicorns he cannot remember, brings power and luxury to the two-footers.

When Jan is chosen as an equinox sacrifice, he sensationally escapes with copper mare Ryhenna in a scene recalling Meredith's childhood dream of horses, in which she leapt from a cliff into the sea. Jan's spiritual guardian, Jah-lila, calls narwhals, or sea unicorns, to guide them safely home. Believing Jan dead, the unicorns suffered a devastating famine, driving Jan's father, Korr, to dictatorship and madness. Korr has banished Jan's mate, Tek, who retreats to her mother Jah-lila's cave to give birth to twins Aiony and Dhattar, a delightful surprise to Jan when they reunite.

Pierce has sent Jan on a hero's journey, a test in which he loses his identity before truly knowing himself. Like Ratha in Clare Bell's cat fantasies, Jan returns home with knowledge of fire, which will help restore his Ring to their rightful home. He also brings Ryhenna, a red mare from the two-footers' world, somehow connected to "Red Mare" Jah-lila. Jan's witnessing of slavery and idolatry among two-footers makes him wary of such power in his own land.

Booklist found *Dark Moon* "carefully plotted with satisfying action and . . . intriguing characters," capable of standing alone, with "Red Mare's repeated promises of more to come as tantalizing lures."[52] Of the opposite opinion, *School Library Journal* claimed that only readers of the previous volume would be interested in this "predictable" story with "one-dimensional" characters and a plot with "everything in it but the kitchen sink."[53]

Fantasy fanatics missed the unheralded publication of the next volume, *Son of the Summer Stars*. Pierce forecast before its publication that Tek would have a pivotal role, revealing the secret of her parentage, and no two-footers would invade the war between unicorns and wyverns. Later volumes may focus on the twins, nudged by Jah-lila toward their destiny. Jah-lila was born among daya, still captive in the City of Fire. "How well do you suppose that sits with the Red Mare?" Pierce hints.

YAFEs on *The Firebringer Trilogy*

Birth of the Firebringer

The book itself is magic.

—Alisa Kotmair, 16

As a kid, I read it all the time and anxiously awaited its sequel. It is my own childhood classic, and I still revisit it.

—Midian Crosby, 15

Dark Moon

After waiting seven years for this sequel, I was disappointed because humans spoiled it by making it less storylike and beautiful. I was distracted by alternating Ring and City storylines, and disliked Jan's changes. Instead I identified with Tek's strong female warrior quality.

—Midian Crosby, 15

Darkangel Monsters

In Meredith Ann Pierce's most acclaimed work, the mesmerizing *Darkangel Trilogy*, Avarclon the Starhorse is a winged steed like Pegasus with a twisted silver horn on his brow. Not a unicorn, Avarclon is one of seven lons guarding each land in *The Dark-*

angel's moon world, each a mythical beast, from a cockatrice to a winged panther. *Darkangel* has more fantastic creatures per square inch than any fantasy since *Circus of Dr. Lao,* monsters cataloged by Pierce: "wingèd vampires, starving gargoyles, wraiths, a ghost, phantom jackals, a red-eyed harridan, weaselhounds, mereguints, a mudlick, and a terrible White Witch."[54] To save her world, young heroine Aeriel "disenchants and rehabilitates a whole slue of monsters" ("Monsters," 107). The moon's creatures and races were created by settlers from Earth who abandoned their moon colony. Revering these departed Ancients, Aeriel's people see Earth as blue-white Oceanus in their sky, an image imprinted on Pierce in childhood from watching Apollo moon shots on television.

As usual with Pierce, story and dreams are entangled. In college, reading psychoanalyst Carl Jung's autobiography, Pierce was intrigued by the delusion of a catatonic girl, who told Jung "she had lived on the moon," where a vampire's murders made women and children almost extinct. This psychotic girl waited with a hidden knife to destroy the vampire. When he landed before her, covered with "several pairs of wings," she was so spellbound by his "unearthly beauty" that she couldn't strike, so he flew off with her.[55] *Darkangel* readers will recognize Pierce's beautiful vampyre with his dozen black wings, and Aeriel waiting with a knife to avenge her mistress, Eoduin, stolen as his 13th bride.

Carried off like Jung's patient, Aeriel is enslaved by the vampyre as caretaker to his wives, who are mere wraiths since the vampyre drank their blood and locked their souls in lead vials on a chain around his neck. Wasted Eoduin does not even recognize her servant Aeriel, who dresses the hideous wraiths in airy fabric spun on a magic spindle of her emotions. Finding her vampyre master both alluringly lovely and repellently evil, Aeriel risks feeding his starving gargoyle guards, and amuses the bored vampyre with tales, which bring tormenting dreams of his human past before the water witch stole his soul. He needs only one more wife to present 14 souls to the witch, which would make him a full vampyre and allow him to join six darkangel brothers in ruling the moon for her.

Aeriel joins the duarough (dwarf) mage Talb's plot to "undo" the vampyre, by fulfilling the prophecy in a magic rime left by the

Ancients. Escaping the vampyre, Aeriel crosses the desert to find the hoof of the starhorse Avarclon, the major ingredient for the vampyre's undoing. Darkangels have destroyed Avarclon and the other Ions which were made by Ravenna, last of the Ancients, to guard the moon. Returning to Talb with the hoof, Aeriel no longer feels the darkangel's power: "there was no splendor to him anymore, no grace or majesty, only menace and vicious petulance."[56] But the vampyre chooses Aeriel for his 14th bride.

In Avarclon's hoof, doomed bride Aeriel feeds the vampyre poisoned brew. When he faints, she retrieves his necklace of souls, returning each vial to its wraithlike owner. "One by one the mummy-women drank, and their bodies fell away, leaving only the bright images of their souls" (*Darkangel*, 229), which rise into the sky to become a constellation of 13 maidens.

But Aeriel cannot plunge her magic knife into the unconscious darkangel, for she loves him despite his evil. Her longing to heal him brings Aeriel's ultimate sacrifice: she replaces his heart with her own, restoring his lost humanity. Talb's magic prevents Aeriel's death, and the vampyre is once again Prince Irrylath. Recalling how the witch kidnapped him as a child of six, Irrylath repents his darkangel crimes and vows to defeat the other darkangels.

This layered novel about the healing power of love fuses myths and fairy tales into a haunting, original whole. In a startling departure from tradition, a vampire, that undead specter from horror literature, is redeemable. Conscious of Jung's inspiration, and one image of a chain of maids' hearts from the folk song "Silver Dagger," Pierce spent a "febrile week when *Darkangel* came roiling out of my subconscious like a wellspring, like a flame" ("Lion," 36). Later she recognized other roots in a favorite fairy tale, "Beauty and the Beast," and a favorite myth, "Psyche and Eros." Alert readers will discover other familiar stories. Like Scheherezade during the 1,001 Arabian nights, Aeriel spins tales to placate the darkangel and also spins thread for the wraiths, like the miller's daughter in "Rumpelstiltskin" and Elise in Andersen's "Wild Swans" ("Lion," 37).

The guardian Ions, which embody the glorious power of lions, stem from Pierce's most traumatic childhood experience. When she was alone, a threatening adult restrained Meredith, intending her harm, and "my anger rose up like some great, tawny cat . . . filling the house with its presence." Through Meredith the anger fixed her persecutor with "its yellow eyes," as her voice rang out: "[T]here is a lion in the room." Like her courageous heroine Aeriel, young Meredith met that "ferocious" essence inside, which refuses to give up and be a victim ("Lion," 39–40).

In her *New York Times* review, Nancy Willard, later to become Pierce's teacher, called *The Darkangel* "one of the best fantasies I've read in a long time," a work that reveals love's "healing power and evil's terrible attractiveness." Willard quotes Pierce's "word pictures" to praise her style. "Though I have met many a magical beast," says Willard, "never have I met in any other story the likes of those who live in this one," which she trusts to "last and be loved by readers of all ages."[57] Two other reviewers were not as laudatory. *VOYA* called *Darkangel* "tightly constructed" and "pleasant" but also found "no surprises for a seasoned fantasy reader."[58] *School Library Journal* saw "an interesting mix of space setting and magic" with "new use . . . of old 'icons' " but also felt it needed "more logic to be first-rate."[59]

These criticisms are outweighed by other praise. *Magazine of Fantasy and Science Fiction* found *The Darkangel* "a marvelous tissue of allusions and evocations . . . [in a] golden life-repleted universe."[60] To *Horn Book,* it was a "personal vision" of "powerful images in a haunting, provocative novel."[61] *The Darkangel* captured many awards. Not only was it a 1982 ALA Best Book for Young Adults but it was also among ALA's Best of the Best 1970–1982 and became a New York Times Notable Children's Book, a Parents' Choice Award winner, and the recipient of the International Reading Association's Children's Book Award. YAFEs also appreciate *The Darkangel's* qualities, though some report confusion in their comments at the end of this section. A style as original as Pierce's both attracts and deflects readers.

Irrylath's "undoing" as a darkangel only fulfilled part of the rime. The next segment of the riddle is delivered to Aeriel in *A Gathering of Gargoyles* by the 13 ex-wraiths, now star maidens. Its solution will also reveal Aeriel's identity. Living with Irrylath's mother and brothers, Aeriel and Irrylath are married in name only, for Irrylath is too haunted by witch-sent nightmares to love anyone. Longing for him, Aeriel must return without him to her homeland, Terrain, where she was sold into slavery, to find the sibyl who can explain the rime. Along her route through lands blighted by darkangels, the ugly gargoyles Aeriel once freed return to her one by one, like loyal dogs. She also gathers two more devoted companions, dark-skinned Erin, whom she rescues from a darkangel, and her unknown twin brother, Roshka. In a horrific climax at the sibyl's temple, Aeriel is nearly consumed by the Feasting Stone, until Talb and Irrylath save her. Cleansed in the temple fire, Aeriel and the gargoyles arise as their true selves; Aeriel is a princess, and the gargoyles are the missing lons, steeds for Irrylath's brothers in the battle against the witch. In this middle book, the reader follows the perplexing riddle with Aeriel by intuition. Aeriel's own story is woven into the rime, which she must enact to make real. Many mysteries are left unresolved for the final volume, which left YAFE Allison Barrett "craving more."

Fantasy author and critic Eleanor Cameron found "echoes of other outstanding fantasies" in *Gargoyles,* describing Pierce as "intensely visual, even poetic in her descriptions and imaginative in her surprising plot turns. And she is strong in her overall conception of a courageous, loving girl who is both compassionate and determined."[62]

As the last *Darkangel* volume opens, Aeriel wanders lost in underground caverns, a pale girl without memory. A silver pin painfully pierces her head behind her ear, and around her neck is a glowing pearl, the title's *Pearl of the Soul of the World.* Through subterreanean passages, she reaches the Ancients' City of Crystalglass, which is not abandoned, as everyone thinks. There Ravenna, the last Ancient, removes the pin so Aeriel's memories flood back: the witch's black bird pinned her at Irrylath's war camp. Revealing the last part of the rime, Ravenna explains that Aeriel must give her pearl to the witch, who is actually Ravenna's daughter Oriencor. Learning she could never visit Oceanus (our Earth), Oriencor unleashed her wrath on the hated moon; perhaps the pearl will sway her to stop plaguing the moon and begin healing it. Giving Aeriel a magic sword, Ravenna pours the Ancients' knowledge of the world into Aeriel's pearl, and so pours out her life.

While Aeriel vainly tries to convince the treacherous witch to reform, her dark companion, Erin—her other half, as in Jane Yolen's *Sister Light, Sister Dark* (see chapter 4)—wields the sword against the witch's hordes beside Irrylath and his brothers on their lon steeds. Though the witch and her underwater palace are destroyed after a war of wits and shocking twists and Irrylath is finally free of the witch's clutches, Aeriel and Irrylath win only one night of love. The pearl shattered by enraged Oriencor has entered Aeriel's blood, a heavy legacy she must carry alone as Ravenna's heir. Aeriel must "regather the lost soul of the world" to save the ravaged moon.[63]

Longing for Aeriel and Irrylath to live happily ever after, few readers can bear the trilogy's ending. YAFE Sarah Luna correctly senses it unfinished. "Anybody who considers that a satisfying ending is nuts," says Pierce. Planning a second *Darkangel* trilogy, she hoped to clue her readers in by ending *Pearl* with "Here end for a time the adventures of Aeriel. The adventures of Irrylath have only begun." Since her editor removed those lines, Pierce urges her readers, "Take heart! I intend to shift focus to Irrylath and show him as a very human character coming to grips with a life . . . [of] duty . . . devoid of personal satisfaction or love. No longer overshadowed by Aeriel, Irrylath must . . . forgive himself for his crimes as a darkangel, regain his wings, and discover the secret that will set both him and Aeriel free." Aeriel will learn "the high personal cost of . . . surrendering herself, however nobly, to Ravenna's planetary rescue plan."

Critics agreed that *The Pearl of the Soul of the World* was "too complex and mystical" to understand without knowledge of previous volumes. "Besides the haunting heroine," says *Horn Book,* its strength is "shimmering, fragile textures and delicate, shadowy descriptions. But the rarefied atmosphere will restrict the audience to sophisticated fantasy lovers."[64] The "intrepid" Aeriel, reinforces *Bulletin of the Center for Children's Books,* "is a truly heroic figure" in this "imaginative and forceful high fantasy."[65]

After Meredith Ann Pierce made a speech about her childhood dream of Queen of the Night, the queen became Ravenna in *The Pearl of the Soul of the World*. As in Meredith's dream, tall, dark Ravenna offers two gifts: a sword and a pearl. The dream Meredith took a silver ring instead, "the silver in my blood" of a storyteller, but Aeriel accepts both sword and pearl.

YAFEs on *The Darkangel*

It is one of the more engaging and original fantasies I have read. Pierce's dreamy style paints very vivid and beautiful pictures of a harsh but wonderful world that appears peaceful and dangerous at the same time. I admire her unusual contrast of beauty with evil in a yin-yang relationship.

—Naomi Perera, 16

It is powerful and simple at the same time, reminding me of "Beauty and the Beast," so lonely and magical and strange, with the taste of lost love.

—Sarah Luna, 17

I love Pierce's exquisite descriptions that vary from typical fantasy patterns, but readers must concentrate to find it rewarding.

—Allison Barrett, 15

I was so confused that I felt completely lost, so I abandoned the series.

—Sam Walter, 15

Though Pierce is a skillful writer, *Darkangel* is too abstract. The plot didn't follow any sort of logical line and was based on totally off-the-wall concepts. It is a matter of taste as to whether you *adore* the books or simply enjoy them.

—Nadia Haddad, 15

Shapeshifters and Transformations

Indebted again to her beloved "Beauty and the Beast," Meredith Ann Pierce created another transforming tale of love in *The Woman Who Loved Reindeer*. On a two-mooned world in a wintry land, Caribou is barely 13 summers old when her brother's wife,

Branja, thrusts a fur-wrapped infant upon her. Seeming fearful of the baby, Branja won't discuss the stranger who fathered it. Wooed by its fathomless golden eyes, Caribou is comforted by its company in the lonely Wilderland, miles from the nearest village.

Never laughing or crying, the baby seems moved only by the thunderous migrating reindeer herds. When a huge golden reindeer stag scoops him into his antlers and carries him off, the baby crows delightedly. This image of a baby "resting unharmed in the rocking cradle of . . . horns" as a speechless woman in doeskin watches came to Pierce as she gazed upon deserted playing fields on the last day of school in ninth grade ("Lion," 37).

Tracking the stag through endless snow, Caribou finds him felled with an arrow, the baby safe in his antlers. So she names the child Reindeer. As he grows, she is shocked to see that the boy's reflection in the water is that of a golden young buck. When Reindeer is 13, Caribou finally accepts that he is a trangl, a halfling fathered by the golden stag with human mother Branja. Transforming to reindeer shape, he must run free with the herd. Though she misses him, Caribou is not alone. The villagers consult her as wisewoman, for "she could read things in flurries of falling snow, hear words in wind, knew all the old tales by heart, and sometimes dreamed."[66] When Reindeer returns to her at 16, he becomes her lover, helping her tribe escape earthquakes and volcanoes that destroy their village.

As in *Darkangel,* love between a supernatural being and a human bridges two worlds. When Caribou dreams solutions to earthly problems, parts of Reindeer's trangl father's body assist her, and the arrow that killed him is the compass pointing to the tribe's destination. "Untouchable by love or sorrow" (*Reindeer,* 62), Reindeer fights his supernatural nature to learn human emotion. When he releases Caribou from her promise to live among the reindeer, he weeps golden tears for the first time, feeling "a great pain in my breast" (*Reindeer,* 239). Transforming into human shape for love, this beast is transformed by that love, which helps Caribou bring the spirit world to her people. Yet their different origins mean they can never truly merge, so Caribou and Reindeer give each other freedom.

Reindeer resonates with borrowings from many spiritual traditions. Pierce sees the trangl as a "supernatural lover archetype" like Eros or the demon-lover. His birth through mortal-supernatural union has Christian overtones. The sea-maidens' parting of the sea so Caribou can lead her people to a promised land recalls Old Testament Moses. The Fireking's cavern recalls Scandinavian myth, and rituals connecting humans to nature mirror those of many tribal peoples.

Though the single volume *The Woman Who Loved Reindeer* seems complete, Pierce hopes to continue the story, shifting focus to Tor, the only person "with whom Caribou has forged even a whisper of a personal relationship." Tor seems likely to lead this transplanted community, and "he could fall in love with the mysterious wisewoman. How would Reindeer react to Tor's interest in Caribou?" Pierce wonders.

YAFEs often name *The Woman Who Loved Reindeer* as a favorite. Reviewers are also impressed. Patty Campbell found the shapechanging lover a fascinating ancient motif used "to create a haunting story of great beauty . . . [which] vibrates with mythic resonance."[67] *Horn Book*'s Ann A. Flowers called it "a remarkably fine fantasy by an emerging master of the genre,"[68] and *VOYA* found it "unique," reading like "a tale from ancient mythology."[69] *The Woman Who Loved Reindeer* became a 1985 ALA Best Book for Young Adults and won a Parents' Choice Award and a citation in New York Public Library's Books for the Teen Age.

Starkly direct in Reindeer's shapeshifting, the underlying theme in all Meredith Ann Pierce's work is transformation. While writing *A Gathering of Gargoyles,* Pierce realized, "[A]ll of my stories are about *changes*." Involved in the basic metamorphosis from childhood to adulthood, Pierce's heroic young leaders Jan in *Firebringer,* Aeriel in *Darkangel,* and Caribou in *Reindeer* also take charge of others in challenging situations. As traditional heroes, they all endure tests of their fitness to lead, finally becoming saviors of their people. Transformations come after they experience "a revolution in thinking: a fundamental realization or epiphany," says Pierce, which she pinpoints: "Jan's re-examination of his people's ancestral hatreds, Aeriel's perceiving the darkangel as ugly rather than beautiful, Caribou's conclusion that seeking to control one's beloved is not the same thing as loving him."

As Pierce's young visionaries change their people's lives, their landscapes endure cataclysms. In *Firebringer,* Jan cannot restore the unicorns' home without an "end of the world scenario." The colony built by Ancients from Earth is expiring in *Darkangel;* the witch's destroyed ice palace becomes restorative rain. Violent earth changes force Caribou's tribe in *Reindeer* to flee to new land. Pierce does not see such upheavals as do the Millennialists, who predict our world's ending in the year 2000. Instead, "ending/renewal is an ongoing process." Her inspiration is Kali, the Hindu goddess of renewal who "perpetually dances in fire, casting down the old so that the new may spring up and take hold." When Pierce writes about the end of the world, "it's really the revamping of my characters' *interior* landscapes I'm most concerned with portraying. If one changes oneself, one has changed the world." Spirituality offers a major route to transformation, and Pierce merges many spiritual traditions to metamorphose her characters. "Good and evil has influenced my writing even though I'm not a Christian and don't belong to an organized religion," she says. "Spirituality pervades the books whether I want it to or not" (*SATA* 67, 162).

Though Jan does not sacrifice himself for his people as Christ does, Christian teachings fill *Firebringer:* Jan is the deliverer foretold, who reveals that all creatures are connected and that evil lies in alienation from others and in putting earthly law above the Creator's. The fire Jan brings is a spiritual purifier, and his dreams are communications from beyond. *Darkangel* is a treasury of spiritual borrowings. To many mythologies are added a striking array of Christian images. Aeriel sacrifices herself, resurrecting the darkangel by giving him her own heart. As Christ was tempted by Satan, Aeriel faces the darkangel's evil magnetism. To heal him, she forgives him. She clothes the wraiths with charity, feeds the starving gargoyles, and uses the Starhoof as a Holy Grail. Like Jan after the wyvern's sting, Aeriel has a near-death experience on the Feasting Stone, which will literally eat her body unless she accepts spiritual truths. In *Reindeer,* Caribou is modeled on the tribal shaman, "whose duty it is, when . . . famine threatens, to descend into the underworld" to appease the gods, says Pierce, also inspired by the real Woman Chief, who led the American Crow tribe ("Lion," 37–38).

Love is also an agent of transformation. Of all love relationships in Pierce's stories, only Jan and Tek's in *Firebringer* is fulfilling; they are life mates and parents. In *Darkangel* and *Reindeer,* love is painfully unrequited. Pierce reports being very affected by Frank Stockton's short story "The Lady, or the Tiger?" in junior high English class ("Lion," 40–41). That the lover's fate was in his lady's hands, that she set up his unknowable choice between her and the devouring tiger, reveals "the tremendous power that lovers have over one another." But since love is one of the "few things worth living for, we risk life, not death. . . . To love is a courageous act. It is to become human, and therefore mortal, vulnerable. It is to transform oneself," says Pierce. So her heroines Caribou and Aeriel risk it, failing to win the love they so desire, since their aloof supernatural lovers have other priorities. While these heroines have Pierce's fierce lion within, they are essentially feminine, unlike the recent fantasy fad of pseudomale women warriors. Caribou and Aeriel win their battles without brawn, through intuition and spirit.

Only when a friend asked why she wrote monster stories did Meredith Ann Pierce realize her books teem with monsters, like her wildly imaginative childhood. A "whirlwind" of trips and frequent moves plunged small Meredith into "dangerous unknowns. . . . A large, loyal following of stuffed animals . . . guarded my bed" from nameless attackers. "We're talking deeply neurotic childhood. . . . Everything was alive. . . . [M]onsters lived behind the bathroom water heater," waiting until you flushed to "eat you up while the howl of the plumbing covered your screams" ("Monsters," 102). Pierce's book monsters are symbolic now. Jan's wyvern is his self-destructive instincts. Aeriel's darkangel is her fear, her temptation. Caribou's sea-maidens cannot love, so she must. All triumph over these monsters, and Aeriel even redeems hers.

Monsters are scary, Pierce believes, because they are incapable of the love that makes us human. Pierce's characters, like us, strive "to become as fully and completely human as we can. . . . The battle to unmake the monsters without and within is a laborious task. . . . I'm still floundering, and so I write monster stories, tales of the struggle to escape servitude, attain selfhood, define love. Dream-visions of the unmaking of monsters" ("Monsters," 108). Teenagers understand transformation: "Like many of my characters, I think young people are furiously struggling to see clearly, re-examine their society's prejudices, learn to trust themselves, and build successful relationships. If young people identify with my protagonists' struggles, I guess that's the reason behind [their] appeal."

As in *The Woman Who Loved Reindeer,* love transforms through shapechanging in *Owl in Love* by Patrice Kindl, a 1995 ALA Best Book for Young Adults. By day, Owl is a 14-year-old schoolgirl. By night, she shapeshifts into an owl, swooping the skies for prey. Being a wereowl does not stop Owl from falling in love with her science teacher, Mr. Lindstrom, but she is awkward with humans. Only when Owl finds another wereowl to love can she accept her dual nature. In Owl's droll voice, both wise and naive, Kindl spins a fable about the wild creature within. A starred *School Library Journal* review predicts, "Owl's adventures should win flocks of readers, especially those who like their humor hard-edged and on the dark side."[70]

A tragic tale of doomed love unfolds in Louise Cooper's 1993 ALA Best Book *The Sleep of Stone.* Ghysla is the last of her ancient race of shapechangers, "alien and grotesque" to humans.[71] To win the love of Prince Anyr, she assumes animal forms. On his wedding eve, Ghysla gives his bride, Sivorne, a potion that traps her in an endless "sleep of stone," then takes Sivorne's form. When Anyr notices, Ghysla faces the bitter truth. Cooper creates a palpable sense of Ghysla's lonely suspension in vast time. While engaging our sympathy for Ghysla, she invokes our distaste for her otherness. Ghysla's dignity and heartbreak stir us in this "lovely, romantically tragic . . . three-handkerchief book that's really worth it," according to *Booklist.*[72] YAFEs echo the sentiment in their comments following. Even Dylan Burns, a 13-year-old boy, succumbed to its spell.

Comparing animal to human nature within one consciousness, stories about shapeshifters offer intriguing commentary on what it means to be human. Sometimes people suffer in comparison to animals. In *Adventures of the Rat Family,* published in 1893 by Jules Verne, the philosopher father Raton chooses to remain a rat when offered the chance to reincarnate as a human. There is another breed of rat in *Kokopelli's Flute* by Will Hobbs. A modern teenaged boy guarding the ancient cliff dwellings near his New Mexico home from thieving pothunters transforms into a packrat for a unique viewpoint on the natural world. When in human form, Tepary meets the mythical Native American seed-bearing flute player Kokopelli, realizing his mission is to learn the secrets of a civilization that disappeared a thousand years ago, to keep our environment healthy today. "Factual details about the Southwest intermingle with moral concerns about nature," observes *VOYA,* in this "engaging and delightful tale."[73]

In *The Woman Who Lives in the Earth,* a mythic fable by Swain Wolfe with Native American echoes, the shapeshifter is a fox who isn't really a fox but an embodiment of the pattern that connects the parts of the natural world. The fox appears to young Sarah, bringing her the spirit messages she needs, not only to save her people from drought but to reconnect them to the natural world. The fox turns out to be an aspect of Sarah herself, and she transforms into various other shapes to learn how to enact her people's transformation. "Besides being a magical adventure story," says *VOYA,* "it also emphasizes the importance of caring for the earth, and so should appeal to lovers of environmental stories as well as fantasy."[74] Teen readers have profound reactions to this striking story, as evidenced in YAFE comments at the end of this section. This first novel by Wolfe was listed among *VOYA*'s 1996 Best Science Fiction, Fantasy, and Horror.

With implications even more cosmic, the hot new fantasy trilogy *His Dark Materials* by Philip Pullman features one of the most inventive uses of shapechanging in all of fantasy. It opened in 1995 with *The Golden Compass* in a richly realized otherworld, part Victorian, part arctic, part alternative future, where feisty young orphan Lyra fights instinctively for independence from her distracted Oxford professor guardians. The most foreign aspect of Lyra's otherwise only slightly off-kilter world is its most fascinating: everyone has a daemon, or animal familiar. Exhibiting a person's character and emotions, a daemon fits its human partner's personality by the type of animal it is, shapechanging continually during childhood. A daemon settles into final shape only after puberty, as identity gels. Lyra's daemon Pantalaimon shifts from moth to mouse to wolverine, among many shapes from cuddly to fierce to nearly invisible, as Lyra experiences shifts in her precarious existence. Not only are daemons bosom companions, personal champions, alter egos, and shadow selves, but they embody the soul. People cannot live without their daemons, so when Lyra discovers evidence of horrifying experiments that sever children from their daemons, it could signal the end of her world. Lyra's intrepid pursuit of the child-stealing villains leads her to a frozen northern landscape, an alliance with an immense white armored bear, the cold truth about her heritage, and eventually another world beyond the Northern Lights in the sequel, *The Subtle Knife.*

With the earmarks of a fresh new classic, Pullman's captivating work has wowed readers of all ages; teachers are using it with enormous success in middle and high school literature classes. *Washington Post* critic Michael Dirda proclaims *The Golden Compass* to be "the best juvenile fantasy novel of the past 20 years," in the same class as other classics from L'Engle to Garner but "more sheerly, breathtakingly, all-stops-out thrilling than any of them." *The Subtle Knife,* he asserts, "full of heroic self-sacrifice" and "moral complexities," loses none of Pullman's grip and pace, "and prepares us for a concluding volume of almost inconceivable cosmological grandeur."[75] Pullman, who acknowledges the presence of every element from myth and folklore to Shakespeare and *Paradise Lost* in his astonishingly original retelling of "the rebellion of the angels and their expulsion from heaven," anticipates the trilogy's much-awaited completion in 1998.[76] *The Golden Compass* won numerous prizes, including Britain's Carnegie Medal and Guardian Fiction Prize, and was included in the Top Ten 1997 ALA Best Books for Young Adults. Its sequels are sure to sustain this well-deserved furor in the world of fantasy fiction.

More shapechanging stories, listed in this chapter's Recommended Reading, challenge us to expand humanity with animal nature.

YAFEs on Shapeshifters and Transformations

Kindl—*Owl in Love*

Owl's ignorant wisdom is charming in this realistic tale of shapeshifters in love.... I really like to think that it could happen.

—Anna Salim, 15

Cooper—*The Sleep of Stone*

It's my favorite book ever.

—Pixy Dougherty, 14

I find it unbearably romantic and sad.

—Allison Barrett, 15

Wolfe—*The Woman Who Lives in the Earth*

I found it very interesting and fitting that Wolfe did not specify the time period or world where it took place. He portrayed evil as coming from fear, in a group mentality that reminded me of *The Grapes of Wrath*, but he showed that people are not truly evil at heart. I like the sort of Native American idea of a person who sees herself from the eyes of a fox. I enjoyed the pace, style, and descriptions in this unusual fantasy fairy tale because I was in the mood for that, but those who want an adventure with more developed characters may get bored. It is a book to be read in a very short time, and then read again.

—Mariah Iseley, 15

The author's main theme is transformation. Throughout the story, Sarah changes into another being for a short time: a bird, a fox, a flower, even a tree. The people of the town have a transformation as they lose their fear and hatred. Finally the rain falls, the drought is over, and the world transforms. The reader also experiences a feeling of transformation when realizing what is 'really' happening.

This wonderful book is bursting at the seams with imaginative ideas. It gives a visual description of the three parts of the soul, like an egg. It explains the imagination and pulls the reader into the story. It teaches a lesson about fear and hatred without seeming to do so. I recommend it to everyone. If they open up to the story, they will find so much there.

—Kylin Follenweider, 17

Recommended Reading

(* denotes title mentioned in text; other titles are additional)

Psychic Beasts

Adams, Richard. *The Plague Dogs*. New York: Knopf, 1978.
———. *Shardik*. New York: Simon & Schuster, 1975.
———. **Watership Down*. New York: Macmillan, 1974.
———. *Tales from Watership Down*. New York: Knopf, 1996.
Andrews, Allen. **Plantagenet* Series. 2 vols. New York: Viking.
    Vol. 1: *The Pig Plantagenet*. 1980.
    Vol. 2: *Castle Crespin*. 1984.
Bach, Richard. *Jonathan Livingston Seagull*. New York: Macmillan, rev. ed. 1990, © 1970.
Carter, Robert. **The Collectors*. New York: Lothrop, Lee & Shepard, 1994.
Clement, Aeron. **The Cold Moons*. New York: Doubleday, 1989.
Ford, Richard. **Quest for the Faradawn*. Illus. Owain Bell. New York: Delacorte, 1982.
Grahame, Kenneth. **The Wind in the Willows*. New York: Knopf, 1993, © 1908.
Gurney, James. **Dinotopia: A Land Apart from Time*. Atlanta: Turner Publishing, 1992.
Hamley, Dennis. **Hare's Choice*. Illus. Meg Rutherford. New York: Delacorte, 1990.
Harris, Joel Chandler. **Uncle Remus*. Random House, 1986, © 1881.
Hawdon, Robin. **A Rustle in the Grass*. New York: Dodd, Mead, 1985.
Horwood, William. **Duncton Wood*. New York: McGraw Hill, 1980.
Jacques, Brian. **Redwall* Series. Illus. Gary Chalk. 10 vols. New York: Philomel.
    Vol. 1: *Redwall*. 1987.
    Vol. 2: *Mossflower*. 1988.
    Vol. 3: *Mattimeo*. 1990.
    Vol. 4: *Mariel of Redwall*. 1992.

Vol. 5: *Salamandastron*. 1993.
Vol. 6: *Martin the Warrior*. 1994.
Vol. 7: *The Bellmaker*. 1995.
Vol. 8: *Outcast of Redwall*. 1996.
Vol. 9: *Pearls of Lutra*. 1997.
Vol. 10: *The Long Patrol*. 1998.
Jekel, Pamela. *The Third Jungle Book*. Illus. Nancy Malick. Niwot, Colo.: Roberts Rinehart Publishers, 1992.
Jordan, Sherryl. *Wolf-Woman*. Boston: Houghton Mifflin, 1994.
Katz, Welwyn Wilton. *Whalesinger*. New York: Margaret K. McElderry Books, 1990.
Kilworth, Garry. *The Foxes of Firstdark*. New York: Doubleday, 1989.
Kipling, Rudyard. *Jungle Book* Series.
Vol. 1: *The Jungle Book*. New York: Knopf, 1994, © 1893.
Vol. 2: *The Second Jungle Book*. New York: Puffin, 1987, © 1895.
———. *Just So Stories*. Illus. Barry Moser. New York: Morrow, 1996, © 1897–1902.
Lester, Julius. *Further Tales of Uncle Remus*. Illus. Jerry Pinkney. New York: Dial, 1990.
Oppel, Kenneth. *Silverwing*. New York: Simon & Schuster, 1997.
Orwell, George. *Animal Farm*. New York: Knopf, 1993, © 1945.
Salten, Felix. *Bambi: A Life in the Woods*. Illus. Michael J. Woods. New York: Simon & Schuster, 1992, © 1928.
Stanton, Mary. *Heavenly Horse* Series. 2 vols. New York: Baen.
Vol. 1: *The Heavenly Horse from the Outermost West*. 1988.
Vol. 2: *Piper at the Gate*. 1989.
Tarr, Judith. *Her Majesty's Elephant*. San Diego: Harcourt Brace, 1993.
Wangerin, Walter, Jr. *Dun Cow* Series. 2 vols. New York: Harper & Row.
Vol. 1: *The Book of the Dun Cow*. 1978.
Vol. 2: *The Book of Sorrows*. 1985.

Cats with Consciousness

Bell, Clare. *The Jaguar Princess*. New York: Tor, 1993.
———. *The Ratha* Series. 4 vols. New York: Atheneum/Margaret K. McElderry Books.
Vol. 1: *Ratha's Creature*. 1983.
Vol. 2: *Clan Ground*. 1984.
Vol. 3: *Ratha and Thistle-Chaser*. 1990.
Vol. 4: *Ratha's Challenge*. 1994.
———. *Tomorrow's Sphinx*. New York: Margaret K. McElderry Books, 1986.
Catfantastic Series. Ed. Andre Norton and Martin H. Greenberg. New York: DAW.

Catfantastic. 1989.
Catfantastic II. 1991.
Catfantastic III. 1994.
Catfantastic IV. 1996.
Eliot, T. S. **Old Possum's Book of Practical Cats.* Drawings by Edward Gorey. New York: Harcourt Brace Jovanovich, 1982, © 1939, 1967.
Ende, Michael. *The Night of Wishes.* Translated from German by Heike Schwarzbauer and Rick Takvorian. Pictures by Regina Kehn. New York: Farrar, Straus & Giroux, 1992.
Gallico, Paul. **The Abandoned.* (Published in U.K. as *Jennie.*) New York: International Polygonics, Ltd., 1991, © 1950.
Greeno, Gayle. *The Ghatti's Tale.* 3 vols. New York: DAW.
    Vol. 1: *Finders-Seekers.* 1993.
    Vol. 2: *Mindspeaker's Call.* 1994.
    Vol. 3: *Exiles Return.* 1995.
Great Cat Tales. Ed. Lesley O'Mara. Illus. William Geldart. New York: Carroll & Graf, 1989.
Leiber, Fritz. *Gummitch and Friends.* Illus. Rodger Gerberding. Hampton Falls, N.H.: Donald M. Grant Publishing, 1992.
McCaffrey, Anne. *No One Noticed the Cat.* New York: ROC, 1996.
McCormick, Malachi. *Cat Tales: Folk Tales Collected and Retold.* New York: Clarkson N. Potter, 1989.
Murphy, Shirley Rousseau. **The Catswold Portal.* New York: Roc, 1992.
———. Joe Gray mystery series. 3 vols. New York: HarperPrism.
    Vol. 1: *Cat on the Edge.* 1996.
    Vol. 2: *Cat under Fire.* 1997.
    Vol. 3: *Cat Raise the Dead.* 1997.
Sheehan, Carolyn and Edmund. **Magnifi-Cat.* New York: Doubleday, 1972.
Westall, Robert. **Blitzcat.* New York: Scholastic, 1989.
———. **Cats of Seroster.* New York: Greenwillow, 1984.
Williams, Tad. **Tailchaser's Song.* New York: DAW, 1985.

Mythical Creatures

Bauer, Steven. *Satyrday.* New York: Berkley, 1980.
Bradshaw, Gillian. *Beyond the North Wind.* New York: Greenwillow, 1993.
de Larrabeiti, Michael. *Borribles* Series. 2 vols.
    Vol. 1: *The Borribles.* New York: Macmillan, 1978.
    Vol. 2: *The Borribles Go for Broke.* New York: Ace, 1982.
Finney, Charles G. **The Circus of Dr. Lao.* New York: Viking, 1935.
Lackey, Mercedes. *Firebird.* New York: Tor, 1996.
McKillip, Patricia A. **The Forgotten Beasts of Eld.* New York: Atheneum, 1974.

Morpurgo, Michael. *King of the Cloud Forests*. New York: Viking, 1988.

O'Donohoe, Nick. **Crossroads* Series. 2 vols. New York: Ace.

   Vol. 1: *The Magic and the Healing*. 1994.

   Vol. 2: *Under the Healing Sun*. 1995.

Pierce, Meredith Ann. **The Darkangel Trilogy*. 3 vols. Boston: Little, Brown.

   Vol. 1: *The Darkangel*. 1982.

   Vol. 2: *A Gathering of Gargoyles*. 1984.

   Vol. 3: *The Pearl of the Soul of the World*. 1990.

Sherman, Josepha. *Gleaming Bright*. New York: Walker, 1994.

Singer, Marilyn. *Horsemaster*. New York: Atheneum, 1985.

Snyder, Zilpha Keatley. *Song of the Gargoyle*. New York: Delacorte, 1991.

Yolen, Jane. **The Stone Silenus*. New York: Philomel, 1984.

Creatures of the Sea

Andersen, Hans Christian. **The Little Mermaid*. Illus. Michael Hague. New York: Henry Holt, 1994, © 1846.

Anderson, Poul. *The Merman's Children*. New York: Berkley/Putnam, 1979.

Cooper, Susan. *Seaward*. New York: Atheneum, 1983.

Doherty, Berlie. *Daughter of the Sea*. New York: DK Ink, 1997.

Hendry, Frances Mary. *Quest for a Kelpie*. New York: Holiday House, 1988.

Hunter, Mollie. *A Stranger Came Ashore*. New York: Harper & Row, 1975.

James, Betsy. *Long Night* Series. 2 vols. New York: Dutton.

   Vol. 1: *Long Night Dance*. 1989.

   Vol. 2: *Dark Heart*. 1992.

Lockley, Ronald. *Seal Woman*. New York: Bradbury, 1975.

McKillip, Patricia A. **The Changeling Sea*. New York: Atheneum, 1988.

———. *Something Rich and Strange*. Brian Froud's *Faerielands* Series. New York: Bantam, 1994.

Nimmo, Jenny. *Ultramarine* Series. 2 vols. New York: Dutton.

   Vol. 1: *Ultramarine*. 1992.

   Vol. 2: *Rainbow and Mr. Zed*. 1994.

Osborne, Mary Pope. **Haunted Waters*. Boston: Candlewick Press, 1994.

Park, Ruth. **My Sister Sif*. New York: Viking, 1991.

Reynolds, Susan Lynn. *Strandia*. New York: Farrar, Straus, & Giroux, 1991.

Senn, Steve. *A Circle in the Sea*. New York: Atheneum, 1981.

Yolen, Jane. **Neptune Rising: Songs and Tales of the Undersea Folk*. New York: Philomel, 1982.

Zindel, Paul. *Loch*. New York: HarperCollins, 1994.

Dragons: Our Favorite Fearsome Creature

Bradshaw, Gillian. Dragon Series. 2 vols. New York: Greenwillow.
    Vol. 1: *The Dragon and the Thief*. 1991.
    Vol. 2: *The Land of Gold*. 1992.
Christian, Peggy. *The Bookstore Mouse*. Illus. Gary Lippincott. San Diego: Harcourt Brace, 1995.
Dickson, Gordon R. *Dragon Knight* Series. 7 vols.
    Vol. 1: *The Dragon and the George*. New York: Doubleday, 1976.
    Vol. 2: *The Dragon Knight*. New York: Tor, 1991.
    Vol. 3: *The Dragon on the Border*. New York: Ace, 1992.
    Vol. 4: *The Dragon at War*. New York: Ace, 1992.
    Vol. 5: *The Dragon, the Earl, and the Troll*. New York: Ace, 1994.
    Vol. 6: *The Dragon and the Djinn*. New York: Ace, 1996.
    Vol. 7: *The Dragon and the Gnarly King*. New York: Tor, 1997.
Dragon Fantastic. Ed. Rosalind M. Greenberg and Martin H. Greenberg. New York: DAW, 1992.
Dragons! Ed. Jack Dann and Gardner Dozois. New York: Ace, 1993.
Dragons & Dreams. Ed. Jane Yolen, Martin H. Greenberg, and Charles G. Waugh. New York: Harper & Row, 1986.
Fletcher, Susan. Dragon Series. 3 vols. New York: Atheneum.
    Vol. 1: *Dragon's Milk*. 1989.
    Vol. 2: *Flight of the Dragon Kyn*. 1993.
    Vol. 3: *Sign of the Dove*. 1996.
Grahame, Kenneth. *The Reluctant Dragon*. Illus. Ernest H. Shepard. New York: Holiday House, 1966, © 1938, 1898.
Hambly, Barbara. *Dragonsbane*. New York: Ballantine, 1985.
Kushner, Donn. *A Book Dragon*. New York: Henry Holt, 1987.
MacAvoy, R. A. *Black Dragon* Series. 2 vols. New York: Bantam.
    Vol. 1: *Tea with the Black Dragon*. 1984.
    Vol. 2: *Twisting the Rope*. 1986.
McCaffrey, Anne. *A Diversity of Dragons*. Illus. John Howe. New York: HarperPrism, 1997.
———. *Dragonriders of Pern* Series. 3 vols. New York: Ballantine.
    Vol. 1: *Dragonflight*. 1968.
    Vol. 2: *Dragonquest*. 1971.
    Vol. 3: *The White Dragon*. 1978.
———. *Dragonsong* Series. 3 vols. New York: Atheneum.
    Vol. 1: *Dragonsong*. 1976.
    Vol. 2: *Dragonsinger*. 1977.
    Vol. 3: *Dragondrums*. 1979.
———. *The Girl Who Heard Dragons*. New York: Tor, 1994.
Murphy, Shirley Rousseau. *The Dragonbards Trilogy*. 3 vols. New York: HarperCollins.

Vol. 1: *Nightpool*. 1985.

Vol. 2: *The Ivory Lyre*. 1987.

Vol. 3: *The Dragonbards*. 1988.

Strickland, Brad. *Dragon's Plunder*. Illus. Wayne D. Barlowe. New York: Atheneum, 1992.

Vande Velde, Vivian. *Dragon's Bait*. San Diego: Harcourt Brace Jovanovich, 1992.

Wrede, Patricia C. *The Enchanted Forest Chronicles*. 4 vols. San Diego: Harcourt Brace.

Vol. 1: *Dealing with Dragons*. 1990.

Vol. 2: *Searching for Dragons*. 1991.

Vol. 3: *Calling on Dragons*. 1993.

Vol. 4: *Talking to Dragons*. 1993, © 1985.

Yep, Laurence. *Dragon of the Lost Sea* Series. 4 vols. New York: HarperCollins.

Vol. 1: *Dragon of the Lost Sea*. 1982.

Vol. 2: *Dragon Steel*. 1985.

Vol. 3: *Dragon Cauldron*. 1991.

Vol. 4: *Dragon War*. 1992.

Yolen, Jane. **The Dragon's Boy*. New York: HarperCollins, 1990.

―――. **The Pit Dragon Trilogy*. 3 vols. New York: Delacorte.

Vol. 1: *Dragon's Blood*. 1982.

Vol. 2: *Heart's Blood*. 1984.

Vol. 3: *A Sending of Dragons*. New York: Delacorte, 1987; San Diego: Harcourt Brace, 1996.

―――. **Here There Be Dragons*. Illus. David Wilgus. San Diego: Harcourt Brace/Jane Yolen Books, 1993.

Unicorns: Believing in Beauty

Anthony, Piers. *The Apprentice Adept* Series. 3 vols. New York: Ballantine.

Vol. 1: *Split Infinity*. 1980.

Vol. 2: *Blue Adept*. 1981.

Vol. 3: *Juxtaposition*. 1982.

Beagle, Peter S. **The Last Unicorn*. New York: Dutton, 1991, © 1968.

―――. *The Unicorn Sonata*. Atlanta: Andrews & McMeel, 1996.

Bishop, Michael. **Unicorn Mountain*. New York: Arbor House, 1988.

Brooks, Terry. **The Black Unicorn*. Book 2 in *Magic Kingdom of Landover* Series. New York: Ballantine, 1987.

Cohen, Barbara. **Unicorns in the Rain*. New York: Atheneum, 1980.

Estey, Dale. *A Lost Tale*. New York: St. Martin's Press, 1980.

Gentle, Mary. *A Hawk in Silver*. New York: Lothrop, Lee & Shepard, 1985, © 1977.

The Immortal Unicorn. Ed. Peter S. Beagle and Janet Berliner. New York: HarperPrism, 1995.

Jones, David Lee. *Unicorn Highway*. New York: Avon, 1992.

Lee, Tanith. Unicorn Trilogy. 3 vols. Vols. 1–2: New York: Atheneum. Vol. 3: New York: Tor.

Vol. 1: *Black Unicorn*. 1991.

Vol. 2: *Gold Unicorn*. 1994.

Vol. 3: *Red Unicorn*. 1997.

Luenn, Nancy. *Arctic Unicorn*. New York: Atheneum, 1986.

Myers, Walter Dean. *Shadow of the Red Moon*. Illus. Christopher Myers. New York: Scholastic, 1995.

Pierce, Meredith Ann. *The Firebringer Trilogy*. 3 vols. Vol. 1: New York: Four Winds Press/Macmillan. Vol. 2–3: Boston: Little, Brown.

Vol. 1: *Birth of the Firebringer*. 1985.

Vol. 2: *Dark Moon*. 1992.

Vol. 3: *Son of the Summer Stars*. 1996.

Salsitz, Rhondi Vilott. *Twilight Gate*. New York: Walker, 1993.

Thurber, James. *"The Unicorn in the Garden" in *Fables for Our Time and Famous Poems Illustrated*. New York: Harper & Row, 1983, © 1940.

The Unicorn Treasury: Stories, Poems, and Unicorn Lore. Comp. and ed. Bruce Coville. Illus. Tim Hildebrandt. New York: Doubleday, 1988.

Unicorns! Ed. Jack Dann and Gardner Dozois. New York: Ace, 1982.

Unicorns II. Ed. Jack Dann and Gardner Dozois. New York: Ace, 1982.

Yolen, Jane. *Here There Be Unicorns*. Illus. David Wilgus. San Diego: Harcourt Brace/Jane Yolen Books, 1994.

Shapeshifters and Transformations

Banks, Lynne Reid. *Melusine*. New York: Harper & Row, 1988.

Brown, Mary. Summer Trilogy. 3 vols. New York: Baen.

Vol. 1: *The Unlikely Ones*. New York: McGraw Hill, 1986; Baen, 1995.

Vol. 2: *Pigs Don't Fly*. 1994.

Vol. 3: *Master of Many Treasures*. 1995.

Cooper, Louise. *The Sleep of Stone*. New York: Atheneum, 1991.

Dalkey, Kara. *Little Sister*. San Diego: Harcourt Brace, 1996.

Hobbs, Will. *Kokopelli's Flute*. New York: Atheneum, 1995.

James, Mary. *Shoebag* Series. New York: Scholastic.

Vol. 1: *Shoebag*. 1990.

Vol. 2: *Shoebag Returns*. 1996.

Jones, Diana Wynne. *The Power of Three*. New York: Greenwillow, 1977.

Kindl, Patrice. *Owl in Love*. Boston: Houghton Mifflin, 1993.

LeVert, John. *The Flight of the Cassowary*. Boston: Atlantic Monthly, 1986.

Levy, Robert. Shape-Changers Series. 2 vols. Boston: Houghton Mifflin.
    Vol. 1: *Clan of the Shape-Changers*. 1994.
    Vol. 2: *The Misfit Apprentice*. 1995.

Mazer, Anne. *The Oxboy*. New York: Knopf, 1993.

McKillip, Patricia A. *The Book of Atrix Wolfe*. New York: Ace, 1995.

Pierce, Meredith Ann. **The Woman Who Loved Reindeer*. Boston: Little, Brown, 1985.

Pullman, Philip. **His Dark Materials Trilogy*. New York: Knopf.
    Vol. 1: *The Golden Compass*. 1996.
    Vol. 2: *The Subtle Knife*. 1997.
    Vol. 3: Forthcoming 1998.

Rubinstein, Gillian. *Foxspell*. New York: Simon & Schuster, 1996.

Smith, Sherwood. *Wren* Series. 3 vols. San Diego: Harcourt Brace.
    Vol. 1: *Wren to the Rescue*. 1990.
    Vol. 2: *Wren's Quest*. 1993.
    Vol. 3: *Wren's War*. 1995.

Verne, Jules. **Adventures of the Rat Family*. Trans. Evelyn Copeland. Illus. Felician Myrbach. New York: Oxford University Press, 1993, © 1893.

Wolfe, Swain. *The Woman Who Lives in the Earth*. New York: Harper-Collins, 1996.

Selected Bibliography

Meredith Ann Pierce

Primary Sources

" 'All Shall Love Me and Despair': The Figure of Lilith in Tolkien, Lewis, Williams, and Sayers." *Mythlore* 31 (Spring 1982): 3–7, 25. [Misprint Meredith Price.]

The Darkangel Trilogy. 3 vols. Boston: Little Brown.
    Vol. 1: *The Darkangel*. 1982.
    Vol. 2: *A Gathering of Gargoyles*. 1984.
    Vol. 3: *The Pearl of the Soul of the World*. 1990.

The Firebringer Trilogy. 3 vols. Vol. 1: New York: Four Winds Press/ Macmillan. Vols. 2–3: Boston: Little, Brown.
    Vol. 1: *Birth of the Firebringer*. 1985.
    Vol. 2: *Dark Moon*. 1992.
    Vol. 3: *Son of the Summer Stars*. 1996.

"A Lion in the Room." *Horn Book* (January/February 1988): 35–41.

"The Magical Moment in Fantasy." *The ALAN Review* (Fall 1988): 39–42.

"Meredith Ann Pierce Autobiographical Sketch." In *Sixth Book of Junior Authors and Illustrators*, 224–25. New York: H. W. Wilson, 1989.

"On the Making of Monsters." *The New Advocate* (Spring 1990): 101–9.

"Out of This World: Science Fiction Booktalks for the Adolescent as Public Library Sponsored Programs in the Schools." *Voice of Youth Advocates* (August 1991): 148–55.

"The Queen of the Night." *The New Advocate* (Fall 1988): 221–29.

"Rampion." Novella in *Four from the Witch World*. Created [and ed.] by Andre Norton. New York: Tor, 1989.

Where the Wild Geese Go. Illus. Jamichael Henterly. New York: Dutton, 1988.

The Woman Who Loved Reindeer. Boston: Little, Brown, 1985.

"The Woman Who Loved Reindeer." Novella in *Moonsinger's Friends: An Anthology in Honor of Andre Norton*. Ed. Susan Schwartz. New York: Bluejay Books, 1985.

Secondary Sources

Barnhouse, Rebecca, and Brown, Sidney. *"The Darkangel."* In *Beacham's Guide to Literature for Young Adults*. Vol. 5. Ed. Kirk H. Beetz. Washington, D.C.: Beacham Publishing, 1991, 2179–84.

Davis, Hazel K. "Meredith Ann Pierce." In *Authors and Artists for Young Adults*. Vol. 13. Ed. Kevin S. Hile and E. A. Des Chenes. Detroit: Gale Research, 1994, 149–55.

MacRae, Cathi Dunn. Interview with Meredith Ann Pierce. Micanopy, Fla., 17 October 1994.

"Pierce, Meredith Ann." In *Major Authors and Illustrators for Children and Young Adults*, 6 vols. Ed. Joyce Nakamura and Laurie Collier. Detroit: Gale Research, 1992, 1882–85.

Telgen, Diane. "Pierce, Meredith Ann." In *Something about the Author*. Vol. 67. Ed. Donna Olendorf. Detroit: Gale Research, 1992, 160–65.

A Magic Bestiary

Dickinson, Peter. *The Flight of Dragons*. Illus. Wayne Anderson. New York: Harper & Row, 1979.

Dragons. The Enchanted World Series. Editors of Time-Life Books. Alexandria, Va.: Time-Life Books, 1984.

Ellis, Richard. *Monsters of the Sea*. New York: Knopf, 1994.

Gaffron, Norma. *Unicorns: Opposing Viewpoints. Great Mysteries* Series. San Diego: Greenhaven Press, 1989.

Giblin, James Cross. *The Truth About Unicorns*. Illus. Michael McDermott. New York: HarperCollins, 1991.

Johnsgard, Paul, and Karin Johnsgard. *Dragons and Unicorns: A Natural History*. New York: St. Martin's Press, 1982.

Magical Beasts. The Enchanted World Series. Editors of Time-Life Books. Alexandria, Va.: Time-Life Books, rev. ed. 1986, © 1985.

Mastin, Colleayn O. *The Magic of Mythical Creatures.* Illus. Jan Sovak. Kamloops, B.C., Canada: Grasshopper Books Publishing, dist. Custer, Wash.: Orca Book Publishers, 1997.

Mythical and Fabulous Creatures: A Source Book and Research Guide. Ed. Malcolm South. Westport, Conn.: Greenwood Press, 1987.

Passes, David. *Dragons: Truth, Myth, and Legend.* Illus. Wayne Anderson. New York: Western Publishing/Artists & Writers Guild Books, 1993.

Peterson, Gail. *Greg Hildebrandt's Book of Three-Dimensional Dragons.* Illus. Greg Hildebrandt. Boston: Little, Brown, 1994.

Poltarnees, Welleran, comp. *A Book of Unicorns.* La Jolla, Calif.: Green Tiger Press/Star and Elephant Books, 1978.

Shepard, Odell. *The Lore of the Unicorn.* Mineola, N.Y.: Dover Publications, 1993, repr. 1930.

7. Time Fantasy: From Now to Then

> The most commonplace way to travel in time, to move through a shift of time, to go backwards or sideways in time, to enter a different space-time continuum, is to open a book.
>
> —Jill Paton Walsh, from "Narrative Time,"
> in *Travelers in Time*

Time fantasy—also called time travel, time warp, time slip, or time shift fiction—is a fascinating genre that propels both characters and readers to the past or future. Visiting other times can be like visiting fantasy otherworlds; we wonder if science will ever make it possible.

Seeing time travel as psychological fantasy, critic Karen Patricia Smith believes "the time journey is linked intricately to the mind of the protagonist. . . . It is the mind which embodies the concept of time," prompting "psychological change" as a result of the trip.[1] Critic Barbara Elleman cautions that readers will not accept time fantasy's "combination of the real and the fantastical" unless it passes a "tightrope test. With magic the integral thread, an author unreels a story out across the time barriers and I, the reader, trustfully follow across unknown terrain. If the magic is not strong and surely woven or if the writer flexes the wire too much, my fragile belief is shattered, the illusion is disrupted, and the story's impact is lost."[2]

Time travel may be fantasy or science fiction, depending on whether magic or science makes travel possible. A group of Fantasy Fanatics, all age 16, argued about which works better. "Time travel needs the logical proof of science fiction to justify it," asserted Sam Walter. "Magic in fantasy defies laws, but time travel needs laws to explain it."

"But time fantasy works if it is written well," insisted Kylin Follenweider. "It asks you to imagine 'what if?' and helps you see how people thought in other times."

Nate Doyle argued, "Time travel is technical. Fantasy has no technical concepts—it says all time is fated to happen, will happen, and is always happening. Characters who time travel in fantasy don't have the knowledge to do so wisely."

"My major problem with fantasy time travel is that it can be so horribly clichéd and romantic," said Allison Barrett.

"And fantasy authors don't deal with the paradoxes in time travel," added Eric Rice.

Paradoxes arise from travelers' interference in times before their own, when their actions might disrupt events to change outcomes, perhaps even threatening their own existence. If, while traveling to the past, you caused your ancestor's death, would you ever be born to travel back in time to kill your ancestor? Arguing Fanatics demand that "tightrope test" of credibility.

Time itself is a challenging concept. In a study of how children perceive time in books, Harvard psychologist Diana Paolitto discovered that time perceptions progress with developmental stages of growth.[3] Children under seven have no sense of chronology, instead relating stories to their own experience. After learning to tell time with clocks, children grasp sequence but have vague notions of calendar time. From ages 10 to 12, children are obsessed with forward-moving events, still uncertain of the past. Only when they reach the level of abstract reasoning in early adolescence can readers analyze ideas, themes, and sequence. Some teenagers under 14 still have trouble conceptualizing times before their own, explaining the lack of appeal of stories with historical settings.

"A sense of time," claims author Peter Dickinson, "is one of the most valuable intellectual gifts one can give to one's children."[4] Penelope Lively, whose novels constantly grapple with time, realizes that children's reality differs from adults':

> Children live in another country; and although it is one we have all passed through, ... we have lost the sense of a continuous present and have moved into an awareness of . . . our own situation in relation to time—both personal time as the context of a life and collective time, history. . . . Awareness of the past . . . is an achievement of the imagination. . . . The writer [must] . . . strike a chord in children so that they recognize, without ever having been there, the wider country into which we are inviting them.[5]

Historical novelist Janni Howker profoundly encapsulates this notion: "There is a moment when a child becomes an adult because he enters time."[6] All these writers spoke at an illuminating 1989 conference at Cambridge University in England, "Travelers in Time: Past, Present, and to Come," examining time in books for youth as "a quality—a flavor, an atmosphere, a psychological phenomenon." As a fortunate participant, I reported on that stimulating week in the article "Timescapes in Cambridge." Not limited to time travel, the conference abounded with mind-expanding ideas, including historian David Lowenthal's conviction that the past, like the title of his book *The Past Is a Foreign Country* (Cambridge University Press, 1985), is so remote and strange that we cannot possibly know it.

Other conference speakers referred to two theories of time: linear—progressing forward, or cyclical—moving round and round as events repeat. Critic Neil Philip found children's literature at the point where the two theories intersect (MacRae, 25). To Newbery Medalist Katherine Paterson, each story halts time's rolling river (26). To author Betty Levin, readers "cup some of time's river in their hands before it rejoins the flow" (28). Ten years after writing *The Dark Is Rising,* (see chapter 5), Susan Cooper realized it was her unconscious attempt to define time. After years living in America, Cooper saw, from an airplane, her patchwork British homeland, "a continuous dialogue between people and land." Growing up amid Neolithic forts, Roman villas, and castles gives British children a deep sense of time's continuum, Cooper explained, whereas America's destruction of early roots "vanquishes place and time." Returning home for a time "fix," Cooper knows why many time fantasy authors are British (MacRae, 26).

Types of Time Fantasy

"Time travel is a notion," declares author John Rowe Townsend. "Look at it too closely and it dissolves."[7] Yet in her essay "The Pleasures and Problems of Time Fantasy," novelist Eleanor Cameron scrutinizes it as an "elegantly played game of chess,"[8] pinpointing three types:

> *Legendary*—stories that bring "contemporary characters into close touch with legendary ones" (Cameron, 170)
> *Historical*—stories that allow modern characters to explore the past with more sense of "eeriness" than in historical fiction (171)
> *Scientific*—stories that use scientific principles or psychological insight to explain time travel but are not as technological or future-oriented as science fiction (172).

Refusing confinement, some time fantasies appear with myths in chapter 4, legends in chapter 5, or magic realism in chapter 3. Most time travel discussed here is historical or scientific.

In his science fiction encyclopedia, John Clute organizes time travel in three other groups:

> *Travel into the future*—"simple" because it cannot affect the present
> *Travel into the past*—"a highly subversive literary device," affecting events
> *Travel from the future to our present or past*—uncommon, "perhaps because it is hard to identify with characters who may be superior to us."[9]

Cameron also identifies elements of time fantasy; imaginative use of these conventions can "truly test the freshness of each new fantasy" (Cameron, 176):

- "The timeless moment"—a "sense of dream, in which events seem insanely warped yet exude a sense of dreadful logic" (177)
- A "flow of inevitability" making time travel seem natural and uncontrived (201)

- A vivid sense of place (174)
- "Time objects"—devices which convey characters through time (196)

Time Triggers

Time travel cannot happen without time objects, or time triggers:

- Physical triggers—characters step through time gates, portals linking one time to another, in old buildings or ancient monuments. One unique gate is a redwood tree, in *The Ancient One,* by T. A. Barron.
- Magical triggers—talismans or artifacts such as keys, charms, portraits, or other items that link their finders with the objects' past owners. A human skull, a bone flute, and a carved stone all bring modern people in touch with past Native American owners in Gary Paulsen's *Canyons,* Will Hobbs's *Kokopelli's Flute* (see chapter 6), and Pamela F. Service's *Vision Quest.*
- Psychological triggers—dreams, visions, or hypnosis, as in Allen Appel's Balfour series, J. Alison James's *Sing for a Gentle Rain,* Richard Matheson's *Somewhere in Time.*
- Scientific triggers—such as computers in Madeleine L'Engle's *Time Trilogy,* drugs in Daphne du Maurier's *House on the Strand,* and an experiment in Jack Finney's *Time and Again.*

Several time triggers might combine. Finney meshes three: scientific experiment, hypnosis, and historical sites. Some trigger holders do not actually travel but alter their perceptions, becoming "stirred up," says author Gregory Maguire.[10] "Once the trigger enters the story," states Barbara Elleman, "then the transition either to the past or to the present can work—the flow of magic can begin." Trigger and transition may be the only fantasy elements in an otherwise realistic story (Elleman, 495).

Pioneers of Time Travel Literature

As in much fantasy, time travel's forerunners are legends and fairy tales. In what John Rowe Townsend calls "time capsule" stories, such characters as Sleeping Beauty, Rip Van Winkle, and King Arthur and his knights simply go to sleep, waking up in the future. In Fairyland time moves at a different pace; returning visitors find that more or less time has passed on earth. Such stories never risk time travel paradoxes.

Time fantasy could not be written until people's ideas about time progressed. Nineteenth-century geologists and evolutionists were the first to propose that time extends beyond 6,000 years, the world's presumed age. Townsend credits L. S. Mercier as the first writer to consider that new vastness in a forgotten French novel of 1771. As in time capsule tales, its narrator falls asleep as a young man, awakening in 2500 at 750 years of age. To Mercier, who contrasts a sensible utopian Paris to his own pre-Revolutionary France, "the idea of technological change seems never to have occurred." The novel ends "fully in the spirit of time-slip fantasy" when Louis XIV contemplates Versailles's ruins, regretting his tyranny (Townsend, 87).

In 1887, American novelist Edward Bellamy had a similar political agenda in *Looking Backward 2000—1887.* His hypnotized narrator, Julian West, awakens in Boston's socialistic welfare state in the year 2000. Bellamy adds a few more technological developments than Mercier—one listens to live concerts by telephone.

Two years later, Mark Twain "opened a Pandora's Box," according to Clute, fiddling with the dangers of changing history in *A Connecticut Yankee in King Arthur's Court* (see chapter 5). An industrial revolution begun in Arthur's time might "undermine the whole course of history," inspiring more writers to time travel backward from Twain's moment onward (Clute, 61). Twain himself has proved a popular figure for recent time travelers to meet, as in David Carkeet's *I Been There Before,* Allen Appel's *Twice Upon a Time,* and Darryl Brock's *If I Never Get Back.*

H. G. Wells first explored time as a fourth dimension; in his famous 1891 novel *The Time Machine,* a "good stout Victorian contraption" (Townsend, 88) moves his Time Traveler thousands of years forward. Wells's "enormously exciting" tale "has never been successfully imitated," declares Clute (60), its mechanical future travel classifying it as science fiction.

Two celebrated British authors published the first children's time fantasies in the same year, 1906. In *Puck of Pook's Hill,* Rudyard Kipling uses one of the earliest magical time triggers, when Dan and Una act out Shakespeare's *Midsummer Night's Dream* on Midsummer's Eve within an ancient Fairy Ring. This potent spell calls out Puck himself, who was young "when Stonehenge was new,"[11] to show the children their living heritage. Unlike time travel, which sends people backward in time, Kipling brings forward past inhabitants of the children's own land, near England's Channel coast; among them are a Norman knight and a Romano-British centurion, who tell Dan and Una vivid tales of their lives there. Though *Puck* and its sequel, *Rewards and Fairies,* are wordy and old fashioned, they still resonate.

Meanwhile, E. Nesbit was taking children back in time to experience history in *The Story of the Amulet,* which Cameron sees as setting "into motion the genre of time fantasy in children's literature" (Cameron, 219). In this sequel to *The Five Children and It* (see chapter 3) and *The Phoenix and the Carpet,* the children find half an amulet in a junk shop, which sends them through time in search of its other half. According to Townsend, not only are their "various cliffhanging adventures in times and places in the past . . . good gripping stuff," but Nesbit also flirts with the paradox of time travel (Townsend, 89). Just when Julius Caesar has decided not to bother invading dull old Britain in 55 B.C., the children change his mind by boasting of its modern wonders, such as hotair balloons. What Townsend admires as Nesbit's "tongue-in-cheek" liberties with time Cameron sees as "a certain toughness, tartness" (218), still pungent to readers 90 years later. In his autobiography, C. S. Lewis refers to Nesbit's *Amulet* as the book that awakened him to "the dark backward and abysm of time," which he still read "with delight" as an adult.[12]

Thirty years after Nesbit, John Masefield probed time in *The Midnight Folk,* when schoolboy Kay Harker steps into his grandfather's portrait and past. In its sequel, *The Box of Delights,* Kay enters past scenes beneath the lid of a magical box, which also has a knob that transports him swiftly across distance or shrinks him to mouse size, as in Lewis Carroll's *Alice.* To foil a villainous gang of kidnappers, Kay zooms about in time, space, and size with great abandon, visiting the Trojan War for a paragraph or two or briefly greeting a Roman centurion. After a frantic finale in which he rescues dozens of kidnapped victims, Kay awakens from his dream. Such sabotage of magic prevents this 1935 swashbuckler from enduring as a classic.

That honor was earned four years later by *A Traveler in Time.* As a child, its author, Alison Uttley, lived next door to the manor house called Thackers in her story. Like her young time traveler, Penelope, Uttley dreamed her way into "secret hidden doorways in the house wall and found myself in another century . . . moving through a life parallel to my own existence."[13] Visiting her great-aunt Cicely's farm Thackers in idyllic Derbyshire, sensitive Penelope slips from a current hallway into past rooms, entering the lives of the aristocratic Babington family, who lived there in Elizabethan times. Learning that Anthony Babington plans to rescue Mary, Queen of Scots, from imprisonment, Penelope knows they are doomed, as both were executed in 1587. But Penelope forgets her foreknowledge, witnessing instead the relentless unfolding of fate.

Beautifully demonstrating all Cameron's elements, *A Traveler in Time* is a touchstone for modern time fantasy. Penelope experiences Cameron's "timeless moment" when past and future intertwine, becoming her now. Penelope's awareness of her "hidden shadowy ones," whose "life was compact with sorrows and joys so intense that I marveled the barrier was not broken down with the flood of their emotions" (Uttley, 139), is certainly a "flow of inevitability." Here also is the sense of place: "The air of house and barn was throbbing with the memory of things once seen and heard" (139), which Uttley makes readers feel with all their senses. The whole brilliantly realized Thackers is Penelope's time trigger. If all time fantasies were as masterful as Uttley's, readers would experience more often the eternal now.

Many writers are captivated by Cameron's "complexities result-ing from the mingling of times"; their novels are reflections on the nature of time itself. Others emphasize "those strange oppor-tunities that only time fantasy can offer" (Cameron, 169), helping time travelers resolve present problems, bringing growth or heal-ing. Though many time fantasies slip among several types, in the next section they are considered as "reflections" or "resolutions."

Reflections: Exploring Time's Mystery

The Nature of Time

Albert Einstein's 1905 and 1915 theories of relativity radically changed our concept of time. His four-dimensional space-time continuum infected public consciousness, inspiring writers to express time's revolutionary new shapes in fiction.

Alan Garner's *Red Shift* "belongs most clearly and insistently to the age of relativity," declares John Rowe Townsend (Townsend, 93). Susan Cooper agrees: "[T]his novel is more pro-foundly concerned with the continuum of place and time than any other."[14] In physics, light waves grow more red as an object moves farther away—the red shift. Garner's oblique, demanding 1973 novel is a time riddle. Its three interwoven narratives about three Thomases in the English county of Cheshire occur in three different times. Macey (an old nickname for Thomas) is a Roman soldier fighting second-century Celts, Thomas fights for Parlia-ment against the king in the 1643 Civil War, and Tom is a mod-ern student at war with his parents. All three are disturbed by fits of madness or seizures, which bring visions these alter egos share across time. Each Thomas is loved by a woman; all watch the stars of Orion. A 3,000-year-old stone axe connects them, each finding the powerful talisman where the previous Thomas left it.

Their stories are not chronological; each one's insight or crisis heralds another's. Through dialog with little description, readers must work out allusions connecting them, which may perplex all but the most savvy. Do all events occur simultaneously? In a lucid study of the novel, Kathleen A. Boardman explains, "Time is bent, pushed around, manipulated—leaving readers with the idea that only place matters."[15] To Susan Cooper, past, present, and future "echo to and fro. Within Garner's piece of Cheshire, all three co-exist, and fierce emotion runs through the continuum, erupting in violent death or in the violence of loving" (Cooper, 100). Garner's view is bleak; massacre, rape, and betrayal culminate in modern Tom's own destruction of his affair with Jan. Though love saves earlier Thomases, Garner implies that we have red-shifted too far from the community of others, leaving us isolated, dislocated from place, and therefore self-destructive.

Red Shift arouses controversy. Is it "Literary Crossword Puzzle . . . or Masterpiece?" asks *Horn Book,* concluding, with many other critics, that this experimental novel is not for young adults.[16] Since teenaged Tom's anguished love story, fraught with parental interference, lies at *Red Shift*'s heart, experimental YA readers will decide if Garner's novel is for them.

No other time travel novel contemplates time's nature as completely as physicist Alan Lightman's 1993 best-seller, *Einstein's Dreams,* which imagines the great scientist's meditations upon infinite varieties of time. Each dream/chapter describes the same Swiss town as it might exist if time had different textures, shapes, or dimensions. One world stands still at the center of time. Another has no time, merely images. Time flows fitfully in stops and starts, or moves backward so one remembers the future while growing younger. One world's people live for only a day; others live knowing when the world will end. Lightman's flowing language is as precise and intuitive as was Einstein himself. This small but enormous book excites thoughtful young adults with enlightening postulations on how people relate to time.

YAFEs on the Nature of Time

Garner—*Red Shift*

The style of writing was hard to follow, but on the whole it is a very imaginative book that challenges your ideas about relationships between different times. Emotions and social relations are essentially the same in every period, leaving it up to the reader to imagine the setting. The stone axe was an interesting way to tie everything together. I recommend this original novel to anybody 16 or over who is willing to put some thought into it.

—Eric Rice, 16

Lightman—*Einstein's Dreams*

In this philosophically challenging set of essays, Lightman sees humans as easily manipulated by time. Time is the only constant in life . . . so what happens in places where time is different? Lightman's simple, elegant style complements the everyday but magical subject. I recommend this beautiful, awesome book to anyone who feels intellectually ready to challenge the very ideas we live by.

—Anne Pizzi, 15

Lightman challenges the most basic human assumptions, creating alternative realities in direct opposition to the expected norm. He expands the minds of his readers in truly unprecedented ways. The distant third-person perspective enhances the surreal nature of this wonderful book. Alan P. Lightman is an intellectual god!

—Colyn Bulthaup, 18

Discovering History

Like historical fiction, time travel can probe history's reality, adding current awareness to the past. No one achieves this feat better than Simon Morley, in Jack Finney's modern classic *Time and Again,* an adult novel chosen as a 1970 ALA Best Book for Young Adults. A young New York illustrator, Si becomes involved in a secret government project based on Einstein's image of time as a river. If the past still exists along the river behind us, we can step out of our present boat to walk back. Si proves adept at this simple but profound time travel method. Steeped in details of his target time and place, 1882 New York, Si moves to a "gateway" location existing now and then, the Dakota building (which current readers associate with John Lennon's 1980 assassination). Through self-hypnosis, Si loosens his 1970 ties, stepping into the snowy, gaslit Central Park of 1882. Swept into blackmail and a devastating fire, Si loses his heart to beautiful Julia.

Tearing through Finney's suspenseful pages, readers share Si's wonder at participating in 1882 life. Si snaps photographs of the street scenes and people that illustrate Finney's novel, comparing them to his own New York. Through Si's eyes, Finney describes exactly how it feels to be in the 1882 city, and how human attitudes differ then and now. Finney's lively catalog of 1882 reality, and Si's emotional investment in it, offer readers all they desire in time travel: the sensation of actually being there. We are not surprised that Si prefers 1882 to 1970. Refusing to follow Project orders to experiment with the ripples of changing events, Si makes a startling decision which ends the Project forever.

"Forever," that is, until the sequel, *From Time to Time,* written 25 years after *Time and Again* but set five years later, when Finney brilliantly manipulates time's river to bring Si back into the Project. Against earlier scruples, Si cannot resist visiting 1912, when he tries to prevent the outbreak of World War I. But the one man who might stop the war is aboard the *Titanic.*

Finney's story collection *About Time* features characters transfixed by time's tricks, such as a man who savors two different but equally engaging wives in alternate time lines and a couple whose strange neighbors arrive from the future. Also known for *Invasion of the Body Snatchers,* Jack Finney won the World Fantasy Convention's 1987 Life Achievement award.

Three other exceptional novels also expand genre conventions. Published only in a 1985 paperback, R. A. MacAvoy's *The Book of Kells* is difficult to locate but worth finding for its richly realized atmosphere. In modern Ireland, Canadian artist John Thornburn copies an illuminated manuscript design, causing a hysterical naked girl to erupt into his apartment. Recognizing her antiquated Irish speech, John's historian friend Derval O'Keane calms Ailesh, victim of a Viking raid. When John and Derval accompany her home to tenth-century Ireland, they become embroiled in the conflict of their modern logic with ancient superstition, mirroring the violent culture clash between Vikings and Gaels 1,000 years ago.

In her 1988 young adult novel *Another Shore,* Nancy Bond makes an unthinkable departure from time travel conventions that would spoil suspense if revealed. For a summer job at Louisbourg National Historic Park in Nova Scotia, a reconstructed 1744 French fortress comparable to colonial Williamsburg, Lyn plays the role of colonist Elisabeth Bernard. When she tumbles into the real 1744 Louisbourg, everyone thinks she is really Elisabeth, the baker's niece.

Like Finney, Bond provides gritty details of daily life, illuminating Lyn's challenge to labor in Elisabeth's place, her freedom strictly curtailed. Lyn also becomes enmeshed with those she meets, but unlike Si Morley she has no choice, no power to leave. Lyn's distress is eased when she meets two other refugees from her own time. Will they find a way home before brutal winter hits, with war on its tail? "A pulsating urgency runs through the book," says a VOYA reviewer, in "a multi-textured look at life's choices that continues to haunt the reader long after the cover is closed."[17] Says a starred *School Library Journal* review: "[T]his intense twist on the time fantasy genre forces readers not only to learn from the past but to accept its reality."[18]

Connie Willis tops every time travel achievement so far with her masterful *Doomsday Book,* which captured both the 1992 Hugo Award and the 1993 Nebula Award. On the border between fantasy and science fiction, it uses a futuristic, scientific method of time travel to visit the Middle Ages. In 2054, time travel is the ultimate history lesson at Britain's Oxford University. Students travel through a "net," its computer calculating probabilities and preventing time paradoxes. Eager to experience medieval England, Kivrin studies Latin, Norman French, Middle English, social customs and politics, spinning, weaving, and milking cows. Inoculated against medieval diseases, she prepares authentic clothing and a pretext for being in 1320 Oxford. But her computer technician succumbs to a virus before confirming that Kivrin arrived safely. As the virus escalates into an epidemic, its tracking alternates with Kivrin's intense encounters with residents of a past she slowly realizes is not 1320 but 1348, the time of the Black Plague.

Juxtaposing past and future plagues to tell the story of "the end of the world," Connie Willis debunks what she calls our "cherished idiocies" that we can control natural forces like disease and that we are superior to superstitious fools of history.[19] Human nature remains the same in any crisis; Kivrin's history lessons were inaccurate, her 1300s reality beyond imagination. Like Finney and Bond, Willis counteracts our ignorant arrogance by forcing us to look deeper into our origins. In a companion novel, *To Say Nothing of the Dog,* Willis balances this bleakness with a *"deeply* comic" look at "the positive side." Another future Oxford historian is sent to Victorian England to recuperate from the stress of time travel, only to find that the Victorians, like us, take themselves too seriously. The Oxford time travel unit first appeared in the short story "Fire Watch," whose title was also used for a 1985 collection. Willis declares, "I could write nothing but time travel stories the rest of my life. . . it's so rich, there's so much you could do" (Willis, 73).

Other time fantasies that reveal history appear in this chapter's Recommended Reading.

YAFEs on Discovering History

Bond—*Another Shore*

An interesting, realistic portrayal of how a teen from the 1980s copes when she is abruptly jarred from her own time.
—Deirdre Kambic, 16

MacAvoy—*The Book of Kells*

Though long, it was very well written, with a lot of attention to detail on the problems of entering another time and a cool form of time travel.
—Pixy Dougherty, 15

Willis—*The Doomsday Book*

This is the best time travel book in existence, because of sheer incredibility. Both past and future are real, visual, believable, and fascinating. As much an adventure science fiction as a fantasy, it reminded me of the movie *Outbreak.*
—Ashley Burns, 17

Though it gave a very vivid feel for the plague era, I found the future scenes boring.
—Allison Barrett, 16

Science Fiction

Inaugurated in 1891 by H. G. Wells's *The Time Machine*, science fiction time travel uses scientific methods instead of psychic or magical means, often involving travel to the future or other planets. Borders between fantastical and scientific approaches are fuzzy, sometimes blended, as in *The Doomsday Book*. Ray Bradbury's short story "A Sound of Thunder," from his 1962 collection *R is for Rocket*, has been called "the most classic exposition of the consequences of interference with the past."[20] From a dinosaur-hunting safari into prehistory, one hunter brings back a butterfly stuck to his shoe, which utterly alters the course of time. Bradbury pursued time safaris in the later *Dinosaur Tales*, recently continued in a paperback series by Stephen Leigh, opening with *Dinosaur World*. Also in 1962, Madeleine L'Engle won the Newbery Medal for *A Wrinkle in Time*, beloved by middle grade readers, which invented the word *tesseract* for time travel. The Murry family tesseracts through sequels *A Wind in the Door* and *A Swiftly Tilting Planet*.

Giant among adult scientific time travel is physicist Gregory Benford's 1981 Nebula winner, *Timescape*, declared "the best time-travel-backwards tale ever written" (Clute, 230). Threatened by environmental disaster, in 1998 Cambridge University physicists send Morse code messages into the past via tachyons, subatomic particles that travel faster than light. Will 1963 scientists understand the warning not to use world-destroying chemicals?

In Robert Charles Wilson's imaginative *A Bridge of Years*, Tom Winter buys an isolated house in the Pacific Northwest, amazed to find it cleaned by cybernetic bugs, caretakers of its time tunnel created by future advanced beings. One of many houses on a network of nodes in time, it is used to study human history. Tom escapes his dull 1989 life to hippie 1962 Greenwich Village, unaware of a threat from a murderous renegade time traveler. This fast-paced adult page turner makes revelations about the immutable past and the indeterminate future. Other time science fiction is listed in this chapter's Recommended Reading.

Resolutions:
Change and Growth through Time

Changing Outcomes

Though Jack Finney's time traveler Si Morley is opposed to tampering with the past, he is still convinced, in *From Time to Time,* that World War I is worth preventing. Si's shocking results prove that outcome cannot be controlled. Speculation on interference with events fuels a lively group of time fantasies, in which inhabitants of different times communicate in order to right a wrong or correct a misconception.

Eleanor Cameron's unsurpassed *Court of the Stone Children,* winner of the children's 1974 National Book Award, mystically connects two girls, past and present. Moving to San Francisco, teenaged loner Nina is drawn to a French museum, enjoying her "Museum Feeling" when holding old objects that once belonged to others, "as if there wasn't any time at all between their lives and mine."[21] There Nina meets Domi, a spirit from Napoleon's time, unseen by anyone else, who inhabits the museum rooms transported from her chateau in France. Domi's father was unjustly executed as a murderer, and Nina must clear his name before his biography is published. Nina finds clues in paintings, an old journal, and two identical past and present cats named Lisabetta. Serving as catalysts and conduits are stone children, statues in the museum garden. Says critic Betty Levin: "a kind of energy resides in the unresolved pasts of the stone children, awaiting the right time, the right person to act for them in the present."[22] Chagall's painting "Time is a River Without Banks" is the unifying image revealing time's nature.

Along with vindication for Domi's father, Nina finds her own direction among supportive museum staff in this rich, penetrating novel. A lingering melancholy surrounds Nina's heightened perceptions, which will always set her apart. Such a complex, meditative novel is mislabeled for children; it appeals to young adults and adults who share Nina's sensitivity. Sometimes classified as a ghost story, *The Court of the Stone Children* embodies the elusive nature of time fantasies that work on many levels.

As critic, Cameron herself notes "a new toughness" in time fantasies of the late 1970s onward (Cameron, 197), exemplified in Robert Westall's 1979 ALA Best Book for Young Adults *The Devil on the Road*. Out for a holiday lark on his motorcycle, college student John Webster follows what he calls "Lady Chance," but it is not merely a traffic jam and storm which forces John to shelter in a barn with a pesky starving kitten. The barn is a time gate, and the cat, who becomes John's cherished pet News, is a time-cat, his escort into 1647, where he meets accused witch Johanna Vavasour. Saving Johanna from hanging involves more than modern explosives and his motorcycle, for Johanna ensnares John with powers he cannot understand. This original, gritty tale has as many twists and folds as the time Johanna kneads. Through plucky John, Westall faces unanswerable questions about spiritual connections across time.

Other authors also confront travelers with Puritan witch hunts, trying to save victims of the 1692 Salem hangings in *A Witch Across Time* by Gilbert B. Cross, and *Witch Hunt* by Wendy Corsi Staub. In Eileen Dunlop's *The Valley of Deer*, a charmstone found in an archaeological dig in Scotland sends Anne back to 1726, to be persecuted as a witch. Experiments with telepathy allow two teenagers to experience another accused Johanna's torments in fifteenth century England, in New Zealander Sherryl Jordan's *The Juniper Game*. In a time travel twist, Abby in Kathryn Reiss's *Pale Phoenix* has been bewitched to stay thirteen for three hundred years, until she seeks shelter in Miranda's home, and a way to return to her 1693 family. Miranda is experienced at time tinkering, finding a dollhouse replica of her own home in 1993 ALA Best Book *Time Windows*, where previous residents replay traumatic scenes from their lives.

In *Playing Beatie Bow*, a 1982 ALA Best Book for Young Adults and a Best Australian Children's Book of the Year, Ruth Park sends another Abby back to fulfill a prophecy. Unable to forgive her father for leaving, Abby escapes her high-rise Sydney apartment to take her little neighbor Natalie to the playground, where children play a chanting game "Beatie Bow." Trying to stop Natalie from following a little girl in ragged old-fashioned dress, Abby stumbles and faints, awakening in Sydney's 1873 slums being nursed by the grandmother of Beatie Bow, the little girl. Noticing Abby's dress, crocheted with a design Granny planned but has not yet made, the Bows believe Abby is the prophesied Stranger who will save their inherited psychic "Gift." When they hide Abby's dress, her passport home, she must stay until she performs this mysterious role. Abby falls in love with sailor Judah Bow, only to learn that saving the "Gift" means losing him. Through sights, smells, and vigorous personalities of everyone Abby meets, Park brings alive daily life among Sydney's Victorian poor. Adjustment to another time is Abby's coming of age; the love she carries home changes Abby as she changes the Bows.

Following Jack Finney's tradition is Allen Appel's New York history professor Alex Balfour, who inherited his time traveling ability from his abusive father. Yet Alex cannot control his forays into history. In 1986 ALA Best Book for Young Adults *Time After Time,* lifelike dreams plummet Alex into the 1917 Russian Revolution, where he witnesses Rasputin's murder, meets Lenin, and is imprisoned as a spy. Agonizing over the ethics of involvement in the past, Alex meets his father leading a band of Cossacks, ruthlessly shaping history for himself. Then Alex finds his guardian, Max Surrey, as a young revolutionary, preserving Max's life so he can later become that guardian. Should Alex also save Tsar Nicholas and his family from assassination?

Barely recovered from these traumas, in *Twice Upon a Time* Alex lands in 1876 Philadelphia for America's Centennial exhibition, where he meets his writer hero Mark Twain, and two Indians on display, treated with outrageous prejudice. Determined to help the Indians by changing the outcome of Custer's Last Stand, Alex is again out of control. His efforts for the Indians parallel his journalist lover Molly's modern coverage of Red Power activism.

In Alex's most recent adventure, *Till the End of Time,* another ALA Best Book for Young Adults, he plunges into the 1941 Japanese attack on Pearl Harbor. With Albert Einstein, he tries to stop America's dropping of the atomic bomb on Hiroshima. Alex even saves young lieutenant John F. Kennedy from drowning in the South Pacific on PT-109, and meets aviator Amelia Earhart six years after her plane disappeared. Meanwhile, Molly visits modern Japan to investigate World War II germ warfare experimentation on American prisoners, placing herself in dire danger from the unscrupulous scientists Alex met in the past.

Appel's Balfour series has irresistible appeal, mixing romance, suspense, intricate plotting, lively images, and Alex's eternal wrestling with moral responsibility, while unavoidably thrust into crises with famous history makers. Does Alex's participation really change history? Though Appel can go enthusiastically overboard, his flawed romantic hero engages us "unashamedly," says the *New York Times,* in "ferociously paced adventure whose chief object is to keep us reading. It does that with grace and skill."[23]

In Alan Brennert's compelling adult novel *Time and Chance,* successful Broadway actor Richard Cochrane grieves when his mother dies, wishing he had spent more time in their small New Hampshire town. Returning there for her funeral, he is shocked to see himself through a window, arguing with his college sweetheart Debra. This other version of himself, Rick, has married Debra, regretting that he never pursued his dream of acting. Realizing they split into two at the point of choice between marrying and acting, Richard and Rick exchange lives, each living the unfulfilled dream. Will their alternate timelines merge again? This superb character study explores choice and destiny, riveting readers with the chance to try the road not taken.

YAFES ON CHANGING OUTCOMES

Appel—*Time After Time*

It throws a lot together successfully: history, romance, fantasy, and family problems each play some role in making this story believable and enjoyable.

—Megan Corrigan, 16

There is so much to be learned from this book: history, vocabulary, an intriguing plot, ideas on dealing with life, and even Nietzsche's idea of eternal recurrence! Not only does Appel have a great style, but he brilliantly incorporates different elements in time.

—Alisa Kotmair, 15

Cameron—*Court of the Stone Children*

I loved the metaphor of the paintings, inquisitive Nina, and her friend who devoted his life to studying time. Vivid description added to the overall clarity of the story, which brought light to the murky darkness of the past. How refreshing that unlike most time travel, there was no sexy, tall, dark stranger!

—Allison Barrett, 16

Jordan—*The Juniper Game*

It was difficult to identify with the main characters, a major loss to the book since it was really tough to understand what was happening to them emotionally. The idea of going back in time through meditation is rarely used, and carried out well. Some scenes were really cheesy, and it was the biggest cliché to have the beautiful psychic and the nerd fall in love. Although oozing with problems, the book was actually enjoyable, very captivating.

—Dylan Burns, 14

Koontz—*Lightning*

This book not only represents destiny, heartbreak, and loss, but it artfully expresses courage on the part of a mind-boggled victim. It is filled with creativity.

—Tricia Brissett, 14

This page-turner has a very good 'what if': you cannot travel into the past or the future before any other of your trips, since you must avoid the paradoxes inherent in possibly meeting yourself. Viewpoint shifts throughout the story were a nice added touch.

—Brian Dunning, 14

It was incredibly clever and fascinating—I couldn't stop reading!

—Amanda Krotki, 15

Park—*Playing Beatie Bow*

With a simple, charming writing style, this lovely book has a plot similar to life itself, seemingly obvious, but not quite what you expect. Very sweet and bittersweet, enjoyable even to people who loathe time travel as much as I do.

—Ashley Burns, 17

Victorian scenes seemed accurate, and the story was cute and fuzzy.

—Allison Barrett, 16

Shapiro—*A Time to Remember*

The storyline about preventing Kennedy's assassination was unique and fabulously carried out. Fast, suspenseful, imaginative, and appealing from the very beginning.

—Ann Rodavitch, 17

Healing Lessons

Instead of changing outcomes, many recent time fantasies focus on changing the time traveler himself or herself. "The emotional climate has deepened," says Barbara Elleman. Time travelers seek relief from "personal despair, . . . [which] also paves the way for readers to accept and become involved in the story" (Elleman, 495). As Karen Patricia Smith puts it, characters "come to terms with internal and external conflict through the presence of a time dimension" (Smith, 45). Time travelers bring new awareness home from the past, healing whatever hurts.

Philippa Pearce pioneered healing time travel with 1958 Carnegie Medal winner *Tom's Midnight Garden,* declared by John Rowe Townsend as "still unsurpassed in the field of children's fiction, . . . profoundly concerned with time" (Townsend, 91). Spending the summer in a small apartment with his aunt and uncle, Tom is homesick and lonely until the grandfather clock strikes 13, allowing him to enter a magical walled garden. There he befriends Hatty, a girl in Victorian dress who grows older with each nightly visit, while Tom stays the same. Eventually Tom realizes that Hatty is old Mrs. Bartholomew, landlady of the apartments that were once her large childhood home. Knowing this old lady as his beloved young Hatty helps Tom grow.

Living in the English millhouse where her father grew up, Philippa Pearce explains that in Tom's garden, "a community of longing brings the two children together over a span of Time that would otherwise separate them forever."[24] Townsend sees Pearce's "deep-lying theme" as "the four-dimensional wholeness of life. In the child the old person is implicit; in the old person the child remains" (Townsend, 91–92). Suggesting the garden of Eden, this evocative classic remains a model for all books in which youth encounter time.

Several British novelists of the 1970s followed Pearce's cue. In Penelope Farmer's *Charlotte Sometimes,* two girls sleep in the same boarding school bed 40 years apart, exchanging lives. In *A Game of Dark* by William Mayne, Donald is guilt stricken at his inability to love his stern, disabled father, becoming a medieval dragonslayer in order to confront his feelings. In a haunting work of deep spirituality, *The Wind Eye,* a 1978 ALA Best Book for Young Adults, Robert Westall repairs a stepfamily's troubled relations by sailing them to the island of seventh-century hermit monk St. Cuthbert. In Eileen Dunlop's engrossing *Elizabeth Elizabeth,* titled *Robinsheugh* in Britain, a girl visiting an old Scottish house connects so deeply with another Elizabeth who lived there in the 1770s that she becomes estranged from her once-fond aunt. In the Dickensian atmosphere of *A Chance Child,* Jill Paton Walsh sends abused child Creep back into the horrifying reality of child labor during the Industrial Revolution while modern Christopher searches for some clue that Creep survives.

Few Americans matched British writers' ability to make time heal wounds until Nancy Bond wrote *A String in the Harp,* a 1977 Newbery Honor Book. After his mother dies, Peter Morgan, 12, is devastated when his father transplants the family from Massachusetts to Wales. In windswept Borth, Peter is friendless and bitter until he finds an ancient key stuck among rocks on the beach. The key brings entrancing visions of another young boy in the same landscape long ago. When he learns that his key tuned the harp of legendary bard Taliesin in sixth-century Wales, Peter becomes obsessed with unfolding scenes from Taliesin's life. Trying to reach remote Peter, his sisters, Becky and Jen, and new Welsh friends also see signs from the past: moving torches, a leather boat, a fishing weir. Peter's distress triggers the key, and his isolation brings family and friends to his aid until grief is transformed, knitting the family together again. Bond skillfully interweaves Taliesin's wandering life with the Morgans' experience of foreign Wales; emotional intensity binds both until they discover home. Story itself is a link, for Taliesin's "story had been entrusted to Peter. He carried it as Taliesin himself had once carried stories."[25]

Around the same time, American Norma Fox Mazer was first to portray the traumatic shock of time travel, in *Saturday, the Twelfth of October,* in which teenaged Zan suddenly slips from New York City to its wilderness past, among primitive cave dwellers. After a year of painful adjustment to this utterly foreign way of life, Zan whisks home to find it still the same day as when she left. No one believes where she has been, and Zan's new awareness of nature, survival, and community again separates her from others. Mazer convincingly details the isolating psychology of the time travel experience.

Though its *Time Trilogy* predecessors were science fiction, Madeleine L'Engle's rich metaphysical allegory *Many Waters* features teenaged Murry twins Sandy and Dennys, who have a fantastical adventure when their father's computer sends them to Noah's family in biblical times before the flood. Drawn before angels were so popular, L'Engle's shimmering portraits of seraphim and nephilim are especially appealing. The flood's looming certainty helps L'Engle's fans forgive lapses in characterization in this 1987 ALA Best Book for Young Adults.

Young readers experience the Nazi Holocaust's horrors through Jane Yolen's 13-year-old Hannah in *The Devil's Arithmetic,* winner of two Jewish book awards. Embarrassed by the outbursts of Holocaust survivor Grandpa Will and impatient with her family's Seder traditions, Hannah reluctantly opens the door to the prophet Elijah. Beyond the door is a 1942 Polish village; inside the mind of another girl, Chaya, Hannah is transported to a death camp. Unable to tell her companions about their dreadful fate, Hannah loses her 1980s self within Chaya's daily struggle for survival. After making the ultimate sacrifice, Hannah returns home, transformed through knowing her grandfather's and great-aunt's suffering. Yolen's achievements in myth and fairy tales are legion (see her chapter 4 biography), but "this thoughtful, compelling novel is unique among them," says *Kirkus* in a pointered review. This "triumphantly moving book"[26] deeply affects young adult readers with tragedy otherwise unimaginable.

A similar testament reaches older teens in Han Nolan's *If I Should Die Before I Wake,* when a 1994 witness experiences Auschwitz. Unlike Yolen's Hannah, neo-Nazi Hilary is no sympathetic Jew. In a coma since her motorcycle accident during a Jew-bashing incident, Hilary enters Polish girl Chana's consciousness in the World War II death camp. As both face death, Hilary and Chana lend their spirits to each other. Nolan's details of privation and torture seem even more horrific than Yolen's; both books are powerful and cautionary transporters of youth into the most devastating encounter with inhumanity in recent history.

What T. A. Barron's intrepid young heroine Kate hopes to heal in *The Ancient One* is human links with all beings. In this lively adventure between Kate's science fantasy *Heartlight* (Philomel, 1990) and her Arthurian connection in *The Merlin Effect* (see chapter 5), the unique time trigger is a hollow redwood tree, inside a volcanic crater in Oregon. Trying to save the tree from loggers, Kate moves 500 years into its past to meet native peoples and magical beings, from shapeshifting lizards to the dinosaur-octopus creature controlling the world by volcano. Barron pairs inventive time travel with a classic quest and a plea for environmental awareness, as Kate restores harmony to all times and creatures. In Barron's local newspaper, critic Payton Knopf, age 12, found his characters "well-depicted and original, and the author's storytelling abilities . . . exceptional."[27]

YAFEs on Healing Lessons

Barron—*The Ancient One*

The redwood is the most unusual time gate ever!
—Nate Doyle, 16, and Eric Rice, 16

L'Engle—*Many Waters*

The story is so intriguing and unpredictable. Both factual and fantasy elements work together to make it readable and enjoyable.

—Megan Corrigan, 17

Much more mature than the earlier three books in the series, it retold a story everyone knows, so it was easier to understand.

—Rachel Libonati, 14

Picturesque and unique; a good twist on a well-known tale.

—Ashley Burns, 17

It didn't have that "zing" that *A Wrinkle in Time* had. It was entertaining, but I didn't really feel for any of the characters.

—Bill Henry, 19

The science part was a little confusing, and I didn't like how the evil angels turned into animals I like—snakes, rats, and vultures. I liked the idea of turning a Biblical story into fantasy, and though it was pretty slow, I enjoyed it anyway.

—Galadriel Wills, 14

Walsh—*A Chance Child*

I loved the idea—child labor can be a touching story—but it was very colorless. It is impossible to beat Katherine Paterson's *Liddy* for a portrayal of this world. There was a very tenuous connection between present and past. Instead of allowing escape to a better world, this book merely made me feel bad for all the characters.

—Anne Pizzi, 15

Yolen—*The Devil's Arithmetic*

It was beautiful, sad, creative—a gorgeous book that majestically dealt with the heartbreaking subject of humanity's oppression of itself.

—Allison Barrett, 16

A disturbing, accurate, and beautiful book about a difficult subject.

—Pixy Dougherty, 15

This is Jane Yolen's best book, and that is saying a lot! It was my favorite book for years. It was so marvelous, I didn't take time to analyze it—I was too enthralled. Yolen writes so beautifully, she pulls off this time travel trick, which brings a spiritual side to the story. Enjoy this perfect story as much as it deserves. I completely recommend it.

—Anne Pizzi, 15

Healing through Reincarnation or Repetition

Some time travelers' healing experiences reflect a cyclical theory of time. Events and people seem fated to repeat themselves through the ages until something left undone is completed. In Phyllis Reynolds Naylor's *York Trilogy,* Dan Roberts, 15, sees life as "a revolving wheel, and he was in the middle of it, watching the same cycles go by again and again."[28]

Struggling to cope with the possibility that he may have inherited disabling Huntington's disease, which could strike at around age 40, Dan visits the English city of York with his parents, searching for ancestors who suffered the illness. There, in *Shadows on the Wall,* Dan meets taxi driver Joe Stanton and the large gypsy family of Ambrose Faw, who seem familiar and haunt him in various forms and times until he discovers why. In the gypsy camp, Dan wrestles with a mysterious Roman centurion, only to find him metamorphosing into Joe. In *Faces in the Water,* Dan as a fourth-century Celtic tribesman replays his fight with Roman Joe. Returning home to Pennsylvania in *Footprints at the Window,* Dan encounters the Faws as the migrant Dawsons. Again Dan is attracted to their daughter Orlenda, now called Oriole. Her face in a stream sends Dan to her aid in plague-ridden 1349 York, where Dan faces his own mortality. His enduring tie to Orlenda vanquishes self-pity at last. Throughout this engrossing trilogy, the River Ouse in York and the Susquehanna in Pennsylvania mesh Einstein's river with cyclical time. A Roman coin connects all ages Dan visits. Spanning violent times, Naylor's tale carries a strong antiwar message, planting seeds of hope in YA readers facing their own uncertain futures.

In *The Druid's Gift,* Caitlin tries to escape her fate as a tenth-century Druid sacrifice in the islands of St. Kilda, over 100 miles west of Scotland. Scottish author Margaret Anderson illuminates the remote islands' history through Caitlin's visions of her destiny as Cathan in Viking times, Catie in the mid-1700s, and Catriona in Victorian times, when St. Kilda was discovered by the outside world. As she reincarnates through 1,000 years, the simple seasonal rhythms of the islands change little; Caitlin's culture is preserved through the continuity of its isolated place. Readers are wrenched to discover that the few remaining islanders abandoned their sparse homes in the 1930s, lured to the modern comforts of the mainland. Today's nature reserve, still difficult to reach, is the only testament left to a lost people.

Other titles in which modern characters reenact the past are listed in this chapter's Recommended Reading.

Healing through Meeting Ancestors

Sometimes modern protagonists meet ancestors to gain understanding of their origins. The 1977 comedy *Hangin' Out with Cici* established Francine Pascal's sympathy with the perils of adolescence before she created the *Sweet Valley High* series. Eighth grader Victoria's mother fails to see that her mischief is just high spirits, not deliberately bad behavior. On a train home to face the consequences of passing a joint at a party, Victoria jolts into an old-fashioned station where she meets familiar-looking Cici, just her age but much wilder. What satisfying insight dawns when Victoria realizes that Cici is her own mother back in 1944!

In Octavia Butler's *Kindred,* African-American Dana helplessly plunges from 1976 California to 1815 Maryland whenever slave owner Rufus needs her to save his life. Learning that Rufus was her many-greats grandfather she never knew was white, Dana realizes she must continue playing the tormenting role of his slave to assure her own eventual birth. Dana's intolerable link to treacherous Rufus, her terrifying lack of control, and her courage in coping with such bizarre imprisonment keep readers breathlessly turning pages. Butler's searing adult novel allows mature teen readers to experience the agonies of slavery. The sexual bondage of slave women to white masters places Dana's modern interracial marriage in stark context.

A Girl Called Boy by Belinda Hurmence has a similar premise for younger YA readers. Like Jane Yolen's Hannah in *The Devil's Arithmetic* (also about meeting relatives), Blanche Overtha Yancy, called Boy for her initials, pays little attention to her parents' honoring of family origins. Not until she becomes a runaway slave in 1853 North Carolina does Boy appreciate the spirit of her people.

In Helen Hughes Vick's 1994 ALA Best Book for Young Adults, *Walker of Time,* Walker fulfills his Hopi uncle's dying wish. Taking a prayer stick to an isolated cave, Walker meets white archaeologist's son Tag before both boys fall into an ancient cliff village. Enduring drought, plague, and hostility, they unravel complicated roles among people 800 years removed, until Walker finds his own past and future entwined. Vick's enthralling tale of vanished Arizona cliff dwellers reveals modern Hopi ties to this ancient culture, continuing in sequels *Walker's Journey Home* and *Tag Against Time.* Other time warp encounters with relatives—and oneself—are listed in this chapter's Recommended Reading.

Romance

Time travel novels of all types often feature star-crossed lovers, for whom intense emotional connection is the powerful lure across time. In time travel romance, love is not merely one strand of a larger story but the abiding theme.

Perhaps more of a ghost fantasy, one of the first time romances is *The Sherwood Ring* by Elizabeth Marie Pope. In gothic romance tradition, its 1958 teenaged heroine, Peggy, is an orphan with nowhere to go but the upstate New York family mansion, where her preoccupied Uncle Enos lives. Lonely Peggy is visited by a succession of ghostly ancestors, each of whom relates a piece of colorful family history during the American Revolution, when they were plagued by roguish British spy Peaceable Sherwood. Their revelations lead Peggy to solve a 200-year-old mystery—and into the arms of her modern lordly English lover. Rather than sending Peggy directly into the past, Pope's charming, clever ghosts help her find her own place among recurring family patterns.

Richard Matheson's striking *Bid Time Return,* winner of the 1976 World Fantasy Award, was retitled *Somewhere in Time* to match Matheson's screenplay of the 1980 movie with Christopher Reeve and Jane Seymour. Stricken with a brain tumor at age 36, writer Richard Collier has just a few months to live. Determined to travel, Richard is drawn to majestic old Hotel del Coronado, on the southern California coast. In its museum, he falls in love with the photograph of famous actress Elise McKenna, who performed there in 1896. Like Si Morley in Finney's *Time and Again,* written just five years previously, Richard uses self-hypnosis to move from 1971 to 1896, to meet Elise and win her love. Richard's journal records intense joy turning to tragedy, the blueprint for all impossible, bittersweet time romances to follow.

John Rowe Townsend brought time romance to young adult literature with *The Visitors,* entitled *The Xanadu Manuscript* in Britain. Townsend reverses custom by sending his time travelers from future 2149 to present 1970s Cambridge, England. Only after falling in love does Katherine learn it would be lethal to stay with Ben. Since her future technology erases all traces of time travelers who return home, Ben will not remember her once she is gone. The tender romance occurs offstage, seen through the eyes of Ben's sensitive brother John, who manages to write about the mysterious visitors before his memory fades.

Prolific YA novelist Caroline B. Cooney's ambitious time romance trilogy opens in *Both Sides of Time,* in which teenaged Annie Lockwood is bruised by her father's extramarital affair and fed up with her unromantic boyfriend Sean. Her dreams of romance swirl her back 100 years to 1895, where she meets truly romantic hero Strat, heir to the Stratton mansion, a ruin in her time. Embroiled in both a murder and a romantic triangle with Strat, Annie reluctantly goes home, only to return in *Out of Time,* rescuing Strat from an insane asylum where he is imprisoned for believing that Annie travels in time. Forced once more to part, Annie and Strat will doubtless meet again in *Prisoner of Time.* Cooney mixes Annie's serious concerns about the meaning of love and the repression of women with a tongue-in-cheek tone. Among her lively cast are characters who either relish or flout standard gothic roles.

Two best-selling adult romance writers have produced time romances with more depth and colorful historic detail than expected from this unfairly maligned genre. In Jude Deveraux's sensual novel *A Knight in Shining Armor,* modern American damsel in distress Dougless, deserted without resources by her fiancé on a tour of England, meets a knight emerging from his 1564 grave in response to her weeping. Diana Gabaldon's epic series *Outlander, Dragonfly in Amber, Voyager,* and *Drums of Autumn* follows spirited World War II nurse Claire Randall and her heart-stoppingly heroic Highland lover, Jamie Fraser, in 1743 Scotland. Gabaldon has it all: expert historical research, romantic thrills, authentic characters, a brilliant landscape. Separated by centuries, will Claire reunite with her husband, Frank, in 1945? These fantastical love stories are savored by older teens.

In infinite varieties of time fantasy, from physics to philosophy, from paradox to history, from healing to romance, young adult readers may travel to the otherworld of time.

Recommended Reading

(* denotes title mentioned in text; other titles are additional)

Pioneers of Time Travel Literature

Bellamy, Edward. *Looking Backward 2000–1887.* Boston: Houghton Mifflin, 1926, © 1987.

Kipling, Rudyard. *Puck Series. 2 vols. New York: Viking Penguin.
    Vol. 1: *Puck of Pook's Hill.* 1987, © 1906.
    Vol. 2: *Rewards & Fairies.* 1991, © 1910.

Masefield, John. *Kay Harker Series. 2 vols. New York: Macmillan.
    Vol. 1: *The Midnight Folk.* 1932.
    Vol. 2: *The Box of Delights.* Abridged by Patricia Crampton. Illus. Faith Jacques. 1984, © 1935.

Nesbit, E. *The Story of the Amulet.* New York: Viking Penguin, 1986, © 1906.

Twain, Mark. *A Connecticut Yankee in King Arthur's Court.* New York: W. W. Norton, 1982, © 1889.

Uttley, Alison. *A Traveler in Time.* New York: Viking Penguin, 1977, © 1939.

Wells, H.G. *The Time Machine.* Cambridge, Mass.: Robert Bentley, Inc., 1973, © 1891.

Reflections: Exploring Time's Mystery

The Nature of Time

Bradbury, Ray. *The Halloween Tree*. New York: Knopf, 1972.

DuMaurier, Daphne. *The House on the Strand*. New York: Doubleday, 1969.

Garner, Alan. **Red Shift*. New York: Macmillan, 1973.

Hidden Turnings: A Collection of Stories Through Time and Space. Ed. Diana Wynne Jones. New York: Greenwillow, 1990.

Lightman, Alan P. **Einstein's Dreams*. New York: Pantheon, 1993.

Lively, Penelope. *The House in Norham Gardens*. New York: Dutton, 1974.

Vonnegut, Kurt. *Slaughterhouse-Five*. 25th Anniversary Edition. New York: Delacorte, 1994, © 1969.

Wesley, Mary. *Haphazard House*. New York: Overlook, 1993.

Discovering History

Bethancourt, T. Ernesto. Richie Gilroy/Matty Owen Series. 2 vols. New York: Holiday House.

Vol. 1: *Tune in Yesterday*. 1978.

Vol. 2: *The Tomorrow Connection*. 1984.

Bond, Nancy. **Another Shore*. New York: Margaret K. McElderry, 1988.

Brock, Darryl. *If I Never Get Back*. New York: Crown, 1990.

Dexter, Catherine. *Mazemaker*. New York: Morrow, 1989.

Finney, Jack. **About Time: Twelve Stories*. New York: Simon & Schuster, 1986.

———. **Simon Morley Series*. 2 vols. New York: Simon & Schuster.

Vol. 1: *Time and Again*. 1995, © 1970.

Vol. 2: *From Time to Time*. 1995.

Goldstein, Lisa. *The Dream Years*. New York: Bantam, 1985.

Goodwin, Marie D. *Where the Towers Pierce the Sky*. New York: Macmillan, 1989.

MacAvoy, R. A. **The Book of Kells*. New York: Bantam, 1985.

Melling, O. R. *The Druid's Tune*. Dublin: O'Brien Press, rev. ed. 1992, © 1983; U.S. Dist. Chester Springs, Penn.: Dufour Editions.

Service, Pamela F. *The Reluctant God*. New York: Atheneum, 1988.

Simpson, George Gaylord. *The Dechronization of Sam Magruder*. New York: St. Martin's, 1996.

Willis, Connie. **Doomsday Book*. New York: Bantam, 1992.

———. **Fire Watch*. New York: Bluejay, 1985.

———. **To Say Nothing of the Dog*. New York: Bantam, 1997.

Science Fiction

Benford, Gregory. *Timescape*. New York: Bantam, 1992, © 1980.

Bradbury, Ray. *R is for Rocket*. New York: Doubleday, 1962, reprint Buccaneer Books, 1994.

———. *Dinosaur Tales*. New York: Bantam, 1983.

Chetwin, Grace. *Collidescope*. New York: Bradbury, 1990.

Jones, Diana Wynne. *A Tale of Time City*. New York: Greenwillow, 1987.

Leigh, Stephen. *Ray Bradbury Presents: Dinosaur World* Series. 6 vols. New York: Avon.

Vol. 1: *Dinosaur World*. 1992.

Vol. 2: *Dinosaur Planet*. 1993.

Vol. 3: *Dinosaur Samurai*. 1993.

Vol. 4: *Dinosaur Warriors*. 1994.

Vol. 5: *Dinosaur Empire*. 1995.

Vol. 6: *Dinosaur Conquest*. 1995.

L'Engle, Madeleine. *Time Trilogy*. 3 vols. New York: Farrar, Straus & Giroux.

Vol. 1: *A Wrinkle in Time*. 1962.

Vol. 2: *A Wind in the Door*. 1973.

Vol. 3: *A Swiftly Tilting Planet*. 1978.

Service, Pamela F. *Storm at the Edge of Time*. New York: Walker, 1994.

Silverberg, Robert. *Letters from Atlantis*. Illus. Robert Gould. New York: Atheneum, 1990.

Sleator, William. *Strange Attractors*. New York: Dutton, 1990.

Wilson, Robert Charles. *A Bridge of Years*. New York: Doubleday, 1991.

Resolutions: Change and Growth through Time

Changing Outcomes

Appel, Allen. *Alex Balfour Series*. 3 vols. Vols. 1–2: New York: Carroll & Graf. Vol. 3: New York: Doubleday.

Vol. 1: *Time After Time*. 1985.

Vol. 2: *Twice Upon a Time*. 1988.

Vol. 3: *Till the End of Time*. 1990.

Avi. *Something Upstairs: A Tale of Ghosts*. New York: Orchard, 1988.

Brennert, Alan. *Time and Chance*. New York: Tor, 1990.

Cameron, Eleanor. *The Court of the Stone Children*. Magnolia, Mass.: Peter Smith, 1994, © 1973.

Card, Orson Scott. *Pastwatch: The Redemption of Christopher Columbus*. New York: Tor, 1996.

Cochran, Molly, and Warren Murphy. *World Without End*. New York: Tor, 1996.

Conrad, Pam. Zoe Series. 2 vols. New York: HarperCollins.

    Vol. 1: *Stonewords: A Ghost Story*. 1990.

    Vol. 2: *Zoe Rising*. 1996.

Cross, Gilbert B. *A Witch Across Time*. New York: Atheneum, 1990.

Dunlop, Eileen. *The Valley of Deer*. New York: Holiday House, 1989.

Hautman, Pete. *Mr. Was*. New York: Simon & Schuster, 1996.

James, J. Alison. *Sing for a Gentle Rain*. New York: Atheneum, 1990.

Jones, Diana Wynne. *Aunt Maria*. New York: Greenwillow, 1991.

Jordan, Sherryl. *The Juniper Game*. New York: Scholastic, 1991.

———. *A Time of Darkness*. New York: Scholastic, 1990.

Koontz, Dean R. *Lightning*. New York: Putnam, 1988.

L'Engle, Madeleine. *An Acceptable Time*. New York: Farrar, Straus & Giroux, 1989.

MacLeod, Charlotte. *The Curse of the Giant Hogweed*. New York: Doubleday, 1985.

Mowry, Jess. *Ghost Train*. New York: Henry Holt, 1996.

Park, Ruth. *Playing Beatie Bow*. New York: Atheneum, 1982.

Paulsen, Gary. *Canyons*. New York: Delacorte, 1990.

Peck, Richard. *Voices After Midnight*. New York: Delacorte, 1989.

Reiss, Kathryn. *Miranda Browne Series. 2 vols. San Diego: Harcourt Brace.

    Vol. 1: *Time Windows*. 1991.

    Vol. 2: *Pale Phoenix*. 1994.

Service, Pamela F. *Vision Quest*. New York: Macmillan, 1989.

Shapiro, Stanley. *A Time to Remember*. New York: Random House, 1986.

Staub, Wendy Corsi. *Witch Hunt*. New York: Kensington Publishing/ Z*FAVE, 1995.

Westall, Robert. *The Devil on the Road*. New York: Greenwillow, 1979.

Wiseman, David. *Jeremy Visick*. Boston: Houghton Mifflin, 1981.

Healing Lessons

Barron, T. A. *The Ancient One*. New York: Philomel, 1992.

Bond, Nancy. *A String in the Harp*. New York: Atheneum, 1976.

Cameron, Eleanor. *Beyond Silence*. New York: Dutton, 1980.

Dunlop, Eileen. *Elizabeth, Elizabeth*. (Published in U.K. as *Robinsheugh*.) New York: Holt, 1977.

Farmer, Penelope. *Charlotte Sometimes*. Magnolia, Mass.: Peter Smith, 1993, © 1969.

Griffin, Peni R. *Switching Well*. New York: Margaret K. McElderry, 1993.

Hoppe, Joanne. *Dream Spinner*. New York: Morrow, 1992.

Lawson, Julie. *White Jade Tiger*. Victoria, B.C., Canada: Beach Holme Publishing, 1993; U.S. Dist. Niagara Falls, N.Y.: General Distribution Services.

L'Engle, Madeleine. *Many Waters*. New York: Farrar, Straus, & Giroux, 1986.

Levin, Betty. *Mercy's Mill*. New York: Greenwillow, 1992.

Mayne, William. *A Game of Dark*. New York: Dutton, 1971.

Mazer, Norma Fox. *Saturday, the Twelfth of October*. New York: Delacorte, 1975.

Nolan, Han. *If I Should Die Before I Wake*. San Diego: Harcourt Brace, 1994.

Pearce, Philippa. *Tom's Midnight Garden*. Illus. Susan Einzig. Harper-Collins, 1992, © 1958.

Peel, John. *Uptime Downtime*. New York: Simon & Schuster, 1992.

Peyton, K. M. *A Pattern of Roses*. New York: Crowell, 1973.

Walsh, Jill Paton. *A Chance Child*. New York: Farrar, Straus, & Giroux, 1991, © 1978.

Westall, Robert. *The Wind Eye*. New York: Greenwillow, 1977.

Willis, Connie. *Lincoln's Dreams*. New York: Bantam, 1987.

Yolen, Jane. *The Devil's Arithmetic*. New York: Viking, 1988.

Healing through Reincarnation or Repetition

Anderson, Margaret. *The Druid's Gift*. New York: Knopf, 1989.

Carkeet, David. *I Been There Before*. New York: Harper, 1985.

Dunlop, Eileen. *Clementina*. New York: Holiday House, 1987.

———. *The Maze Stone*. New York: Coward, 1983.

Naylor, Phyllis Reynolds. *York Trilogy*. 3 vols. New York: Atheneum.
   Vol. 1: *Shadows on the Wall*. 1980.
   Vol. 2: *Faces in the Water*. 1981.
   Vol. 3: *Footprints at the Window*. 1981.

Reiss, Kathryn. *Dreadful Sorry*. San Diego: Harcourt Brace, 1993.

Healing through Meeting Ancestors

Adkins, Jan. *A Storm Without Rain*. New York: Morrow, 1993.

Aiken, Joan. *The Shadow Guests*. New York: Delacorte, 1980.

Butler, Octavia. *Kindred*. New York: Doubleday, 1979.

Curry, Jane Louise. *Me, Myself, and I: A Tale of Time Travel*. New York: Margaret K. McElderry, 1987.

Eubank, Judith. *Crossover*. New York: Carroll & Graf, 1992.

Griffin, Peni. *A Dig in Time*. New York: Margaret K. McElderry, 1991.

Hurmence, Belinda. *A Girl Called Boy*. Boston: Houghton Mifflin, 1982.

Pascal, Francine. *Hangin' Out With Cici*. New York: Viking Penguin, 1991, © 1977.

Pearson, Kit. *A Handful of Time*. New York: Viking, 1988.

Sleator, William. *The Green Futures of Tycho*. Magnolia, Mass.: Peter Smith, 1995, © 1981.

Vick, Helen Hughes. *Walker Series. 3 vols. Vols. 1–2: Tucson, Ariz.:
    Harbinger House. Vol. 3: Boulder, Colo.: Roberts Rinehart.
    Vol. 1: *Walker of Time*. 1993.
    Vol. 2: *Walker's Journey Home*. 1995.
    Vol. 3: *Tag Against Time*. 1996.
Voigt, Cynthia. *Building Blocks*. New York: Atheneum, 1984.
Wilde, Nicholas. *Down Came a Blackbird*. New York: Henry Holt, 1992.

Romance

Cooney, Caroline B. *Annie Lockwood Series. 3 vols. New York: Dela-
    corte.
    Vol. 1: *Both Sides of Time* 1995.
    Vol. 2: *Out of Time*. 1996.
    Vol. 3: *Prisoner of Time*. Forthcoming in 1998.
Deveraux, Jude. *A Knight in Shining Armor*. New York: Pocket Books,
    1989.
Gabaldon, Diana. *Claire Randall Series. 4 vols. New York: Delacorte.
    Vol. 1: *Outlander*. 1991.
    Vol. 2: *A Dragonfly in Amber*. 1992.
    Vol. 3: *Voyager*. 1994.
    Vol. 4: *Drums of Autumn*. 1997.
Marzollo, Jean. *Halfway Down Paddy Lane*. New York: Dial, 1981.
    Paperback title *Out of Time, Into Love*. New York: Scholastic, 1984.
Matheson, Richard. *Bid Time Return*. Title change: *Somewhere in
    Time*. Edition includes *What Dreams May Come: Two Novels of Love
    and Fantasy*. Los Angeles: DreamPress, 1991, © 1975.
Pope, Elizabeth Marie. *The Sherwood Ring*. Viking Penguin, 1992, © 1958.
Schurfranz, Vivian. *Another Time, Another Love*. New York: Scholastic,
    1995.
Townsend, John Rowe. *The Visitors*. (U.K. title: *The Xanadu Manu-
    script*.) New York: Lippincott, 1977.

Selected Bibliography

*(Note: For Primary Fiction Sources, see starred titles in Chapter 7 Recom-
mended Reading List)*

Secondary Sources

Boardman, Kathleen A. "*Red Shift*." In *Beacham's Guide to Literature
    for Young Adults*. Vol. 5. Ed. Kirk H. Beetz. Washington, D.C.:
    Beacham Publishing, 1991, 2537–45.

Cameron, Eleanor. *The Seed and the Vision: On the Writing and Appreciation of Children's Books*. New York: Dutton, 1993.

Clute, John. *Science Fiction: The Illustrated Encyclopedia*. New York: Dorling Kindersley, 1995.

Elleman, Barbara. "A Game of Catch." *Booklist* (15 November 1985): 494–96.

Innocence and Experience: Essays and Conversations on Children's Literature. Comp. and ed. Barbara Harrison and Gregory Maguire. New York: Lothrop, Lee & Shepard, 1987.

MacRae, Cathi. "Timescapes in Cambridge." *Wilson Library Bulletin* (November 1989): 22–28.

Smith, Karen Patricia. "The English Psychological Fantasy Novel: A Bequest of Time." *School Library Journal* (May 1985): 44–45.

Travelers in Time: Past, Present, and to Come, Children's Literature New England, preface by Barbara Harrison. Proceedings of the summer institute at Newnham College, Cambridge University, England, 6–12 August 1989. Cambridge, U.K.: Green Bay Publications, 1990.

Notes and References

Preface: *Young Adults and Fantasy*

1. Diana Tixier Herald, "Fantasy Novels for Young Adults" speech, Young Adult Literature Conference, Denver, 27 April 1991.

1. *Defining Fantasy: The Impossible Made Real*

1. Terri Windling, introduction to *The Faces of Fantasy* (New York: Tor, 1996), 24; hereafter cited in text.
2. Orson Scott Card, "Fantasy Genre," speech, Genrecon, American Library Association Conference, Atlanta, 28 June 1991; hereafter cited in text.
3. Orson Scott Card, introduction to *Speaker for the Dead,* rev. ed. (New York: Tor, 1994), xvi–xvii.
4. Tamora Pierce, "Fantasy: Why Kids Read It, Why Kids Need It," *School Library Journal* (October 1993): 50–51; hereafter cited in text.
5. Ruth Nadelman Lynn, *Fantasy Literature for Children and Young Adults,* 4th ed. (New Providence, N.J.: R. R. Bowker, 1995), xliii; hereafter cited in text.
6. Betty Rosenberg and Diana Tixier Herald, *Genreflecting: A Guide to Reading Interests in Genre Fiction,* 3d ed. (Englewood, Colo.: Libraries Unlimited, 1991), 242–43.
7. Emma Bull, "Interpreting the World," *Locus* (April 1992): 4.
8. David Pringle, *Modern Fantasy: The Hundred Best Novels* (New York: Peter Bedrick Books, 1989), 13, 18; hereafter cited in text.
9. Marshall B. Tymn, Kenneth J. Zahorski, and Robert H. Boyer, *Fantasy Literature: A Core Collection and Reference Guide* (New Providence, N.J.: R. R. Bowker, 1979), 3–4.
10. Ann Swinfen, *In Defence of Fantasy: A Study of the Genre in English and American Literature Since 1945* (London: Routledge & Kegan Paul, 1984), 5.
11. Sheila Egoff, *Worlds Within: Children's Fantasy from the Middle Ages to Today* (Chicago: American Library Association, 1988), 19.

12.   Baird Searles, Beth Meacham, and Michael Franklin, *A Reader's Guide to Fantasy* (New York: Facts on File, 1982), 171.

13.   Ursula K. Le Guin, "From Elfland to Poughkeepsie," in *The Language of the Night: Essays on Fantasy and Science Fiction* (New York: Putnam/Perigee, 1979), 84, 93.

14.   Susan Cooper, "Fantasy in the Real World," *Horn Book* (May/June 1990): 305, 308–9, 314.

15.   Jane Yolen, "The Mask on the Lapel" and "Tough Magic," in Yolen, *Touch Magic: Fantasy, Faerie and Folklore in the Literature of Childhood* (New York: Philomel, 1981), 64, 73.

16.   Cathi Dunn MacRae, interview with Meredith Ann Pierce, Micanopy, Florida, 17 October 1994.

17.   Eleanor Cameron, "The Pleasures and Problems of Time Fantasy," in *The Seed and the Vision: On the Writing and Appreciation of Children's Books* (New York: Dutton, 1993), 186.

18.   Natalie Babbitt, "The Purposes of Fantasy," in *Innocence and Experience: Essays and Conversations on Children's Literature,* comp. and ed. Barbara Harrison and Gregory Maguire (New York: Lothrop, Lee & Shepard, 1987), 174, 176.

19.   Diana Paxson, *The Faces of Fantasy* (New York: Tor, 1996), 204; hereafter cited in text as *Faces*.

20.   "Exploring Alternative Worlds," *Publishers Weekly* (2 August 1993): 54.

21.   John Clute and John Grant, *The Encyclopedia of Fantasy* (New York: St. Martin's Press, 1997), viii.

22.   Wayne Douglas Barlowe, *Barlowe's Guide to Fantasy* (New York: HarperPrism, 1996), ix.

2. Alternate Worlds: Beyond the Walls of the World

1.   J. R. R. Tolkien, "On Fairy-stories," in *Tree and Leaf* (London: Allen & Unwin, 1964), 50; hereafter cited in text as *Tree*.

2.   Ann Swinfen, *In Defence of Fantasy: A Study of the Genre in English and American Literature Since 1945* (London: Routledge & Kegan Paul, 1984), 3; hereafter cited in text.

3.   Kenneth L. Donelson and Alleen Pace Nilsen, *Literature for Today's Young Adults,* 3d ed. (Glenview, Ill.: Scott, Foresman, 1989), 187.

4.   Lin Carter, introduction to William Morris, *The Wood Beyond the World* (1895; reprint, New York: Ballantine, 1969), xii; hereafter cited in text as Carter or Morris (depending on whether the introduction or the work is being cited).

5.   Baird Searles, Beth Meacham, and Michael Franklin, *A Reader's Guide to Fantasy* (New York: Facts on File, 1982), 40; hereafter cited in text.

6.	David Pringle, *Modern Fantasy: The Hundred Best Novels* (New York: Peter Bedrick Books, 1989), 27; hereafter cited in text.

7.	L. Sprague de Camp, "The Miscast Barbarian: Robert E. Howard," in de Camp, *Literary Swordsmen and Sorcerers: The Makers of Heroic Fantasy* (Sauk City, Wis.: Arkham House, 1976), 158; hereafter cited in text as "Barbarian."

8.	Marshall B. Tymn, Kenneth J. Zahorski, and Robert H. Boyer, *Fantasy Literature: A Core Collection and Reference Guide* (New Providence, N.J.: R. R. Bowker, 1979), 22–23; hereafter cited in text.

9.	David G. Hartwell, "Dollars and Dragons: The Truth about Fantasy," *New York Times Book Review* (29 April 1990): 1.

10.	Donald L. Lawler, "Tolkien, John Ronald Reuel," in *Twentieth Century Science Fiction Writers,* 3d ed., ed. Noelle Watson and Paul E. Schellinger (Chicago: St. James Press, 1991), 800; hereafter cited in text.

11.	Robin McKinley, "J. R. R. Tolkien," in *Writers for Children: Critical Studies of Major Authors Since the Seventeenth Century,* ed. Jane Bingham (New York: Scribner's, 1988), 562; hereafter cited in text.

12.	Humphrey Carpenter, *Tolkien: A Biography* (New York: Ballantine, 1978, ©1977), 197; hereafter cited in text.

13.	L. Sprague de Camp, "Merlin in Tweeds: J. R. R. Tolkien," in de Camp, *Literary Swordsmen and Sorcerers: The Makers of Heroic Fantasy* (Sauk City, Wis.: Arkham House, 1976), 218; hereafter cited in text as "Merlin."

14.	Anne E. Niemark, *Myth Maker: J. R. R. Tolkien* (San Diego: Harcourt Brace, 1996), 73.

15.	David R. Collins, *J. R. R. Tolkien: Master of Fantasy* (Minneapolis: Lerner, 1992), 101.

16.	Sheila A. Egoff, "The New Fantasy," in Egoff, *Thursday's Child: Trends and Patterns in Contemporary Children's Literature* (Chicago: American Library Association, 1981), 81–82; hereafter cited in text.

17.	Diana Paxson, "The Tolkien Tradition," *Mythlore* 39 (Summer 1984): 23; hereafter cited in text as Paxson 1984.

18.	Mary J. Du Mont, "Images of Women in Young Adult Science Fiction and Fantasy 1970, 1980, and 1990: A Comparative Content Analysis," *Voice of Youth Advocates* (April 1993): 13–14.

19.	Ursula K. Le Guin, "Dreams Must Explain Themselves," in Le Guin, *The Language of the Night: Essays on Fantasy and Science Fiction* (New York: Putnam's, 1979), 49–50; hereafter cited in text as "Dreams."

20.	Rosemary Herbert, "Le Guin, Ursula K.," in *Twentieth Century Science Fiction Writers,* 3d. ed., ed. Noelle Watson and Paul E. Schellinger (Chicago: St. James Press, 1991), 477; hereafter cited in text.

21.	John Clute and John Grant, *Encyclopedia of Fantasy* (New York: St. Martin's Press, 1997), 573, 572; hereafter cited in text.

22.   Le Guin, *The Tombs of Atuan* (New York: Atheneum, 1971), 106.

23.   Paul Heins, *Horn Book* (October 1971): 490.

24.   Margery Fisher, "Things Counter, Original, Spare, Strange," *Growing Point* (June 1972): 1972–73.

25.   Millicent Lenz, "Ursula K. Le Guin's *The Tombs of Atuan*: Moving toward Completion," in *The Phoenix Award of the Children's Literature Association 1990–1994,* ed. Alethea Helbig and Agnes Perkins (Lanham, Md.: Scarecrow Press, 1996), 96; hereafter cited in text.

26.   Le Guin, *The Farthest Shore* (New York: Atheneum, 1972), 122; hereafter cited in text as *Shore*.

27.   Ann Welton, "Earthsea Revisited: *Tehanu* and Feminism," *Voice of Youth Advocates* (April 1991): 15; hereafter cited in text.

28.   Le Guin, "The Last Book of Earthsea," *Locus* (January 1990): 5.

29.   Le Guin, *Tehanu: The Last Book of Earthsea* (New York: Bantam, 1991, © 1990), 34; hereafter cited in text as *Tehanu*.

30.   Eleanor Cameron, "High Fantasy: *A Wizard of Earthsea*," *Horn Book* (April 1971): 129–38.

31.   Robin McKinley, "The Woman Wizard's Triumph," *New York Times Book Review* (20 May 1990): 38.

32.   Le Guin, *Ursula Kroeber Interviews Ursula K. Le Guin,* pamphlet (New York: Atheneum, 1989).

33.   "Brooks, Terry," in *Something About the Author,* vol. 60, ed. Agnes Garrett and Helga P. McCue (Detroit: Gale Research, 1990), 15; hereafter cited in text as *SATA*.

34.   Cathi Dunn MacRae, interview with Terry Brooks, Boulder, Colorado, 7 May 1994. All further personal quotes from Brooks are from this interview, unless otherwise cited.

35.   Robert Dahlin, "Ballantine and Random House Join Their Imaginations to Publish a Fantasy of Epic Size," *Publishers Weekly* (3 January 1977): 38; hereafter cited in text.

36.   Louise J. Winters, "Brooks, Terry," in *Twentieth Century Young Adult Writers,* ed. Laura Standley Berger (Detroit: St. James Press, 1994), 80; hereafter cited in text.

37.   Daniel Francisco, "An Interview with Terry Brooks," in Corey Cole and Lori Cole, *Shannara: The Official Strategy Guide* (Rocklin, Calif.: Prima Publishing, 1996), 178; hereafter cited in text.

38.   Emily Narvaes, "Author and Fantasist Promotes Book in Boulder," *The Boulder, Colorado Sunday Camera* (22 May 1994): hereafter cited in text.

39.   *The Faces of Fantasy,* photographs by Patti Perret (New York: Tor, 1996), 212.

40.   Marilyn Achiron and Nick Gallo, "Laying Down the Law," *People* (10 May 1993): 54; hereafter cited in text.

41.   Joe Wilson, "Swords, Sorcery and Space Opera," *USA Today* (29 February 1996).

42.   Brooks, introduction to Philip Pullman, *The Golden Compass* (New York: Ballantine/Del Rey, 1997, © 1995), n.p.

43.   Brooks, *The Sword of Shannara* (New York: Ballantine/ Del Rey, 1978, © 1977), 18; hereafter cited in text as *Sword*.

44.   Brooks, *The Tangle Box* (New York: Ballantine/Del Rey, 1994), 42; hereafter cited in text as *Tangle*.

45.   Frank Herbert, "Some Arthur, Some Tolkien," *New York Times Book Review* (10 April 1977): 15, 25; hereafter cited in text.

46.   *Choice* (July/August 1977): 678.

47.   *Saturday Review* (28 May 1977): 30.

48.   Christine Watson, *"The Sword of Shannara,"* in *Survey of Modern Fantasy Literature,* vol. 4, ed. Frank N. Magill (Englewood Cliffs, N.J.: Salem Press, 1983), 1867; hereafter cited in text.

49.   *Library Journal* (15 June 1982): 1244.

50.   *Booklist* (January 1982): 1282.

51.   Brooks, *The Wishsong of Shannara* (New York: Ballantine/ Del Rey, 1985), 2; hereafter cited in text as *Wishsong*.

52.   *School Library Journal* (August 1985): 85.

53.   W. Keith McCoy, *Voice of Youth Advocates* (December 1985): 323.

54.   Gene LaFaille, *Wilson Library Bulletin* (January 1991): 115.

55.   Barbara A. Lynn, *School Library Journal* (September 1990): 266.

56.   Nancy Choice, *Voice of Youth Advocates* (October 1990): 224.

57.   Brooks, *The Druid of Shannara* (New York: Ballantine/Del Rey, 1991), 71; hereafter cited in text as *Druid*.

58.   Choice, *Voice of Youth Advocates* (October 1991): 237.

59.   Brooks, *The Elf Queen of Shannara* (New York: Ballantine/Del Rey, 1992), 106; hereafter cited in text as *Elf Queen*.

60.   *Library Journal* (15 February 1992): 200.

61.   John O. Christensen, *Voice of Youth Advocates* (August 1992): 172.

62.   *Publishers Weekly* (20 December 1991): 68.

63.   Brooks, *The Talismans of Shannara* (New York: Ballantine/Del Rey, 1993), 406; hereafter cited in text as *Talismans*.

64.   *Publishers Weekly* (29 March 1993): 39.

65.   *Library Journal* (15 February 1993): 196.

66.   Roland Green, *Booklist* (1 January 1993): 770.

67.   Brooks, *The First King of Shannara* (New York: Ballantine/ Del Rey, 1996), 8.

68.   Brenda Moses-Allen, *Voice of Youth Advocates* (October 1996): 216.

69.   *Publishers Weekly* (25 March 1996): 66.

70.   Brooks, *Magic Kingdom for Sale—Sold!* (New York: Ballantine/ Del Rey, 1986), 19.

71. *Booklist* (1 March 1986): 913.

72. *Library Journal* (15 April 1986): 98.

73. Brooks, *The Black Unicorn* (New York: Ballantine/Del Rey, 1987), 260; hereafter cited in text as *Unicorn.*

74. *Booklist* (15 September 1987): 90.

75. *Library Journal* (15 October 1987): 95.

76. *Publishers Weekly* (25 September 1987): 98.

77. *Booklist* (1 September 1988): 3.

78. Ann Welton, *Voice of Youth Advocates* (April 1989): 40.

79. *Publishers Weekly* (4 April 1994): 62.

80. Ruth Dishnow Cox, *Voice of Youth Advocates* (August 1994): 154.

81. Brooks, *Witches' Brew* (New York: Ballantine/Del Rey, 1995), 43.

82. *Booklist* (15 April 1995): 1484.

83. *Publishers Weekly* (20 February 1995): 199.

84. Brooks, *Hook* (New York: Ballantine/Ivy, 1992, © 1991), 173; hereafter cited in text as *Hook.*

85. Suzanne Julian, *Voice of Youth Advocates* (June 1992): 106.

86. Brooks, "Imaginary Friends," in *Once Upon a Time: A Treasury of Modern Fairy Tales,* ed. Lester del Rey and Risa Kessler (New York: Ballantine/Del Rey, 1991), 37; hereafter cited in text as "Friends."

87. Ray Olson, *Booklist* (July 1997): 1773.

88. *Kirkus Reviews* (15 July 1997): 1072.

89. *Publishers Weekly* (28 July 1997): 58.

90. Charlotte Spivack, *Merlin's Daughters: Contemporary Women Writers of Fantasy* (Westport, Conn.: Greenwood Press, 1987), 124–25.

91. Donna R. White, "McKillip, Patricia A.," in *Twentieth Century Young Adult Writers,* ed. Laura Standley Berger, 1st ed. (Detroit: St. James Press, 1994), 442.

92. Patricia A. McKillip, "Moving Forward," *Locus* (August 1992): 69; hereafter cited in text as "Moving."

93. Robin McKinley, "Newbery Medal Acceptance," *Horn Book* (July/August 1985): 399; hereafter cited in text as "Newbery."

94. "McKinley, Robin," in *Authors and Artists for Young Adults,* vol. 4, ed. Agnes Garrett and Helga P. McCue (Detroit: Gale Research, 1990), 197; hereafter cited in text as *AAYA.*

95. Robin McKinley, *The Blue Sword* (New York: Greenwillow, 1982), 73; hereafter cited in text as *Blue Sword.*

96. Robin McKinley, *The Hero and the Crown* (New York: Greenwillow, 1984), 174.

97. Lyle Black Smythers, *School Library Journal* (October 1984): 169.

98. Anna E. Altmann, "Welding Brass Tits on the Armor: An Examination of the Quest Metaphor in Robin McKinley's *The Hero and*

the Crown," *Children's Literature in Education* 23.3 (1992): 144; hereafter cited in text.

99.　Barbara Hambly, *The Ladies of Mandrigyn* (New York: Ballantine/Del Rey, 1984), 6–7; hereafter cited in text as *Ladies*.

100.　Hambly, *The Witches of Wenshar* (New York: Ballantine/Del Rey, 1987), 154.

101.　*Booklist* (1 September 1987): 31.

102.　Hambly, *The Dark Hand of Magic* (New York: Ballantine/Del Rey, 1990), 293; hereafter cited in text as *Dark Hand.*

103.　*Horn Book* (May 1986): 333.

104.　Sally Estes, *Booklist* (1 and 15 June 1995): 1757.

105.　Sylvia C. Mitchell, *Voice of Youth Advocates* (April 1997): 46.

106.　Rebecca Taylor, Gayle Keresey, and Margaret Miles, "Interview with Mercedes," *Voice of Youth Advocates* (October 1992): 214; hereafter cited in text.

107.　Mercedes Lackey, in *Queen's Own: The Mercedes Lackey Fan Club* 5.1 (1991): 1.

108.　Mary K. Chelton, *Voice of Youth Advocates* (April 1992): 44.

109.　Margaret Miles, *Voice of Youth Advocates* (April 1992): 46.

110.　*Booklist* (1 September 1987): 31.

111.　Rebecca Sue Taylor, *Voice of Youth Advocates* (June 1991): 110.

112.　Louise J. Winters, "Lackey, Mercedes R.," in *Twentieth Century Young Adult Writers,* ed. Laura Standley Berger (Detroit: St. James Press, 1994), 370.

113.　Rebecca Taylor, *Voice of Youth Advocates* (December 1990): 299.

114.　*Publishers Weekly* (1 November 1993): 70.

115.　Donna L. Scanlon, *Voice of Youth Advocates* (August 1996): 170.

116.　Mary Arnold, *Voice of Youth Advocates* (August 1993): 159.

117.　Roland Green, *Booklist* (1 January 1995): 803.

118.　Don D'Ammassa, "Anthony, Piers," in *Twentieth Century Science Fiction Writers,* 3d ed., ed. Noelle Watson and Paul E. Schellinger (Chicago: St. James Press, 1991), 14.

119.　Libby Bergstrom, *Voice of Youth Advocates* (December 1993): 314.

120.　Michael Cule, "Eddings, David," in *Twentieth Century Science Fiction Writers,* 3d ed., ed. Noelle Watson and Paul E. Schellinger (Chicago: St. James Press, 1991), 233–34, hereafter cited in text.

121.　Roland Green, *Booklist* (1 March 1987): 947.

122.　Green, *Booklist* (15 February 1991): 1163.

123.　Gene LaFaille, *Wilson Library Bulletin* (May 1991): 129.

124.　Denice M. Thornhill, *Voice of Youth Advocates* (June 1992): 108.

125.　*Publishers Weekly* (2 August 1993): 66.

126.　David Eddings, author's note in *Belgarath the Sorcerer* (New York: Ballantine/Del Rey, 1995).

127.   Laura Staley, *Voice of Youth Advocates* (June 1990): 116.

128.   Catherine M. Dwyer, *Voice of Youth Advocates* (April 1993): 41.

129.   *Publishers Weekly* (17 October 1994): 67–68.

3. Magic Realism: Magic Here, There, and Everywhere

1.   Baird Searles, Beth Meacham, and Michael Franklin, *A Reader's Guide to Fantasy* (New York: Facts on File, 1982), 9; hereafter cited in text.

2.   Marshall B. Tymn, Kenneth J. Zahorski, and Robert H. Boyer, *Fantasy Literature: A Core Collection and Reference Guide* (New Providence, N.J.: R. R. Bowker, 1979), 121; hereafter cited in text.

3.   See fantasy questionnaire results in chapter 1.

4.   Alan Garner, *Elidor* (New York: Dell, 1993, © 1965), 42.

5.   Andre Norton, *Witch World* (New York: Ace, 1978, © 1963), 13.

6.   Cathi Dunn MacRae, interview with Barbara Hambly, Los Angeles, 15 March 1993. All further personal quotes from Hambly are from this interview unless otherwise cited.

7.   Barbara Hambly, "Barbara Hambly: Saved by the Ax," *Locus* (June 1986): 39.

8.   Donna Scanlon, *Voice of Youth Advocates* (April 1996): 44.

9.   Diana L. Paxson, "What a Piece of Work: An Appreciation of Barbara Hambly," Disclave Convention Program (Washington, D.C., 1988), n.p.; hereafter cited in text as Paxson 1988.

10.   Hambly, "The Man Who Loved His Craft: A Guidebook to the Mountains of Madness," in H. P. Lovecraft, *The Road to Madness: The Transition of H. P. Lovecraft* (New York: Ballantine/Del Rey, 1996), viii.

11.   Hambly, *The Time of the Dark* (New York: Ballantine/Del Rey, 1982), 18; hereafter cited in text as *Time*.

12.   Hambly, *The Rainbow Abyss* (New York: Ballantine/Del Rey, 1991), 17; hereafter cited in text as *Rainbow*.

13.   Hambly, *The Armies of Daylight* (New York: Ballantine/Del Rey, 1983), 22–23; hereafter cited in text as *Armies*.

14.   Hambly, *The Silent Tower* (New York: Ballantine/Del Rey, 1986), 12; hereafter cited in text as *Tower*.

15.   *Library Journal* (15 May 1982): 1014.

16.   *Library Journal* (15 March 1983): 603.

17.   *Booklist* (1 September 1983): 31.

18.   *Voice of Youth Advocates* (April 1997): 42.

19.   *Library Journal* (December 1986): 142.

20.   Hambly, *The Silicon Mage* (New York: Ballantine/Del Rey, 1988), 1; hereafter cited in text as *Silicon*.

21.   *Booklist* (15 April 1988): 1395.

22.   *Voice of Youth Advocates* (August 1993): 165.

23. *Publishers Weekly* (14 March 1994): 68.

24. *Voice of Youth Advocates* (February 1992): 382.

25. *Booklist* (1 February 1992): 1014.

26. Hambly, *The Walls of Air* (New York: Ballantine/Del Rey, 1983), 106; hereafter cited in text as *Walls*.

27. Hambly, *Dog Wizard* (New York: Ballantine/Del Rey, 1993), 94; hereafter cited in text as *Dog*.

28. David Pringle, *Modern Fantasy: The Hundred Best Novels* (New York: Peter Bedrick Books, 1989), 225.

29. *Booklist* (1 November 1988): 450.

30. Robert K. J. Killheffer, "Fantasy Charts New Realms," *Publishers Weekly* (16 June 1997): 35.

31. Rick Swan, *The Complete Guide to Role-Playing Games* (New York: St. Martin's, 1990), 28; hereafter cited in text.

32. Margaret Weis and Tracy Hickman, DRAGONLACE *Chronicles* (Lake Geneva, Wis.: TSR, Inc., 1988), ix.

33. *Voice of Youth Advocates* (August 1993): 166.

34. Christopher Schelling, quoted in Robert K. J. Killheffer, "Exploring Alternative Worlds," *Publishers Weekly* (2 August 1993): 55.

35. Quoted in William Dear, *The Dungeon Master: The Disappearance of James Dallas Egbert III* (Boston: Houghton Mifflin, 1984), 33.

4. Myth: Dreams of the Soul's Adventure

1. Curtis Church, foreword to James G. Frazer, *The Golden Bough: The Roots of Religion and Folklore* (1890; reprint, New York: Gramercy Books, 1993, © 1981), vii.

2. Charles Mills Gayley, *The Classic Myths in English Literature and Art,* rev. ed. (Boston: Ginn and Company, 1939, 1893, 1911), 431.

3. Alan W. Watts, *Myth and Ritual in Christianity* (New York: Vanguard, 1954), 7.

4. Stith Thompson, "Myth and Folktales," in *Myth: A Symposium,* ed. Thomas A. Sebeok (1955; reprint, Bloomington: Indiana University Press, 1970), 171.

5. Joseph Campbell, *The Hero with a Thousand Faces,* rev. ed. (Princeton, N.J.: Princeton University Press, 1968, 1949), 4; hereafter cited in text as Campbell 1968.

6. Campbell, with Bill Moyers, *The Power of Myth,* ed. Betty Sue Flowers (New York: Doubleday, 1988), 14; hereafter cited in text as Campbell 1988.

7. Robert Holdstock, *Mythago Wood* (New York: Arbor House, 1985), 96.

8. *Locus* (October 1988): 15.

9. *Booklist* (July 1994): 1928.

10.   *Twentieth Century Science Fiction Writers,* ed. Noelle Watson and Paul E. Schellinger (Detroit: St. James Press, 1991), 384.

11.   Jane Yolen, *Touch Magic: Fantasy, Faerie, and Folklore in the Literature of Childhood* (New York: Philomel, 1981), 14; hereafter cited in text as *Touch Magic.*

12.   Yolen, introduction to Yolen, *Favorite Folktales from Around the World* (New York: Pantheon, 1988), 11; hereafter cited in text as *Folktales.*

13.   Yolen, "The Modern Mythmakers," *Language Arts* (May 1976): 491; hereafter cited in text as "Mythmakers."

14.   Yolen, "The Creative Process: The Route to Story," *The New Advocate* (Summer 1991): 144; hereafter cited in text as "Route."

15.   Yolen, "An Empress of Thieves," *Horn Book* (November–December 1994): 702–3.

16.   Yolen, "Jane Yolen," in *Speaking for Ourselves: Autobiographical Sketches by Notable Authors of Books for Young Adults,* ed. Donald R. Gallo (Urbana, Ill.: National Council of Teachers of English, 1990), 225; hereafter cited in text as Gallo.

17.   "Jane Yolen," in *Authors and Artists for Young Adults,* vol. 4, ed. Agnes Garrett and Helga P. McCue (Detroit: Gale Research, 1990), 234; hereafter cited in text as *AAYA.*

18.   Yolen, "The Wood Between the Worlds," *Mythlore* 41 (Winter-Spring 1985): 6; hereafter cited in text as "Wood."

19.   "Yolen, Jane," in *Major Authors and Illustrators for Children and Young Adults,* ed. Joyce Nakamura and Laurie Collier (Detroit: Gale Research, 1992), 2529; hereafter cited in text as *Major Authors.*

20.   Jane Yolen, interview by Jim Roginski, in *Behind the Covers: Interviews with Authors and Illustrators of Books for Children and Young Adults* (Englewood, Colo.: Libraries Unlimited, 1985), 225; hereafter cited in text as Roginski.

21.   Yolen, *Guide to Writing for Children* (Boston: The Writer, Inc., 1989), vi; hereafter cited in text as *Guide.*

22.   Brooks Whitney, "Jane Yolen Sails Ocean of Ideas," *Denver Post* (13 June 1995): 2E.

23.   Yolen, *A Letter from Phoenix Farm* (Katonah, N.Y.: Richard C. Owen Publishers, 1992), 7.

24.   Yolen, *Here There Be Unicorns* (San Diego: Harcourt Brace, 1994), 88; hereafter cited in text as *Unicorns.*

25.   Donald R. Gallo, "What They Did on *Their* Summer Vacations," *English Journal* (September 1993): 93.

26.   *Jane Yolen,* Putnam Publishing Group publicity brochure, 1991, n.p.

27.   Yolen, *Here There Be Dragons* (San Diego: Harcourt Brace, 1993), 52.

28.   Yolen, "Traveling the Road to Ithaca," in *Innocence and Experience: Essays and Conversations on Children's Literature,* comp. and ed. Barbara Harrison and Gregory Maguire (New York: Lothrop, Lee & Shepard, 1987), 188.

29.   Cathi Dunn MacRae, interview with Jane Yolen, St. Andrews, Fife, Scotland, 29 April 1992; hereafter cited in text as "Interview."

30.   Yolen, "Old Herald," in Yolen, *Tales of Wonder* (New York: Schocken Books, 1983) 85.

31.   *Publisher's Weekly* (7 October 1983): 91.

32.   *SF and Fantasy Review* (March 1984): 36–37.

33.   *School Library Journal* (September 1989): 258.

34.   "An Interview with Jane Yolen," *Mythlore* 47 (Autumn 1986): 35.

35.   *Fantasy Review* (June 1985): 32–33.

36.   *Analog Science Fiction/Science Fact* (July 1985): 182–83.

37.   *Voice of Youth Advocates* (June 1985): 141.

38.   Yolen, *Sister Light, Sister Dark* (New York: Tor, 1988), 206.

39.   Yolen, *White Jenna* (New York: Tor, 1989), 78.

40.   *Locus* (August 1989): 19.

5. Legends: The Shaping of Heroes

1.   Caitlín Matthews, *The Elements of the Celtic Tradition* (Shaftesbury, Dorset, England: Element Books, 1989), 73; hereafter cited in text as C. Matthews.

2.   Jeffry Gantz, introduction to *The Mabinogion* (New York: Penguin, 1976), 10; hereafter cited in text.

3.   Morgan Llewelyn, *Bard: The Odyssey of the Irish* (Boston: Houghton Mifflin, 1984), 448; hereafter cited in text as *Bard*.

4.   Llewelyn, "Morgan Llewelyn on Irish myth and history and how they relate to her novels," Tor press release, New York, n.d.

5.   Marshall B. Tymn, Kenneth J. Zahorski, and Robert H. Boyer, *Fantasy Literature: A Core Collection and Reference Guide* (New York: R. R. Bowker, 1979), 40; hereafter cited in text.

6.   "Lloyd Alexander," in *Authors and Artists for Young Adults,* vol. 1, ed. Agnes Garrett and Helga P. McCue (Detroit: Gale Research, 1989), 22.

7.   Margery Fisher, "Special Review: *The Owl Service,*" *Growing Point* (September 1967), 950, quoted in *Major Authors and Illustrators for Children and Young Adults,* 1st ed., ed. Joyce Nakamura and Laurie Collier (Detroit: Gale Research, 1992), 925.

8.   Alan Garner, interview by Justin Wintle and Emma Fisher, in *The Pied Pipers: Interviews with the Influential Creators of Children's Literature* (London: Paddington Press, 1975), n.p., quoted in *Major Authors,* 925.

9.   Kathleen A. Boardman, *"Elidor,"* in *Beacham's Guide to Literature for Young Adults,* vol. 5, ed. Kirk H. Beetz (Washington, D.C.: Beacham Publishing, 1991), 2217.

10.   Alan Garner, "Alan Garner," in *Speaking for Ourselves: Autobiographical Sketches by Notable Authors of Books for Young Adults,* ed. Donald R. Gallo (Urbana, Ill.: National Council of Teachers of English, 1990), 73.

11.   Graham Phillips and Martin Keatman, *King Arthur: The True Story* (Douglas, Isle of Man, British Isles: Arrow Books, Ltd., 1993), 189; hereafter cited in text.

12.   Richard Wunderli, "Who Was Arthur? The Legendary Figure as He Emerged after Geoffrey of Monmouth," lecture for "The Many Realms of King Arthur Symposium," Boulder Public Library, Boulder, Colorado, 2 April 1995.

13.   Catherine M. Andronik, *Quest for a King: Searching for the Real King Arthur* (New York: Atheneum, 1989), 10; hereafter cited in text.

14.   Geoffrey Ashe, *The Discovery of King Arthur* (New York: Henry Holt, 1985), 13; hereafter cited in text.

15.   Tom Napierkowski, *"Le Morte D'Arthur:* A Defining Moment in Arthurian Legend," lecture for King Arthur Book Discussion Series, Boulder Public Library, Boulder, Colorado, 17 April 1995.

16.   Raymond H. Thompson, *The Return from Avalon: A Study of the Arthurian Legend in Modern Fiction* (Westport, Conn.: Greenwood Press, 1985), 17; hereafter cited in text.

17.   John Wright, "Celtic Heroic Precursors of Arthur and the Bardic Tradition Related to the Transmission of the Legend," lecture for "The Many Realms of King Arthur Symposium," Boulder Public Library, Boulder, Colorado, 2 April 1995.

18.   John Matthews, *The Elements of the Arthurian Tradition* (Shaftesbury, Dorset, England: Element Books, 1989), 10.

19.   "An Interview with Jane Yolen," *Mythlore* 47 (Autumn 1986): 36.

20.   Parke Godwin, *Firelord* (New York: Doubleday, 1980), 2; hereafter cited in text as *Firelord.*

21.   Rosemary Sutcliff, "Rosemary Sutcliff," in *Speaking for Ourselves: Autobiographical Sketches by Notable Authors of Books for Young Adults,* ed. Donald R. Gallo (Urbana, Ill.: National Council of Teachers of English, 1990), 207.

22.   Sutcliff, *The Lantern Bearers* (1959; reprint, New York: Farrar, Straus, & Giroux, 1994), 279.

23.   Sutcliff, *Sword at Sunset* (New York: Coward-McCann, 1963), viii.

24.   Charlotte Spivack, *Merlin's Daughters: Contemporary Women Writers of Fantasy* (Westport, Conn.: Greenwood Press, 1987), 101; hereafter cited in text.

25. *Voice of Youth Advocates* (December 1993): 314.

26. *Kirkus Reviews* (1 September 1993): 1153.

27. Persia Woolley, *Guinevere: The Legend in Autumn* (New York: Pocket Books, 1993), xv.

28. *Booklist* (15 May 1987): 1410.

29. Parke Godwin, "Finding Firelord," *Avalon to Camelot,* 1.4 (Summer 1984): 25.

30. Sylvia Townsend Warner, "The Story of the Book," in T. H. White, *The Book of Merlyn* (New York: Ace Books, 1987, © 1977), xx.

31. Marion Zimmer Bradley, *The Mists of Avalon* (New York: Ballantine, 1984), 788; hereafter cited in text as *Mists.*

32. Thelma J. Shinn, *Worlds Within Women: Myth and Mythmaking in Fantastic Literature by Women* (Westport, Conn.: Greenwood Press, 1986), 37.

33. Allison Barrett, "Women in the Arthurian Legend: A Growing Trend in Fantasy Literature," *Booklook* (Spring 1995), Boulder Public Library, Boulder, Colorado, 7; all other quotes are from this article.

34. Kathleen Marszycki, *Voice of Youth Advocates* (October 1996): 216.

35. H. Alan Stewart, "King Arthur in the Comics," *Avalon to Camelot* 2.1 (1986): 14.

36. *Christian Science Monitor* (6 February 1987): B5.

37. Jane Yolen, *Merlin's Booke* (Minneapolis: SteelDragon Press, 1986), xii; hereafter cited in text as *Merlin's.*

38. Judith L. Kellogg, "The Dynamics of Dumbing: The Case of Merlin," *The Lion and the Unicorn* 17 (1993): 70.

39. "Dream Weaver: An Interview with Jane Yolen," *Avalon to Camelot* 1.4, (1987): 21.

40. *School Library Journal* (December 1988): 120.

41. *Twentieth Century Science Fiction Writers,* ed. Noelle Watson and Paul E. Schellinger (Detroit: St. James Press, 1991), 158.

42. "A Note about the Author," in Robert Nathan, *The Elixir* (New York: Alfred A. Knopf, 1971), n.p.

43. David Pringle, *Modern Fantasy: The Hundred Best Novels* (New York: Peter Bedrick Books, 1989), 252.

44. Robertson Davies, *The Lyre of Orpheus* (New York: Penguin, 1990), 146.

45. Arthur Quiller-Couch and Daphne Du Maurier, *Castle Dor* (New York: Doubleday, 1961), 273.

46. Howard Pyle, *The Merry Adventures of Robin Hood* (1883; reprint, Chicago: World Book, 1988), vi–vii.

47. Robin McKinley, *The Outlaws of Sherwood* (New York: Greenwillow, 1988), 281; hereafter cited in text as *Outlaws.*

48. James C. Holt, *Robin Hood* (New York: Thames and Hudson, 1982), 7; hereafter cited in text.

49.   *Kirkus Reviews* (15 October 1988): 1530.

50.   *Booklist* (15 December 1988): 703.

51.   *School Library Journal* (January 1989): 94.

52.   Parke Godwin, *Sherwood* (New York: Avon, 1992), 391.

53.   Jennifer Roberson, *Lady of the Forest* (New York: Kensington Publishing/Zebra Books, 1992), 669.

6. A Magic Bestiary

1.   Mary Ellmann, introduction to Kenneth Grahame, *The Wind in the Willows* (New York: New American Library, 1969), ix, xiii.

2.   "Science Fiction Universe," *Wilson Library Bulletin* (September 1993): 102.

3.   *Kliatt Reviews* (January 1993): 17.

4.   T. S. Eliot, "The Naming of Cats," in Eliot, *Old Possum's Book of Practical Cats,* with drawings by Edward Gorey (1939; reprint, New York: Harvest/Harcourt Brace Jovanovich, 1982), 2, ll. 25–31.

5.   Clare Bell, *Ratha's Creature* (New York: Atheneum/Margaret K. McElderry, 1983), 107–8; hereafter cited in text as *Creature*.

6.   Bell, *Clan Ground* (New York: Atheneum/Margaret K. McElderry, 1984), 175; hereafter cited in text as *Ground*.

7.   Bell, *Ratha and Thistle-chaser* (New York: Margaret K. McElderry Books, 1990), 224.

8.   Bell, *Tomorrow's Sphinx,* (New York: Margaret K. McElderry Books, 1986), 37; hereafter cited in text as *Sphinx*.

9.   *Booklist,* 15 October 1993, 417.

10.   *Mythical and Fabulous Creatures: A Source Book and Research Guide,* ed. Malcolm South (Westport, Conn.: Greenwood Press, 1987), xix; hereafter cited in text.

11.   *The Enchanted World: Magical Beasts* (Alexandria, Va.: Time-Life Books, 1986), 17; hereafter cited in text as *Magical Beasts*.

12.   Jane Yolen, *The Stone Silenus* (New York: Philomel, 1984), 17.

13.   Richard Ellis, *Monsters of the Sea* (New York: Knopf, 1994), 79–82.

14.   Yolen, "The Undine," in Yolen, *Neptune Rising: Songs and Tales of the Undersea Folk* (New York: Philomel, 1982), 28.

15.   Mary Pope Osborne, *Haunted Waters* (Cambridge, Mass.: Candlewick Press, 1994), 108.

16.   *Voice of Youth Advocates* (December 1988): 247.

17.   *Dragon Fantastic,* ed. Rosalind M. and Martin H. Greenberg (New York: DAW Books, 1992), 14.

18.   Peter Dickinson, *The Flight of Dragons* (New York: Harper, 1979), 58.

19.   Kenneth Grahame, *The Reluctant Dragon* (1938; reprint, New York: Holiday House, 1989), 10.

20. Jonathan D. Evans, "The Dragon," in South, 50; hereafter cited in text.

21. R. Bretnor, *Science Fiction and Fantasy Literature,* vol. 2, quoted in *AAYA,* 147; hereafter cited in notes as *AAYA6.*

22. Melanie Belviso, "Anne McCaffrey," in *Twentieth Century Young Adult Writers,* 1st ed., ed. Laura Standley Berger (Detroit: St. James Press, 1994), 434; hereafter cited in notes as *YA Writers.*

23. Anne McCaffrey, "On Pernography," *Algol* (Fall 1968), in *AAYA6,* 148.

24. Jane Yolen, interview by author, St. Andrews, Scotland, 29 April 1992. All further personal quotes from Yolen are from this interview unless otherwise cited.

25. *Voice of Youth Advocates* (October 1982): 51.

26. *School Library Journal* (September 1982): 146.

27. *Voice of Youth Advocates* (February 1988): 293.

28. Yolen, *Here There Be Dragons* (San Diego: Harcourt Brace, 1993), 90.

29. Barbara Hambly, *Dragonsbane* (New York: Ballantine, 1985), 187.

30. *Booklist* (15 February 1986): 860.

31. *Voice of Youth Advocates* (August/October 1986): 21.

32. James Cross Giblin, *The Truth About Unicorns* (New York: HarperCollins, 1991), 104; hereafter cited in text.

33. Malcolm South, "The Unicorn," in South, 12; hereafter cited in text as South, "Unicorn."

34. Odell Shepard, *The Lore of the Unicorn* (New York: Avenel Books, 1930), 21.

35. James Thurber, "The Unicorn in the Garden," in Thurber, *Fables for Our Time and Famous Poems Illustrated* (New York: Harper & Brothers, 1940), 65.

36. Yolen, *Here There Be Unicorns* (San Diego: Harcourt Brace, 1994), 59.

37. Peter S. Beagle, *The Last Unicorn* (New York: Viking, 1968), 96; hereafter cited in text.

38. *School Library Journal* (November 1991): 134.

39. Terry Brooks, *The Black Unicorn* (New York: Ballantine, 1987), 298.

40. Meredith Ann Pierce, "The Queen of the Night," *The New Advocate* (Fall 1988): 221; hereafter cited in text as "Queen."

41. Diane Telgen, *Something about the Author,* vol. 67, ed. Donna Olendorf (Detroit: Gale Research, 1992), 160; hereafter cited in text as *SATA* 67.

42. Cathi Dunn MacRae, interview with Meredith Ann Pierce, Micanopy, Florida, 17 October 1994. All further personal quotes from Pierce are from this interview unless otherwise cited.

43.   Pierce, "A Lion in the Room," *Horn Book* (January/February 1988): 36; hereafter cited in text as "Lion."

44.   Pierce, autobiographical sketch in *Sixth Book of Junior Authors and Illustrators* (New York: H. W. Wilson, 1989), 225; hereafter cited in text as *Sixth Book.*

45.   Pierce, *Where the Wild Geese Go* (New York: Dutton, 1988), n.p.

46.   *Kirkus Reviews* (1 February 1988): 205.

47.   Pierce, "Rampion," in *Four from the Witch World,* created by Andre Norton (New York: Tor, 1989), 197.

48.   Sketch in *Major Authors and Illustrators for Children and Young Adults,* ed. Joyce Nakamura and Laurie Collier, 6 vols. (Detroit: Gale Research, 1992), 1885.

49.   Pierce, *Birth of the Firebringer* (New York: Four Winds/ Macmillan, 1985), 50.

50.   *School Library Journal* (January 1986): 70.

51.   *Booklist* (15 February 1986): 870.

52.   *Booklist* (15 May 1992): 1674.

53.   *School Library Journal* (June 1992): 140.

54.   Pierce, "On the Making of Monsters," *The New Advocate* (Spring 1990): 101; hereafter cited in text as "Monsters."

55.   C. G. Jung, *Memories, Dreams, Reflections,* rev. ed. by Aniela Jaffé, trans. from German by Richard and Clara Winston (1963; reprint, New York: Vintage Books, 1989), 129.

56.   Pierce, *The Darkangel* (New York: Tor, 1984, © 1982), 195; hereafter cited in text as *Darkangel.*

57.   Nancy Willard, "Vampire on the Moon," *New York Times Book Review* (25 April 1982): 35, 47.

58.   *Voice of Youth Advocates* (June 1982): 40.

59.   *School Library Journal* (March 1982): 160.

60.   *Magazine of Fantasy and Science Fiction* (November 1984): 38.

61.   *Horn Book* (August 1982): 416.

62.   Eleanor Cameron, *New York Times Book Review* (30 December 1984): 19.

63.   Pierce, *The Pearl of the Soul of the World* (Boston: Little Brown, 1990), 228.

64.   *Horn Book* (May 1990): 340.

65.   *Bulletin of the Center for Children's Books* (April 1990): 195.

66.   Pierce, *The Woman Who Loved Reindeer* (Boston: Little Brown, 1985), 3–4; hereafter cited in text as *Reindeer.*

67.   Patty Campbell, "The Young Adult Perplex," *Wilson Library Bulletin* (March 1986): 51.

68.   *Horn Book* (March–April 1986): 208–9.

69.   *Voice of Youth Advocates* (April 1986): 41.

70.   *School Library Journal* (August 1993): 186.

71.   Louise Cooper, *The Sleep of Stone* (New York: Atheneum, 1991), 84.

72.   *Booklist* (1 January 1992): 819, 821.

73.   *Voice of Youth Advocates* (February 1996): 372.

74.   *Voice of Youth Advocates* (February 1997): 342.

75.   Michael Dirda, *Washington Post Book World* (3 August 1997): 1.

76.   Philip Pullman, "Fantasy Fiction in the Classroom—Why Not?" speech, National Conference of Teachers of English, Detroit: 23 November 1997.

7. Time Fantasy: From Now to Then

1.   Karen Patricia Smith, "The English Psychological Fantasy Novel: A Bequest of Time," *School Library Journal* (May 1985): 44; hereafter cited in text.

2.   Barbara Elleman, "A Game of Catch," *Booklist* (15 November 1985): 494; hereafter cited in text.

3.   Diana Paolitto, "The Child's Perception of Time in Children's Books," in *Travelers in Time: Past, Present, and to Come* (Cambridge, U.K.: Green Bay Publications, 1990), 36–46. Compilation hereafter cited as *Travelers*.

4.   Peter Dickinson, "The Burden of the Past," in *Innocence and Experience: Essays and Conversations on Children's Literature,* comp. and ed. Barbara Harrison and Gregory Maguire (New York: Lothrop, Lee & Shepard, 1987), 99; compilation hereafter cited as *Innocence*.

5.   Penelope Lively, "Bones in the Sand," in *Innocence,* 13–15.

6.   Cathi MacRae, "Timescapes in Cambridge," *Wilson Library Bulletin* (November 1989): 28; hereafter cited in text as MacRae.

7.   John Rowe Townsend, "Slippery Time," in *Travelers,* 93; hereafter cited in text.

8.   Eleanor Cameron, *The Seed and the Vision: On the Writing and Appreciation of Children's Books* (New York: Dutton, 1993), 168; hereafter cited in text.

9.   John Clute, *Science Fiction: The Illustrated Encyclopedia* (New York: Dorling Kindersley, 1995), 60–61; hereafter cited in text.

10.   Gregory Maguire, "Memory," in *Travelers,* 55.

11.   Rudyard Kipling, *Puck of Pook's Hill* (1906; reprint, New York: Puffin, 1987), 14.

12.   C. S. Lewis, *Surprised by Joy: The Shape of My Early Life* (New York: Harcourt, 1956), 14.

13.   Allison Uttley, *A Traveler in Time* (1939; reprint, New York: Puffin, 1977), 9–10; hereafter cited in text.

14.   Susan Cooper, "Long Ago and Far Away," in *Travelers,* 100; hereafter cited in text.

15.   Kathleen A. Boardman, *"Red Shift,"* in *Beacham's Guide to Literature for Young Adults,* vol. 5, ed. Kirk H. Beetz (Washington, D.C.: Beacham Publishing, 1991), 2539.

16.   Aidan Chambers, *Horn Book* (October 1973): 494–97.

17.   Elaine Mersol, *Voice of Youth Advocates* (December 1988): 246.

18.   Barbara Chatton, *School Library Journal* (October 1988): 159.

19.   "Connie Willis: Talking Back to Shakespeare," *Locus* (July 1992): 4; hereafter cited in text.

20.   Jane Langton, "Time Thirst," in *Travelers,* 135.

21.   Eleanor Cameron, *The Court of the Stone Children* (1973; reprint, New York: Puffin, 1990), 79.

22.   Betty Levin, "Past and Future—Time's Eye," in *Travelers,* 117.

23.   Perry Glasser, *New York Times Book Review* (26 January 1986): 1.

24.   Philippa Pearce, "Time Present," in *Travelers,* 72.

25.   Nancy Bond, *A String in the Harp* (New York: Puffin, 1987, © 1976), 347.

26.   *Kirkus Reviews* (15 August 1988): 1248.

27.   Payton Knopf, *The Boulder, Colorado, Sunday Camera* (24 January 1993): 1B.

28.   Phyllis Reynolds Naylor, *Faces in the Water* (New York: Atheneum, 1981), 139.

Selected Bibliography

General Fantasy Reference Sources

Authors and Artists for Young Adults. 22 vols. Various editors. Detroit: Gale Research, 1989– (semiannual).

Barron, Neil, ed. *Fantasy Literature: A Reader's Guide*. New York: Garland Publishing, 1990.

Barron, Neil, ed. *What Fantastic Fiction Do I Read Next?* Detroit: Gale Research, 1998.

Beetz, Kirk H., ed. *Beacham's Guide to Literature for Young Adults*. Vol. 5 (fantasy and gothic novels). Washington, D.C.: Beacham Publishing, 1991.

Berger, Laura Standley, ed. *Twentieth Century Young Adult Writers*. 1st ed. Detroit: St. James Press, 1994.

Cawthorn, James, and Michael Moorcock. *Fantasy: The 100 Best Books*. New York: Carroll & Graf, 1988.

Clute, John, and John Grant. *The Encyclopedia of Fantasy*. New York: St. Martin's Press, 1997.

De Camp, L. Sprague. *Literary Swordsmen and Sorcerers: The Makers of Heroic Fantasy*. Sauk City, Wis.: Arkham House, 1976.

Egoff, Sheila A. "The New Fantasy." In *Thursday's Child: Trends and Patterns in Contemporary Children's Literature*, 80–125. Chicago: American Library Association, 1981.

The Faces of Fantasy. Photographs by Patti Perret. Introduction by Terri Windling. New York: Tor, 1996.

Gallo, Donald R., ed. *Speaking for Ourselves: Autobiographical Sketches by Notable Authors of Books for Young Adults*. Urbana, Ill.: National Council of Teachers of English, 1990.

Herald, Diana Tixier. *Teen Genreflecting*. Englewood, Colo.: Libraries Unlimited, 1997.

Le Guin, Ursula K. *The Language of the Night: Essays on Fantasy and Science Fiction*. Edited and with introductions by Susan Wood. New York: Putnam's, 1979.

Lynn, Ruth Nadelman. *Fantasy Literature for Children and Young Adults: An Annotated Bibliography*. 4th ed. New Providence, N.J.: R. R. Bowker, 1995.

MacNee, Marie J. *Science Fiction, Fantasy, and Horror Writers*. 2 vols. Detroit: UXL/Gale Research, 1995.

Nakamura, Joyce, and Laurie Collier, eds. *Major Authors and Illustrators for Children and Young Adults*. 6 vols. Detroit: Gale Research, 1992.

Pringle, David. *Modern Fantasy: The Hundred Best Novels*. New York: Peter Bedrick Books, 1989.

Pringle, David, ed. *St. James Guide to Fantasy Writers*. Detroit: St. James Press, 1996.

Rosenberg, Betty, and Diana Tixier Herald. *Genreflecting: A Guide to Reading Interests in Genre Fiction*. 3rd ed. Englewood, Colo.: Libraries Unlimited, 1991.

Searles, Baird, Beth Meacham, and Michael Franklin. *A Reader's Guide to Fantasy*. New York: Facts on File, 1982.

Spencer, Pam. *What Do Young Adults Read Next? A Reader's Guide to Fiction for Young Adults*. 2 vols. Detroit: Gale Research, 1994, 1997.

Spivack, Charlotte. *Merlin's Daughters: Contemporary Women Writers of Fantasy*. Westport, Conn.: Greenwood Press, 1987.

Swinfen, Ann. *In Defence of Fantasy: A Study of the Genre in English and American Literature Since 1945*. London: Routledge & Kegan Paul, 1984.

Tymn, Marshall B., Kenneth J. Zahorski, and Robert H. Boyer. *Fantasy Literature: A Core Collection and Reference Guide*. New Providence, N.J.: R. R. Bowker, 1979.

Watson, Noelle, and Paul E. Schellinger, eds. *Twentieth-Century Science Fiction Writers*. 3rd ed. Chicago: St. James Press, 1991.

What Do I Read Next? A Reader's Guide to Current Genre Fiction. 8 vols. Detroit: Gale Research, 1990– (annual).

Yolen, Jane. *Touch Magic: Fantasy, Faerie, and Folklore in the Literature of Childhood*. New York: Philomel, 1981.

Guides to Fantasy Realms, Characters, and Creatures

Barlowe, Wayne Douglas, and Neil Duskis. *Barlowe's Guide to Fantasy*. New York: HarperPrism, 1996.

Edwards, Malcolm, and Robert Holdstock. *Realms of Fantasy*. Illustrated by Stephen Bradbury, Bill Donohoe, Chris Foss, Mark Harrison, Michael Johnson, Ian Miller, Paul Monteagle, David O'Connor, and Dan Woods. Garden City, N.Y.: Doubleday, 1983.

The Enchanted World Series. 18 vols., unno'd. Alexandria, Va.: Time-Life Books. *Dragons*. 1984. *Ghosts*. 1984. *Legends of Valor*. 1984. *Wizards and Witches*. 1984. *Dwarfs*. 1985. *Fairies and Elves*. 1985.

Giants and Ogres. 1985. *Magical Beasts*. 1985. *Night Creatures*. 1985. *Spells and Bindings*. 1985. *Water Spirits*. 1985. *The Book of Christmas*. 1986. *Fabled Lands*. 1986. *The Fall of Camelot*. 1986. *Magical Justice*. 1986. *Seekers and Saviors*. 1986. *The Lore of Love*. 1987. *Tales of Terror*. 1987.

Holdstock, Robert, and Malcolm Edwards. *Lost Realms*. Illustrated by John Avon, Bill Donohoe, Godfrey Dowson, Dick French, Mark Harrison, Michael Johnson, Pauline Martin, David O'Connor, Colleen Payne, Scitex 350, and Carolyn Scrace. N.p.: Salem House, 1985.

Manguel, Alberto, and Gianni Guadalupi. *The Dictionary of Imaginary Places*. Expanded edition. Illustrated by Graham Greenfield. Maps and Charts by James Cook. San Diego: Harcourt Brace Jovanovich, 1987.

Page, Michael, and Robert Ingpen. *Encyclopedia of Things That Never Were*. New York: Viking, 1985.

Appendix A

Literary Awards
and Fantasy Fiction

Many fine fantasy novels have won youth book awards, from the annual Boston Globe–Horn Book Award to the Phoenix Award, which honors 20-year-old books that have become classics. Many titles covered in this book have won the Newbery or Carnegie Medals or other English language awards from Australia to Canada. A good resource for extracting fantasy titles from winners of children's and adult awards is Ruth Nadelman Lynn's *Fantasy Literature for Children and Young Adults,* fourth edition (Bowker, 1995), updated through 1993.

Fantasy novels are often cited for book awards chosen by teenagers themselves, usually sponsored by state library associations, such as Colorado's Blue Spruce Award and Texas's Blue Bonnet Award. The International Reading Association compiles "Young Adult Choices" by gathering votes from junior and senior high school students. A few book awards are entirely youth-produced, often by groups who meet voluntarily in public libraries. It is worth noting that such awards designed by teens give special attention to fantasy. The Golden Pen Awards, produced annually by the Young Adult Advisory Committee at Spokane Public Library in Washington, has a fantasy section among winning titles. They also choose a favorite author of the year as recipient of the Golden Pen; in 1989, *ElfQuest*'s Wendy and Richard Pini shared it as "authors who have given us the most reading pleasure." Favorite books published in 1988 were selected by the Young Adult Advisory Board at Enoch Pratt Free Library in Baltimore, Maryland, for "Youth-to-Youth Books: A List for Imagination and Survival," including a science fiction/fantasy section. The annual Gold Seal Booklist comes from the Youth Review Board at Stratford Library Association in Connecticut; their five-year compilation from 1988 to 1992 covered many topics, including fantasy. Many local youth book awards are not nationally publicized; it would be a revealing research project to locate as many state and local youth-produced book awards as possible to see how heavily fantasy titles are represented.

Recently access to the names of winners of all sorts of book awards has become readily available through the Internet. One especially helpful Web site, with links to many others, is "AwardWeb: Collections of Literary Award Information" at http://www. city-net.com/.

Because this study focuses on fantasy books especially enjoyed by teenagers, the following list is divided into two sections: awards limited to adult fantasy and lists of recommended books that combine titles intended for both adult and young adult readers. Awards for individual books generally go to titles intended for the adult reader, many of which are favored by teenagers.

Adult Fantasy Awards

British Fantasy Award
Since 1976, authors of any nationality are eligible for annual awards from the British Fantasy Society. For the best novel category, the winner receives the August Derleth Fantasy Award.

Gandalf Award
The World Science Fiction Convention, which chooses Hugo Awards for science fiction, names writers for lifetime contributions to fantasy literature. The official name of the award is the

Grand Master of Fantasy Award, but it is affectionately known as the Gandalf. J. R. R. Tolkien won it in its inaugural year, 1974.

Locus Poll

The magazine *Locus* reviews science fiction, fantasy, and horror, taking an annual poll of readers, which it has done since 1971, to rank their top choices of works in many categories. Results of the poll appear in each August issue and can also be found on the magazine's Web page at http://www.locusmag.com/. The top fantasy novel in the 1996 poll was Orson Scott Card's *Alvin Journeyman*. Occasionally *Locus* combines poll results over several years to name "Best All-Time" novels and novelists. Their first compilation ran in 1975; another appears in their August 1987 issue, with Tolkien's *The Lord of the Rings* named as "All-Time Best Fantasy Novel."

Mythopoeic Awards

Members of the Mythopoeic Society annually select a top fantasy work in both adult and children's categories, which reflects "the spirit of the Inklings": J. R. R. Tolkien, C. S. Lewis, and Charles Williams among others (see chapter 2). In 1997 the adult and children's categories were combined for the winning book, *The Wood Wife* by Terri Windling.

Nebula Award

Since 1966 the Science Fiction Writers of America have chosen the best novel, novella, novelette, and short story published during the previous year in science fiction or fantasy; each year's single best novel may be in either genre.

World Fantasy Awards

From a ballot of nominees, the World Fantasy Convention selects annual awards for Best Novel, Best Anthology, and Life Achievement. The first World Fantasy Award for Best Novel in 1975 was won by Patricia McKillip for *The Forgotten Beasts of Eld*. Other winners of interest to young adult readers are Robert

Holdstock for *Mythago Wood* in 1985, Robin McKinley for her anthology *Imaginary Lands* in 1986, and Ellen Kushner for *Thomas the Rhymer* in 1991.

Lists of Recommended Fantasy Titles

Booklist's Fantasy Highlights of the 80s

A "highly selective retrospective bibliography of fantasy series and individual titles published in the 1980s" appeared in the January 1, 1990, issue of *Booklist*. It lists series titles in order, and its annotations and superior choices make it an excellent reading guide.

Locus Recommended Reading Lists

Editors choose these lists of books in several categories, including nonfiction reference and literary criticism, appearing in each February issue of *Locus*.

VOYA's Best Science Fiction, Fantasy, and Horror

Since 1985, volunteer reviewers for *Voice of Youth Advocates (VOYA)*, devoted exclusively to books for young adults, have nominated their choices for this annual list, which appears in each April issue (with the exception of the first list, which was published in the February 1986 *VOYA*). This list consciously combines adult and young adult genre fiction of appeal to teenagers, with Q ratings for quality and P ratings for popularity given equal measure. Recommendations for appropriate reader age levels are also made. Among the 1996 fantasy choices were *Mother of Winter* by Barbara Hambly; *The Sandman Book of Dreams,* edited by Neil Gaiman and Ed Kramer; and *The Woman Who Lives in the Earth* by Swain Wolfe—all fine titles overlooked by other lists.

Fantasy Genre Lists from the Young Adult Library Services Association

Committees of librarians from the Young Adult Library Services Association (YALSA) division of the American Library Association produce booklists of paperbacks for teens in several popular genres each year, from humor to mystery, romance to outdoor adventure. Fantasy genre lists were published in 1991 and 1993 both as annotated booklists and as bookmarks. Tips for professionals on using fantasy literature with young adults were also distributed. The 1991 list recognized favorite modern fantasy classics, from T. H. White's *The Once and Future King* to Robin McKinley's *The Hero and the Crown*. The 1993 list included more recent titles, such as Terry Brooks's *Magic Kingdom for Sale— Sold!*, Mercedes Lackey's *Arrows of the Queen*, and Robert Jordan's *The Eye of the World*. For the most recent fantasy genre list, write to the YALSA Office at American Library Association, 50 E. Huron St., Chicago, IL 60611.

A list of fantasy titles compiled from 27 years' worth of YALSA's Best Books for Young Adults lists is included in appendix B, "Best Fantasy Books for Young Adults."

Appendix B

Best Fantasy Books
for Young Adults

(Compiled from American Library Association's Best Books for Young Adults Lists 1970–1997)

Adams, Richard. *Watership Down*. New York: Macmillan, 1974.

Alcock, Vivien. *Singer to the Sea God*. New York: Delacorte, 1993.

Alexander, Lloyd. *The Westmark Trilogy*. 3 vols. New York: Dutton.
> Vol. 1: *Westmark*. 1981.
> Vol. 2: *The Kestrel*. 1982.
> Vol. 3: *The Beggar Queen*. 1984.

Andronik, Catherine M. *Quest for a King: Searching for the Real King Arthur*. New York: Atheneum, 1990.

Anthony, Piers. *On a Pale Horse*. New York: Ballantine/Del Rey, 1984.

Appel, Allen. *Till the End of Time*. New York: Doubleday, 1991.

———. *Time After Time*. New York: Carroll & Graf, 1986.

Barron, T.A. *The Lost Years of Merlin*. New York: Philomel, 1996.

Bauer, Steven. *Satyrday: A Fable*. New York: Putnam's, 1981.

Bell, Clare. *Ratha and Thistle-Chaser*. New York: Margaret K. McElderry, 1991.

———. *Ratha's Creature*. New York: Atheneum, 1983.

Bradley, Marion Zimmer. *Hawkmistress!* New York: NAL/DAW, 1982.

Bradshaw, Gillian. *Hawk of May*. New York: Simon & Schuster, 1980.

Brooks, Terry. *Magic Kingdom for Sale—Sold!* New York: Ballantine/Del Rey, 1986.

———. *The Sword of Shannara*. New York: Random/Ballantine/Del Rey, 1977.

Brown, Mary. *Pigs Don't Fly*. New York: Baen, 1994.

428

Bruchac, Joseph. *Dawn Land*. Golden, Colo.: Fulcrum, 1993.

Bull, Emma. *Finder: A Novel of the Borderlands*. New York: Tor, 1994.

———. *War for the Oaks*. New York: Berkley/Ace, 1987.

Card, Orson Scott. *Pastwatch: The Redemption of Christopher Columbus*. New York: Tor, 1996.

———. *Seventh Son*. New York: Tor, 1987.

Cohen, Barbara. *Unicorns in the Rain*. New York: Atheneum, 1980.

Cohen, Barbara, and Bahija Lovejoy. *Seven Daughters and Seven Sons*. New York: Atheneum, 1982.

Cooper, Louise. *The Sleep of Stone*. New York: Atheneum, 1993.

Cormier, Robert. *Fade*. New York: Doubleday/Delacorte, 1988.

De Larrabeiti, Michael. *The Borribles*. New York: Macmillan, 1978.

Dear, William. *Dungeon Master: The Disappearance of James Dallas Egbert III*. Boston: Houghton Mifflin, 1984.

Dickinson, Peter, and Wayne Anderson. *The Flight of Dragons*. New York: Harper, 1979.

Finney, Jack. *Time and Again*. New York: Simon & Schuster, 1970.

Fletcher, Susan. *Flight of the Dragon Kyn*. New York: Atheneum, 1993.

Ford, Richard. *Quest for the Faradawn*. New York: Delacorte, 1982.

Gaiman, Neil, and Terry Pratchett. *Good Omens: The Nice and Accurate Prophecies of Agnes Nutter, Witch*. New York: Workman, 1992.

Galloway, Priscilla. *Truly Grim Tales*. New York: Delacorte, 1995.

Gilmore, Kate. *Enter Three Witches*. Boston: Houghton Mifflin, 1991.

Gurney, James. *Dinotopia: A Land Apart from Time*. Atlanta: Turner Publishing, 1992.

Hambly, Barbara. *Dragonsbane*. New York: Ballantine/Del Rey, 1986.

———. *Stranger at the Wedding*. New York: Ballantine/Del Rey, 1994.

Hamilton, Virginia. *In the Beginning: Creation Stories from Around the World*. San Diego: Harcourt Brace Jovanovich, 1988.

Hautman, Pete. *Mr. Was*. New York: Simon & Schuster, 1996.

Hendry, Frances Mary. *Quest for a Maid*. New York: Farrar, Straus & Giroux, 1991.

Hoover, H. M. *Dawn Palace: The Story of Medea*. New York: Dutton, 1988.

Huygen, Wil, and Rien Poortvliet. *Gnomes*. New York: Abrams, 1977.

Jacques, Brian. *Redwall*. New York: Philomel, 1987.

Jaffe, Rona. *Mazes and Monsters*. New York: Delacorte, 1981.

James, J. Alison. *Sing for a Gentle Rain*. New York: Atheneum, 1991.

Jones, Diana Wynne. *Archer's Goon*. New York: Greenwillow, 1984.

———. *Castle in the Air*. New York: Greenwillow, 1992.

———. *Homeward Bounders*. New York: Greenwillow, 1981.

———. *Howl's Moving Castle*. New York: Greenwillow, 1986.

———. *Sudden Wild Magic*. New York: Morrow, 1992.

Jordan, Robert. *Eye of the World*. New York: Tor, 1990.

Jordan, Sherryl. *Winter of Fire*. New York: Scholastic, 1993.

———. *Wolf-Woman*. Boston: Houghton Mifflin, 1994.

Kilworth, Garry. *The Foxes of Firstdark*. New York: Doubleday, 1991.

Kindl, Patrice. *Owl in Love*. Boston: Houghton Mifflin, 1993.

L'Engle, Madeleine. *Many Waters*. New York: Farrar, Straus, & Giroux, 1987.

Lackey, Mercedes. *Arrows of the Queen*. New York: NAL/DAW, 1987.

———. *Bardic Voices: The Lark and the Wren*. New York: Baen, 1993.

Le Guin, Ursula K. *The Beginning Place*. New York: Harper, 1980.

Lee, Tanith. *Black Unicorn*. New York: Atheneum, 1992.

———. *Red as Blood; or, Tales from the Sisters Grimmer*. New York: NAL/DAW, 1983.

LeVert, John. *Flight of the Cassowary*. New York: Atlantic Monthly Press, 1986.

Levitin, Sonia. *Escape from Egypt*. Boston: Little, Brown, 1994.

Llywelyn, Morgan. *The Horse Goddess*. Boston: Houghton Mifflin, 1982.

Lockley, Ronald. *Seal Woman*. New York: Bradbury, 1975.

Marzollo, Jean. *Halfway Down Paddy Lane*. New York: Dial, 1981.

Mayhar, Ardath. *Soul Singer of Tyrnos*. New York: Atheneum, 1981.

McKinley, Robin. *Beauty*. New York: Harper, 1978.

———. *The Blue Sword*. New York: Greenwillow, 1982.

———. *Deerskin*. New York: Ace, 1993.

———. *The Hero and the Crown*. New York: Greenwillow, 1985.

———. *Outlaws of Sherwood*. New York: Greenwillow, 1988.

Napoli, Donna Jo. *The Magic Circle*. New York: Dutton, 1993.

Nix, Garth. *Sabriel*. New York: HarperCollins, 1996.

O'Donohoe, Nick. *The Magic and the Healing*. New York: Ace, 1994.

Park, Ruth. *Playing Beatie Bow*. New York: Atheneum, 1982.

Pierce, Meredith Ann. *Darkangel*. New York: Atlantic Monthly Press, 1982.

———. *The Pearl of the Soul of the World*. Boston: Little Brown, 1991.

———. *The Woman Who Loved Reindeer*. New York: Atlantic Monthly Press, 1985.

Pierce, Tamora. *Emperor Mage*. New York: Atheneum, 1995.

Pullman, Philip. *The Golden Compass*. New York: Knopf, 1996.

Reiss, Kathryn. *Time Windows*. San Diego: Harcourt Brace Jovanovich, 1993.

Rice, Robert. *The Last Pendragon*. New York: Walker, 1993.

Roberson, Jennifer. *Lady of the Forest*. New York: Kensington Publishing/Zebra Books, 1992.

Scieszka, Jon, and Lane Smith. *The Stinky Cheese Man and Other Fairly Stupid Tales*. New York: Viking, 1993.

Senn, Steve. *Circle in the Sea.* New York: Atheneum, 1981.

Sherman, Josepha. *Child of Faerie, Child of Earth.* New York: Walker, 1992.

Stewart, Mary. *The Crystal Cave.* New York: Morrow, 1970.

———. *The Hollow Hills.* New York: Morrow, 1973.

Strauss, Gwen. *Trail of Stones.* New York: Knopf, 1991.

Sutcliff, Rosemary. *Black Ships Before Troy: The Story of the Iliad.* New York: Delacorte, 1993.

———. *The Road to Camlann: The Death of King Arthur.* New York: Dutton, 1983.

Tepper, Sheri S. *Beauty.* New York: Doubleday, 1992.

Turner, Megan Whalen. *The Thief.* New York: Greenwillow, 1996.

Vick, Helen Hughes. *Walker of Time.* Tucson, Ariz.: Harbinger House, 1993.

Voigt, Cynthia. *On Fortune's Wheel.* New York: Atheneum, 1991.

Wells, Rosemary. *Through the Hidden Door.* New York: Dial, 1987.

Westall, Robert. *Devil on the Road.* New York: Greenwillow, 1979.

———. *The Wind Eye.* New York: Greenwillow, 1978.

Willard, Nancy. *Things Invisible to See.* New York: Knopf, 1985.

Wilson, David Henry. *The Coachman Rat.* New York: Carroll & Graf, 1990.

Woolley, Persia. *Child of the Northern Spring.* New York: Poseidon, 1987.

———. *Queen of the Summer Stars.* New York: Poseidon, 1991.

Wrede, Patricia C. *Dealing with Dragons.* San Diego: Harcourt Brace Jovanovich, 1991.

———. *Searching for Dragons.* San Diego: Harcourt Brace Jovanovich, 1991.

Yolen, Jane. *Briar Rose.* New York: Tor, 1993.

———. *Dragon's Blood.* New York: Delacorte, 1982.

———. *Heart's Blood.* New York: Delacorte, 1984.

Zambreno, Mary Frances. *A Plague of Sorcerers.* San Diego: Harcourt Brace Jovanovich, 1993.

Appendix C

Surveys and Questionnaires Used in this Study

Distribution details and teen responses to the Fantasy Fanatics Questionnaire are described in the preface, which also explains how the Young Adult Fantasy Evaluator Report (YAFER) was used in this book. Comments from teen evaluators were extracted from YAFERs and set apart to conclude relevant sections throughout the text. The use of the Fantasy Gaming Survey is discussed in the Fantasy Gaming section of chapter 3.

Fantasy Fanatics Questionnaire

If you are:
   —a fan of fantasy books,
   —between the ages of twelve and eighteen,
   —interested in joining the Fantasy Fanatics Reading Group at Boulder Public Library, OR
   —interested in being a long-distance Young Adult Fantasy Evaluator (YAFE) for a book on teenagers' favorite fantasy authors,
complete this fantastical questionnaire and return it to:
Cathi MacRae at Boulder Public Library.

PART I. FANTASY AUTHORS

Check each author's name on the list below, if you have read
book(s) by him or her. If you recall titles, write them beside their
names. Star (*) your favorites:

Check	AUTHOR NAME	TITLES
_____	*Piers Anthony*	_____
_____	*Clare Bell*	_____
_____	*Nancy Bond*	_____
_____	*Marion Zimmer Bradley*	_____
_____	*Terry Brooks*	_____
_____	*Orson Scott Card*	_____
_____	*David Eddings*	_____
_____	*Raymond Feist*	_____
_____	*Barbara Hambly*	_____
_____	*M. Weis & T. Hickman*	_____
_____	*Mercedes Lackey*	_____
_____	*Ursula K. Le Guin*	_____
_____	*R. A. MacAvoy*	_____
_____	*Anne McCaffrey*	_____
_____	*Suzy McKee Charnas*	_____
_____	*Robin McKinley*	_____
_____	*Patricia McKillip*	_____
_____	*Meredith Ann Pierce*	_____
_____	*Tamora Pierce*	_____
_____	*Wendy & Richard Pini*	_____
_____	*Terry Pratchett*	_____
_____	*Nancy Springer*	_____
_____	*Jane Yolen*	_____

Name any fantasy authors NOT in the above list who you especially enjoy, and your favorite titles by them:

Who is your all-time favorite fantasy author?

What is your absolute favorite fantasy title?

PART II. FANTASY STORY TYPES

Check ALL that apply. What I like about fantasy is:

_____ Alternate worlds in which the story is set.

_____ Magic that occurs in everyday world.

_____ Stories of normal people involved in fantasy gaming.

_____ Stories based on mythology or legends.

_____ Stories based on the King Arthur legend.

_____ Books based on fairy tales.

_____ Books about invisible "faerie folk" in our world.

_____ Books about witches and wizards.

_____ Animal books with psychic beasts or mythical creatures.

_____ Time travel or time-slip stories.

_____ Humorous stories.

_____ Adventure or quest stories.

_____ "Sword and sorcery" stories.

_____ Stories of supernatural beings.

Referring to the list above, and adding more detail if you like, identify what qualities of fantasy are in your favorite fantasy books:

PART III. FANTASY AUTHOR NATIONALITIES
Check whatever applies:
Do you prefer

_____ British authors
_____ American authors
_____ other nationalities. Which? _____
_____ no preference

PART IV. FANTASY DEFINITION
A simple definition of fantasy might be: "stories or novels which take place in the realm of magic." Expand this definition; compare fantasy to science fiction if you wish:

PART V. YOUR PERSONAL INFORMATION
Name _____
Address _____ City _____
State _____ Zip _____
Phone ( ) _____ Age _____
School _____
Public library used most often _____

(Check one) I wish to:
_____ Attend Fantasy Fanatics Reading Group at Boulder Public Library
_____ Become a long-distance Young Adult Fantasy Evaluator (YAFE) for a book on fantasy.

Fantasy Gaming Survey

A. Fantasy Gameplayers

1. Do you like to read books about people who play fantasy role-playing games? Yes___ No___

2. Place a checkmark next to each title you have read. Leave others blank.

_____ Anthony - *Killobyte*
_____ Anderson - *Gameplay;* ___ *Gamearth;* ___ *Game's End*
_____ Beagle - *Folk of the Air*
_____ Bowkett - *Gameplayers*
_____ Carpenter - *The Twilight Realm*
_____ Cross - *A Map of Nowhere*
_____ Dear - *The Dungeon Master: The Disappearance of James Dallas Egbert III*
_____ Hall - *Fair Maiden*
_____ Jaffe - *Mazes and Monsters*
_____ Locke - *Game Over*
_____ Mace - *Under Siege*
_____ Norman - *Albion's Dream*
_____ Scott - *Burning Bright*
_____ Posner - *Sparrow's Flight*
_____ Pulver - *Murder at the War*
_____ Rosenberg - *The Sleeping Dragon;*
    ___ *The Sword and the Chain;* ___ *The Silver Crown;*
    ___ *The Heir Apparent;* ___ *The Warrior Lives;*
    ___ *The Road to Ehvenor:*
_____ Rubinstein - *Beyond the Labyrinth;* ___ *Space Demons;*
    ___ *Skymaze*
_____ Vande Velde - *User Unfriendly*
_____ Walker - *War Gamers' World;* ___ *Army of Darkness;*
    ___ *Messengers of Darkness*
_____ Other titles? _____

Next to your checkmarks above, show your opinion of the books using these symbols: ☺ = Excellent   ☺ = OK   ☹ = Pretty lame

3. *Elements of Gameplayer Books*

Place a + or − next to each of these elements found in books about gamers:

+ for important quality that adds to your enjoyment of the book

− for quality you dislike

_____ Story based on actual case of gamers getting carried away, confusing fantasy with reality

_____ Gamers are real world characters who seem very realistic and believable

_____ Gamers' involvement in game is a way to cope with problems in their lives

_____ Gamers are deluded into thinking they are in game world; they are psychologically escaping, but do not really enter alternate world

_____ Gamers actually enter alternate world of game

_____ There are connections between gamers' real personalities and conflicts, and those within the fantasy roles they play

_____ Fantasy adventure within the game world is as compelling as in any good fantasy novel

_____ The story makes you "suspend your disbelief," convincing you that game worlds really can come alive.

Additional comments: Add any other observation or explanation of your opinions above.

B. Books Set in Game Worlds

1. Do you play any fantasy role-playing games? Yes___ No___

2. If yes, please name the games you have played, starring (*) those you enjoy most.

3. In your opinion, what are the most popular fantasy role-playing games among teenagers?

4. In your gaming group or groups, what age are players? Teens___ Adults___ Mixed___

5. Do you read fantasy novels set in worlds that tie in with fantasy games? Yes___ No___

6. If yes, do you also play the games that go with the novels? Yes___ No___

7. In your opinion, do most gamers enjoy connected novels as an enhancement to playing? Yes___ No___ Explain why if you like.

8. In your opinion, can related novels be enjoyed with no reference to the actual games? Yes___ No___ Explain why if you like.

9. If you wish, elaborate on the relationship between games and novels, especially *Dragonlance* and *Forgotten Realms*. Mention other books if you like.

10. Please mark the four TSR booklists of *Dragonlance, Forgotten Realms,* other game series starting with *Dungeons and Dragons,* and single titles, with checkmarks to the left of each title you have read. Leave others blank. (You may mark trilogies as one item if you reacted the same way to all titles in it.)

Next to your checkmarks, show your opinion of the books using these symbols:

☺ = Excellent, one of the best in whole game series
☹ = OK, readable, but not essential for anyone but fans
☹ = Pretty lame, only for desperate series fans

Additional comments: Add any other observation or explanation of your opinions above.

Your name _____   *Age* _____

(Return to: **Cathi MacRae, Children's Dept., Boulder Public Library**)

YAFER (YOUNG ADULT FANTASY EVALUATOR REPORT)

Author _____

Title _____

Book Number ___ in series named _____ (if in series)*

Or, you may choose to complete one form for an entire series.

Publisher _____ Publication Date_____

Your Name_____ Your Age_____

Your Library Group_____ Librarian_____

Circle book's fantasy type or types below:

Alternate worlds	Science fantasy	Magic realism
Fantasy gaming	Myths	Arthurian legends
Fairy tales	Faery folk	Animal tales
Witches and wizards	Time travel	Humorous
Other		

_____

Standards Rating:
Use this scale to fill in numbers:

Poor		**O.K.**		**Excellent**	
0	1	2	3	4	5	*Number*

Relevant to young adults _____
Offers guidance _____
Challenges imagination _____
Good plot & characters _____
Visual appeal/cover _____
Innovative style/content _____
Universal value _____
Enjoyable reading _____
_____
Add total: _____

Popularity Rating:
Circle statement that most applies:

4 - Most teen fantasy fans would love this.
3 - Many teen fantasy fans would love it.
2 - A few teen fantasy fans would love it.
1 - Most teen fantasy fans would hate it.

Age Rating:
Check all that apply:

_____ages 11–13
_____ages 14–15
_____ages 16–18
_____other (specify:_____)

Guidelines for Responding to Questions

The finest fantasy is not just escape from reality—it expands imagination and awareness to help us understand more about our inner and outer worlds.

Keeping that in mind, please give your honest opinion about how meaningful and enjoyable this book is to you, and perhaps to other young adults (ages 11–18).

Your responses may be quoted in my book *Presenting Young Adult Fantasy Fiction*. This critical biography highlights fantasy authors enjoyed and valued by young adults. The lives and works of four contemporary American authors are featured: Terry Brooks, Barbara Hambly, Meredith Ann Pierce, and Jane Yolen. Piers Anthony, David Eddings, and others will be mentioned.

Please answer as many questions as you can.

1. List some of the author's most imaginative ideas.

2. With which character did you identify most, and why?

3. What do you see as the author's main theme or themes?

4. Comment on how the author portrayed good vs. evil. Consider plot, characters, setting, and symbols.

5. What myths, legends, or fairy tales did you recognize within the story? ALSO, did this book remind you of similar fantasies by other authors? If so, name title(s).

6. Did the author's writing style enhance, or interfere with your enjoyment? Give examples: *I enjoyed the fast pace* or *It moved too slowly*.

7. What makes this book better or worse than some of the very best fantasy you have read?

8. Would you recommend this book only to fantasy fanatics, or also to friends who don't usually read fantasy? Why or why not?

Check here if you would **NOT** recommend this book to **ANYONE**____.

9. What else do you feel is important to say about this book?

YAFER DEADLINES
Please mail YAFERs **monthly** *to:* Cathi Dunn MacRae

DOOMSDAY DEADLINE: *July 31, 1996*
Sending YAFERs sooner and regularly gives your comments more chance to be used.
If this is your first YAFER, fill in:
Name _____
Address _____
City/State _____ Zip _____
Phone (   ) _____ Age _____ Library _____
Favorite fantasy author _____

Return completed Fantasy Fanatics Questionnaire with this form, if available. In return, you will receive book's writing schedule and reading list.

Index

Index

461

Thurber, James, "Unicorn in the Garden,
The" (short story), 324
Tiger Burning Bright, 137–38
Till the End of Time, 381–82
time: concept of, 365–66, 372; theories of,
366, 372–73, 389
Time After Time, 381, 382–83
Time and Again, 368, 374–75, 392
Time and Chance, 382
time fantasy (time travel). *See* fantasy,
time
Time of the Dark, The, 181, 187, 188, 189,
190, 195, 196, 198
Timescape, 378
Time to Remember, A, 384
time travel, triggers, 368. *See also* fantasy,
time
Time Trilogy, The, 368, 386
Titus Alone, 17
Titus Groan, 17–18
Tolkien, J. R. R., xviii, xix, xxii, 13, 17, 18,
19, 20, 22, 23–34, 36, 47, 48, 49, 53, 55,
56, 58, 87, 122, 147, 150, 156, 157, 186,
201, 279; best-sellers, 30; bibliography,
170; Carpenter, Humphrey (biographer),
26; criticism of work, 27–29; good *vs.* evil
theme, 26, 29, 31; Inklings, 19; language
studies, 24; legacy to fantasy literature,
26, 32–34; Middle Earth, creation of, 24,
26–27; mythology, creation of, 24–25, 27,
32–33; ordinary heroes, theme, 30, 33;
publishing, 24, 25; readers' responses,
24, 25–26, 29, 30–32; Recommended
Reading, 158–59; self-description (epigraph), 23; story elements, 34

WORKS
Book of Lost Tales, The, 24
Hobbit, The, 17, 19, 24, 25, 30, 172, 316
Lord of the Rings Trilogy, The, 12, 25–30,
31–32, 34, 55, 79, 80, 81, 100, 120, 159;
Fellowship of the Ring, The, 17, 25, 27;
Return of the King, The, 25, 120; *Two
Towers, The*, 25, 32
"On Fairy-stories" (essay), 12, 26
Silmarillion, The, 24–25, 27

Tolve, Melissa (Fantasy Fanatic), 130, 131,
140, 141, 142, 143, 190, 192, 206, 209,
210, 283, 322
Tombs of Atuan, The, 38–40, 41, 42, 43, 45,
46, 48–49
Tomlinson, Theresa, *Forestwife, The*, 290
Tomorrow's Sphinx, 307–8, 309
Tom's Midnight Garden, 384–85
To Say Nothing of the Dog, 377
*Touch Magic: Fantasy, Faerie, and
Folklore in the Literature of Childhood*,
225–26

Townsend, John Rowe, 367, 369, 370, 372,
384, 385; *Visitors, The (Xanadu
Manuscript, The*, in Britain), 392
Traveler in Time, A, 371
"Travelers in Time: Past, Present, and to
Come" (conference), 366
Treasure Island, 232
"Tree's Wife, The" (short story), 246
Tris's Book, 132
Tristan and Iseult, 266
Tritonian Ring, The, 22
Troyes, Chretien de (12th-century poet),
262
Truth About Unicorns, The, 322–23
Turner, Megan Whalen, *Thief, The*, 150
Twain, Mark, 15, 381; *Connecticut Yankee
in King Arthur's Court, A*, 271, 369
*Twelve Impossible Things Before Breakfast:
Stories*, 239
Twice Upon a Time, 369, 381
Twisting the Rope, 200
Tymn, Marshall B. *See Fantasy Literature:
A Core Collection and Reference Guide*

Uncle Remus stories, 302
Under Siege, 209
Under the Healing Sun, 312
Undine, 313–14
"Unicorn in the Garden, The" (short story),
324
Unicorn Mountain, 325
unicorns, 107, 312, 322–26, 336–39; read-
ers' responses, 326, 339; Recommended
Reading, 359–60
Unicorns in the Rain, 325, 326
unicorn tapestries, 323, 326
"Unicorn Tapestry" (short story), 326
Unicorn Treasury, 325
Unicorn Trilogy (Lee), 325, 360
Unknown (magazine), 20
Unwin, Sir Stanley, 24, 25
urban fantasy. *See* fantasy, urban
Uttley, Alison, *Traveler in Time, A*, 371

Valdemar Sequence, The, 134, 138–39,
161–62
Valley of Deer, The, 380
vampires, xix, 183, 332, 340–45
Verne, Jules, 15; *Adventures of the Rat
Family*, 351
Vick, Helen Hughes, *Tag Against Time*,
391; *Walker of Time*, 391; Walker series,
391, 398; *Walker's Journey Home*, 391
Virta, Gary (YAFE), 31
Virtual Mode, 175, 176
Visa for Avalon, A, 280
Vision Quest, 368
Visitors, The (Xanadu Manuscript, The, in
Britain), 392

The Author

After 19 years as a young adult specialist in Maryland and Colorado libraries, Cathi Dunn MacRae became editor of *Voice of Youth Advocates* (*VOYA*), a national journal for librarians and educators who serve young adults. Known for her pioneering work in youth participation, MacRae is also a YA library consultant and critic. For seven years she wrote "The Young Adult Perplex" review column for *Wilson Library Bulletin,* until publication ceased in 1995.

MacRae graduated cum laude with a B.A. in English literature from Drew University in New Jersey in 1972 and received her M.A. in librarianship from the University of Denver in 1978. Among other intellectual freedom awards, for her youth-produced anticensorship play *Don't Read This!* she won the 1995 Econo-Clad/American Library Association/YALSA Award for Outstanding Achievement in the Development of a Literature Program for Young Adults. Some of the same students who produced the play were members of her Fantasy Fanatics book discussion group at Boulder Public Library in Colorado and also served as consultants for this book.

MacRae lives in Annapolis, Maryland, with her Scots writer husband and cat, Rhubarb.

The Editor

Patricia J. Campbell is an author and critic specializing in books for young adults. She has taught adolescent literature at UCLA and is the former Assistant Coordinator of Young Adult Services for the Los Angeles Public Library. Her literary criticism has been published in the *New York Times Book Review* and many other journals. From 1978 to 1988 her column "The Young Adult Perplex," a monthly review of young adult books, appeared in the *Wilson Library Bulletin*.

She now writes a column on controversial issues in adolescent literature for *Horn Book* magazine, "The Sand in the Oyster." Recently she has been traveling the country to lead "YA Biblioramas," intensive workshops on young adult fiction for teachers and librarians.

Campbell is the author of five books, among them *Presenting Robert Cormier,* the first volume in the Twayne Young Adult Author Series. In 1989 she was the recipient of the American Library Association Grolier Award for distinguished achievement with young people and books. A native of Los Angeles, Campbell now lives on an avocado ranch near San Diego, where she and her husband, David Shore, write and publish books on overseas motorhome travel.